The Magic of Computer Graphics

The Magic of Computer Graphics

Landmarks in Rendering

Noriko Kurachi

edited by Michael M. Stark

CRC Press
Taylor & Francis Group
Boca Raton London New York

CRC Press is an imprint of the
Taylor & Francis Group, an **informa** business

AN A K PETERS BOOK

Translation rights arranged with Ohmsha, Ltd.

Original Japanese edition published as
"CG Magic: Rendering" by Noriko Kurachi
Copyright © 2007 by Noriko Kurachi
Published by Ohmsha, Ltd.,
3-1 Kanda Nishikicho, Chiyodaku, Tokyo, Japan

CRC Press
Taylor & Francis Group
6000 Broken Sound Parkway NW, Suite 300
Boca Raton, FL 33487-2742

English edition © 2011 by Taylor and Francis Group, LLC
CRC Press is an imprint of Taylor & Francis Group, an Informa business

No claim to original U.S. Government works

Printed in the United States of America on acid-free paper
Version Date: 20110505

International Standard Book Number: 978-1-56881-577-0 (Paperback)

Library of Congress Cataloging-in-Publication Data

Kurachi, Noriko.
  [CG magic. English]
  The magic of computer graphics : landmarks in rendering / Noriko Kurachi ; edited by
  Michael M. Stark.
    p. cm.
  Includes bibliographical references and index.
  ISBN 978-1-56881-577-0 (alk. paper)
   1. Rendering (Computer graphics) I. Stark, Michael M. II. Title.

  T385.K82813 2010
  006.6−dc22
                                                               2010029397

Visit the Taylor & Francis Web site at
http://www.taylorandfrancis.com

and the CRC Press Web site at
http://www.crcpress.com

Contents

Foreword

In broad terms, computer graphics is the use of computers to create images. CG has come to be the dominant form of content creation for video games, movie special effects, and many other forms of entertainment. One of the principal things CG does for creatives is to free them from the bounds of what can be held in front of a camera. From the standpoint of a naive observer, CG really is magic. Vision is entwined with our sense of reality, "seeing is believing" as they say, and when the line between physical experience and imagination is crossed, there is simply no other word for it.

The mathematical basis for computer graphics was established in the late '60s, some might say before that, though there were no computers capable of realizing its potential at the time. The best they could do was draw lines on the screen that were reminiscent of 3-D shapes. Early advances included hidden line removal and the ability to fill polygons with color(!) Later on, basic ray-tracing techniques were introduced to model how light really interacts with surfaces. This was a breakthrough compared to what came before, and as the years and decades passed, graphics researchers continued to push the boundaries of what was possible, and how real faking it could look.

Make no mistake, CG is, has been, and always will be a bag of tricks. CG artists don't reproduce the real world, even in simulation. The physics of light is simply too complex to model exactly. In the time it took you to read the word "physics," over a trillion photons struck your retina. The computations required to completely reproduce what we see are not only beyond reach, they are largely unnecessary. You didn't notice most of those photons, anyway. Computer graphics is all about finding good approximations to reality, or magic tricks of the light.

Once we have an approximation of reality that fools most of the people most of the time, we can expand our canvas to include things not found in the real world, such as flying logos and even (wait for it) space ships! Besides offering Hollywood the ability to remake every science fiction movie ever made, CG reduces the cost of realistic depictions of the past, of thousands of actors in orc costumes, or knocking down a famous building the producer doesn't have the money to rebuild.

Speaking of buildings, computer graphics is also quite useful to those designing structures and wanting to know how daylight will enter a space before it is built. Many of the same approximations used in movies, with proper care and validation, can be used for accurate lighting predictions as well. Again, we stop short of counting every photon, but a well-designed CG trick not only looks right, but to a reasonable degree, it *is* right. Many of the established methods in CG rendering, such as Monte Carlo ray sampling, radiosity, and image-based lighting, started out as simulation techniques for building design.

Computer graphics is a vast field, and getting larger every day. It is impossible to cover every topic of interest, even within a specialization such as CG rendering. For many years, Noriko Kurachi has reported on the latest developments for Japanese readers in her monthly column for CG World. Being something of a pioneer herself, she selected topics that represented original and promising new directions for research, as opposed to the tried and true methods. Many of these novel ideas paid off handsomely, and these are the topics covered in this book.

Starting from the basic behavior of light, Ms. Kurachi introduces the most useful techniques for global and local illumination using geometric descriptions of an environment in the first section. She then goes on in the second section to describe image-based techniques that rely on captured data to do their magic. In the final section, she looks at the synthesis of these two complimentary approaches and what they mean for the future of computer graphics. Being ever careful to check her facts with the original researchers, she offers in these pages a journalist's view of the evolution of computer graphics over the past twenty years in a style that is accessible and thorough, tailored for and by an artist who is also a technician.

—Gregory J. Ward

Preface

The origin of this book was the technical column that I wrote every month in a computer graphics-related Japanese magazine (called *CGWORLD*). My column had two distinguishing characteristics: its topics and style.

I daringly selected topics whose value had not been well-established in the CG community but that nevertheless looked like they would have potential to make the CG scene evolve to the next stage. The writing style of the column was also unique. I communicated personally with the researchers and developers whose methods I described. These interviews enabled me to include added details about what challenges motivated their work and where their inspiration came from, as well as their insights for the future or their suggestions for practical application of their work that they couldn't include in the technical papers.

Sometime after I started this column, people came to expect that its contents would be summed up in the form of a book. The column itself spans a wide range of CG technologies and, in the beginning, it was intended for the book to cover all of them. However, as the writing went on, I discovered that it was unrealistic to cover such a huge volume of material all at once. Therefore I decided to focus on rendering technologies—the first quarter of the original plan. The book, published by the Japanese publisher Ohmsha, was released at the end of 2007 as *CG Magic: Rendering*.

From the responses of researchers and the developers that I had spoken with while writing the book, I knew that even outside of Japan it is uncommon to find a book with contents like this one. I became convinced that it would be meaningful if this book were translated into English and could be read by a wider range of people. Therefore, as soon as the Japanese book was released, I started translating it into English, and when half of translation was completed, I told Greg Ward, who had always been supportive of my writing the book, about my plan of releasing an English edition. He was very positive and gave me the opportunity to meet with Alice Peters at SIGGRAPH 2008, which led to the birth of this book. Even though this started as simply a translated version of the previous Japanese book, I wanted to include descriptions of new developments occurring on the CG scene since the release of the Japanese book. For example, the new sections on hair rendering were added because hair rendering technologies, from a practical viewpoint, had reached a turning point in physical accuracy. In addition, a new section has been added at the end of each chapter in order to describe how the technologies introduced in the chapter are in progress.

Finally I should note two things. One is that the stories in this book focus mainly on technologies invented after 2000; therefore, I recommend that people refer to more traditional books in order to study the fundamentals of CG rendering. The other is that even though this book describes the content of professional technical papers, it has been adapted to be more accessible to people who are non-professionals in CG rendering. Therefore, I refer those people interested in further study to the original technical papers (listed in the references).

Admitting such imperfections, I hope that the stories about how these new ideas were born and eventually became widespread will be valuable for all those who are interested in the magic that CG enables. I also expect that this book will find a place with people who are interested in visual effects because this book includes many stories about how new CG theories came to be used in this area.

In general, the developing theories and the process of making them practical are very different areas; however, when combined they can make new CG technologies a reality and lead to a true revolution. The stories in this book describe efforts in both areas, and I hope that this feature of the book can inspire those who will lead the progress of CG technologies.

Acknowledgments

This book was well supported by a large number of researchers and developers. Special thanks to Greg Ward, Tony Apodaca, Holly Rushmeier, Henrik Wann Jensen, Toshiya Hachisuka, Timothy Purcell, Pat Hanrahan, Jos Stam, Craig Donner, Eugene D'Eon, Christophe Hery, Peter Sand, Paul Devebec, Mark Sagar, Pierre Buffin, Marc Levoy, Radek Grzezczuk, Ren Ng, Sing Bing Kang, Ravi Ramamoorthi, Sameer Agrawal, Eric Lafortune, Wojcjech Matusik, Shree Nayar, Steve Marshner, Arno Zink, Wenzel Jakob, Martin Hill, Gero Muller, Xin Tong, Ko Nishino, Alex Vasilescu, Peter-Pike Sloan, Jan Kautz, Doug James, Changxi Zheng, Mark Sagar, Larry Gritz, Sven Woop, Tomoyuki Nishita, Yoshinori Dobashi, Yosuke Bando, Takeshi Naemura, and Masao Takakuwa for revising the book from a more current perspective, providing new stories and images in some cases, and contributing to the technical reviewing. Those were very time-consuming tasks which required a lot of work, so I honestly feel grateful to have received such contributions.

In addition, there were people who supported me even before the project started, because releasing a book for an English-speaking audience started as my personal plan. Thanks to Nick Foster, Mike Milne, Agent Xray, Andre Corwin Mazzone, Yoshiharu Gotanda, and Katsutsugu Kurachi, who helped my efforts to make the project actually happen.

One significant aspect of the project was the translation into English from Japanese because, in addition to the gap between Japanese and English colloquialisms, the technical nature of the book required the translators to have a high-level knowledge of CG rendering. Thanks to Chuk Tang, Yoshihiro Kanamori, Paul Caristino, Ryusuke Villemin, Witawat Rungjiratananon, Paulo Silva, Kiminori Tsukazaki, and Ayako Ogawa, who accomplished this difficult job.

Many thanks to A K Peters. I greatly appreciate Alice Peters, who made the project happen. Special thanks to Michael Stark, who did an excellent job revising the chapters, uniting all of the voices in the book, and smoothing the English. Thanks to the staff at A K Peters, particularly Sarah Cutler, for leading the project and often giving me advice. Thanks to Ohmsha for clearing the rights issues smoothly. Thanks to Taku Kimura for approving the use of the beautiful cover image in the English edition.

Finally, thanks to my family, friends, and colleagues who kept on encouraging me; I think I couldn't have reached the goal without their warm voices.

I

Geometry-Based Approaches

In computer graphics, *rendering* is the process of creating an image of an object or a general scene from a mathematical representation. Just as styles of painting and drawing in art range from the representational to the abstract, there are different styles of rendering. Early rendering methods, much like early artwork, concentrated on producing recognizable representations of objects—early renderings did not look at all real. *Photorealistic rendering* is the process of reproducing what an object or scene would look like if it were constructed and photographed, and this involves simulating how reflected and scattered light illuminate a real environment.

The interaction of light and matter in nature is very complicated, and has been studied in the natural sciences for many years. By the mid-twentieth centuryit had become commonplace in manufacturing to represent objects using spatial coordinates and mathematical expressions. New approaches for representing curved surfaces emerged by the 1960s. By then, the theoretical foundations of light transport were mostly complete, but the application of physically based light simulation was not feasible until sufficient computer processing power became available in the early 1980s. Since then photorealism has been a major goal of research in computer graphics.

Just like studies in any field of science, researchers in photorealistic rendering took the approach of starting simple. Specifically, basic surface reflection was modeled first, and illumination effects were studied in very simple scenes. More complex environments and volume effects such as smoke and fog were considered later. Research then shifted to scattering and re-emission of light from beneath a surface, an effect observed in hair and skin. Since 2000, much research has focused on generating photorealistic renderings at interactive rates, driven in part by the emergence of high-speed graphics hardware technology. In Part I, methods of photorealistic rendering that work on geometric models are introduced along with methods for implementing them on graphics hardware.

1

Introduction to Photorealistic Rendering

Photorealistic rendering is the process of image generation by simulating the physical interaction of light in an environment. Specifically, the simulation involves how light from *light sources* is reflected and scattered throughout the environment. The environment, or scene, as it is sometimes called, consists of a collection of mathematically described geometric objects. The shape description of the objects is known as the *geometric model* of the environment; however, this is only part of the complete model needed for rendering. Surface properties, such as color and reflection characteristics, as well as volume elements such as smoke and fog, affect the light propagation and are therefore a necessary part of the model. These elements, and a model for the light propagation itself all require a mathematical representation that can be incorporated into the rendering simulation.

In this chapter, the basic physical concepts used in rendering are presented. The model of light propagation most often used in rendering, radiant power carried along light paths in the form of rays, is developed in conjunction with related physical quantities of light measurement. The basic surface reflectance model used in rendering is also introduced, and the chapter concludes with a description of the two primary methods of image generation: scanline rendering and ray tracing.

1.1 Physical Quantities of Light

Modeling light interaction involves the physical quantities associated with light as electromagnetic radiation. Physically, light consists of electromagnetic waves

Figure 1.1   Flux is a measure of radiant power.

formed from simultaneously changing electric and magnetic fields. At a very small scale, light also behaves as if it exists in discrete bundles or packets (photons). However, at the macroscopic scale where rendering is normally done, particle effects really do not come into play, and wave effects have limited impact. In real environments, light is more naturally regarded as a flow of energy, the measurement of which is known as *radiometry*. The physical quantities of light measurement are called *radiometric* quantities.[1]

1.1.1   Radiant Energy and Flux

A basic physical (radiometric) quantity of light is *flux* Φ, which is defined as the *radiant energy Q* per time:

$$\Phi = \frac{dQ}{dt}. \tag{1.1}$$

Flux, the temporal flow of radiant energy, is thus a measurement of radiant power and is typically expressed in watts. Flux normally refers to the radiant power reaching or flowing through some real or hypothetical surface. In the case of a light source, the flux through an imaginary sphere centered at the source represents the total flux output of the source (Figure 1.1). This flux divided by 4π, the area of a unit sphere, is the *intensity* of the source.

1.1.2   Irradiance

Flux measures the total radiant power reaching a surface, but without regard to surface position: the power might be concentrated on only part of the surface, or spread evenly across it. A position-dependent measure of radiant power is flux

---

[1] Terminology of radiometry is not entirely standardized. The notation here follows Chapter 2 of *Radiosity and Realistic Image Synthesis* by Cohen and Wallace [Cohen and Wallace 93]; the chapter was written by Pat Hanrahan.

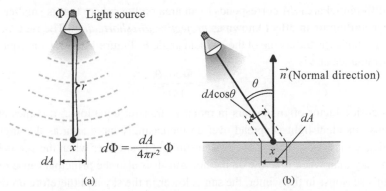

Figure 1.2   Irradiance caused by a light source. (a) The flux at a distance r from the source is spread out over a sphere of radius r. (b) When the flux hits a surface at an angle, the differential surface area dA gets the flux of a smaller differential area on the sphere: the irradiance is reduced by the cosine of the angle of incidence.

per area, the *irradiance* at the area. The irradiance $E(x)$ at a point x on a surface is the differential flux on a differential area dA at x divided by that area:

$$E(x) = \frac{d\Phi}{dA}, \tag{1.2}$$

where dA is perpendicular to the surface normal direction at x, i.e., is parallel to the surface at x. Irradiance is thus a measure of the radiant energy per area per time. The function $E(x)$ is formalized as a function of surface position; it is the limit of the flux in a small region containing x divided by the area of the region, as the region shrinks uniformly to x. Irradiance is also known as *flux density*, as it measures the local density of flux at the surface point.

Radiant emission of a sufficiently small light source can be regarded as a collection of expanding concentric spheres centered at the light source, each having constant flux Φ. When one of these spheres hits a surface point x, its radius r is the distance from x to the source (Figure 1.2(a)). If the light source lies directly above the surface, i.e., in the direction of the surface normal, then the differential flux $d\Phi$ incident on the differential area dA at x is the total flux Φ times the fraction of the sphere area that hits dA, which is $dA/4\pi r^2$. The irradiance at x is therefore

$$E(x) = \frac{d\Phi}{dA} = \frac{\frac{dA}{4\pi r^2}\Phi}{dA} = \frac{\Phi}{4\pi r^2}, \tag{1.3}$$

which is the familiar inverse square law of illumination.

Of course, light sources do not generally lie directly above the illuminated surface; the incident flux sphere usually hits the surface at an angle θ. In this case the differential area dA corresponds to an area on the sphere that is smaller than dA, according to an effect known as *projective foreshortening*. The ratio of this foreshortening is the cosine of the incident angle θ (Figure 1.2(b)). Consequently, the irradiance at x is

$$E(x) = \frac{\Phi \cos \theta}{4\pi r^2}. \tag{1.4}$$

This cosine factor often appears in radiative transfer equations. It comes about because incident light is spread over an increasingly large area as the angle of incidence increases. This is one reason sunlight is stronger when the sun is high in the sky than when it is low on the horizon. It is also the principal cause of the Earth's seasons: in the winter, the sun is lower in the sky and therefore produces less irradiance.

While irradiance $E(x)$ is the radiant power received at a point x, the radiant power *leaving* a surface at x is the known as the *radiant exitance* or *radiosity*, denoted by $M(x)$ or $B(x)$. The definition is the same as that of irradiance, flux per area, but the flux is regarded as leaving the surface rather than arriving. The term "radiant exitance" has become the preferred term in recent years, to avoid confusion with the "radiosity method" for computing global illumination. (described in Chapter 2).

1.1.3   Radiance

Just as flux does not depend on surface position, irradiance and radiant exitance do not depend on direction. But light emission and reflection clearly do depend on direction: the color and strength of light perceived at a photoreceptor in the human eye is dependent on the particular direction. The radiant power exiting from (or incident on) a point x in a direction $\vec{\omega}$ is called the *radiance* $L(x, \vec{\omega})$.[2]

Radiance is essentially a directional restriction of irradiance or radiant exitance: it is the flux per area in a differential cone of directions (Figure 1.3). As a matter of convenience, the surface through which the flux is measured need not be perpendicular to the direction $\vec{\omega}$. If θ is the angle the surface normal makes with the direction $\vec{\omega}$, then $dA \cos \theta$ is the *projected differential area*—the $\cos \theta$ factor accounts for the projective foreshortening. If $d\omega$ denotes the differential solid angle[3] about the direction $\vec{\omega}$, as illustrated in Figure 1.3, radiance can be

---

[2]Although directions are often represented by 3D vectors, it is also convenient to represent directions from a point x as points on the unit sphere centered at x. Each point on the unit sphere corresponds to a unique direction. By convention, directions are often denoted by $\vec{\omega}$

[3]A set of directions corresponds to a subset of the unit sphere; the *solid angle* of the set is the area of the corresponding spherical subset. The set of all directions therefore has solid angle 4π, the area of the unit sphere. The differential solid angle $d\omega$ of a differential cone is the differential area of the unit sphere subtended by the cone.

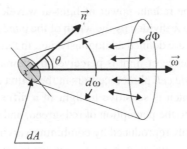

Figure 1.3   Definition of radiance. The radiance is the flux in a differential cone from a differential area dA.

defined in terms of differentials as

$$L(x, \vec{\omega}) = \frac{d\Phi}{d\omega\, dA \cos\theta}.$$ (1.5)

This definition removes the dependence on the specific surface orientation without losing the area dependence, so that radiance is well defined at any point in space.

Radiance has a fundamental property that is particularly relevant to computer graphics: as it travels through a transparent medium, *radiance is constant along a line*. This is not obvious from the definition and may seem unintuitive. It is a result of the fact that the solid angle subtended by a small area, which is inversely proportional to the square of the distance to the area, cancels the effect of inverse square decrease of flux density with distance. A real-world example of this phenomenon is that an area on a wall (or a book page, or a computer monitor) appears to have the same brightness as an observer moves toward it or away from it. The fact that radiance is constant along a line is the basis of geometric optics, in which light is treated as propagating along rays, and also serves as the physical foundation of ray tracing (Section 1.3.3).

Radiance is in some sense the most fundamental physical quantity of light used in photorealistic rendering. The definition of Equation (1.5) is not very intuitive. It is probably more helpful to think of radiance as the general strength of light at a point in a particular direction, or equivalently, as the radiant power carried along a ray.

1.1.4   Spectral Quantities and Color

As defined above, radiance and the other radiometric quantities include energy across the electromagnetic spectrum. They can be made to depend on wavelength by limiting the quantity to the power in a small wavelength band. For example, *spectral flux* $\Phi(\lambda)$ is the radiant power of light at wavelengths in a differential wavelength band around λ divided by the width of the band $d\lambda$. *Spectral radiance* and *spectral irradiance* are defined analogously, i.e., in terms of the spectral flux.

Wavelength dependence of light is perceived by humans as color. Color vision comes from the *cone cell* photoreceptors in the retina of which humans have three types, each of which is sensitive to light in a different wavelength band, corresponding roughly to the perception of red, green, and blue.

Color can be plausibly reproduced by combining varying strengths of light in the red, green, and blue wavelength bands; most display systems work using this principle. It is therefore common to use a *trichromatic* (three color) representation for spectral quantities. In the RGB representation, each value has a separate red, green, and blue component. Other trichromatic formats are described in Chapter 6.

1.2   Modeling the Behavior of Light

1.2.1   Local Illumination and Global Illumination

Modeling of light interaction for photorealistic rendering can be loosely split into two basic problems. How the surface of an object responds to incident illumination is called *local illumination*. This includes reflection from the surface, transmission through the surface, and the more complicated problem of subsurface scattering, which describes how light bounces around below the surface before leaving it.

In contrast, *global illumination* is concerned with the problem of how the environment is illuminated as a whole. In particular, global illumination includes light that reaches a surface indirectly by reflection and scattering from other objects in the environment. In fact, the term has become almost synonymous with the computation of indirect illumination. Of course, good local illumination models are essential to indirect illumination computation, as it involves the transport (reflection and scattering) of light throughout the environment. Likewise, effective models of local illumination depend on global requirements. Local and global illumination are thus intertwined, and there is not always a clear distinction between them.

1.2.2   Calculation of Illumination

Irradiance produced on a surface by a light source is one form of *direct illumination*. Equation (1.4) provides a formula for direct illumination from small or

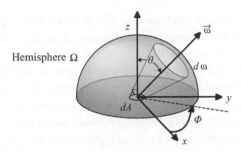

Figure 1.4   Radiance at a surface point. Directions above the surface correspond to points on the hemisphere Ω; the differential area in the direction $\vec{\omega}$ is smaller than differential surface area by the $\cos\theta$ factor.

sufficiently distant light source. The formula depends only on the flux (intensity) of the light source, not its size, and therefore remains valid if the source is shrunk to a single point. Such a light source is known as a *point source*. When a point source is far enough away, neither the direction of nor the relative distance to the point change appreciably across a surface. In this case, the point source becomes a *directional source*.

Point and directional sources were used almost exclusively in the early days of graphics, and remain in use for many applications. However, they have limited applicability in photorealistic rendering, because real light sources have some effective nonnegligible surface area. Such sources are called *area sources*. While the radiance from a point or directional source comes from a single direction, an area source subtends a nonzero solid angle from a surface point. The irradiance due to an area source is computed by integrating the radiance over the set of directions to the source.

In real environments, incident radiance comes not only from light sources, but also from light reflected off other objects. This is known as *indirect illumination*. To account for this, the irradiance at a surface point must be computed by integrating the incoming radiance in all directions above the surface, not just the directions to the light source. More precisely, irradiance $E(x)$ at a surface point x comes from integrating the cosine-weighted incident radiance $L_i(x, \vec{\omega})$ function over the hemisphere Ω above the surface at x (Figure 1.4):

$$E(x) = \int_{\Omega} L_i(x, \vec{\omega}')(\vec{n} \cdot \vec{\omega}') \, d\omega'. \tag{1.6}$$

Here $\vec{n}$ is the unit normal vector; $\vec{n} \cdot \vec{\omega}' = \cos\theta'$, where θ' the incident angle. Multiplication by $\cos\theta'$ essentially undoes the projective foreshortening and thereby accounts for the spreading out of flux coming in at an angle.

The incident radiance function $L_i(x, \vec{\omega}')$ is an abstract representation of the directional distribution of light reaching a surface point—only in the simplest cases can it be expressed directly as a mathematical expression. If a direction $\vec{\omega}'$ corresponds to a light source, the value of L_i is normally the radiance emitted by the source. Otherwise it represents indirect light, which might include light reflected from the point x itself. (This interdependence is part of what makes photorealistic rendering such a difficult problem, and is discussed extensively in coming chapters.) In the case of a point light source, $L_i(x, \vec{\omega}')$ has a singularity where $\vec{\omega}'$ is the direction to the light source; elsewhere the value is zero. This can be modeled in terms of a Dirac δ, which is a function that has an infinitely thin "spike" at a single point, and is zero elsewhere.[4] The radiance produced by a point source can thus be regarded as being infinite.

1.2.3   Surface Reflection and BRDFs

A *bidirectional reflectance distribution function* (BRDF) provides one model of local reflection. A BRDF is a function $f_r(x, \vec{\omega}', \vec{\omega})$ that determines how much light coming in from direction $\vec{\omega}'$ is reflected out in direction $\vec{\omega}$ at surface point x.

It might seem natural to define the BRDF as the ratio of the outgoing radiance $L_r(x, \vec{\omega})$ to the incoming radiance $L_i(x, \vec{\omega}')$; however, it is actually defined in terms of the *irradiance* at the surface point caused by light in a thin cone around the incident direction $\vec{\omega}'$. More formally, the BRDF is defined as the ratio of the differential outgoing radiance $L_r(x, \vec{\omega})$ to the differential surface *irradiance* at x caused by the incoming radiance $L_i(x, \vec{\omega}')$ spread through a thin cone of directions $d\omega'$ about the incident direction $\vec{\omega}'$:

$$f_r(x, \vec{\omega}', \vec{\omega}) = \frac{dL_r(x, \vec{\omega})}{dE_i(x)} = \frac{dL_r(x, \vec{\omega})}{dL_i(x, \vec{\omega}') \cos \theta' \, d\omega'}. \tag{1.7}$$

While perhaps less intuitive, this definition has proven more useful.

One way of visualizing a BRDF is to fix the surface point x and the incoming direction $\vec{\omega}'$, and consider the behavior of f_r as a function of only the outgoing direction $\vec{\omega}$ (see Figure 1.5). The shaded area, known as a *lobe*, represents the relative distribution of the surface reflection of light from the fixed direction $\vec{\omega}'$ at point x.

The BRDF of a highly reflective surface has long thin lobes centered near the mirror direction of $\vec{\omega}'$, while dull surfaces have more uniform BRDF lobes. It is worth mentioning that the value of a BRDF, while never negative, can get

---

[4]In its basic form, the Dirac δ, or *impulse function* is a function of a single variable that satisfies $\int_{-\infty}^{\infty} \delta(x) \, dx = 1$ and, for any function f, $\int_{-\infty}^{\infty} \delta(x) f(x) \, dx = f(0)$. To be precise, δ is a kind of generalized function—no real function can satisfy these properties.

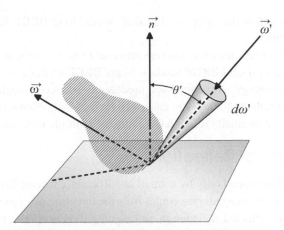

Figure 1.5   Notion of a bidirectional reflectance distribution function (BRDF). Radiance coming from $\vec{\omega}'$ (in differential cone) is reflected by the surface according to the BRDF function. The shaded area shows the relative distribution of reflection intensity, which is often largest in the direction of mirror reflection (in this figure the outgoing direction $\vec{\omega}$ lies well away from the mirror direction).

arbitrarily large if most of the light is reflected in one direction, such as the mirror direction. This may also seem unintuitive, but it comes from the definition of radiance as power (irradiance) per solid angle: if radiant power is concentrated in a thin cone, the power per solid angle in the cone can be very large.

As the name suggests, a BRDF satisfies the property of *bidirectionality*: the BRDF value remains the same if the incoming and outgoing directions are exchanged; i.e.,

$$f_r(x, \vec{\omega}', \vec{\omega}) = f_r(x, \vec{\omega}, \vec{\omega}'). \tag{1.8}$$

This means that light paths can be traced in the opposite direction that light would normally travel. Some of the global illumination methods described in the coming chapters rely on this property. BRDF bidirectionality is also known as *symmetry*.

A physically plausible BRDF must also satisfy energy conservation. For each incoming direction $\vec{\omega}$, the total power output, computed by integrating the cosine-weighted BRDF value in all directions on the hemisphere, cannot exceed the power coming in from $\vec{\omega}$; i.e.,

$$\int_{\Omega} f_r(x, \vec{\omega}', \vec{\omega})(\vec{n} \cdot \vec{\omega}') \, d\omega' \leq 1 \tag{1.9}$$

for each outgoing direction $\vec{\omega}$.

This does not bound the BRDF $f_r(x, \vec{\omega}', \vec{\omega})$ itself, but it does mean that it can be large only on a commensurately small set of directions $\vec{\omega}$ so that total value averages out in the integral. In other words, long BRDF lobes must be appropriately thin.

The energy conservation requirement turns out to be a significant challenge in the development of useful BRDF models. Many BRDF formulas in common use do not conserve energy. Although such models can produce visually acceptable results for local reflection, they can cause errors in global illumination computation that grow exponentially through the course of multiple reflections.

1.2.4 Calculation of Reflection

If a surface is illuminated only by a small or sufficiently distant light source, essentially all the incoming radiance comes from the direction $\vec{\omega}'$ of the light source. In this case, the reflected radiance in an outgoing direction $\vec{\omega}$ is the irradiance from the source multiplied by the BRDF value:

$$L_r(x, \vec{\omega}) = f_r(x, \vec{\omega}', \vec{\omega})(\vec{n} \cdot \vec{\omega}') \frac{\Phi}{4\pi r^2}, \qquad (1.10)$$

as follows from Equation (1.4), where Φ is the flux (intensity) of the source.

If indirect illumination is considered, the reflectance computation involves integrating the incoming radiance against the BRDF in all directions (Figure 1.6). The irradiance caused by incoming radiance $L_i(x, \vec{\omega}')$ incident on a surface point x from direction $\vec{\omega}'$ is given by $L_i(x, \vec{\omega}')(\vec{n} \cdot \vec{\omega}')$. The total outgoing radiance in a direction $\vec{\omega}$ is thus

$$L_r(x, \vec{\omega}) = \int_\Omega f_r(x, \vec{\omega}', \vec{\omega})(\vec{n} \cdot \vec{\omega}') L_i(x, \vec{\omega}') \, d\omega'. \qquad (1.11)$$

The conservation of energy requirement assures that the outgoing power does not exceed the collected incoming power. Equation (1.11) is the fundamental expres-

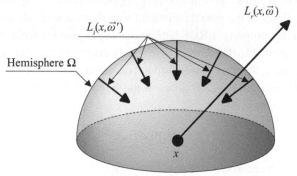

Figure 1.6   Calculation of reflection including indirect illumination must consider light from all directions on the hemisphere.

sion governing surface reflection (although it does not account for transmission or subsurface scattering).

1.2.5 Types of Reflection

The notion of a BRDF is an abstract framework for surface reflection. For practical rendering, explicit representations for BRDFs are needed. Such a representation can be constructed from actual measurements taken from real surfaces, but most often a BRDF is expressed as a mathematical formula known as a *reflection model* or *BRDF model*.

Surface reflection can be categorized into two basic types: *diffuse* and *specular*. Diffuse reflection occurs when incoming light is scattered, or diffused, uniformly in all directions. A diffusely reflecting surface looks about the same from any viewpoint, because the reflected radiance is essentially constant. In contrast, specular reflection is directionally dependent. Light incident on a specular surface is reflected most strongly near the direction of mirror reflection, which makes the object appear shiny or glossy.

In ideal diffuse reflection, which is also known as *Lambertian reflection*, the radiance $L_r(x)$ reflected from a surface point x is identical in all directions in the hemisphere above the surface (Figure 1.7(a)). The value of $L_r(x)$ is proportional to the radiant exitance (radiosity) at x, which is in turn proportional to the surface irradiance at x. The fraction of irradiance that is reflected as radiant exitance is known as the *albedo*, defined by

$$\rho_d(x) = \frac{B(x)}{E(x)} = \frac{\int_\Omega L_r(x)\,(\vec{n} \cdot \vec{\omega})\,d\omega}{E(x)} = \frac{L_r(x)\pi}{E(x)}. \tag{1.12}$$

The integral in the numerator is the radiant exitance, computed as in Equation (1.6) but with the incident radiance term $L_i(x)$ replaced with the reflected radiance $L_r(x)$. Because $L_r(x)$ is constant, it factors out of the integral. The factor of π is the result of integrating the value of $\vec{n} \cdot \vec{\omega} = \cos\theta$ over the hemisphere.

A surface that exhibits purely Lambertian reflection is said to be a *Lambertian surface*. It follows from Equation (1.12) that the BRDF of a Lambertian surface is

$$f_{r,d}(x) = \frac{\rho_d(x)}{\pi} \tag{1.13}$$

and thus depends only on the surface position.

Ideal or perfect specular reflection (also known as *mirror reflection*) is exhibited by a perfectly smooth surface, such as a mirror (Figure 1.7(b)).

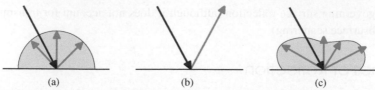

       (a)   (b)   (c)

Figure 1.7   Basic types of reflection. (a) Ideal diffuse reflection, from a Lambertian surface, is uniform in all directions. (b) A perfectly specular (mirror) surface reflects light only in the mirror direction. (c) Reflection from real surfaces can be quite complex.

All incident light from a particular direction that is not absorbed by the surface is reflected in the specular direction, the direction of mirror reflection. (Unreflected light is actually transmitted into the surface according to physical properties of the materials as described in Section 1.2.6.) Ideal specular reflection does not fit well into the BRDF framework, because BRDFs normally describe how incident light is spread out by reflection, and ideal specular reflection exhibits no such spread. The BRDF of a mirror surface therefore behaves like a Dirac δ function, with the lobes having the shape of infinitely long spikes in the direction of mirror reflection. In practice, mirror reflection is often handled as a special case in rendering algorithms.

In reality, perfectly specular surfaces do not actually exist, because surfaces are neither perfectly smooth nor entirely clean. Roughness causes the reflected radiance to spread out near the direction of mirror reflection. As the spread increases, the *specularity* of the surface is said to decrease. Highly specular surfaces exhibit near mirror reflection, while less specular surfaces appear more dull. Surfaces of medium to high specularity are sometimes described as *glossy*. Lambertian surfaces can be said to have no specularity; however, perfectly Lambertian surfaces do not exist, either. Real "Lambertian" surfaces normally exhibit some specularity, and this tends to increase at grazing angles. BRDF models frequently include a mix of Lambertian and specular behavior to better model real surfaces.

1.2.6   Fresnel Reflectance

Maxwell's equations, which govern the propagation of electromagnetic waves, determine the behavior of light at a boundary between two spatial regions having different physical properties. In this context, a spatial region through which light travels is called a *medium*. Regarding light as an electromagnetic wave, Maxwell's equations apply to reflection at a smooth homogeneous surface, such as a metal surface or a *dielectric* material such as glass or clear plastic. The sur-

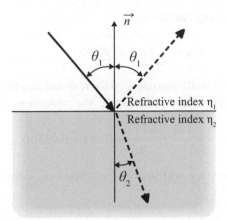

Figure 1.8 Reflection and refraction of light at the interface between two media. The angle of incidence is the angle of reflection, and the amount of reflected light is the Fresnel reflectance. The angle of refraction is governed by Snell's law. Both depend on the refractive indices of the media.

face of water is another example. The boundary is between the surface and the air, or whatever medium lies above the surface.

The ratio of the reflected flux to the incident flux as derived from Maxwell's equations is called the *Fresnel reflectance*. In terms of the incoming angle θ_1 and the angle of refraction θ_2, the Fresnel reflectance F_r is given by

$$F_r = \frac{1}{2} \left\{ \frac{\sin^2(\theta_1 - \theta_2)}{\sin^2(\theta_1 + \theta_2)} + \frac{\tan^2(\theta_1 - \theta_2)}{\tan^2(\theta_1 + \theta_2)} \right\}. \qquad (1.14)$$

Snell's law provides the relationship between the angle of incidence and the angle of refraction:

$$\eta_1 \sin \theta_1 = \eta_2 \sin \theta_2 \qquad (1.15)$$

where η_1 and η_2 are the refractive indexes of the outside and inside media, respectively (Figure 1.8). The complement of the Fresnel reflectance

$$F_t = 1 - F_r \qquad (1.16)$$

is the *Fresnel transmittance*, which is the ratio of transmitted flux to the incident flux at a surface.

The Fresnel reflectance is defined for purely specular reflection, but it can be extended to other surfaces by averaging the Fresnel reflection from all incoming directions. If $\eta = \eta_1 / \eta_2$ is the ratio of the refractive indices, the *diffuse Fresnel reflectance* is defined for any surface as

$$F_{dr} = \int_{\Omega} F_r(\eta, \vec{n} \cdot \vec{\omega}') \, d\omega'. \tag{1.17}$$

The value is known to be well approximated for real surfaces by a rational poly-nomial (truncated Laurent series). For example, the expression

$$F_{dr} = -\frac{1.440}{\eta^2} + \frac{0.710}{\eta} + 0.668 + 0.0636\eta. \tag{1.18}$$

for diffuse Fresnel reflectance is utilized in the subsurface scattering models dis-cussed in Chapter 4.

1.3   Structure of Rendering

Rendering is the process of generating an image of an environment or scene from a model. As noted previously, the model consists of the geometric shapes of the objects in the environment together with reflection characteristics (BRDFs) and other properties, such as the emission of the light sources. The problem of constructing and representing geometric models, which is aptly known as *geomet-ric modeling*, is a major subfield of computer graphics and is an active research field in itself. Rendering and modeling are usually considered separate prob-lems, although there is some overlap. As this book is about rendering, geometric modeling and the related field of animation are not really considered—rendering algorithms that depend on geometry assume the geometric model has been con-structed. It is important to remember though, that generating and animating re-alistic models for CG characters is a *very* difficult task that involves both human artistry and extensive technology resulting from many years of research.

1.3.1   Notion of Rendering

The conceptual process of rendering a scene (which can be a single object) amounts to projecting the scene from a chosen viewpoint onto an imaginary *image plane*. The *image* is a cropped rectangular section of the image plane that is divided into a fine rectangular grid. Ultimately each grid cell corresponds to a *pixel* (picture element) in the *rasterized* image. Each pixel normally stores three color compo-nents, and it may store other values as well, such as depth, opacity, or percentage coverage. The color values of a pixel come from the color of the object or objects that project into the pixel. The process of determining the color of a scene object at a point is known as *shading*.

In modern computer graphics, there are two basic approaches to rendering a scene. The first is to project each object onto the image plane and color all the pixels it hits accordingly. The second is to trace a ray from the viewpoint through each pixel and determine the object that the ray hits, then color the pixel by shading the object. The first approach is generally known as *scanline rendering*, because the objects are typically rasterized by scanning through the pixels. Rendering methods employing the second method are collectively described as *ray tracing*, although this term properly refers to rendering by tracing not only rays through pixels, but also tracing reflected and transmitted rays in scene objects. The term *ray casting* usually means that the rays are not traced further than the first object they hit, while *path tracing* refers to the more general process of tracing light paths.

1.3.2 Scanline Rendering

In scanline rendering, each scene element is projected to the image plane, clipped to the image, and rendered by filling in the affected pixels. The projection is effected by a projective (perspective) transformation represented by a 4×4 matrix constructed at the outset. The process of filling a projected polygon is sufficiently simple that it was among the first operations implemented in the earliest dedicated graphics hardware. Contemporary graphics hardware now allows the shading of pixels for basic graphics primitives to be done according to a user-defined program. One measure of the power of graphics hardware is the number of polygons that can be rendered per second. Real-time rendering systems (such as video game systems) have almost universally used some form of scanline rendering, but this is beginning to change as improvements in hardware have made other approaches, such as ray tracing, more practical.

In scanline rendering, care must be taken to assure that the rendering process respects the apparent depth of the scene objects: if an object appears in front of another, it has to be rendered accordingly. This is known as *hidden surface removal*. The *painter's algorithm* works by rendering the objects from back to front, but is seldom used because it requires sorting by depth, and does not properly handle mutually occluding objects. A modified form of the algorithm places the scene objects in a tree data structure, with all potential mutually occluding objects appropriately split. The tree structure, which is known as a *binary space partitioning tree* (BSP tree) is then traversed to render the objects in the proper depth order from any viewpoint. The method does, however, require extra storage and significant preprocessing time.

The *Z-buffer algorithm* handles hidden surfaces by adding a depth channel to the color channels in each pixel to store the depth of the object corresponding to the pixel. When an object is rendered, a pixel is only drawn if the depth value is less than the existing pixel depth. The objects can therefore be rendered in any order. This approach, also called a *depth buffer*, has proven very effective and is now a standard part of graphics hardware. However, it is not without its drawbacks. The extra depth channel does require extra memory, and it must have enough precision to adequately distinguish the depths of scene objects. When points on different objects project to the same pixel at the same depth, the results can be unpredictable. Such "Z-fighting" as it is called can cause unwanted visible *artifacts* in the image resulting from incorrect pixels being drawn.

1.3.3   Ray Tracing

As described above, ray tracing works by following the ray from the viewpoint through each pixel and coloring the pixel according to the shading of the object. Ray tracing naturally performs hidden surface elimination, because a pixel is shaded according to the first object the ray hits. Furthermore, reflected and transmitted light can be captured by tracing secondary reflected and refracted rays when a ray hits a reflective or refractive surface. Multiple rays can be fired through each pixel and the results averaged to produce better looking images, a technique known as *antialiasing*. However, ray tracing is computationally expensive, primarily because of the cost of computing the intersection of rays with the scene objects. Many of the rendering methods discussed in this book use some form of ray tracing, so the basic method is briefly described here.

Light emitted from a light source can be regarded as a collection of rays, each carrying a radiance value. These light rays are reflected and scattered between objects, and some of the light ends up reaching the eye of a human observer (or the lens of a camera making a photographic record of the scene). Rendering by tracing rays from the light source ends up being extremely wasteful, because the probability that a tracked ray hits the eye or camera is small. Rendering methods based on ray tracing therefore usually start from the viewpoint or camera and trace rays in the reverse direction. This way, light paths are followed that are known to hit the viewpoint. The approach is physically sensible because of the reversibility property of light propagation: essentially the same physical laws apply if the direction of light travel is reversed. The bidirectional requirement of a BRDF assures this is true for surface reflection.

In ray tracing, the value of a pixel is determined from the radiance carried by the ray (in the reverse direction) from the viewpoint through the pixel. When the ray hits an object, the radiance is the outgoing surface radiance reflected from the light source according to the BRDF (Figure 1.9). Ray tracing that stops at the first object is known as *ray casting*. General *recursive* ray tracing involves tracing

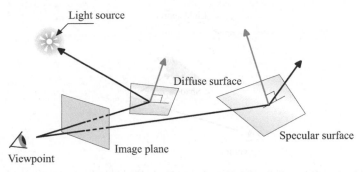

Figure 1.9 Whitted-style recursive ray tracing. Rays are traced from the viewpoint through pixels on the image plane. When a ray hits a diffuse surface, the illumination is calculated from the light source; at a reflective/refractive surface, secondary rays are traced.

reflection and refraction rays. If an object has a perfectly specular (mirrored) surface, the radiance comes from tracing the reflected ray at the surface intersection. When an object exhibits Fresnel reflection with transparency, separate rays are traced for the reflected and refracted paths, and the resulting radiance is the sum of the two values weighted by the reflectance and transmittance as described in Section 1.2.6.

The radiance carried by the ray at the intersection with a nonspecular surface is computed from Equation (1.10) with a modification to account for occlusion (shadowing):

$$L_r(x, \vec{\omega}) = f_r(x, \vec{\omega}', \vec{\omega})(\vec{n} \cdot \vec{\omega}') V(x, p) \frac{\Phi}{4\pi r^2}. \qquad (1.19)$$

The new term $V(x, p)$ is the *visibility function*; it is 0 if points x and p do not see each other, and 1 otherwise. Consequently, the radiance $L_r(x, \vec{\omega})$ is zero if the light source at point p is not visible from the surface point x. Otherwise, $L_r(x, \vec{\omega})$ is the radiance from direct illumination on the surface, and its value is added to the value of the pixel.

The visibility function $V(x, p)$ is computed by tracing a special *shadow ray* from x to p (or vice versa). This shadow ray is traced merely to see if it hits an object in between x and p; which object is hit first and how it is shaded are not considered (Figure 1.10). Shadow rays are therefore less expensive computationally.

The first practical implementation of a recursive ray-tracing algorithm was developed by Turner Whitted [Whitted 79], and basic recursive ray tracing is therefore known as *Whitted-style* or simply *Whitted* ray tracing.[5] Whitted-style ray

---

[5]Whitted-style ray tracing is sometimes called *classical ray tracing*. The term is avoided in this book, to avoid ambiguity with ray-tracing methods used in optics that are centuries old.

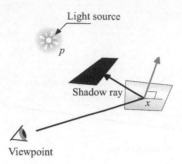

Figure 1.10   Shadows are determined by tracing a shadow ray to the light; the point is in shadow if the
ray hits any surface before it hits the light.

tracing faithfully simulates mirror reflection and refraction, and direct illumination of diffuse objects illuminated by point light sources. However, it has some
fundamental limitations that make it unsuitable for photorealistic rendering of
general scenes. The main drawback is that it does not account for indirect illumination. Global illumination requires integration over the entire hemisphere above
the surface. In Whitted's algorithm, radiance at a diffuse surface is determined
from only one direction: that of the light source. Indirect illumination coming
from light reflected off other surfaces is not considered.

The lack of indirect illumination is a major drawback, because diffuse interreflection is a primary component of global illumination and is key to photorealism. For example, shadows appear entirely black in the absence of indirect illumination. In real environments shadows are merely darker than their surroundings.
A very simple trick to mitigate dark shadows is to add a constant *ambient* value to
each pixel. The ambient value is a rough approximation—a guess, really—to the
average indirect illumination throughout the scene. Although it falls well short
of the expectations of photorealism, the ambient term is remarkably effective for
such a simple trick.

Shadows raise another limitation of Whitted-style ray tracing—it only handles
point and directional light sources. Each surface point is either totally illuminated
or totally in shadow, so the shadow boundaries in the rendered image appear to
have sharp edges. In reality, light sources have a nonzero surface area, so surface
points that "see" part of the light are partially illuminated. This causes real shadows to have blurred or "soft" edges in the transition between fully lit and totally
shadowed areas. Whitted-style ray tracing does not capture this effect.

Ray tracing can be extended to solve these problems by tracing more rays
at each surface intersection. For example, the reflection integral can be approximated by tracing many rays over the hemisphere above the intersection point

and averaging the results. When one of these rays hits another surface, the process is repeated until the light source is hit, or a sufficient depth is reached. This approach can produce some very realistic images, but at high computational cost. The problem is that because many rays are spawned at each intersection point, the number of traced rays grows exponentially with the number of bounces. Methods for making this more efficient are discussed in the next chapter.

2

Global Illumination

The basic ray-tracing method implemented by Whitted was a significant advance in realistic rendering. However, it does not account for the indirect light reflected between diffuse surfaces, which is an important component of illumination in real environments. As discussed in the previous chapter, *global illumination* (GI) refers to the overall lighting of an environment, particularly indirect illumination caused by light bouncing between objects.

The mathematical foundations of GI were essentially complete by the middle of the 1980s, but the cost of computing indirect lighting to a visually acceptable accuracy was a major obstacle to its practical use. Techniques such as image-based lighting were developed to mimic some of the effects of GI in a more cost-effective way. Even as computing power has increased, much of the research in GI continues to be about achieving the essential effects in GI efficiently. This chapter explores the history of GI and some of the most recent developments in its computation.

2.1 The Rendering Equation and Its Solutions

2.1.1 The Rendering Equation

Whitted's original ray-tracing paper was published in 1979. The early and middle 1980s saw major developments in algorithms for indirect lighting, such as the radiosity method and Monte Carlo ray tracing (MCRT). Jim Kajiya formulated the GI problem as a single integral *rendering equation* in a classic 1986 paper of the same name [Kajiya 86]. How to solve this equation efficiently has since become the ultimate goal of much of GI research.

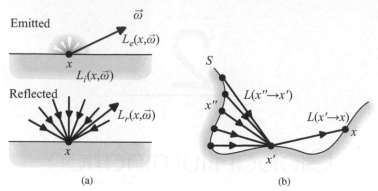

Figure 2.1   Geometry for the rendering equation. (a) Radiance coming off a surface is the sum of the surface emission (top) and the reflected light (bottom). (b) The reflected light can be taken from all visible surface points in the scene rather than the hemisphere of directions.

The rendering equation models light transport between object surfaces. The radiance L_o of the light coming off a surface at a point in a particular direction is the sum of the radiance L_e emitted from the surface at the point and the radiance L_r reflected from all incoming directions (Figure 2.1(a)). The reflected radiance is computed by integrating the incoming radiance over the hemisphere of directions above the surface point against the BRDF, as in Equation (1.13). The outgoing radiance is therefore

$$L_o(x, \vec{\omega}) = L_e(x, \vec{\omega}) + L_r(x, \vec{\omega}) \tag{2.1}$$

$$= L_e(x, \vec{\omega}) + \int_{\Omega} f_r(x, \vec{\omega}', \vec{\omega}) L_i(x, \vec{\omega}')(\vec{n} \cdot \vec{\omega}') d\vec{\omega}'. \tag{2.2}$$

The emission is intrinsic to the surface; note that emissive surfaces also reflect light. Equation (2.2), which is one form of the *rendering equation*, is deceptively simple in its appearance. The incoming light $L_i(x, \vec{\omega}')$ at x from a direction $\vec{\omega}'$ may be light emitted from a light source, or reflected from another surface; in fact, it includes light bouncing back from the surface point x itself. In other words, $L_i(x, \vec{\omega}')$ depends on $L_r(x, \vec{\omega})$, which in turns depends on $L_i(x, \vec{\omega})$, ad infinitum. This complex and intricate interdependence is what makes GI such a difficult problem.

Because the incoming light comes from other surface points, either by reflection or direct emission, Equation (2.2) can be reformulated as a summation over the points x' of all the surfaces in the environment (Figure 2.1(b)). This requires two extra terms: one to encode the visibility of the other surfaces (light from x' cannot be reflected at x if x' is not visible from x), and another to account for

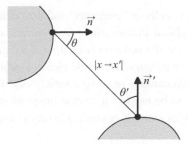

Figure 2.2   The geometry term for the rendering equation.

the distance to x' and projective foreshortening. The latter can be expressed as a *geometry term* as suggested by Figure 2.2:

$$G(x,x') = \frac{\cos\theta \cos\theta'}{\|x - x'\|^2} \qquad (2.3)$$

where $\cos\theta' = (\vec{n} \cdot \vec{\omega}')$. The $V(x,x')$ term is the visibility function described in Chapter 1: $V(x,x')$ is 1 if x and x' are visible to each other, and 0 otherwise. In this form, the rendering equation thus becomes

$$L(x'\to x) = L_e(x'\to x) + \int_S f_r(x',x''\to x',x'\to x)V(x',x'')G(x',x'')L(x''\to x')dA'$$
$$(2.4)$$

where the integral is taken over all surfaces S in the environment, and the notation $x\to y$ indicates the direction of light transport is from point x to point y.

Even for the simplest environments, the rendering equation is too complicated to solve in the traditional sense of finding a mathematical formula for the radiance L. Instead, "solving" the equation means to find a sufficiently accurate numerical approximation. Integral equations are well studied in mathematics, but computer graphics presents its own challenges. Numeric accuracy is often less important than an approximation that is visually plausible, and accurate numerical solutions can have visually unacceptable artifacts. There are two basic methods for solving the rendering equation: the radiosity method and Monte Carlo path tracing (MCPT). Radiosity works by splitting the environment into many small sections, while Monte Carlo path tracing works by tracing light paths from the scene in random directions.

2.2   The Radiosity Method

The radiosity method employs the *finite element method* to solve the rendering equation. The basic idea of the finite element method is to divide up a system

into a collection of discrete cells or "elements" and then deal with the interaction
of these elements. For global illumination, each surface of an environment is
split into small *patches*, and the solution is computed by modeling the effect of
light transfer between these patches. The finite element method was developed in
the middle of the twentieth century to solve a variety of differential and integral
equations, and continues to be used in a diverse range of engineering problems.
Its use in computer graphics extends beyond radiosity to the simulation of fluids
and deformable bodies.

In the basic radiosity method, the surface are assumed to be Lambertian: all
reflection is assumed to be perfectly diffuse. Each surface BRDF is then constant,
so Equation (2.4) simplifies to

$$B(x) \quad = \quad B_e(x) + \int_S f_{r,d}(x)B(x')V(x',x)G(x,x')dA' \tag{2.5}$$

$$= \quad B_e(x) + \frac{\rho_d(x)}{\pi} \int_S B(x')V(x,x')G(x,x')dA' \tag{2.6}$$

where ρ_d is the surface albedo at x, and the radiance L is replaced by the radiant
exitance (radiosity) $B(x)$. Each patch is assumed to have constant illumination
(and emission, in the case of a light source) and therefore the radiant exitance
of each patch is the albedo of the patch times the irradiance, plus any emission.
The value of the integral in Equation (2.6) is therefore constant for each pair of
patches. This allows the rendering equation to be *discretized* into a system of
linear equations with one equation for each surface patch. The radiant exitance of
patch i is

$$B_i = B_{e,i} + \rho_d \sum_1^N B_j F_{ij}. \tag{2.7}$$

The constant value F_{ij} is the fraction of the light leaving patch i that arrives at
patch j; it is called the *form factor* between the patches.

Because the radiant exitance is constant on each surface patch, so is the outgoing radiance. An image rendered directly with the radiosity solution comes out
looking like the scene is made from patchwork quilts. The discretization is visually unacceptable, even though the values may be numerically close to the correct
solution. In practice, rendering an image from a radiosity solution requires an
extra processing step known as *radiosity reconstruction*. A simple reconstruction
method is to interpolate or otherwise smooth out the radiosity values between
patches. Another approach is to perform a *final gather* at each point by sampling the hemisphere of directions using ray tracing: the radiance in each ray
comes directly from the radiant exitance of the surface patch it hits. Radiosity

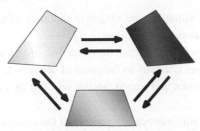

Figure 2.3   In the radiosity method, each surface patch gets a fraction of the radiant exitance of each other patch. This interdependence is the essence of global illumination.

reconstruction may also include the addition of ray-traced specular highlights and mirror reflections.

The radiosity method can produce accurate results, but it is both memory intensive and time consuming. How the surfaces are subdivided into patches has a significant effect on the final solution. When an object has a lot of detail, its surfaces have to be subdivided into very small patches, causing an explosion in the size of the problem. On top of that, the radiosity method only handles purely diffuse reflection (the finite element method can be used for nondiffuse light transfer, but it is a lot more complicated).

2.3 Monte Carlo Ray and Path Tracing

The rendering equation in the form given by Equation (2.2), expressed in terms of all incoming directions above a surface point, is inherently recursive. The incoming radiance $L_i(x, \vec{\omega}')$ at x from some arbitrary direction $\vec{\omega}'$ is the outgoing radiance at another surface point x'. The point x', can be found by tracing the ray from x in direction $\vec{\omega}'$. The outgoing radiance at this secondary point x' is again given by Equation (2.2) at x'. The incoming radiance at x' from another arbitrary direction can in turn be found by tracing the ray from x' in that direction, and so on.

One approach to approximating Equation (2.2) is to apply a kind of numerical integration to the incoming radiance sampled at points (directions) on the hemisphere. At each sample point, the ray is traced in the corresponding direction to find the surface point at which the light originates. The same approximation process applies at the secondary point, and so it goes. The total number of samples therefore increases exponentially with the number of reflections, but this can be mitigated somewhat by using fewer sample points at deeper depths; in fact, some fixed approximation can be substituted at a prescribed depth. For example, in a "one-bounce" approximation, the outgoing radiance at all secondary points is approximated by the direct illumination.

Path tracing comes from a "depth first" version of this approach. One sample direction is chosen from x, the ray to the point of origin x' is traced, where another sample direction is chosen and traced, and so on. The process stops when a light source is reached.

BRDF bidirectionality assures that reverse of the collected path, from the light through each surface bounce to x, is a valid light path.[1] The radiance coming into x along a given light path is the radiance from the light source multiplied by the surface BRDF value at each bounce. The basic idea of computing GI by path tracing is to sum the incoming radiance along all light paths.

Ray tracing in which the sample directions are chosen based on random numbers is called *Monte Carlo ray tracing* (MCRT); *Monte Carlo path tracing* (MCPT) is the extension to general light paths. The idea is similar to Whitted-style ray tracing, in that rays are shot from the viewpoint into the environment. The difference is that reflected rays are shot in all directions rather than just following the path of mirror reflection or refraction. Path tracing in general is a straightforward and effective method for GI computation. It handles reflection using any BRDF model, from purely diffuse surfaces to true mirror reflection, as well as transmission and refraction, and even wavelength-dependent refraction (dispersion). Furthermore, it works well with complicated geometry. The drawback is that a very large number of samples is usually necessary to achieve accurate results: rendering an image of moderate complexity can require tracing *billions* of rays.

2.3.1 The Origin of Monte Carlo Methods

A *Monte Carlo method* is a general name applied to any numerical method that relies on some kind of sampling based on random numbers.[2] Monte Carlo integration is a typical example. The integral of a function can be viewed as the average value of the function times the measure of the domain of integration (e.g., its length, area, or volume). Monte Carlo integration works by averaging many function values at random points in the domain. As more samples are included, the computed average $\times$ the measure of the domain converges to the value of the in-

---

[1] The feasibility of reversing light paths is sometimes called *Helmholtz reciprocity*. Path reversal in general involves principles of *thermodynamics*; Eric Veach provides an extensive discussion of this in his dissertation [Veach 97].

[2] The term "Monte Carlo method" was coined by Los Alamos scientists, in reference to the famous casino in Monte Carlo, Monaco. The connection to gambling is that outcomes of enough random events, such as rolling dice or spinning a roulette wheel, eventually follows an expected distribution; i.e., the house always wins.

tegral. Monte Carlo ray tracing is a form of Monte Carlo integration: the random points in the domain of integration are the random ray directions. Monte Carlo methods are sometimes called *stochastic* methods.

2.3.2 Basic MCRT

The first ray-tracing implementation using a Monte Carlo method was described in a SIGGRAPH paper entitled "Distributed Ray Tracing" by Rob Cook, Thomas Porter, and Loren Carpenter [Cook et al. 84]. Distributed ray tracing makes effective use of *supersampling*, the casting of many rays at each pixel and from each intersection point (Figure 2.4(a)). Glossy reflection at a surface point is computed by averaging multiple reflected rays according to the spread *distribution* of the specular reflection. In the original paper, the implied BRDF is rather simple: the reflected rays are sampled uniformly in a narrow cone about the direction of mirror reflection as if the BRDF has the shape of the cone. The width of the cone thus determines the specularity. The implementation also uses Monte Carlo sampling of area light sources to generate "soft shadows" (Figure 2.4(b)).

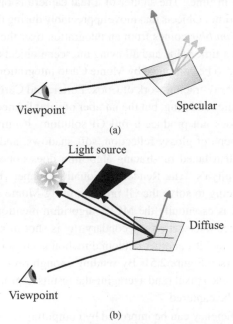

Figure 2.4   Distributed ray tracing averages the results of a collection of sample rays. (a) Reflection is computed by tracing a bundle of rays distributed according to the BRDF; (b) tracing rays to enough points distributed across an area light source produces soft shadows.

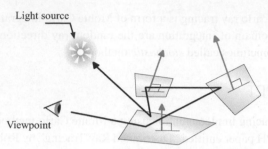

Figure 2.5   Monte Carlo path tracing (MCPT) traces light paths starting from the viewpoint, continuing in a random direction at each surface intersection until the light source is reached.

In this approach, sample points are chosen on the light source, and rays are traced from each surface point to compute the visibility and the radiance. The shadow value (irradiance) is then determined from the average value of these rays in the usual Monte Carlo fashion. The work also extends ray tracing to the simulation of real cameras. Focus and depth of field are rendered by tracing multiple rays through the optics of a virtual camera. The paper also shows how sampling can be distributed in time. The shutter of a real camera is open for a short, but nonzero exposure time. Objects that move appreciably during the exposure appear blurred. This *motion blur* comes from an integration over the time the shutter is open. Giving rays a time value and allowing the scene objects to depend on time allows motion blur to be computed by Monte Carlo integration.

The distributed ray-tracing work of Cook, Porter, and Carpenter was a significant step in realistic rendering, but the number of samples needed is prohibitive. Furthermore, it does not produce a full GI solution: it only accounts for the "blurred" phenomena of glossy reflection, soft shadows, and focus and motion blur. The basic distributed ray-tracing algorithm does not account for diffuse interreflection. Kajiya's "The Rendering Equation" paper [Kajiya 86] extends distributed ray tracing to solve the GI problem using Monte Carlo path tracing. Kajiya's approach is essentially the MCPT algorithm mentioned in Section 2.3. At every ray-surface intersection a secondary ray is shot in a random direction; at the surface that ray hits, another random direction is chosen; and so on, until a light source is hit (see Figure 2.5). By sending enough rays from the viewpoint or camera through each pixel (and averaging the results appropriately) essentially all light paths can be captured.

In practice, efficiency can be improved by computing the direct lighting separately at each intersection point x' on the path by directly sampling rays to the light. In this case, a different path termination criterion is usually employed, such as stopping at a prescribed depth. This approach or something similar actually has to be employed if the scene contains point sources—the probability of a random path or ray hitting a point source is zero; there is literally no chance of ever hitting it.

How well MCPT works in practice depends on the number of samples and how they are chosen. If the number of samples is too low, there are not enough paths to be sufficiently representative and the resulting error will show in the final image as excessive or objectionable noise. But increasing the number of samples increases the rendering time. Unfortunately the number of samples required to get the error below a certain threshold is quadratic: four times as many samples are needed to get half the error.

How the samples are chosen is also critical to the success of MCPT. As Kajiya showed, certain light paths are more "important" than others, in the sense that they carry more radiant power. For example, in a highly specular environment, light paths that are close to the path of mirror reflection carry most of the power. In contrast, the light following a path that bounces away from the specular direction carries far less light to the viewpoint. Avoiding these paths in favor of the more important paths can make MCPT more efficient, but it can also introduce bias. For example, if only specular paths are followed, diffuse reflection will not appear in the final image. When paths are chosen according to a nonuniform distribution, they must be weighed accordingly in the final average. Much research has gone into how sample points and light paths can be chosen judiciously without biasing the results.

2.3.3 Bidirectional Path Tracing

Basic MCPT depends on random paths from the viewpoint eventually finding their way to a light source. In a purely Lambertian environment with a large light source, a sufficient number of paths can be expected to do so. However, following random paths is generally too wasteful. A different approach is to start tracing paths from the light source and track them to the viewpoint, so that all paths carry light. But the problem then becomes how to get enough paths to actually reach the camera. The idea of *bidirectional path tracing* [Lafortune and Willems 93] is to trace paths from both the viewpoint and the light, then join them somehow to get a collection of representative light-to-viewpoint paths.

2.3.4 Metropolis Light Transport

Another method that traces paths from the light and the viewpoint separately is *photon mapping*, developed by Henrik Wann Jensen. The method is described in detail in Section 2.4. Basically the approach has two phases: the first involves a

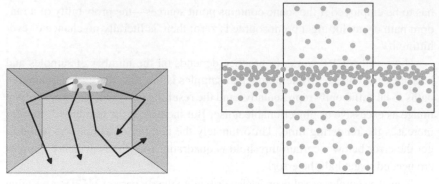

Figure 2.6   The principle of photon mapping. In a first phase, particles are shot from the light source and surface intersections are recorded in a "photon map." The second phase renders the scene using the photon map to estimate illumination at surface points.

form of particle transport simulation starting from the light sources; the second involves tracing rays from the viewpoint, with radiance calculated from the result of the particle simulation. In the simulation phase, a collection of packets called "photons" are fired in random directions from the light source following normal light paths. At a surface intersection, a photon is either absorbed by the surface or it loses some of its power and continues along another path, or possibly splits into two photons. In either case, information about the collision, including the power deposited at the surface, is recorded in the *photon map*. Eventually each photon is absorbed at some surface. The second phase consists of basic ray tracing from the viewpoint. At each ray intersection, the photon map is queried to determine the illumination, much like a final gather in the radiosity method. Photon mapping is a form of Monte Carlo simulation

For MCPT, it may seem more natural to consider only paths that start at the light and end at the viewpoint. However, constructing such paths according to a uniform random distribution is a significant challenge. One method for doing this was presented in a 1997 SIGGRAPH paper by Eric Veach and Leonidas J. Guibas. The method, known as *Metropolis light transport* (MLT), starts from a few simple light paths and develops many more through guided randomized mutations of each path. The construction of paths is based on the *Metropolis* algorithm.[3] The MLT algorithm is significantly more efficient than ordinary MCPT in most environments.

---

[3]This algorithm is named after its primary developer Nicholas Metropolis, a physicist who pioneered the use of Monte Carlo methods. It is also known as the Metropolis-Hastings algorithm.

2.3.5   Sampling Techniques

The final results of Monte Carlo simulations is highly dependent on how the samples are chosen. A good sampling scheme uses a small number of samples, produces little noise, and results in less error. Purely random sampling is unbiased, but inefficient. Although there may not be an "ideal" sampling method, a number of good sampling schemes have been proposed.

Random samples are rarely evenly distributed; they often end up close to each other in a phenomenon known as *clustering*. The effect on Monte Carlo sampling is that values near clustered points are overemphasized in the average. For example, if it is probabilistically expected that only one ray on the hemisphere above a surface point will hit the light source, but three rays end up hitting it, that surface point will get too much light. Although clustering is not unavoidable, it can be mitigated by dividing the domain into small regions and then sampling in these regions separately. This is known as *stratified sampling*. Figure 2.7 illustrates unstratified and stratified sampling, with three different ways of dividing up the domain.

Clustering is made worse by another practical problem with Monte Carlo sampling: truly random numbers are not easy to generate, especially at the rates needed for rendering.[4] Implementations normally depend on *pseudorandom sequences*, which typically exhibit worse clustering than truly random numbers and the lack of randomness can bias sampling in other ways. Alexander Keller began advocating the use of *quasi-Monte Carlo* (QMC) sampling for rendering in the mid-1990s [Keller 96]. QMC sampling constructs sample points from a fixed sequence, known as a *low discrepancy sequence*, rather than from a pseudorandom sequence. A low discrepancy sequence avoids clustering by construction, as the bottom row of Figure 2.7 illustrates. A variety of such sequences are known, although some are difficult to compute.

As noted above, some light paths carry more power than others, but finding those more "important" paths is not easy. General Monte Carlo integration can be made more efficient by concentrating samples where the function being integrated is largest, a technique known as *importance sampling*. Something similar can be done with Monte Carlo ray tracing. Instead of firing rays distributed uniformly on the hemisphere, they can be concentrated in areas of the hemisphere in which the incoming radiance (times the BRDF value) is largest. The trick, of course, is to determine what those areas are, and the only way to do that is to actually sample

---

[4]Hardware random number generators are currently available that produce values based on theoretically unpredictable physical processes, but they only give a few hundred numbers per second. A MCRT algorithm may need millions per second.

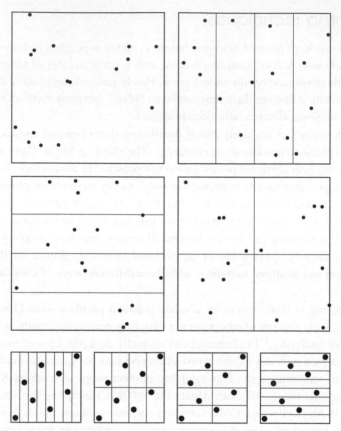

Figure 2.7   Sample point clustering and ways to avoid it. Random samples sometimes end up too
close to each other (top left). This can be mitigated by first partitioning (stratifying) the
region and choosing a fixed number of samples in each subregion (top right and middle).
In contrast, quasi-Monte Carlo sampling uses a fixed sequence of sample points designed
to adequately cover the sampling region (bottom). (Courtesy of Alexander Keller.)

them. One approach is to start with a coarse sampling on the hemisphere and then
use that to guide the importance sampling.

A nonuniform sample distribution is governed by an *importance function*. The
BRDF is largest where the reflection is most significant, so it is a natural choice for
an importance function in GI integration. However, the BRDF says nothing about
the directions of the strongest incoming light. Photon simulation can be used to
precompute the dominant light directions. When this information is used in conjunction with the BRDF, better sampling can be achieved. Figure 2.8 illustrates
such an approach. In the figure, the hemisphere is divided into smaller patches

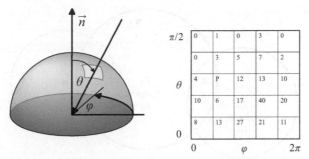

Figure 2.8   Importance sampling deliberately spreads out samples according to some known distribution. Stratifying the hemisphere and sampling more points in sections of known importance is one example (right).

(in spherical coordinates), and an approximate incoming radiance for each patch has been precomputed. Sampling is then done separately in each patch, with the number of samples proportional to the precomputed value in the patch. Importance sampling the BRDF further improves the sampling quality.

2.3.6   Interpolation and Irradiance Caching

Monte Carlo methods assume that obtaining each sample is computationally inexpensive. In ray and path tracing, the cost of firing a ray or tracing a path is relatively small, but is significant nonetheless. Running times can be improved if some of the samples can be obtained by interpolating existing values at nearby sample points rather than by tracing new rays. If most sample values are interpolated rather than traced, the improvement can be significant. Interpolation is well suited to situations where the lighting changes gradually, such as diffuse interreflection, but fails to reproduce fine details such as highly specular reflection and sharp shadows. This is one motivation for separating diffuse indirect lighting from specular reflections. The diffuse contribution normally requires integration over the entire hemisphere, but relatively few samples are needed. More samples can be dedicated to the specular reflection by sampling according to the specular part of the BRDF.

Interpolation of irradiance (more properly, radiant exitance) across surfaces was applied in the radiosity method from the beginning: interpolating the constant radiosity between patches is one way of performing the final reconstruction step. Radiosity interpolation is straightforward, although it becomes more difficult when the objects have geometrically complicated surfaces or the subdivision has complicated geometry. The values and the arrangement of the patches are fixed at the time of reconstruction, and the patches are typically arranged in

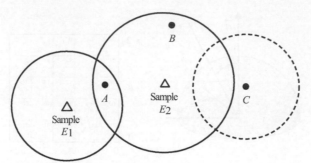

Figure 2.9   The irradiance interpolation scheme of Ward et al. works by interpolating sample points in overlapping discs. (After [Ward et al. 88].)

a somewhat regular rectangular grid. In contrast, samples in MCPT are poorly suited to interpolation. The method does not record the values of the secondary sample points; they are discarded after they are added to the summation for the particular pixel. But even if the values are stored, they occur at scattered points, which poses a more difficult interpolation problem.

In the late 1980s Greg Ward and his colleagues developed a novel scheme for interpolating stored surface irradiance samples—now known as *irradiance caching*—that is well suited to ray tracing [Ward et al. 88]. The method works by computing the irradiance at a collection of surface points by Monte Carlo integration over the hemisphere of directions above the surface (recall that diffuse reflection depends only on the irradiance).

The method maintains bounds on the expected accuracy of the integration, and the sample points are chosen judiciously so that the number of samples can be kept minimal while maintaining a prescribed accuracy.

Ward's interpolation scheme is based on circular regions centered at sample points at which the irradiance has been calculated. Figure 2.9 illustrates. When a point lies in overlapping regions (point A in the figure), irradiance is interpolated from the sample values at the centers of the overlapping circles (E_1 and E_2 in the figure). At a point inside a single region (point B), irradiance is extrapolated by weighting the sample value (E_2) of the circle, under the assumption that the irradiance changes slowly inside each circle. Irradiance outside any region (point C) cannot be approximated from the existing samples, so it must be computed by tracing rays.

The basic questions are how to choose sample points, and how to weight their contributions. To answer this, the authors first consider a "worst case" arrangement where each point is contained in sphere with a light (luminous) hemisphere and a dark hemisphere, arranged so the boundary between the two lies directly

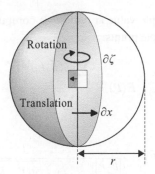

Figure 2.10   Light-dark sphere model around a surface element. (After [Ward et al. 88].)

above the surface point (Figure 2.10). Then they look at how the irradiance changes when the sphere is rotated or translated. The reasoning is that this causes as much of a change as any real incoming radiance, so an error bound for this case bounds that of any real radiance distribution.

More precisely, the goal is to express the change in irradiance as a function of the sphere rotation angle ζ and the displacement x. The exact formula is messy, but a first-order Taylor series expansion serves as a reasonable approximation:

$$\varepsilon \leq \left| \frac{\partial E}{\partial x}(x - x_0) + \frac{\partial E}{\partial \zeta}(\zeta - \zeta_0) \right|. \tag{2.8}$$

Inside the disc of radius R_i,

$$\varepsilon \leq \frac{4}{\pi} \frac{E}{R} |x - x_0| + E |\zeta - \zeta_0|. \tag{2.9}$$

The right side of Equation (2.9) can be viewed as the maximum irradiance gradient inside the disc. The change in irradiance caused by translating and rotating the sphere at a point is equivalent to the irradiance at a nearby point. Let $\vec{P}_i$ denote the original point and $\vec{N}_i$ the surface normal at $\vec{P}_i$. At a nearby point $\vec{P}$, where the surface normal is $\vec{N}$, Equation (2.9) can be expressed as

$$\varepsilon(\vec{P}) \leq E_i \left[\frac{4}{\pi} \frac{\left\| \vec{P} - \vec{P}_i \right\|}{R_i} + \sqrt{2 - 2\vec{N}(\vec{P}) \cdot \vec{N}(\vec{P}_i)} \right], \tag{2.10}$$

and this represents the maximum variation of the irradiance in the disc. The irradiance recorded at $\vec{P}_i$ is considered usable in the disc when this variation is sufficiently small.

The interpolated sample value at point $\vec{P}$ is computed as a weighted average of the nearby usable sample points:

$$E(\vec{P}) = \frac{\sum_{i \in s} w_i(\vec{P}) E_i(\vec{P})}{\sum_{i \in s} w_i(\vec{P})} \qquad (2.11)$$

where

$$w_i(\vec{P}) = \frac{1}{\frac{\|\vec{P} - \vec{P_i}\|}{R_i} + \sqrt{1 - \vec{N}(\vec{P}) \cdot \vec{N}(\vec{P_i})}} \qquad (2.12)$$

is the relative weight of sample point i (and implicitly depends on the surface normal $\vec{N}$ at $\vec{P}$).

The weighting function given in Equation (2.12) comes from the light-dark sphere, and is therefore an estimate of the maximum change in irradiance in the region. In 1992, Ward and Paul Heckbert presented a more precise approximation to the change in irradiance called the *irradiance gradient* that comes from interpreting the incident radiation over the hemisphere [Ward and Heckbert 92]. This irradiance gradient produces a better weighting function for the surrounding sample points and thereby results in a better irradiance approximation.

In the late 1980s radiosity was the most popular global illumination method, but the versatility of ray-tracing methods coupled with improvements in computer processor speeds made MCRT increasingly attractive. Irradiance caching was originally invented with the goal of fast MCRT in mind. However, it should be noted that the use of caching and interpolation has become widespread in modern computer graphics outside of ray tracing, particularly in real-time applications and graphics hardware.

2.4   Photon Mapping

2.4.1   Foundations of Photon Mapping

The technique known as *photon mapping* was first introduced by Henrik Wann Jensen in 1996 [Jensen 96]. One of the original goals was to improve the rendering of focused light effects, such as the moving patterns of light seen at the bottom of a pool on a sunny day, or the bright pattern created on a table from light transmitted through a glass of wine. These effects are known as *caustics*. They are caused by a lensing effect, where light is concentrated by refraction through curved surfaces. The term "caustic" comes from optics: when enough radiant power is focused on a small area, it can literally burn like a caustic substance.

In basic Monte Carlo ray tracing, rays are shot from the viewpoint or camera. When a ray hits a surface point of a caustic, finding the path to the light through the refractive media relies on random paths eventually hitting the light—there is no "shortcut" straight to the light as there is for the direct illumination. The probability of hitting the light source depends on the size of the light. If the light is large enough, it is likely that enough random paths will hit the source to capture the caustic. However, the most visually interesting caustics come from small light sources and therefore require a prohibitively large number of samples to capture effectively.

A solution is to trace paths from both the light sources and the camera. But bidirectional path tracing is complex, and is not particularly suited to rendering caustics. Photon mapping traces paths in both directions, but in two separate phases. The first phase is a particle simulation starting from the light sources, which distributes the particles throughout the scene. The second phase uses ray tracing from the viewpoint. The radiance at each surface intersection is computed from the locations of the shot particles, much like the final gather in radiosity, except that the photon map replaces the surface patches. The second phase is the main rendering stage; the first is a preprocessing phase that is the essential component of photon mapping.

In photon simulation, particles simulating the transport of light energy are fired in random directions from the light sources and then are used to simulate the interactions between light and surfaces in the scene. Particle intersections at the surface are recorded for use in the rendering phase. The particles are called "photons" but they are not true photons in the sense of quantum optics; they merely represent packets of radiant energy.

In the particle simulation phase each photon is given a fraction of the radiant power (flux) of the light source from which it is emitted along with a direction vector (Figure 2.11). The radiant flux of a photon is denoted by

$$\Delta\Phi_p(x, \vec{\omega}_p). \tag{2.13}$$

Every time a photon interacts with a surface, it stores its incoming direction, power, and position into a 3D map called the *photon map*. The photon may also be reflected, or "split" by transmission, according to the physical properties of light rays. Caustics are created by firing enough photons to make the photon map dense enough for faithful representation of the caustic.

Photon mapping can be used to make MCRT more efficient in general, as it provides an alternate form of irradiance caching. Basic irradiance caching only records the direct irradiance from the first diffuse bounce (although path tracing can be applied to compute secondary bounces). The photon map accounts

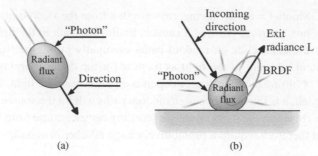

Figure 2.11   Photon mapping. (a) In the simulation (photon tracing) phase each "photon" has a flux value and a direction. (b) Both are recorded at a surface collision; the photon is reflected according the BRDF.

for multiple bounces. Also, BRDF-based importance sampling in MCRT tacitly assumes incoming light is constant in all directions, or at least in the stratified sections described above. But the incoming light can vary significantly with direction. The photon map can be used to guide the sampling based on directions where the light is strongest. Combining this information with the BRDF leads to better sampling and therefore improves MCRT efficiency.

The photon simulation is done differently depending on whether the goal is to render or to do a GI computation. For example, it is normally better to concentrate photons toward the refractive surfaces in caustic rendering, and there may not be any need to represent general diffuse interreflection. On the other hand, nonuniform photon distribution can bias the GI solution.

2.4.2   Photon Map Creation

In the first phase of photon mapping, photons are shot from light sources in random directions and then scattered at object surfaces. The position, incoming direction, and radiant power are stored at each surface intersection. After that, a probability test is performed to decide whether this photon is scattered or absorbed. If it is scattered, the photon is reflected in a random direction and the tracing continues. Otherwise the photon is terminated.

The difference between caustic photon mapping and global photon mapping in this first stage is that in caustic photon mapping, only photons that can contribute to the caustic are stored. Caustics come from reflected or refracted light, so a photon cannot contribute to a caustic unless it has been reflected or refracted at least once (Figure 2.12(a)). In global photon mapping, the goal is to get an approximation of the light density in order to guide subsequent MCRT, so all photons are traced and stored (Figure 2.12(b)).

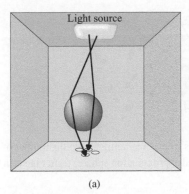 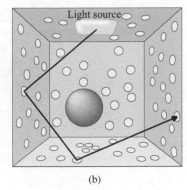

(a)   (b)

Figure 2.12   (a) When photon mapping is used for caustics, photons are only fired through the refractive object and only recorded where the caustic appears. (b) For global illumination, photons are fired in all directions and are recorded everywhere.

In either case, the photon map is initially stored as a list. Once the particle simulation phase is complete, they are moved to a structure called a kd-tree. This kd-tree is sometimes what is meant by the "photon map." The kd-tree not only compresses the data, but also accelerates lookup of surrounding photons independent of the scene geometry. This decoupling of geometry from lighting is one of the major advantages of photon mapping.

2.4.3   Rendering Using a Photon Map

In the second stage of photon mapping, the rendering stage, the reflected radiance at a point is interpolated from information contained in surrounding photons contained in the map. The calculation is based on a density estimation in an approximation sphere around the point to be shaded. The incoming radiance is regarded as coming from the collection of photons in the sphere (Figure 2.13), which is determined by finding the k photons nearest the sample point for some fixed k. The sum of these photons, each normalized by the cross-sectional area of the sphere and scaled by the BRDF value in the appropriate direction, produces the outgoing radiance:

$$L(x, \vec{\omega}) \approx \sum_{p=1}^{n} f_r(x, \vec{\omega}'_p, \vec{\omega}) \frac{\Delta \Phi_p(x, \vec{\omega}'_p)}{\pi r^2}. \qquad (2.14)$$

Note that storing the direction as well as its power is necessary for this calculation. Equation (2.14) may seem a crude approximation compared to the error-driven approach of irradiance caching, but the results are visually plausible and it has the advantage of being very fast to compute.

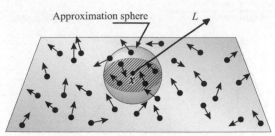

Figure 2.13   Radiance estimation from a photon map comes from a averaging a specific number of photons near the sample point, but limited to a fixed approximation sphere. (After [Jensen 96].)

There is also a difference between photon mapping for caustics and global illumination in the rendering stage. In global photon mapping, the photon computation is not done at every point to be shaded. Rather, the lighting computation is
done in the usual MCRT manner of sampling over light sources. The photon map
can be used to approximate the irradiance and determine the appropriate number
of samples. It can be used in a similar way for importance sampling: the distribution of photons represents the relative importance of incoming light directions
and can be used to guide the choice of directions to shoot reflected rays.

2.4.4   Improving Photon Mapping

Constructing photon maps is computationally expensive. Theoretically, an infinite
number of photons is necessary to obtain accurate results (just as infinitely many
rays are theoretically needed for Monte Carlo ray tracing). In practice, though, it
is only necessary to shoot the minimum number of photons needed to get adequate
visual quality. One improvement is to introduce a more principled method for
shooting photons from the light instead of just firing in random directions. The
same techniques used to improve Monte Carlo sampling, such as stratification or
a quasi-Monte Carlo approach, can lead to a more even distribution from fewer
photons.

In real environments, light is typically concentrated in particular parts of the
scene. Furthermore, not all surfaces of a scene are visible from a particular viewpoint; examples include back-facing walls, undersides of tables, objects behind
the camera, etc. These surfaces contribute to global illumination, but only through
reflection. A coarser photon representation may suffice for that. Ingmar Peter and
Georg Pietrek proposed adding a kind of dual precomputation to Jensen's photon
mapping algorithm that fires imaginary particles known as *importons* from the
viewpoint [Peter and Pietrek 98]. Importons are stored in an *importon map* in
the same manner as a photon map, but they travel in the opposite direction. The

importon map is used to guide the construction of the photon map. For example, when rendering a room inside a building, photons from the sun hitting the outside walls of a building can be discarded. In practice however, the importon map may not correspond well to areas that a human observer would see as visually important.

The main problem in effective photon mapping is how to predict where and how many photons to shoot so that the map is sufficiently populated to capture enough detail in visually significant areas. Graphics hardware can help with this. The sheer speed of hardware rendering provides quick feedback, and has the potential to allow a user to visually check and update the photon map at interactive rates. This does, however, still require human intervention. The problem of automatically predicting good photon distributions remains for future work, although a recent paper by Toshiya Hachisuka and Jensen contains an interesting approach [Hachisuka and Jensen 09].

2.5 Programmable Graphics Hardware and GI

2.5.1 Programmable Graphics Hardware

The *graphics hardware* is the part of computer hardware responsible for actually controlling the pixels on the display. The simplest graphics hardware merely maintains a segment of memory that stores the pixels to be displayed, which is known as a *framebuffer*, and then constructs the corresponding electrical signal sent to the display device. Modern graphics hardware has become much more complex. The central component is the *graphics processing unit* (GPU), a specialized microprocessor designed for graphics. Early GPUs were capable only of executing hard-wired instructions for drawing graphics primitives, such as lines and polygons with basic shading effects. They also handled hardware storage and manipulation of *texture maps*, which are essentially just small images to be drawn onto graphics primitives. Basic graphics hardware typically includes auxiliary framebuffers and related data objects. For example, a *stencil buffer* is a grid of integer pixels often used to mask parts of a texture or graphics primitive.

Recently *programmable* graphics hardware has emerged—GPUs can now execute programs in a specialized instruction set much like the central processing unit (CPU) of the computer. The first programmable GPUs had limited capabilities: there were restrictions on program lengths, and constructs for conditional execution and looping were restricted when they were even available. But each generation of hardware came with fewer limitations and now GPUs have about as much programming flexibility as CPUs; in fact, GPUs have become more

powerful than typical CPUs. At the same time, software has been developed
to provide higher-level cross-platform GPU programming interfaces. 3DLabs developed a GPU programming language called GPLP, which was included in the
OpenGL 2.0[5] specification in 2004. Another high-level GPU language is Cg,
developed by NVIDIA. Both of these are C-like languages designed to allow pro-
grammers to develop code for GPUs without having to know the underlying instruction sets.

2.5.2 Vertex and Fragment Programs

The two basic types of user programs are *vertex programs* and *fragment programs*;
each is applied at a different point in the pipeline (Figure 2.14). In a vertex program, the vertices of a primitive are available for access and modification. The
vertex program passes the vertices and associated data to the *rasterization* stage
where it is rendered as pixels, or more precisely, *fragments*. A fragment program
is applied to each fragment (pixel) before it is passed on to the framebuffer or texture map. Vertex and fragment programs are also called *shaders*. A *pixel shader*
is another name for a fragment shader.

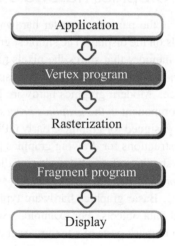

Figure 2.14   Flow of the GPU rendering pipeline. User programs are applied at the two shaded entry
points: a vertex program can change the geometry of a primitive being rendered; a fragment
program overrides the rendering of the individual pixels. (After [Purcell et al. 02].)

---

[5]OpenGL was originally developed by Silicon Graphics Industries (SGI) as a cross-platform interface for earlier nonprogrammable GPUs

2.5.3   GPU Ray Tracing

In 2002, Timothy J. Purcell, Ian Buck, William R. Mark, and Pat Hanrahan published a paper entitled "Ray Tracing on Programmable Graphics Hardware" [Purcell et al. 02] that describes how to do ray tracing entirely on graphics hardware. This was a significant accomplishment, because GPU programming was still very limited at the time. The algorithm works on scenes composed only of triangles (this is not very restrictive; CG environments are often triangulated). An efficiency structure is employed to minimize unnecessary ray intersection tests. The structure is a uniform 3D grid consisting of 3D rectangular cells. Each cell contains a list of the triangles that intersect the cell.

The paper describes the algorithm in terms of an abstraction of GPU pipelines known as *streams*, which are essentially arbitrarily long sequences of data. In general, *input streams* are converted to *output streams*, and the same computation applies to each element in a stream. Operations can be performed on multiple streams in parallel. The instructions that convert the input stream to the output stream are called a *kernel*. In Purcell's approach, ray tracing is done in four steps, each with its own kernel:

1. creation of rays (from the point of view),

2. traversing the efficiency (grid) structure,

3. ray-triangle intersection tests, and

4. shading.

The processes and associated data arrangements are illustrated in Figure 2.15.

In Step 1 a ray is shot from each pixel of the framebuffer. In Step 2 these rays are traced through the grid cells. In Step 3 objects within each grid cell are tested for intersection. If an intersection is found, the next step is Step 4, in which the pixel color is computed, and then secondary rays are shot. Every time a pixel value changes, the whole framebuffer is redrawn, and the process continues until each ray has stopped.

Although the algorithm described above was well known at the time, Purcell's paper showed how to implement it entirely on a GPU. A major limitation to GPU programming is the lack of data structures. About the only structures available are the framebuffer, stencil buffer, and texture maps. A *texture map* is a simply a rectangular array of pixels, normally of three (RGB) or four (RGB) channels, but other formats are available. Texture map pixels are known as *texels*. In Purcell's algorithm, the scene triangles are stored in texture maps. The grid is stored sequentially in an integer-valued texture map, with one texel for each grid cell.

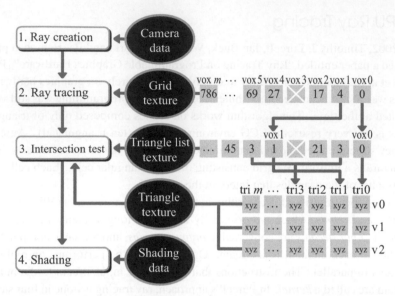

Figure 2.15   Flow of the GPU ray tracing method proposed by Purcell et al. (After [Purcell et al. 02].)

That texel holds the index of the first texel in another texture map containing the scene triangles arranged by grid cell. Each triangle is represented as an index into a group of three RGB texture maps: the x-, y-, and z-coordinates of a triangle vertex are stored in the red, green, and blue components of an RGB texel. There are three texture maps; corresponding texels in these maps contain the three vertices of each triangle. Another triad of texture maps stores the triangle vertex normals, and the colors are stored in yet another texture map. This configuration makes it possible to perform the intersection tests and shading computations entirely with texture map operations.

By defining all the data in textures it is possible to formulate the process in terms of input and output streams. The kernel can access each pixel from the input texture (stream) and store the result in the output texture (stream). The algorithm starts by creating a screen-sized rectangle texture map used to store the rays from the viewpoint (Step 1) with each pixel corresponding to a ray. Step 2 is the process of traversing the grid. This requires multiple passes, as each ray must pass through only one cell at a time. At each cell, the ray/cell pair is streamed through the intersection test kernel (Step 3), which tests for intersection with each triangle in the triangle list texture. If there is a hit, it is passed to the shader (Step 4). The current state of each ray is recorded in the stencil buffer.

Whitted-style ray tracing is recursive, but in 2002 graphics hardware was not; in fact, nested loops were not even available then. Purcell's algorithm works around this by repeatedly executing the same loops but with iteration-dependent state data stored in texture maps. The use of the stencil buffer to record the state of each ray so that the appropriate kernel can be dispatched was an innovation for efficiency. The algorithm can be extended to path tracing by using different shading kernels, making it possible to do true GI in graphics hardware.

2.5.4   GPU Photon Mapping

In 2003, a year after the publication of the GPU ray-tracing paper, Purcell and others authored a paper describing how to do photon mapping on a GPU [Purcell et al. 03]. This offers a significant advantage in addition to the speedup gained by using hardware rendering: it allows the photon-map construction to be visualized, and even directed, during the photon particle simulation. GPU programming had limitations at the time (and still does) that make it difficult to implement complex algorithms, so the algorithm implemented in Purcell's 2003 paper is a modified form of photon mapping that lacks the power of a full implementation. Nonetheless, it introduced a new way of rendering using particle simulation.

The main problems of implementing photon mapping on the GPU are how to do the particle-simulation phase, and how to do the photon map lookup in the rendering phase. The rendering phase is essentially just ray tracing with map lookup, and the ray-tracing part was already done. The method proposed in the 2003 paper stores all the photons in a texture called the *photon texture* or *photon frame* (Figure 2.16). This texture contains all the photon positions, directions, and power at a particular bounce depth for the entire scene. At each bounce, the photons at the current bounce are stored in a frame taken as the input for the process that computes the next bounce. The photons in the subsequent bounce are stored into the next photon texture. The simulation can be viewed as it evolves by displaying the texture for each bounce.

The second problem, that of photon lookup in the rendering phase, is handled by transferring the photon-map information into a framebuffer. Ideally there would be one photon per pixel, and each pixel would contain the index of the photon in the photon texture. But implementing this ends up being too slow and cumbersome. Instead, the photons are arranged in a uniform grid for efficiency, and each grid cell corresponding to a square group of pixels in the framebuffer is known as a *point* (Figure 2.17). Each "point" thus consists of multiple pixels, and each pixel corresponds to a photon. The value of each pixel contains the index of the photon in the final photon texture. The collection of all the pixels makes up the photon map.

The pixels of each point are drawn using the glPoint function; a vertex program handles mapping the grid cells to the points in the framebuffer. An added

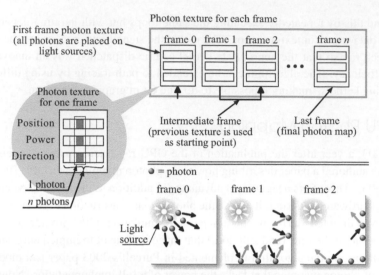

Figure 2.16   Encoding of photon frames and texture maps in GPU rendering.

complication is that the photons in each grid cell are not stored in any particular order—they have to be routed to the proper pixels as they are drawn. This is done by a fragment program, which intercepts the drawing of each pixel (fragment) in the point. The stencil buffer is used to control to what pixels a particular photon index is written. This is best illustrated by an example (Figure 2.18), in which each point is a 2×2 square of pixels indexed by 1 through 4. The photon value is only written where the stencil buffer is the maximum index of 4. The stencil values are incremented each time, so the maximum value shifts backward by one.

   In practice each grid cell may contain more photons than the point in the framebuffer. The stencil-buffer scheme tracks the number of photons destined for each grid cell point and how many were actually written. The total power in

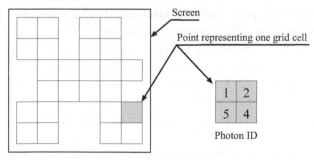

Figure 2.17   A photon map in the framebuffer.

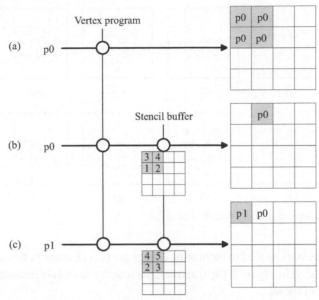

Figure 2.18   GPU photon map creation by fragment shader application. (After [Purcell et al. 03].)

the grid can be distributed (approximately) over the stored photons by scaling the power of each by the ratio of stored photons to actual grid photons. Computing the radiance from only the stored photons thus gives the true strength, although the accuracy depends on the assumption that all grid photons have approximately the same power.

As described above, the radiance estimate in photon mapping is done by averaging the k nearest neighboring photons at the shading point. An approximation to this is employed in the hardware implementation; Jensen's kd-tree representation is too complicated. In any case, the search has to be performed in the framebuffer. The method queries the grid by starting at the pixel in the framebuffer containing the shading point, following pixels in concentric "circles" centered at this point until at least k photons are found. Again, an example is the best way to describe the method. In this example, illustrated in Figure 2.19, $k = 4$. The algorithm employs a maximum search radius to limit the search, and a running search radius bounding all the photons discovered so far. The general steps are as follows.

1. The maximum lookup radius is set, corresponding to the maximum radius of the search sphere (this is the radius of the circle shown in Figure 2.19(a)).

2. The radiance of up to k photons inside the grid cell containing the query point are added to the radiance sum. As each photon is added, the search

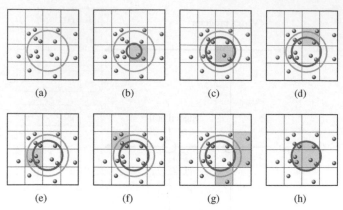

Figure 2.19   GPU photon lookup. (After [Purcell et al. 03].)

radius is expanded to include it. (There are two photons in this cell, which is shaded in Figure 2.19(b) and (c); the search radius is increased with each photon found.)

3. The search moves outward to the pixels corresponding to the current search radius, then Step 2 is applied at each pixel. Once k photons have been added, the search radius stops expanding, but photons continue to be added. This assures that the *nearest* photons are always included, although there may be more than k of them. (This is shown in Figure 2.19(d)–(f). In Figure 2.19(d), one photon is added, but the photon outside the maximum search radius is excluded. In Figure 2.19(e), the two photons inside the search radius are added, which brings the total to five—one more than needed. The one photon outside the search radius but inside the maximum radius is excluded because enough have been added. In Figure 2.19(f) a sixth photon is added.)

4. Step 3 is repeated until at least k photons are found, or only pixels outside the maximum search radius remain. (As shown in Figure 2.19(g), the search circle hits three more pixels, but none contain contributing photons.)

The shaded circle in Figure 2.19(h) shows the effective search radius and the collected photons. The algorithm differs from the original photon lookup algorithm in that it computes the radius estimate of at least k *near* neighbors rather than exactly the k nearest neighbors.

The photon lookup, the calculation of the radiance, and the storage of the result in the final image framebuffer pixel are all done in one pass. The image framebuffer is updated at each bounce, so it is possible to watch the simulation evolve. Presumably, each update will give a more precise result. The rendering is completed when all the pixels are updated. If the resolution is low enough, interactive rates can be achieved, which make is possible for a user to interactively move lights or change the scene geometry. In practice it takes time and a lot of passes to complete the final image. If it is too slow, the image can be *tiled* into smaller images that can be rendered independently. Fast tiles finish sooner, and may provide the user enough information to modify the scene without having to wait for the slowest tiles to finish.

The implementation of photon mapping in hardware is useful in itself, as is the ability to view the photon simulation as it evolves. In addition, the approach used by Purcell and his colleagues opened the door to a different way of looking at the problem, and also GPU programming in general. The techniques they developed may be useful in other areas of GPU computing.

2.5.5   The Progress of GPU Computing

The use of the GPU in photorealistic rendering developed in multiple directions, broadly classified into two categories: using hardware for specialized rendering situations, and using hardware to improve current techniques. A representative example of the former is the *ray processing unit* (RPU) described in a 2005 paper by Sven Woop, Jörg Schmittler, and Philipp Slusallek [Woop et al. 05] The work is notable in its development of hardware dedicated to ray tracing. Not only does it implement some acceleration techniques used in software rendering, such as kd-trees, but it also leverages the strengths of GPU computing to accelerate ray-tracing calculations in general. It clearly shows the potential power of the GPU.

An example of using hardware to improve existing techniques is the Lightspeed Automatic Preview System developed in 2007 at the Massachusetts Institute of Technology (MIT) and Industrial Light & Magic (ILM) [Ragan-Kelley et al. 07]. This system is capable of re-rendering RenderMan[6] scenes with different lighting at interactive rates. Although it is not the first such system, Lightspeed has some significant new abilities. For example, it performs an automatic translation from the RenderMan shading language to a hardware shading language. Also it employs two separate framebuffers: one for shading and another custom "indirect" framebuffer for the final pixels. Lightspeed became the first interactive relighting system able to handle complex effects such as transparency, motion blur, high quality antialiasing, subsurface scattering, ambient occlusion, and color bleeding. Furthermore, existing systems were aimed at game development while Lightspeed was intended for use in feature film production; its creation was

---

[6]RenderMan is the name a photorealistic specification and rendering system developed by Pixar.

driven by the increasing need for interactive feedback in film projects. It has been used in production at ILM. RenderAnt, a similar system developed by Kun Zhou at Zhejiang University and his colleagues at Tsinghua University and Microsoft Research Asia, presented in 2009, runs the entire Reyes[7] algorithm entirely in hardware.

Another GPU-accelerated rendering system developed for the motion picture industry is "Gelato" [Wexler et al. 05]. Released by NVIDIA in 2004, Gelato was a hybrid GPU-CPU rendering system. At the time GPUs alone were not sufficiently advanced to provide the high-quality results demanded by the movie industry, so NVIDIA took the approach of leveraging the best features of CPU and GPU computing. Although the development of Gelato was suspended in 2008, it paved the way for important advances in GPU computing.

As GPU programming has increased in power and flexibility, GPU programming environments have become much more user friendly. This has led to the idea of using GPUs for a wide range of tasks beyond rendering, a philosophy that has come to be called *general purpose GPU* (GPGPU) computing. In line with this philosophy, NVIDIA released a new GPU programming language in 2006 named *CUDA* (from *compute unified device architecture*). CUDA is a C-like language for parallel computing using a shared-memory model. A primary advantage of CUDA over direct GPU programming is the shared random-access memory (recall that ray tracing and photon mapping on the GPU originally required data to be encoded in texture maps and other buffers). The release of CUDA has made it possible to exploit the power of graphics hardware for general-purpose programming.

Since 2008, the use of ray tracing has become more and more prevalent in the entertainment industry and in the CG industry in general. In 2009 NVIDIA announced plans to release a GPU ray-tracing engine known as OptiX. At its heart, OptiX is a ray-tracing library for CUDA. It has the appeal of lowering the development costs of producing high-performance ray-tracing software. It is still in the early stages at the time of this writing, but expectations are high and the hope is that it will contribute to widespread use of ray tracing in the future.

Since the emergence of commercial programmable graphics hardware around the year 2000, research into GPU rendering has become a major trend in the CG industry. Much of the work has gone into implementing existing algorithms on GPUs. Now that this has largely been done, research is being aimed at what is really needed from graphics hardware. The field of GPU computing is still new and rapidly evolving. The industry is anxiously looking forward to future developments.

---

[7]Reyes is an algorithm and rendering system developed at Pixar for rendering RenderMan images.

3

Volume Rendering and Participating Media

3.1 Volume Visualization Techniques

3.1.1 Volumes: The General Idea

Photorealistic rendering is concerned with generating synthetic images that mimic how a scene would look if it were actually constructed and photographed. Computer graphics originated in the more humble problem of simply drawing pictures with a computer. As 3D rendering developed, primarily in the 1970s, it became apparent that computer-generated images lacked a certain realism. Indirect lighting was identified as a missing element, and beginning in the 1980s this drove research into global illumination methods.

Photorealism is not always the goal of computer-generated images. The way we view things depends on the purpose of viewing them. In medical imaging, for example, a photorealistic rendering of the human body is not particularly useful to doctors—they can get that by just looking at the patient! What is needed instead is a way to view the internal organs, layers of tissue, and dynamic elements such as blood flow. Modeling the surfaces and light reflection is not enough to display internal structures of normally opaque objects.

Surface reflection alone does not capture all light interaction within an environment. The basic rendering methods described in the previous chapter all assume that light rays travel through space without interference. This assumption is not always valid. Airborne particles such as smoke, pollution, and even water molecules interfere with the propagation of light. The sky gets bright well before sunrise due to scattering, and another form of scattering causes the daytime sky to appear blue. In fact, the appearance of some objects, such as clouds and smoke, comes from the way light is affected as it passes through them. Such objects are really volume objects and do not even have well-defined surface boundaries. Even when surfaces are well defined, BRDF-based rendering is limited in that it does not account for the diffuse transmission of light exhibited by translucent objects, nor does it properly handle subsurface scattering. Light penetrates the surfaces of real materials at least slightly.

In the late 1980s these issues prompted more research into volume-based material properties, such as particle composition per volume. The term *volume* or *volume data* is used to describe an object that has some particular internal structure or data distribution of interest. A volume may not even have a well-defined boundary surface; a *point cloud* of scattered data points is an example of such a volume. *Volume rendering* and *volume visualization* refer to the process of generating images of volumes or volume data. This chapter introduces some basic volume-rendering techniques.

3.1.2 Two Purposes of Volume Rendering

In CG, some of the first volume-visualization techniques developed were geared toward medical data visualization. The objective was to allow the visualization of the internal organs before performing surgery, or to use it as an interactive visual reference tool while performing the actual surgery. Photorealism was not a priority. What was needed was a way to quickly visualize the structure of body parts. One technique developed early on is to divide the data set for the body into a regular 3D rectangular grid, each cell of which is called a *voxel*. The attenuation or occlusion of light is determined in each voxel. Voxels with high density block a larger amount of light, so their color becomes darker. The light takes a different path through the voxel grid depending on the viewpoint and pixel positions: each light ray crosses a different set of voxels. The color of the surface pixel in the rendered image is computed by traversing the set of voxels for the pixel while accumulating the net color. This is one form of volume rendering.

The volume-rendering techniques used in medical imaging were soon applied to rendering natural phenomena such as smoke, clouds, and fog. As noted above, these objects are really volumes of distributed particles and their appearance comes from light scattering and absorption. A medium that attenuates or scatters light is known as a *participating medium*, a term taken from the optics and radiative transfer literature. The only truly transparent nonparticipating medium is a vacuum, but pure materials such as water, clear glass, and air come close at small scales. Earth's atmosphere becomes a participating medium at larger scales. Light scattering is responsible for a wide variety of natural phenomena.

In the previous chapters, light was assumed to interact with the environment only at object surfaces (other than the slowing of light due to refraction, which was only relevant at intersections). Participating media were not included—radiance along a ray was considered constant. This assumption becomes invalid in the presence of participating media, e.g., when the environment is filled with particles such as smoke, or when refractive elements are not entirely transparent. Participating media can affect light considerably, and were studied in optics and general radiative transfer theory well before the advent of computer graphics. One approach to handing participating media is to construct a mathematical expression for its effect in a small differential volume. This is well suited to volume rendering, because each voxel can be treated as a differential volume.

3.2 Volume Rendering

3.2.1 Basics of Volume Rendering

The term *volume rendering* in general refers to any method for rendering volume data. To distinguish volume rendering from rendering based on object surfaces, the latter can be called *surface rendering*. Surface rendering computes colors (radiance) at sample points on object surfaces, while volume rendering computes colors at sample points throughout the entire 3D volume of the object. The method of using a 3D rectangular grid of voxels to split up the volume described above is one way of constructing sample points. The color of each voxel is typically computed in a preprocessing step to speed the final rendering.

As noted above, an important aspect of volume rendering is the effect on light as it passes through a volume. Each voxel thus has a fixed *opacity* value in addition to an intrinsic color. The opacity, which is almost universally denoted by α, is the fraction of the light that is absorbed by the voxel: when $\alpha = 1$ the voxel is totally opaque; when $\alpha = 0$ it is totally transparent. The term $1 - \alpha$ is the *transparency*, the fraction of incoming light transmitted through the voxel.

The color C_{out} of light coming out of a voxel is defined by the equation

$$C_{\text{out}} = C_{\text{in}} \cdot (1 - \alpha) + C \cdot \alpha \tag{3.1}$$

where C_{in} is the incoming color (or spectral radiance) and C is the intrinsic color of the voxel. The color of light passing through multiple voxels is defined recursively; the light coming into a voxel is the light coming out of a previous voxel:

$$
\begin{aligned}
C(i)_{\text{in}} &= C(i-1)_{\text{Out}}, \\
C(i)_{\text{out}} &= C(i)_{\text{in}} \cdot (1 - \alpha_i) + C(i) \cdot \alpha_i.
\end{aligned}
\tag{3.2}
$$

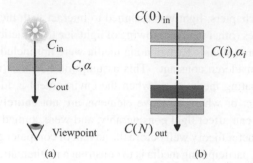

Figure 3.1   Overview of volume rendering with voxels. (a) Light is attenuated by each voxel according to its opacity α. (b) The effect is cumulative through a sequence of voxels.

Given the formulas for light-voxel interaction, the problem remains of how to render the volume into a final image. There are two basic approaches. One is to project all the voxels onto an image plane and draw each projected voxel into a framebuffer (Figure 3.1). This is aided by the depth component of the framebuffer available in modern graphics hardware. Along with the RGB color and the depth information, hardware depth buffers an α channel and can perform the computation of Equation (3.1). Voxels do, however, have to be rendered from "back to front", so that the voxel closest to the viewpoint is rendered last.

The second approach is to trace rays through the volume. This is normally done by tracing each ray from the viewpoint through the voxel grid (Figure 3.2). The voxels are traversed in "front to back" order in this method; the recursive formula of Equation (3.2) is applied to compute the final color.

Tracing rays through the voxels can result in a much better sampling of the voxel than the image-plane projection approach. The typical technique, which is

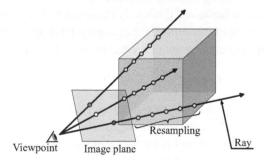

Figure 3.2   The ray-casting technique for volume rendering. Opacity can be sampled at many points in each voxel.

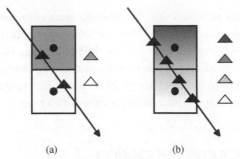

(a)   (b)

Figure 3.3   Ray sampling through voxels. The black triangles represent sample points; the corresponding values are shown in the grayscale triangles at the right. (a) Normally the value is
assumed to be at the center of the voxel, so the sample point is the point on the ray closest
to the center. (b) Resampling works by sampling interpolated values at more points along
the ray.

known as *ray casting* in volume rendering, resamples the volume data along the
ray. In the simplest form, the sampled value comes from the value at the center of
a voxel (Figure 3.3(a)). A smoother resampling can be obtained by interpolating
the volume data between voxels. In effect, this amounts to giving each voxel a
color (and opacity) gradation rather than a fixed value. More sample points using
the interpolated values produces a better overall result (Figure 3.3(b)).

The error introduced in ray casting is largest where the volume data changes
most abruptly. Ray casting can sometimes be optimized by using adaptive sampling (Figure 3.4), where more sample points are taken in sections where the
volume data is changing more quickly. The sampling interval is made narrower
when the difference in adjacent voxels values is large.

Volume

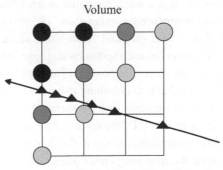

Figure 3.4   Adaptive ray sampling works by taking more samples where the density changes more
rapidly.

The ray-casting technique has become the most common method used for real-time rendering of volume data. This may seem surprising, because ray tracing has a reputation of being too slow for real-time rendering. However, ray tracing is slow for surface rendering because of the cost of computing ray intersections. Ray/voxel intersections are much simpler because of the regular placement of the voxels and the simplicity of intersecting a cube with a ray.

3.2.2   History of Volume Rendering

The emergence of computed tomography (CT) in the 1970s was a driving force behind volume data visualization research in the medical field. CT data is obtained from a scanning machine that records absorption of X-rays fired from a rotating emitter. The scan proceeds along an axis perpendicular to the plane of rotation so that the data consists of cross-sectional "slices" of a human body (or whatever object is being scanned). The result is a collection of tissue-density data distributed in a volume. Different types of tissue have different densities: air, soft tissue, fat, and bone can be distinguished in CT data..

Changes in density—boundaries between a region of identical or similar density—and a region of a different density—correspond to the surfaces of internal objects. Known as *isosurfaces*, these are the 3D analogue of contour lines on a 2D plot. The problem of how to render or "image" isosurfaces is part of volume rendering. Early techniques for volume rendering attempted to isolate and render these isosurfaces using standard surface-rendering techniques.

The *marching cubes* algorithm is an established technique for isosurface visualization. It was originally presented in a 1987 paper by William E. Lorensen and Harvey E. Cline [Lorensen and Cline 87]. The marching cubes algorithm is voxel based. It works by approximating the isosurface inside each voxel as a plane, which becomes a polygon when restricted to the voxel, and this becomes a facet of the computed isosurface representation. The surface is constructed by starting at one end of the voxel grid and "marching" along the grid in one dimension, connecting the facets in each section with those of the previous section. The resulting isosurfaces are piecewise polygonal and are limited to the precision of the voxel grid. One drawback to marching cubes for medical imaging comes from the "all-or-nothing" assumption that the surface is strictly bounded by the plane in the voxel. Surfaces in a CT data set are often fuzzier; the all-or-nothing assumption can produce noticeable artifacts in the final image.

In 1988, a year after the marching cubes paper was published, Marc Levoy introduced a fundamentally different technique for rendering isosurfaces based on the data points only, without explicit surface reconstruction [Levoy 88]. The method was based on his earlier work in representing and rendering objects as a collection of scattered points. It is said that this technique was the initial idea for the volume rendering technique.

Active research into volume rendering was being done at Pixar in the mid-1980s. A technical report written by Alvy Ray Smith at Pixar was said to be the first volume-rendering paper in CG; however, it was not made public at the time [Smith 87]. The original goal was to develop a commercial medical imaging system; the volume visualization research team at Pixar included the now famous radiologist Elliot Fishman. The system was completed and released, but its high cost and the fact that it was perhaps too technologically advanced for its time prevented it from having much success as a commercial product. The work was eventually summarized in a SIGGRAPH paper entitled "Volume Rendering" authored by Robert A. Drebin along with Loren Carpenter and Pat Hanrahan [Drebin et al. 88]. This paper introduces a highly accurate method for rendering images of volumes in CT data that is particularly suited for imaging the human body. The ideas represented a significant leap forward in volume rendering and greatly influenced subsequent research, in both volume rendering in general and the visualization of the human body based on scientific data.

A great advantage of the volume rendering technique presented in this paper is its speed. The algorithm is also useful for rendering both isosurfaces and volumes, and is well suited to hardware rendering. For these reasons it can be said that the algorithm is the most suitable technique for real-time medical imaging. Its use in imaging the human body is described in the next subsection. The approach is also useful for rendering environments that contain participating media. Realistic simulation of smoke, fog, and clouds in fluid dynamics typically use voxel-based finite-element methods. Discrete-time simulation stores the current fluid speed, pressure, and density in voxels at each time step. When these methods are applied in CG, the same voxels can be used for volume rendering.

3.2.3 Volume Rendering of the Human Body

Figure 3.5 illustrates the algorithm described in the SIGGRAPH "Volume Rendering" paper [Drebin et al. 88]. Each slice of data captured by a CT scan is processed in parallel, and then the results are synthesized into the final 3D rendering. The approach was originally developed to visually reconstruct the internal structure of the human body from the complex CT data, but it can be applied to other volume data sets.

One of the most significant advances was the method of handling region boundaries without explicitly reconstructing the boundary surfaces. Before that, most visualization techniques required a geometric representation of the surface

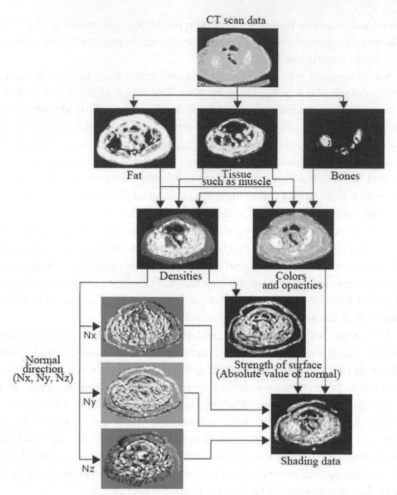

Figure 3.5   Volume rendering technique presented by Robert A. Drebin, Loren Carpenter, and Pat
               Hanrahan. (From [Drebin et al. 88] © 1988 ACM, Inc. Included here by permission.)

as a collection of polygons or other surface primitives. The marching cubes algorithm has trouble reconstructing a surface with fine detail because of the huge
number of polygons needed. Furthermore, connectivity issues arise when surfaces
have too many branches.

The method described in the "Volume Rendering" paper assumes that several
substances are mixed in a voxel. In human CT data these substances are air, soft
tissue, fat, and bone. The first step is to compute the percentage of each material
in each voxel, then a voxel density is computed from the product of the physical

density of the substance and the percentage contained in the voxel. A boundary occurs when there is a sharp change in this density, which can be detected by examining the gradient (differential rate of change) of the density. The gradient is a 3D vector that is large in magnitude when there is a sharp transition between materials of different densities. Away from a surface the density variation is small, and so is the gradient. The magnitude of the gradient, described as the "surface strength," serves to estimate the amount of surface present. The direction of the gradient is perpendicular to the boundary surface. The surface strength plays an important role in the process of color computation.

The color computation depends on the color properties in three regions in a voxel: the region in front of the surface, the region behind the surface, and a thin region corresponding to the surface itself. Each region has a color and an opacity, and can also emit light. Light passing through a voxel is colored by a composition of the colors in the three regions; opacity is included, but attenuation inside the voxel is not.

The color produced by light reflection from the implied surface is computed much as in surface rendering, i.e., as a function of the viewpoint, the surface normal, and the light source. The surface shading is split into a diffuse and specular component: the diffuse component comes from the color of the surface; the specular component, from the color of the light source. The diffuse surface color is that of the region behind the surface, which prevents color bleeding between neighboring materials. An additional step not applied in normal surface rendering is to scale the final color by the strength of the surface. A voxel that contains no surface has a surface strength of (nearly) zero, so the surface reflectance contribution is very small. The appearance of the surface so rendered therefore depends on the gradient, which depends on the density. The algorithm ensures the continuity of the data at each step, so the method produces the appearance of a smooth surface without actually reconstructing the surface geometry.

The final image is constructed by first using fast image-warping techniques to transform each of the two-dimensional slices of the volume into the viewing coordinate system so that voxel boundaries are parallel to view rays. Projection onto the image plane then amounts to compositing the sequential run of voxels corresponding to each pixel. The density and gradient computation can actually be done independently in each slice of CT data, and if the viewpoint is placed at "infinity," perpendicular to the slice planes, no transformation is necessary. This is another feature of the method.

The volume visualization algorithm described in the paper assumes the material percentages for each voxel are available from the data set. The paper also contains an algorithm for classifying measured CT data, which is composed purely of X-ray absorption values, into separate substances. It works using a probabilistic classifier on histograms of data values. However, information about the approximate densities and their relative distribution of the constituent materials is needed to make this work. Because of this, the method detailed in the "Volume Visualization" paper requires a certain amount of a priori knowledge of the materials being imaged.

However, CT scans of the human body are not the only use of 3D imaging by X-ray absorption, and in some cases, very different CT scans of the human body are not the only form of 3D imaging by X-ray absorption. Very different substances can have similar absorption densities. For example, if plastic explosives and cheese have nearly the same X-ray absorption, an airport security scanner could not distinguish between a bomb and a block of vintage cheddar using only the method described in the paper. On the other hand, the usefulness of the method is enhanced by a good understanding of the materials being visualized. Known conditions such as "fat is never contained in the bone" and "muscle does not exist in the skull" can be applied to better distinguish features when visualizing the human body. Although it was not clearly described in the paper, basing the rendering on the density offers a lot of flexibility in visualization. This is because a lookup table can be added to convert "true" densities of the various materials into virtual densities and opacities for the purposes of visualizing particular aspects of the data. For example, the skeletal structure alone can be displayed by setting the virtual density of fat and flesh to zero. This can be generalized: manually varying the percentage and the material histogram assignments allows the user to control many aspects of the visualization, although creating an ideal rendering can require a lot of trial and error.

The "Volume Visualization" paper described in this section is part theoretical, but at the same time it presents a practical and flexible volume rendering method. In the latter sense it is closer to the recent trend in SIGGRAPH presentations, which tend to emphasize practical rendering methods. This paper continues to be referenced in the context of rendering humans, especially in the motion picture industry.

3.3 Participating Media

3.3.1 Participating Media Visualization

As described previously, a spatial region is said to contain (or be) a *participating medium* if the effects of absorption and scattering of light is significant. Participating media are so named because they "participate" in light transport. In contrast to surface rendering, which considers only reflection and scattering at object sur-

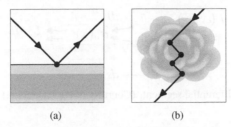

(a)   (b)

Figure 3.6   Surface reflection compared to scattering by a participating medium.

faces (Figure 3.6(a)), rendering of environments that contain participating media has to account for how light is affected by the media (Figure 3.6(b)).

The effect of light passing through a medium (unless otherwise stated, "medium" implies "participating medium" hereafter) falls in the domain of *transport theory*, which is the study of how particles such as electrons, mesons, and photons are affected as they travel through other materials. Transport theory was actively studied in statistical physics in the 1950s. The *light transport equation* (LTE) describes the physical effect on light as it propagates through a medium. Light transport includes not only the loss of light energy by absorption and scattering, but also the gain in energy from *emission* within the medium. The LTE governs the gain and loss of this energy by relating the differential change in radiance to the physical properties of the medium. The behavior of light in a medium is generally computed by solving the volume rendering equation. In computer graphics, the integral of the LTE along the the line segment from a viewpoint to a light source is called the *volume rendering equation*.

3.3.2 The Light Transport Equation (LTE)

The light transport equation is formulated in terms of the differential change in radiance $dL(x, \vec{\omega})$ at a point x in space along a differential section ds of the ray in a direction $\vec{\omega}$ (Figure 3.7). More precisely, $dL(x, \vec{\omega})/ds$ denotes the derivative of the radiance function $L(x + s\vec{\omega}, \vec{\omega})$ with respect to s. There are two basic causes of light attenuation along a ray: particles in the medium absorb some of the light, and collisions with particles deflect the light in other directions. The *absorption* is defined as the amount of light lost as it travels a differential distance ds. It is assumed that the differential absorption is proportional to the radiance:

$$dL(x, \vec{\omega}) = -\sigma_a(x)L(x, \vec{\omega})ds;$$

i.e., the differential light loss from absorption is a fraction of the strength of light (Figure 3.7). The proportionality constant $\sigma_a(x)$ is the *absorption coefficient* or

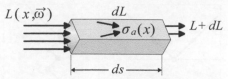

Figure 3.7   Absorption along a differential segment. (Courtesy of Pat Hanrahan.)

absorption cross section. Note that it depends on position in the medium, much as surface albedo depends on the surface position.

Radiance is also lost when light is diverted by collisions with particles in the medium. This phenomenon is known as *out-scattering.* Like absorption, the change in radiance due to out-scattering is proportional to the incident radiance:

$$dL(x, \vec{\omega}) = -\sigma_s(x)L(x, \vec{\omega})ds,$$

where the constant $\sigma_s(x)$ is the *scattering coefficient* or *scattering cross-section* (Figure 3.8).

The sum of the absorption and scattering coefficients, the *extinction coefficient* (*extinction cross-section*)

$$\sigma_t = \sigma_a + \sigma_s,$$

accounts for the total differential attenuation of light:

$$dL(x, \vec{\omega}) = -\sigma_t(x)L(x, \vec{\omega})ds.$$

When a medium emits light internally it is said to be *emissive* or *luminous.* Flame is an example. The light produced by a candle flame is a result of a combination of physical processes. The most significant is the yellowish glowing part, which is caused by hot microscopic soot particles. These particles are said to be *incandescent,* meaning they produce light due to their high temperature.

The light produced by incandescent particles is usually modeled as *black-body radiation.* A *black body* absorbs all radiation incident upon it, and the absorbed

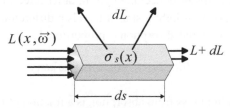

Figure 3.8   Out-scattering from a differential segment. (Courtesy of Pat Hanrahan.)

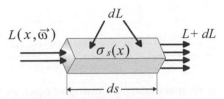

Figure 3.9   In-scattering at a differential segment. (Courtesy of Pat Hanrahan.)

energy takes the form of heat. As the temperature of the body increases it emits radiation according to a known spectral emission. In other words, the hot soot particles absorb light even as they emit it, and the emission depends on the temperature, which depends on the rate of absorption; i.e., the emission is related to the absorption. The differential change in radiance at a point is actually the emission function $L_e(x, \vec{\omega})$ times the absorption coefficient:

$$dL(x, \vec{\omega}) = \sigma_a(x)L_e(x, \vec{\omega})ds.$$

Absorbed light is assumed to be lost in the medium (in reality it is just converted to a different form of energy). In contrast, scattered light is merely diverted to a different direction. This results in an increase in radiance in this other direction, a phenomenon known as *in-scattering* at the point in that direction (Figure 3.9). The radiance $L(x, \vec{\omega})$ at any point can be increased by in-scattered light from any other direction. Computing the in-scattered contribution is similar to computing surface reflection: incoming light has to be integrated over all directions. The in-scattered integral encompasses the entire sphere about the point rather than just the hemisphere above the surface.

Light scattering in a medium is governed by a *phase function* $p(x, \vec{\omega}', \vec{\omega})$, which is something like a BRDF: $p(x, \vec{\omega}', \vec{\omega})$ represents the fraction of light incident from direction $\vec{\omega}'$ that is scattered at x into direction $\vec{\omega}$. The phase function is normalized so that its value integrated over the sphere becomes 1 (recall that a BRDF is not normalized). The increase in radiance from in-scattering is computed by integrating the incoming radiance against the phase function over the sphere, then scaling the result by the scattering coefficient:

$$S(x, \vec{\omega}) = \sigma_s(x) \int_{\Omega_{4\pi}} p(x, \vec{\omega}', \vec{\omega})L(x, \vec{\omega}') d\vec{\omega}' ds \qquad (3.3)$$

($\Omega_{4\pi}$ denotes the full sphere). A larger value of the phase function thus implies greater in-scattering.

The effects of emission, absorption, out-scattering, and in-scattering combine to produce the total differential change in the strength of light in direction $\vec{\omega}$ at point x:

$$dL(x, \vec{\omega}) = \underbrace{\sigma_a(x)L_e(x, \vec{\omega})}_{\text{emission}} + \underbrace{S(x, \vec{\omega})}_{\text{in-scattering}} - \underbrace{\sigma_t(x)L(x, \vec{\omega})}_{\text{absorption+out-scattering}} \quad . \tag{3.4}$$

Equation (3.4) is one version of the *light transport equation* (LTE). The emission term is usually omitted because the emission of light in the medium is seldom significant. The most common form of the LTE is thus

$$dL(x, \vec{\omega}) = -\sigma_t(x)L(x, \vec{\omega}) + S(x, \vec{\omega}).$$

The LTE is an integro-differential equation: a derivative of the radiance appears on the left side, and the scattering term $S(x, \vec{\omega})$ contains an integral of the radiance.

3.3.3 Characteristics of Participating Media

Like surface reflection, scattering can be quite complicated. One way of quantifying the degree of scattering is to compare the amount of scattering to the total attenuation in the medium. Accordingly, the ratio of the scattering coefficient to the extinction coefficient,

$$W = \frac{\sigma_s}{\sigma_t},$$

is the *scattering albedo* of the medium. A larger scattering albedo indicates a greater degree of scattering.

As described above, the computation of in-scattered light is a significant complication in solving the LTE. When the effect of in-scattering is considered negligible, the LTE is much simpler; in fact, it can be solved in closed form if the extinction coefficient σ_t is constant:

$$L(x + \Delta x, \vec{\omega}) = e^{-\sigma_t \Delta x} L(x, \vec{\omega}). \tag{3.5}$$

Equation (3.5) thus expresses the attenuation of radiance as it travels a distance of Δx along a ray in direction $\vec{\omega}$ through a homogeneous participating medium in which the in-scattering is negligible.

The influence of in-scattering cannot be excluded if the degree of scattering is very large. The in-scattering term is computed by integrating the incoming light

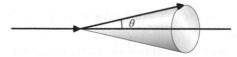

Figure 3.10   The phase function depends on the angle of deflection θ.

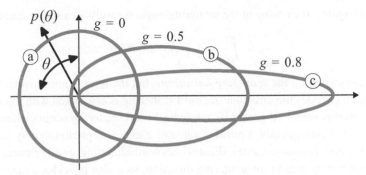

Figure 3.11   Polar plots of several phase function. The plot marked (a) is that of an isotropic phase function; (b) and (c) show examples of forward (anisotropic) scattering with increasing anisotropy.

against the phase function as in Equation (3.3). The phase function $p(x, \vec{\omega}', \vec{\omega})$ fully characterizes the scattering in the medium, much like the BRDF characterizes surface reflection. However, practical phase functions are much simpler than BRDFs: it is known that the phase functions for most media depends only on the angle between the incident and scattering directions (the angle θ in Figure 3.10), which is known as the *angle of deflection.*

The dependence of phase functions on the single angle θ makes them suitable for plotting in polar coordinates. The graph is usually circular or is roughly elliptical (Figure 3.11).[1] If the phase function is constant, then the graph is a circle. Scattering by a constant phase function is called *isotropic scattering.* A nonconstant phase function implies *anisotropic scattering,* which has a directional element. The graph of an anisotropic phase function usually looks like an ellipse with its long axis on the horizontal axis where $\theta = 0$ or $\theta = \pi$. If the ellipse is elongated toward the $\theta = 0$, then scattering is predominately in the form of a small deflection of the angle of incoming light. This is known as *forward scattering.* If the elongation is in the opposite direction, most light is scattered back toward the direction from which it came. This is *backward scattering.*

In practice, anisotropic scattering can usually be categorized as either forward or backward. For the purposes of rendering participating medium, it is helpful to know which. The notion of forward and backward scattering can be formalized in terms of an average scattering direction. More precisely, integrating the phase

---

[1] An important counterexample is the Rayleigh scattering function, which has a two-lobed shape with equal forward and backward scattering. This shape is a result of the nature of the scattering, in which the particles are assumed to be much smaller than the wavelength of light. Rayleigh scattering is the cause of the blue color of the sky and its reddening at sunset. It is also the primary cause of blue eye color.

function against the cosine of the scattering angle θ results in a single number

$$g = \int_{\Omega_{4\pi}} p(x, \vec{\omega}', \vec{\omega}) \cos\theta d\vec{\omega}'.$$

Some authors call g the *scattering anisotropy*, but the term is not universal. The $\cos\theta$ term encodes the direction: forward scattering is associated with directions where $\cos\theta$ is near 1 (θ is near 0), while backward scattering occurs when $\cos\theta$ is near -1. Consequently, a positive value of g indicates predominately forward scattering and a negative value indicates backward scattering. Furthermore, larger $|g|$ implies more bias in the scattering direction, so g also provides a measure of anisotropy.

The usefulness of g in characterizing scattering anisotropy has led to the development of phase function models that use g (or something similar) as a parameter. This makes tuning the model more intuitive. An example is the Henyey-Greenstein function

$$p(\theta) = \frac{1}{4\pi} \frac{1-g^2}{(1+g^2-2g\cos\theta)^{3/2}},$$

which is often used for modeling light scattering in natural objects such as smoke, clouds, flame, and human skin.

3.3.4   Participating Media and CG Rendering

The introduction of the light transport equation into computer graphics in the early 1980s marked the beginning of the connection between rendering and transport theory. As described previously, transport theory was well established in physics and engineering by then. Much of the development of transport theory actually came out of the Manhattan Project during World War II; in fact, it is said to have been key to the development of the atomic bomb. The *Radiative Transfer* textbook originally published in 1950 by Subrahmanyan Chandrasekhar, is considered the "bible" of the field [Chandrasekhar 50]. Early CG efforts in solving the LTE came out of this work. However, the primary goal of general transport theory is to achieve accurate numerical results, for which it is necessary to solve a lot of differential equations at a high computational cost. The original purpose of the LTE for rendering was to simulate light transmission in the medium in order to render phenomena such as smoke, fog, and coulds with greater realism. The CG field therefore needed efficient algorithms to simulate the overall behavior of light in participating media.

In 1982, Jim Blinn presented the first rendering paper that approaches the solution of the LTE , although the paper considers only a restricted version of the problem [Blinn 82]. The degree of scattering is assumed to be small, and only single scattering is considered. Under these assumptions, all light paths start at the light source, end at the viewpoint, and lie in a plane. A further simplification, that the only variable is the depth of light travel in the medium, reduces the problem to a one-dimensional differential equation that is solved analytically in the paper.

James Kajiya and Brian P. von Herzen extended Blinn's technique to the 3D LTE in a 1984 paper entitled "Ray Tracing Volume Densities", which was aimed primarily at rendering clouds (Blinn's work had been motivated by rendering the rings of Saturn) [Kajiya and Von Herzen 84]. In Kajiya's paper, the solution of the LTE is handled differently if the degree of scattering in the medium is small or large. In the case of a relatively small degree of scattering, a "low albedo approximation" is applied, in which in-scattering is only considered from the light; i.e., only single in-scattering is computed. A voxel grid is constructed that initially contains only the voxel densities. In the first step, the ray from the light source to each voxel is traced through the grid, with the radiance attenuated at each voxel according to Equation (3.5). The next stage traces rays from the viewpoint through the voxel, accumulating radiance from each voxel and attenuating it accordingly.

While the low albedo approximation is likely to be sufficient for many applications, a cloud rendering that illustrates some obvious shortcomings of the low albedo approximation is shown in the paper. Accordingly, Kajiya and von Herzen developed a separate method for solving the LTE for media of high albedo. The approach relies on an empirical observation known in transport theory: scattering becomes more isotropic as the degree of scattering increases. By recognizing this, the authors were able to better approximate in-scattering in high albedo media by approximating how it varies from true isotropic scattering. The method reformulates the LTE in terms of *spherical harmonics*, which are a collection of basis functions on the sphere analogous to trigonometric series. Spherical harmonics work well for low-frequency (slowly changing) functions like the incident light in clouds, in the sense that only a few terms are needed to produce a good approximation. In spherical harmonics, the LTE becomes a set of coupled partial differential equations that can be solved analytically. Although not much attention was paid to this solution method at the time of its publication, it had a major influence on multiple scattering work in the latter half of the 1990s.

The early work of Blinn and Kajiya placed significant restrictions on the characteristics of the participating media and the conditions in the environment. This was partially to simplify the equations involved, but also arose out of necessity, as computing power was limited at the time. However, the work paved the way for more general solutions that came later.

3.3.5 Solving the LTE: Radiosity for Volumes

A solution to the light transport equation can be obtained by integrating the equation for a fixed direction over a fixed interval. In CG rendering, the fixed direction is normally that of the viewpoint, as the goal is ultimately to compute the color of a pixel. The integral of the LTE in the view direction is known as the *volume rendering equation*, being a kind of volume extension to the rendering equation. The term is confusing though, because "volume rendering" methods may have nothing to do with the volume rendering equation. However, numerical methods are necessary to solve the equation, as it generally has no analytical solution. Some of the same numerical techniques used in volume rendering can be used in solving (approximating) the volume rendering equation.

For example, the finite-element method can be applied to the volume rendering equation in a manner analogous to the radiosity method for surface rendering. In the surface-based radiosity method, each surface is split into small patches of constant radiosity. Under the assumption of purely diffuse reflection, light transfer between patches is modeled as a linear expression. The interaction between all patches becomes a system of linear equations, thereby discretizing the (surface) rendering equation. The "volumetric radiosity method" works analogously: the entire environment is split into voxels, under the additional assumption that all scattering is isotropic. Light transport between voxels is linear, so the volume rendering equation becomes a system of linear equations.

Holly Rushmeier and Kenneth E. Torrance presented the first general solution of the LTE for CG rendering in a paper entitled "The Zonal Method for Calculating Light Intensities in the Presence of a Participating Medium" [Rushmeier and Torrance 87]. The method described in the paper extends the ordinary (surface-to-surface) radiosity method to include volume elements. The volume containing the participating medium is split into voxels (zones), and form factors (analogous to surface patch form factors) representing light transfer between the voxels are computed. A notable aspect of the method is that the volume elements are incorporated into the surface-to-surface radiosity form factors: the geometric form factors include surface-to-volume and volume-to-surface as well as volume-to-volume interaction. As a result, the entire radiative transfer reduces to a single system of linear equations.

The solution of the equations consists of the constant radiosity of the surface patches, and the volumes (the volume "radiosity" is the radiant power emitted and scattered by the volume). Like the surface radiosity method, a reconstruction step is needed to produce a visually acceptable rendered image. This step also requires integrating over the rays to the eye in order to determine the collected in-scattered and attenuated light. In Rushmeier and Torrance's method, this integration is accomplished by tracing rays through the volumes and adjusting the radiance of the ray at each voxel boundary. The authors show how this can be done efficiently using a depth buffer accumulation method.

3.3.6 Ray Marching

The method of traversing rays through a voxel grid is similar to a more direct form of numerical integration along a path known as *ray marching*. Each ray from the environment to the viewpoint is partitioned into small segments, and the effects of scattering and absorption are computed separately on each segment. At a particular segment, the in-scattering within the segment is computed and added to the accumulated value carried in from the previous segment, attenuated according to the length of the segment (Figure 3.12). In symbols,

$$\underbrace{L_n}_{\substack{\text{Radiance of} \\ \text{segment } N}} = \underbrace{Sx_n}_{\substack{\text{In-scattering at} \\ \text{segment } N}} + \underbrace{e^{-\sigma_t \Delta x}}_{\substack{\text{Attenuation between} \\ \text{segments } N-1 \text{ and } N}} \cdot \underbrace{L_{n-1}}_{\substack{\text{Radiance of} \\ \text{segment } N-1}}$$

where L_n is the accumulated (integrated) radiance carried out of segment N. The process starts at the segment furthest from the viewpoint and sequentially follows the ray. Upon completion, the last segment carries the final radiance, the approximation to the volume rendering equation. Ray marching can be applied to media with general scattering properties, while the volume radiosity method is limited to isotropic scattering. The method also fits in well with surface ray tracing. It is also well suited to hardware rendering. Various methods for improving the efficiency have been developed.

The key to accuracy and efficiency in ray marching is the method of segmenting the ray. In some media, such as smoke and fog, the scattering varies greatly

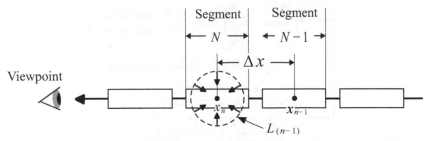

Figure 3.12   The ray marching technique partitions a ray into segments on which the properties of the medium are assumed constant. The radiance is computed by "marching" the accumulated radiance from each segment to the next.

with position. Such cases often require a very fine subdivision of the rays to produce sufficiently accurate results, but this is only necessary where the scattering (or the illumination, or the emission) is large or rapidly changing. Elsewhere a coarse subdivision of the ray suffices. Refining the subdivision uniformly to capture detail along a few small sections of the ray is very inefficient. One improvement is to start with a coarse uniform subdivision, then recursively subdivide segments on which a finer approximation is necessary. This technique is called *adaptive ray marching*.

In the basic adaptive ray marching method, the radiance is computed at both ends of each segment (Figure 3.13). When the difference of two values exceeds a certain threshold, the segment is divided in half and the same test is performed on each new segment. This segmenting process is repeated until the difference is below the threshold. However, subdividing according to the magnitude of the radiance alone can be prone to error if, for example, there is a significant change in the color of participating media. Similarly, an abrupt change in the scattering coefficient might also warrant further subdivision. Any number of different subdivision criteria might be applied; there is no particular "best" way to do it. Sampling the segment only at the endpoints can be problematic if there is significant high frequency (quickly changing) variation in the medium over the segment,

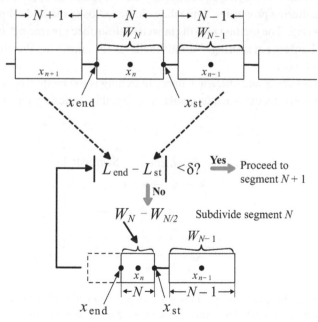

Figure 3.13   Adaptive ray marching splits a segment if the radiance changes more than a threshold δ.

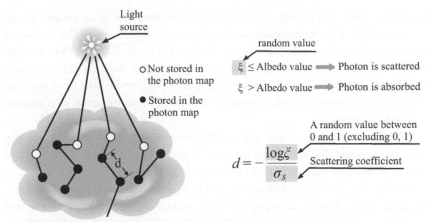

Figure 3.14 Volume photon simulation. At a collision, each particle is either absorbed or scattered according to a random number ξ. A scattered photon travels distance d to the next collision. Only secondary scattering events are stored, because the volume photon map is only used for indirect lighting.

because it is possible that the values at the endpoints end up close purely by co-incidence. The initial ray subdivision has to take that into account. Nonetheless, adaptive ray marching has proven to be a useful technique for optimizing ray marching performance, particularly in inhomogeneous media.

Accurate computation of the in-scattered light in each segment is critical to the success of the ray marching method. Another way efficiency can be improved is to separate direct and indirect incident light in the in-scattering computation. Direct light comes from a specific set of directions, those of the light sources; therefore direct light can be sampled by tracing rays to the light source. In contrast, the indirect light comes from all directions, so the entire sphere of directions has to be sampled. In-scattering from indirect lighting is often small, so fewer samples can be used and therein lies the optimization. However, more samples are needed as the degree of scattering increases, and this increases the computational load.

Henrik Wann Jensen and Per H. Christensen proposed an extension to the photon mapping method to improve the in-scattering computation efficiency [Jensen and Christensen 98]. Instead of using sampled rays, their method uses particle simulation in the medium as a preprocess to the ray marching method (Figure 3.14). The approach is similar to the surface-based photon mapping method, the primary difference being that the simulation for participating media also includes scattering. Each photon is assumed to have a logarithmic probability of colliding with a scattering particle along a free path in the medium. At a collision, a random number ξ in the range from 0 to 1 is chosen. If ξ does not exceed the albedo value, the particle is sent in a random direction (with respect to the phase function) a logarithmically random distance proportional to the inverse of the scattering coefficient. Otherwise it is absorbed. The position, the radiance carried by the photon, and the direction of travel are stored in the *volume photon map* at each *secondary* collision. Values from photons coming directly from the light are not stored, because the photon map is only used to compute the in-scattering from indirect light.

In the ray marching stage, during the in-scattering computation for a ray marching segment, the volume photon map is queried by searching for a constant number of photons near the center of the segment (Figure 3.15).

The desired number of photons are contained in a bounding sphere of radius r. The in-scattered light from a photon is the product of the phase function and the power carried by the photon, divided by the volume of the bounding sphere. The direction $\vec{\omega}'$ of the photon is necessary to find the value of the phase function, which is why photon directions are stored in the photon map. The radiance L_s, the strength of the in-scattered light at point x, from N photons in the bounding sphere of point x is therefore

$$
\begin{aligned}
L_s(x, \vec{\omega}) &= \frac{1}{\sigma_s(x)} \int_\Omega p(x, \vec{\omega}', \vec{\omega}) L(x, \vec{\omega}') d\omega' \\
&= \frac{1}{\sigma_s(x)} \int_\Omega p(x, \vec{\omega}', \vec{\omega}) \frac{d^2\Phi(x, \vec{\omega}')}{dV} \\
&\approx \frac{1}{\sigma_s(x)} \sum_{i=1}^{N} p\left(x, \vec{\omega}_i', \vec{\omega}\right) \frac{\Delta\Phi_i(x, \vec{\omega}_i')}{\frac{4}{3}\pi r^3},
\end{aligned}
$$

where Φ_i and $\vec{\omega}_i'$ are the flux and incident direction, respectively, of photon i.

Using the volumetric photon map in place of direct integral sampling in ray marching considerably improves efficiency for media having a large degree of

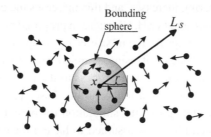

Figure 3.15   In-scattering radiance estimation from a volume photon map works by averaging photons limited to a bounding approximation sphere. (After [Jensen and Christensen 98].)

Figure 3.16   Results of rendering an outdoor scene using a volume photon map; from the top, the sun is positioned at noon, near sunset, and just after sunset. (Image rendered by Henrik Wann Jensen.)

scattering. Dense smoke and clouds are examples of such media. Figure 3.16 shows the results of rendering an outdoor scene under a partly cloudy sky using the volume photon mapping technique.

3.3.7   Rendering of Natural Phenomena

Tomoyuki Nishita and Heihachiro Nakamae published a series of papers in the late 1980s and the early 1990s on the rendering of natural phenomena [Nishita et al. 87, Nishita et al. 93, Nishita and Nakamae 94]. Much of the work was concerned with scattering in the Earth's atmosphere. Their work was primarily voxel based, in line with mainstream approaches to participating media at the time. The ray marching technique became more actively used around the year 2000, driven in part by the rapid growth in hardware. Another change around that time was a shift toward dynamic environments with participating media having time-varying properties: in reality, clouds drift and smoke swirls. Demands for such effects were increasing.

Just as reflection and participating media had been studied for many years in the radiative transfer field, the simulation of atmospheric phenomena lies in the domain of fluid dynamics: clouds and smoke are fluids. Like radiative transfer, *computational fluid dynamics* (CFD) is an active research field in itself. The 1984 volume densities paper by Kajiya and von Herzen was the first to simulate fluids by solving the equations of fluid flow directly; however, progress was impeded by limitations in computing power. Interest in fluid simulation grew in the mid-1990s. Jos Stam presented a stable algorithm for fluid simulation in a 1999 paper [Stam 99] that produced convincing results for smoke, but it tended to lose details observed in real smoke, such as fine swirling eddies.

In 2001, Ronald Fedkiw, Stam, and Henrik Wann Jensen presented a paper entitled "Visual Simulation of Smoke" that combines several methods of fluid simulation into an algorithm suited to computer graphics [Fedkiw et al. 01]. The approach is based on an a *semi-Lagrangian integration* scheme, and the authors apply a technique known as "vortex confinement" to mitigate numerical issues. The algorithm reproduces small vortices and correctly handles interaction of smoke simulation with boundaries and other objects, including moving objects. The rendering is done by two methods based on the density computed in the fluid simulation.

The first rendering method the authors describe is a fast hardware-based algorithm intended to provide a preview of the results. The algorithm is voxel based. In the first pass, the amount of light that reaches each voxel is computed by tracing rays through the grid using a fast algorithm. A ray maintains a transparency that is updated at each voxel it hits. The transparency of the voxel comes from an exponential attenuation according to the voxel density, as in Equation (3.5), and the voxel radiance value is set accordingly. In a second pass, the voxels are rendered in a front-to-back hardware compositing algorithm.

The second rendering method uses ray marching. The attenuation of light is the same exponential function used in the first method, but the in-scattering is computed using a photon map. Also, the authors introduce a variant of ray marching called *forward ray marching* (Figure 3.17). Ordinary ray marching normally starts from the innermost segment and proceeds toward the viewpoint. Forward ray marching proceeds in the opposite direction. It is based on the recurrence

$$L_n = \underbrace{e^{-\sigma_t \Delta x'}}_{\substack{\text{attenuation in} \\ \text{segment of} \\ \text{length } \Delta x'}} \cdot \underbrace{S x'_n}_{\substack{\text{in-scattering at} \\ \text{segment } N}} + L_{n-1}$$

where x'_n is a point chosen at random on segment n. The principal advantage of forward ray marching is that the total attenuation and collected in-scattering

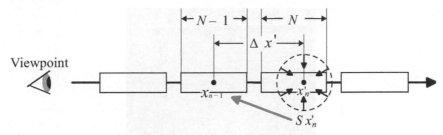

Figure 3.17   Forward ray marching.

contribution all the way back to the viewpoint are known at each segment. In other words, the algorithm tracks how optically deep it is into the medium at each step. As it goes deeper, a less precise approximation to in-scattering is needed, which means that the segment size can be increased and fewer photons are needed from the map. In fact, when the collected in-scattering and attenuation are large enough, the rest of the ray can be ignored outright—light deep enough inside dense smoke does not get out.

A year after the smoke simulation paper, Duc Q. Nguyen, Fedkiw, and Jensen presented a paper entitled "Physically Based Modeling and Animation of Fire" [Nguyen et al. 02]. The physical basis of the model is preserved through the lifetime of the flame (ignition, radiation, and extinction). Figure 3.18 shows an image of fire rendered using the methods described in the paper. Flame is an example of a luminous participating medium—it emits light throughout its volume. Although there is some scattering and attenuation, the basic appearance of flame comes from emission of light within the flame. The light comes primarily from two sources: a blue "core" caused by emission from heated ionized gas molecules, and a yellowish envelope caused by glowing hot uncombusted soot particles.

When an object gets hot enough it begins to emit a visible glow in a phenomenon known as *incandescence*. The emission spectrum of an incandescent source is typically modeled as a *black body*, which is an object that absorbs all incident irradiance. The absorbed energy is re-emitted in a spectral distribution according to a *Plank curve*. The apparent color of a black body changes with temperature: as an object is heated it first appears a dull reddish orange, then shifts to a yellowish color and eventually to almost white (this is the origin of *color temperature*). Soot particles in flame are initially hot enough to appear yellowish, but they cool as they rise, making the flame appear redder near the top. Eventually the particles cool enough to stop emitting light, at which point the visible part of the flame ends and an observer sees a stream of smoke. This is the third primary visible component of flame.

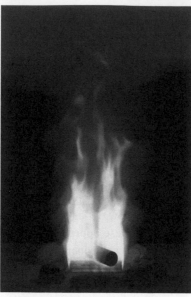

Figure 3.18   Rendered image of fire. (From [Nguyen et al. 02] © 2002 ACM, Inc. Included here by permission.) (See Color Plate I.)

The flame is then rendered using ray marching, but because the emission characteristics are modeled as spectral distributions, the ordinary RGB model, which essentially has three spectral samples, is not sufficient. Such cases require a more finely sampled spectral representation which is later converted to RGB for display on a monitor. The process, which was developed by color scientists early in the twentieth century, works by integrating the spectral representation against three empirical *tristimulus* response curves to produce three components for the color. Normally these are converted to RGB via a linear transformation based on the characteristics of the monitor, but the authors found that the usual conversion process causes the flame to appear too red. The reason is that flame is usually seen only in dark conditions where human vision has become dark adapted. (Flames do appear much redder in daylight.) To account for this, the authors employ a color shift to mimic the perceptual change in color caused by dark adaptation. This shift is applied when the Plank curve is integrated, so the rest of the implementation can use the usual RGB representation.

Scattering within flame is comparatively small, so the in-scattering computation can be done with relatively few samples. In this case it turns out to be more efficient to approximate the in-scattering integral directly from sample rays, rather than incurring the overhead of the volume photon map construction.

3.3.8   Volumetric Shadows

Although shadows are often thought of as 2D projections onto objects, they are really volumes consisting of regions in space where a light source appears partially or totally occluded. A shadow on a surface is the intersection of the shadow volume with the surface. Volumetric shadows become visible in the presence of participating media, although the complement of volumetric shadows—beams of light—are typically more noticeable. Volumetric shadows within a participating medium appear completely dark in the absence of indirect in-scattering, just a surface shadows appear entirely black without indirect illumination. This is a limitation of rendering systems that ignore in-scattering, as many do because of its high computational cost.

Regarding shadows as volumetric objects puts them in the domain of volume rendering. A *shadow map* in its most basic form is a volume function that indicates whether a point is in shadow. The notion was originally developed by Lance Williams in a 1978 paper that showed how a shadow map can be represented in a simplified depth buffer [Williams 78]. It works by placing a hypothetical *shadow camera* at the light source, and rendering the scene into a frame buffer with depth information. However, pixel colors are ignored—only the depth of the object nearest the light source is stored. The result, a rectangular array of depth values, is the shadow map. Later, a point can be tested for shadow by transforming it to the shadow camera coordinate system and comparing the depth against the corresponding pixel in the shadow map: if the point is further from the shadow camera than the shadow map pixel then the point is in shadow; otherwise it is lit.

The shadow map technique is very fast and has been widely used, either in its original form or in one of the many generalizations. A problem though, is that the presence of detail such as fur or hair can require a very high resolution shadow map. The notion of a *deep shadow map* was presented by Lokovic and Veach in 2000, originally developed to render fur of the character "Sully" in the movie *Monsters, Inc.* [Docter 01]. Like an ordinary shadow map, a deep shadow map is a rectangular array of "pixels," each representing the depth of shadowing elements in a particular direction from the shadow camera. The pixels in a deep shadow map contain functions of depth that compute the apparent visibility of the light at a particular depth. These *visibility functions* generalize the simple visible/invisible function described in Chapter 1 by including effects such as fractional visibility of the light source, transmittance, and even scattering effects.

The visibility function for each pixel is created by sampling the *transmittance function* along the rays from the shadow camera through the shadow map pixel; points along the ray correspond to depth values. Each point has a transmittance function, which gives the fraction of light that reaches that depth. The total trans-

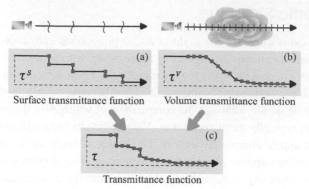

Figure 3.19   The net transmittance function (c) of a deep shadow map is the product of the surface transmittance function (a), which steps through translucent surfaces, and the volume transmittance function (b) of the participating media. (After [Lokovic and Veach 00].)

mittance function is the product of two different transmittance functions: the *surface transmittance function* (Figure 3.19(a)), and the *volume transmittance function* (Figure 3.19(b)). The surface transmittance function ignores participating media and tracks changes in the net transmission at surface points. It is therefore a step function: the value starts at 1 at the light source, then drops at each surface intersection according to the opacity of the surface material. The volume transmittance function is the same as the transmittance function for participating media. The net transmittance function is stored as a series of sample points; the function value is estimated between samples using an exponential interpolation.

The visibility function for a pixel in the deep shadow map is constructed by sampling and averaging the transmittance functions over a set of sample rays covering the pixel. This is essentially the same process used in Monte Carlo ray tracing and serves to antialias the resulting shadows. In addition, a variety of filtering effects can be applied in computing the visibility functions. In particular, a multiresolution prefiltering technique used for rendering at various levels of detail known as *mipmapping*[2] can be applied. Such filtering is particularly important for moving images.

Separating the transmittance functions by surface and volume allows artists to design the surface characteristics without concern for the participating media. Because they are independently integrated, the deep shadow map can be rebuilt for different media without resampling the object geometry. Pixar artists started

---

[2]*Mipmapping* is a technique developed by Lance Williams that stores a texture or other image in a sequence of different sizes [Williams 83]. In a preprocess, the image is repeatedly downsampled by a factor of two until it is reduced to a single pixel; all the downsampled images are stored in the mipmap. A version of the image appropriate for any scale is then readily available at render time.

to use deep shadow maps in movie production without expecting them to apply to smoke or fog or to translucent objects. However, its applicability to participating media was soon discovered by the artists. Afterwards, the deep shadow map method was added to the in-house production renderer and also to commercial rendering software. It has since established itself as the most efficient method for generating shadows in dense volumetric environments.

4

Subsurface Scattering

4.1 Subsurface Scattering

4.1.1 What is Subsurface Scattering?

The general BRDF approach to modeling surface light reflection implicitly assumes that light is reflected immediately at the intersection point. In reality, however, some of the incident light penetrates the object, bounces around below the surface, then emerges at some different point. This behavior is called *subsurface scattering*. While most materials in the real world exhibit some amount of subsurface scattering, it is a significant part of the appearance of translucent materials such as marble, milk, and skin.

Various models for subsurface scattering have been proposed. These models typically split the behavior into two parts: pure surface reflection and scattering below the surface. However, the use of physically accurate subsurface scattering models for practical rendering had long been avoided, due to the high computational cost. This situation has changed recently with the increasing demand for more realistic rendering of natural materials, especially in the motion picture industry. Subsurface scattering has been identified as a key component of realism, so emphasis has been placed on its practical implementation. More efficient models with greater flexibility have been actively studied.

4.1.2 BRDF and BSSRDF

In optics, light reflection at a surface was first modeled in terms of a surface entrance point and a surface exit point. The scattering is measured as the ratio of the radiance exiting the surface at the exit point in a particular direction, to the *irradiance* caused at the entry by light at the entry point from a separate incoming

(a)   (b)

Figure 4.1   (a) A BRDF models light reflection at a surface point. (b) A BSSRDF models light coming
               from a surface including light that has been scattered inside the material below the surface.
               (After [Jensen et al. 01b].)

direction. The function that represents this quantity is the *bidirectional subsurface scattering reflectance distribution function* (BSSRDF) (Figure 4.1(b)). A
BSSRDF is a function of *eight* parameters: a pair of values is needed to represent
each of the surface points, and another pair is needed for each direction (there
are two spherical coordinates for each direction). This made the BSSRDF model
too cumbersome to use for most practical purposes, so the model was simplified
to assume that the entry point and exit point were the same. The result is the
ordinary surface BRDF described in the previous chapters (Figure 4.1(a)).

    Subsurface scattering was actively studied in the field of optics during the
1970s. Computer graphics researchers began applying these models in the late
1980s. The complexity of BSSRDFs prevented them from being used much in
computer graphics, so BRDF-based approximations were used instead. This trend
continued until the mid-1990s. Although BRDFs are defined strictly in terms
of surface reflection, they can and do include subsurface scattering, but only in
a limited way. Except for pure mirror reflection, a BRDF is really a kind of
locally averaged BSSRDF. It assumes that a small neighborhood of the surface
around a point is illuminated, and some of the "reflected" light at a point comes
from subsurface scattering in this neighborhood. The limitation of BRDFs in
representing subsurface scattering comes in the lack of control of the size of the
neighborhood.

4.1.3 Single Scattering and Multiple Scattering

Since the 1990s subsurface scattering has been described using the light transport
equation introduced in the previous chapter, by treating the material below the

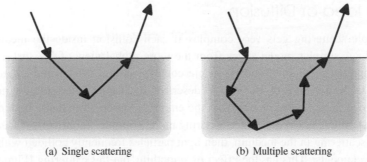

(a) Single scattering   (b) Multiple scattering

Figure 4.2   (a) Single scattering involves light paths that have one scattering event below the surface; (b) multiple scattering involves paths having more than one scattering event.

surface as a participating medium. Subsurface scattering is often modeled by separating it into two components: *single scattering*, which describes the light leaving the surface after only a single scattering event, and *multiple scattering*, which involves several scattering events. This separation was not a new idea when it was first applied to subsurface scattering. As described in the previous chapter, similar approaches had already been proposed by Jim Blinn and Jim Kajiya in the early 1980s in their work that introduced the LTE into CG rendering. By the time it was applied to subsurface scattering in the 1990s, the volume rendering equation was formulated and a number of versatile techniques were available for solving it.

Single scattering (Figure 4.2(a)) can be described as a solution to the volume rendering equation because each light path is fixed. The solution is obtained by integrating both sides of the LTE along the light path from the viewpoint to the light source. For example, Blinn used this scheme to handle single scattering inside a participating medium having a small scattering albedo [Blinn 82]. Hanrahan and Krueger proposed a multilayer subsurface scattering model based on single scattering in 1994 [Hanrahan and Krueger 93]. Multiple scattering (Figure 4.2(b)) is much more difficult, because light can change direction many times along a single path. Consequently, simpler alternative methods were employed to approximate the full volume rendering equation.

The single scattering model was the dominant method for subsurface scattering until the mid-1990s, although its limitations were well understood. As demand for more accurate subsurface rendering grew, interest shifted to the daunting problem of multiple scattering in subsurface light transport. It remains an active area of research in computer graphics.

4.1.4   The Idea of Diffusion

Multiple scattering gets very complex if each collision inside the medium is traced. A simpler model arises from the more global view of the surface as a participating medium. The key insight comes from the 1984 volume rendering paper by Kajiya and von Herzen. As described in Chapter 3, the solution method described in that paper comes from the empirical observation that a high degree of scattering tends to make the scattering more isotropic. Intuitively, if there is a lot of scattering in the medium, then light particles frequently collided with scattering elements. This has the effect of smoothing out the scattering (Figure 4.3) and reducing the directionality. This is one form of the phenomenon known as *diffusion*.

Diffusion is a general physical phenomenon that occurs whenever one medium is spread throughout another by collisions or random motion. It can be observed not only in light scattering but also in other situations where a region is filled with high-density particles. For example, when a drop of liquid coloring is put in a glass of water, the color spreads through the liquid to create a uniform color within a few minutes. This is caused in part by collisions between pigments in the coloring and water molecules.

The process of diffusion can be described with the *diffusion equation*, which is known to have solutions under appropriate boundary conditions. In 1995, Jos Stam proposed modeling multiple scattering as a diffusion process and provided a solution to the resulting diffusion equation [Stam 95]. Although his approach had theoretical significance, the solution was based on a system of differential equations and was not very practical at the time. A 2001 paper by Henrik Wann Jensen, Stephen R. Marschner, Marc Levoy, and Pat Hanrahan introduced a technique for approximating the diffusion equation solution without solving the system of differential equations. It works by approximating the effect of multiple scattering in

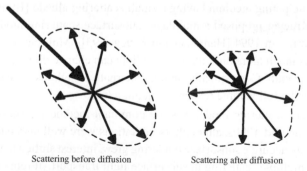

Scattering before diffusion   Scattering after diffusion

Figure 4.3   Scattering as a diffusion process.

terms of elementary functions [Jensen et al. 01b]. The paper presents a BSSRDF model that combines this multiple scattering model with an improved version of the single scattering model developed by Hanrahan [Hanrahan and Krueger 93]. The resulting model, which is effective yet simple, helped launch subsurface scattering into mainstream movie production and game systems.

4.2 Modeling Subsurface Scattering

4.2.1 Modeling Single Scattering

A *multilayer* approach for subsurface scattering was used in the field of optics in the 1970s. In a multilayer model, the material is divided into several homogeneous layers, each parallel to the material surface. This kind of model is appropriate for materials that vary in consistency primarily by depth. Human skin is an example; Figure 4.4 illustrates light transport between multiple skin layers. Multilayer models were adopted in computer graphics in the late 1980s. However, at the time these models did not properly consider scattering within the layers because the light transport was described with BRDFs at the layer interfaces.

The first multilayer subsurface scattering model to properly account for scattering within the media was presented in the 1993 paper "Reflection from Layered Surfaces due to Subsurface Scattering" [Hanrahan and Krueger 93]. In this paper, the layers themselves are regarded as participating media; scattering in the layers and the behavior of light at the interfaces between layers are computed according to the light transport equation.

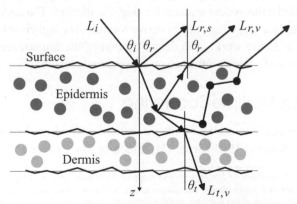

Figure 4.4   A multilayer model for human skin. (After [Hanrahan and Krueger 93].)

The LTE cannot generally be solved analytically. Hanrahan and Krueger made two simplifications in approximating the solution. The first is that the scattering is independent of surface position, and depends only on the depth of penetration into each layer. This reduces the LTE to a one-dimensional equation in the direction perpendicular to the surface. The in-scattering term is then expanded as a generalized geometric series known as a Neumann series. The degree of each term in the series corresponds to the number of scatter events inside the material. That is, the linear term corresponds to single scattering, the quadratic term to double scattering, and higher-degree terms to multiple scattering. However, only the linear term is included. With this simplification, the LTE can be solved analytically. The solution amounts to a surface BRDF that includes single scattering inside the surface.

Although approximating subsurface scattering with only single scattering might seem mathematically reasonable, mathematical models do not always represent natural phenomena correctly. Hanrahan and Krueger's paper actually contains a comparison of the single scattering subsurface model to the results of a Monte Carlo simulation. The simulation works as follows. It begins with a particle simulation in which a large number of particles are shot from the light source. The particles are scattered inside the surface according to a scattering probability function, and the power carried by each scattered particle is stored at the position of the scattering event. The stored intensity of light is then gathered during a second rendering phase, which uses Monte Carlo ray tracing.[1] The results of the simulation can then be compared to the single scattering model. The experiments revealed that the difference increases with the degree of scattering in the medium. This verified the importance of multiple scattering in materials having a large scattering albedo.

The layered scattering paper by Hanrahan and Krueger was significant in that it presented a theoretical solution for single scattering. The authors note that the same technique can be applied to derive formulas for higher-order scattering, but left that as future work. The demonstration of the importance of multiple scattering also had a strong influence on subsequent research.

4.2.2 Modeling Multiple Scattering

The first approach that modeled multiple scattering based on diffusion was proposed by Jos Stam in 1995 [Stam 95]. Much of Stam's research has involved

---

[1]This approach is similar to Jensen's photon mapping technique, and in fact predates it. Particle simulation was not new when photon mapping was developed; its principal novel aspects were the storage and representation of the particles, and the use of the "nearest neighbors" interpolation method for photon map lookup.

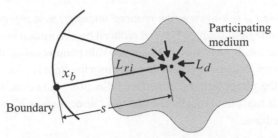

Figure 4.5   Separation of light inside a participating medium. Light reaching a point x comes directly from the source or from scattering inside the medium. The external light is treated as a thin beam, which is assumed to come from point x_b on the surface boundary. The radiance L_{ri} from the source is the reduced intensity (direct radiance). (After [Stam 95].)

the simulation, rendering, and animation of natural phenomena, and he is well known for his work in physically based fluid simulations. In fact, the 1995 multiple scattering paper was motivated by the goal of rendering smoke and fire more realistically. Stam's work built on that of Kajiya and von Herzen.

The light transport equation of Equation (3.3.2) relates the differential change in radiance to the emission plus the in-scattered radiance minus the loss through out-scattering and absorption:

$$(\vec{\omega} \cdot \nabla)L(x, \vec{\omega}) = \sigma_a L_e(x, \vec{\omega}) - \sigma_t L(x, \vec{\omega}) + S(x, \vec{\omega}). \qquad (4.1)$$

The spatial dependence of the coefficients has been dropped in Equation (4.1), as a diffuse medium is normally assumed to be homogeneous. The phase function also does not depend on position, so the scattering term becomes

$$S(x, \vec{\omega}) = \sigma_s \int_{\Omega_{4\pi}} p(\vec{\omega}', \vec{\omega}) L(x, \vec{\omega}') d\vec{\omega}'$$

where $\Omega_{4\pi}$ denotes the sphere of directions $\vec{\omega}$ at x.

Subsurface scattering is concerned with scattering of light coming from outside a surface, so the scattering medium itself is assumed to have no emission. The light at a point inside the medium can be split into two components: the "direct" radiance reaching the point from the outside light source, and the radiance from scattering within the medium. As shown in Figure 4.5, the radiance at x along the ray from the outside source can be treated as coming from a point x_b on the surface boundary. The radiance from x_b is attenuated within the (homogeneous) medium according to Equation (3.5):

$$L_{ri}(x, \vec{\omega}) = e^{-\sigma_t s} L_i(x_b, \vec{\omega}).$$

The variable L_{ri} is known as the *reduced intensity*, as it represents the intensity of the outside light source after it is reduced by absorption and out-scattering within the medium. It is, however, a radiance value and is called the "direct radiance" in this work because it comes directly from the light source and is therefore analogous to the direct lighting in surface reflection. However, this term is not standard, and it must be remembered that this "direct radiance" has been attenuated by the medium.

All the scattered light in the medium ultimately comes from multiple scattering of the direct radiance. The radiance due to single scattering is governed by the phase function:

$$Q(x, \vec{\omega}) = \sigma_s \int_{\Omega_{4\pi}} p(\vec{\omega}', \vec{\omega}) L_{ri}(x, \vec{\omega}) d\vec{\omega}'.$$

This single-scattering function $Q(x, \vec{\omega})$ can be regarded as source of radiance inside the medium; in fact, it is no different than a directional emission function. In other words, single-scattered light can be treated as volumetric emission, and can therefore be used in place of the emission term in the LTE:

$$(\vec{\omega} \cdot \nabla) L(x, \vec{\omega}) = -\sigma_t L(x, \vec{\omega}) + S_d(x, \vec{\omega}) + Q(x, \vec{\omega}). \tag{4.2}$$

The term Q is sometimes called the *source term*, as it amounts to a source of radiance inside the medium (also it comes from the light source). Moving the single scattering into the source term $Q(x, \vec{\omega})$ means the scattering term $S_d(x, \vec{\omega})$ in Equation (4.2) depends only on multiple scattering. The advantage to this comes from the notion of diffusion: multiply scattered light tends to lose its directional dependence. This suggests that a simple approximation to diffuse scattering $S_d(x, \vec{\omega})$ might be sufficient.

Some extra definitions are required to make this precise. The quantities

$$\phi(x) = \int_{\Omega_{4\pi}} L(x, \vec{\omega}) d\vec{\omega},$$

$$\vec{E}(x) = \int_{\Omega_{4\pi}} L(x, \vec{\omega}) \vec{\omega} d\vec{\omega}$$

are known as the *fluence* and the *vector irradiance*, respectively. The vector irradiance is a generalization of surface irradiance: $\vec{E}(x) \cdot \vec{n}$ gives the irradiance through a hypothetical surface perpendicular to $\vec{n}$ at x. Analogous quantities can be defined for any radiance distribution; e.g.,

$$Q_0(x) = \int_{\Omega_{4\pi}} Q(x, \vec{\omega}) \, d\vec{\omega},$$

$$\vec{Q}_1(x) = \int_{\Omega_{4\pi}} Q(x, \vec{\omega}) \vec{\omega} \, d\vec{\omega}$$

are sometimes called the *moments* of degree 0 and 1, respectively, of $Q(x, \vec{\omega})$. If the scattering is isotropic, integrating the LTE of Equation (4.1) produces the expression

$$\nabla \cdot \vec{E}(x) = -\sigma_a \phi(x) + Q_0(x) \tag{4.3}$$

which relates the vector irradiance, the fluence, and the first-order scattering (or the emission). Note that Equation (4.3) is not explicitly dependent on direction.

The idea that light is diffused by multiple scattering is formalized by assuming the diffused radiance $L_d(x, \vec{\omega})$ is well approximated by the sum of the fluence and the surface irradiance in the direction $\vec{\omega}$:

$$L_d(x, \vec{\omega}) \approx \frac{1}{4\pi} \phi(x) + \frac{3}{4\pi} \vec{E}(x) \cdot \vec{\omega}. \tag{4.4}$$

This is called the *diffusion approximation*. Substituting Equation (4.4) into Equation (4.2) and integrating over all directions ultimately gives

$$\nabla \phi(x) = -3\sigma'_t \vec{E}(x) + \vec{Q}_1(x). \tag{4.5}$$

Here $\sigma'_t = \sigma'_s + \sigma_a$, $\sigma'_s = (1-g)\sigma_s$. The value σ'_s is known as the *reduced scattering coefficient*; g is the "scattering anisotropy" from Equation (3.3.3). As g approaches 1 the scattering has a stronger forward bias, which has less influence on the net flux. Combining Equations (4.3) and (4.5) produces

$$\nabla^2 \phi(x) = 3\sigma_a \sigma'_t \phi(x) - 3\sigma'_t Q_0(x) + \nabla \cdot \vec{Q}_1(x), \tag{4.6}$$

which is one form of the *diffusion equation*.

The diffusion equation given in Equation (4.6) describes how particles are diffused within a medium. It also applies to any situation in which flux can be defined, such as in fluid simulations. The simplicity of the equation hides the complexity of the process it governs, as physical equations often do. How easy it is to solve depends on the boundary of the medium and the conditions imposed at the boundary. The basic boundary condition for diffusion inside a medium is that diffuse light cannot come from outside the medium. Stam points out that the diffusion approximation itself prevents this from being satisfied exactly. Instead, he uses the condition that the *net* inward flux is zero; i.e., the amount of light entering at a surface is balanced by the amount leaving it. This condition is popular in fluid dynamics, and much subsequent research in subsurface scattering used this same condition.

A number of solutions are known for simple sources in media with easily modeled boundaries, but not for more complex environments. Stam explored the use of multigrid numerical methods for a thin strip geometry, but notes that deeper simulation requires excessive computation and storage. As an alternative, he proposed using a finite-element method based on approximating the radiance distribution with Gaussian basis functions.

4.3   BSSRDF Models

4.3.1   The BSSRDF Model for Subsurface Scattering

Jensen, Marschner, Levoy, and Hanrahan presented a paper entitled "A Practical Model for Subsurface Light Transport" at SIGGRAPH that described a simple yet fairly general BSSRDF model appropriate for computer graphics [Jensen et al. 01b]. The rendered images demonstrating the technique were some of the most convincing images of translucent materials ever produced. The accompanying video was even shown as part of the SIGGRAPH Electronic Theater, which usually only showcases the winning entries from the annual animated film competition.

The concept of the 2001 paper was to develop a BSSRDF model by combining an exact single scattering solution with an approximate solution to the diffusion equation. The single scattering solution came from a 3D generalization of Hanrahan and Krueger's 1993 model. The multiple scattering solution was the primary contribution. It was well known that the diffusion equation is difficult to solve. Jensen therefore sought functions to approximate the solutions of the diffusion equation without numerically solving it. Applying these functions to multiple scattering yields a very simple BSSRDF function that depends only on the distance between the incident and exitant positions of the light and material properties. This was a major advancement in the practical application of physically based multiple scattering, and the work has had significant impact.

4.3.2   Inspiration from Medical Physics

Jensen's interest in subsurface scattering came out of an interest in more realistic rendering of natural phenomena, in which multiple scattering is a key element (e.g., [Jensen et al. 01a]). His first attempts at rendering subsurface scattering employed his volumetric photon mapping method. However, he discovered that for materials exhibiting a high degree of scattering, the computation and memory requirements become excessive because of the large number of photon collisions needed. The result of each collision has to be stored in the photon map.

While working as a postdoctoral researcher at MIT, Jensen joined a project in the field of medical physics developing skin treatments. Through this project he became more familiar with existing transport theory literature, as transport theory is widely used in medical physics. For example, conditions inside a blood vessel can be estimated from light scattering that occurs around its external wall by applying transport theory. The method observes the transition of photon densities in a local region by capturing light scattering in the whole region. This concept, which is totally different from particle simulation, seemed very promising to Jensen.

4.3.3 The Dipole Model

Of all the publications on the subject of transport theory, a book written by Akira Ishimaru influenced Stam and Jensen the most [Ishimaru 78]. This paper inspired the separation into single scattering and multiple scattering and also the use of an approximation to represent multiple scattering. While Stam was interested in numerical solutions to the equations, Jensen sought an approximate analytical solution.

For the simple environment consisting of a single point light source in an infinite medium, the diffusion equation (Equation (4.6)) is known to have a closed-form solution:

$$\phi(x) = \frac{3\sigma_t'\Phi}{4\pi} \frac{e^{-\sigma_{tr}r(x)}}{r(x)}. \tag{4.7}$$

Here Φ is the intensity (flux) of the point light source, $r(x)$ is the distance to the source to x, and $\sigma_{tr} = \sqrt{3\sigma_a\sigma_t'}$. But this solution is not much use for subsurface scattering—by definition, an infinite medium has no surface! A simple, commonly used geometric model for subsurface scattering is a half-space, which is the collection of points in space that lie on one side of an arbitrary plane. In this model the surface is a plane, and the material extends infinitely deep below the surface. Solutions for simple light source arrangements are known for this case, but they involve infinite series and Jensen was looking for a simple formula. A hint came from a 1970s medical physics paper by G. Eason et al. concerning the scattering of light by blood [Eason et al. 78].

The BSSRDF relates the incident flux coming from a particular direction at an entry point on a surface to the outgoing radiance in another direction at another exit point. When the incident flux is regarded as a thin beam, the resulting radiance distribution inside the medium up to single scattering is represented by

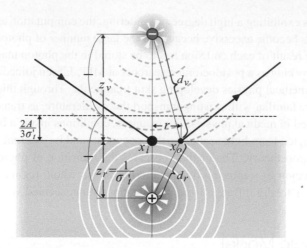

Figure 4.6   The dipole model of multiple scattering. The dipole consists of a virtual point light source below the surface and a virtual "negative" point source above the surface that has the negative intensity of the lower source. The sources are symmetric about the dashed line. The resulting radiance distribution approximates diffuse multiple scattering from light incident at x_i (independent of the incident direction).

the Q term in the light transport equation given by Equation (4.2). According to Eason's paper, this source term Q in the LTE can be reasonably approximated by placing a virtual point light source directly under the point where the outside light enters the medium, and a second *negative* virtual point source directly above it. This negative source is assumed to emit *negative light*, in the sense that the emitted radiance is negative. (This is a hypothetical concept of course—negative light sources do not really exist.) Intuitively, the negative light cancels light that erroneously leaves the medium from the positive source below the surface. The arrangement is known as a *dipole model*.

Figure 4.6 illustrates the dipole arrangement: x_i is the point at which light enters the medium, the sources are arranged so that the line joining them hits x_i and is perpendicular to the surface. The model has been studied in the medical physics community, primarily in the context of noninvasive tissue examination. The particular dipole model employed in the 2001 subsurface scattering paper by Jensen et al. follows the work of cancer researchers Farrell and Patterson. The positive source is placed at a distance of one mean free path below the surface; i.e., $z_v = 1/\sigma_t'$. The position of the negative source is determined by the boundary condition described in the previous subsection: the net inward flux at the surface is zero. More precisely, the integral of the incoming flux over the hemisphere

below the surface must equal that of the outgoing flux over the hemisphere above
the surface. In symbols,

$$\int_{\Omega_-} L(x, \vec{\omega})(\vec{\omega} \cdot \vec{n}_-) \, d\omega = F_{dr} \int_{\Omega_+} L(x, \vec{\omega})(\vec{\omega} \cdot \vec{n}_+) \, d\omega, \qquad (4.8)$$

where Ω_- and $\vec{n}_-$ denote the hemisphere and surface normal below the surface,
respectively; Ω_+ and $\vec{n}_+$ are those above the surface. Under the diffuse assumption, this is satisfied if

$$\phi(x_s) - \frac{2A}{3\sigma_t'}(\vec{n} \cdot \nabla)\phi(x_s) = 0, \qquad (4.9)$$

where x_s is any point on the surface, $\vec{n}$ is the surface normal,

$$A = \frac{1 + F_{dr}}{1 - F_{dr}} \qquad (4.10)$$

and F_{dr} is the diffuse Fresnel reflectance (Section 1.2.6). The two sources have
complementary intensities (the flux of the negative source is the negative of the
flux of the positive source), so it follows from Equation (4.9) that the sources must
cancel each other at the line situated a distance of $2A/(3\sigma_t')$ above the surface.

The fluence function in the dipole approximation is the sum of the two sources
as if they were each in their own infinite medium. Applying Equation (4.7) gives
a formula for the fluence:

$$\phi(x) = \frac{3\sigma_t'\Phi}{4\pi}\left(\frac{e^{-\sigma_{tr}d_r}}{d_r} - \frac{e^{-\sigma_{tr}d_v}}{d_v}\right), \qquad (4.11)$$

where d_r and d_v are the distances from x to the positive and negative sources,
respectively, and Φ is the incident flux. The goal is to find an expression for
the multiple scattering component, which comes from the radiance exiting the
surface (the single scattering component came from the earlier work of Hanrahan
and Krueger). Equation (4.3) relates the fluence, the vector irradiance, and the
first-degree single scattering moment. In the absence of the single scattering term,
Equation (4.3) relates the vector irradiance directly to the fluence:

$$\vec{E}(x) = -\frac{1}{3\sigma_t'}\vec{\nabla}\phi(x). \qquad (4.12)$$

Substituting Equation (4.11) into Equation (4.12) produces a formula for the vector radiant exitance at the surface due to multiple scattering, according to the
dipole model. To see how this applies to the construction of a BSSRDF model,
recall that the BSSRDF relates the incident flux to the outgoing radiance. The

underlying assumption is that multiply scattered light loses its directional dependence. Consequently, the radiance from multiple subsurface scattering does not depend on direction. It is proportional to the radiant exitance $M(x)$ at each surface point, which is the irradiance at the surface due to light coming from beneath the surface. This is where Equation (4.12) comes in. The irradiance from inside the surface is the scalar product of the vector irradiance with the inward surface normal: $M(x) = \vec{E}(x) \cdot \vec{n}$. The ratio of the radiant exitance to the (differential) incident flux therefore comes from combining Equations (4.11) and (4.12):

$$R_d(r) = \frac{\alpha'}{4\pi} \left\{ z_r \left(\sigma_{tr} + \frac{1}{d_r} \right) \frac{e^{-\sigma_{tr}d_r}}{d_r^2} + z_v \left(\sigma_{tr} + \frac{1}{d_v} \right) \frac{e^{-\sigma_{tr}d_v}}{d_v^2} \right\} \qquad (4.13)$$

where $\sigma_{tr} = \sqrt{3\sigma_a\sigma_t'}$ as above, $r = \|x_i - x_o\|$, and $d_r = \sqrt{r^2 + z_r^2}$ and $d_v = \sqrt{r^2 + z_v^2}$ are the distances from x_o to the virtual sources. The value of

$$\alpha' = \frac{\sigma_s'}{\sigma_t'}$$

provides a measure of the relative importance of scattering compared to absorption. The function $R_d(r)$ is sometimes called the diffuse *reflectance profile* of the surface.

Jensen and his coauthors refer to R_d as the *diffuse BSSRDF*, although this is somewhat imprecise because the actual diffuse (multiple scattering) component of the BSSRDF has to be multiplied by the Fresnel transmittance terms for incoming and outgoing light. The true multiple scattering BSSRDF component is thus

$$S_d(r, \theta_i, \theta_o) = \frac{1}{\pi} F_t(\eta, \theta_i) R_d(r) F_t(\eta, \theta_o)$$

where θ_i and θ_o are the angles of incidence and exitance measured from the surface normal. The factor of $1/\pi$ comes from converting radiant exitance to radiance. The Fresnel terms do introduce a directional dependence, but S_d remains rotationally invariant. It is also "separable" as the product of three functions of single independent variables. The final BSSRDF model is the sum of S_d and the single scattering BSSRDF model developed by Hanrahan and Krueger.

Verification of the Dipole BSSRDF model. The multiple scattering dipole model ultimately depends only on two material properties: the absorption coefficient σ_a and the scattering coefficient σ_s'. These values can be measured, approximately, for a real surface. The physical accuracy of the model can therefore be verified by comparing values computed from the dipole model to measurements from an illuminated surface sample. The authors developed a method for doing this based on photographs of the sample under controlled lighting conditions.

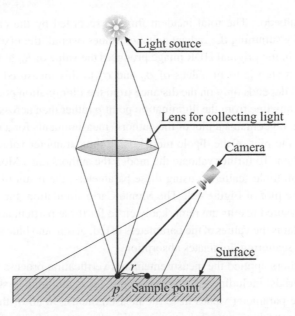

Figure 4.7   The arrangement for measuring multiple subsurface scattering used by Henrik Wann Jensen et al. (After [Jensen et al. 01b].)

The method is based on the assumption that the absorption in the medium is small compared to the degree of scattering, so multiple scattering dominates.

The process works by photographing a physical sample of the surface (Figure 4.7). The surface sample is illuminated by a light source focused into a small beam, which simulates the incident light assumed in the derivation of the diffusion equation. The camera is placed at a fixed angle from the light source (so the Fresnel terms are constant), and a series of digital photographs is taken with increasing exposure times. These are then combined into a *high dynamic range* (HDR) image (see Chapter 6), which has a much greater range of values than is possible from a single exposure. Under the assumption that diffuse multiple scattering is the dominant effect, the value of each pixel in the image is a constant factor times $R_d(r)$, where r is the distance from the illumination point p to the point corresponding to the pixel.

This constant factor actually depends on two unknowns: the incident flux of the light source, and how the camera converts the incoming light to pixel values. Although there are ways to measure each of these, the authors found a way to determine the constant factor more directly using a second image as a reference, in which the original sample is replaced by a (nearly) ideal Lambertian standard of known albedo. The total incident flux, as recorded by the camera, can be computed by summing the radiant exitance values over all the pixels. Dividing a pixel value in the original HDR image produces the value of R_d at that point.

The next step is to fit values of σ_a and σ_s' to this measured R_d data. Because $R_d(r)$ depends only on the distance from the illumination point, this can be done along any line from the illumination point p rather than across the entire image. Figure 4.8 contains a plot of the authors' measurements for a slab of marble along with the plot of the dipole model using the parameter values fit from the measured data. To further validate the model, the authors ran a Monte Carlo simulation of multiple scattering using these parameters, the result of which is also shown in the plot of Figure 4.8. The Monte Carlo simulation, the dipole model, and the measured results are remarkably close for these particular materials. Table 4.1 contains the values of the parameters in red, green, and blue spectral bands. Notice that scattering dominates absorption.

The authors applied the measurement and verification process to several different materials, including the marble sample, milk, and human skin. Table 4.1 contains the parameter values fit to the measurements. In all of these cases, the degree of scattering is much larger than the absorption. Subsurface scattering is likely to be important in such materials, so the authors concluded the model

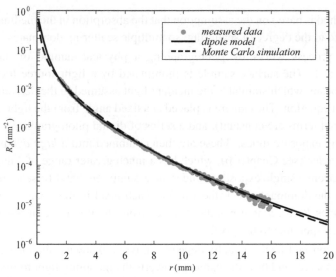

Figure 4.8   Verification of the dipole model for a marble slab, comparing the dipole-based BSSRDF model and a Monte Carlo simulation of scattering in the material to measured data. (From [Jensen et al. 01b] © 2001 ACM, Inc. Included here by permission.)

Material	$\sigma_s'\,[\mathrm{mm}^{-1}]$			$\sigma_a\,[\mathrm{mm}^{-1}]$			η **Refractive**
	R	G	B	R	G	B	**index**
Marble	2.19	2.62	3.00	0.0021	0.0041	0.0071	1.5
Skimmed milk	0.70	1.22	1.90	0.0014	0.0025	0.0142	1.3
Whole milk	2.55	3.21	3.77	0.0011	0.0024	0.014	1.3
Skin 1	0.74	0.88	1.01	0.032	0.17	0.48	1.3
Skin 2	1.09	1.59	1.79	0.013	0.070	0.145	1.3

Table 4.1   Estimated parameters for the dipole-based BSSRDF obtained by fitting measured data.

would be useful. However, they were also aware of its limitations: in addition to the diffusion approximation, it assumes a infinitely deep homogeneous material and a perfectly smooth surface.

Rendering with dipoles. Whether the rendering method employs ray tracing or uses a scanline approach, the outgoing radiance has to be computed at points on the surface of each object being rendered. For ordinary surface rendering, this comes from integrating the BRDF over the set of directions of the light source, or, if indirect illumination is considered, over all directions above the surface. In the case of subsurface scattering the BSSRDF has to be integrated over all light source directions *and over the entire surface* (although in practice the integration can be restricted to a region near the exit point). The integration is done using a Monte Carlo sampling of points near the point of incident illumination (Figure 4.9(a)). Another advantage of separating the BSSRDF into single and multiple scattering

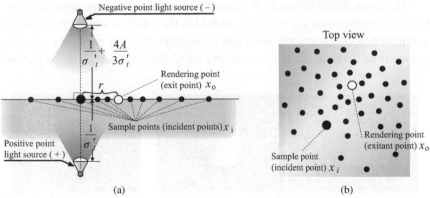

(a)   (b)

Figure 4.9   Rendering using the dipole-based BSSRDF. At a "rendering point" x_o where the outgoing radiance is needed, the BSSRDF is integrated by sampling points x_i over the surface where light is incident. (a) A dipole is constructed at each sample point. (b) The sample points are concentrated near x_o to improve efficiency.

shows up here. Single scattering requires integration over the refracted rays and it has a different distribution than multiple scattering. For the multiple scattering integral, a dipole model is constructed for each sample point: the positive and negative virtual sources are placed directly below and above the sample point, respectively, with the flux of each computed according to the actual illumination. In the case of an area source, sample points can be taken concurrently over the light source. Because the value of $R_d(r)$ falls off exponentially, it is more efficient to concentrate the samples near the evaluation point x_o and spread them out more as the distance from x_o increases (Figure 4.9(b)).

The dipole model is derived and verified assuming the geometry of a plane surface and infinitely deep material. Object geometry in CG scenes is seldom this simple. The authors therefore had to devise a way of applying the dipole model to geometrically more complicated objects. Their method works by constructing the dipole as usual, but places the positive source so that it is always at least $1/\sigma_t'$ below each surface point. This ensures that d_r is bounded away from zero; otherwise, the value of R_d could get arbitrarily large. The model breaks down if the object is thinner than $1/\sigma_t'$.

Images of a glass of milk rendered with a BSSRDF model using measured parameters for skim and whole milk are shown in Figure 4.10(b) and (c), respectively. The image in Figure 4.10(a) is rendered using a BRDF model derived from the dipole model. The BSSRDF model adds a lot: the BRDF image looks more like a glass of paint. Figure 4.11(a) shows an image of a human face model rendered with the BRDF model; Figure 4.11(b) shows the same model rendered with the BSSRDF using the measured parameters for human skin.

The dipole BSSRDF model developed by Jensen et al. fits naturally into a ray-tracing renderer using the method described in the paper. The multiple scattering component is computed only from surface samples; the only need for ray tracing comes from sending shadow rays to the light, and shadowing can be handled

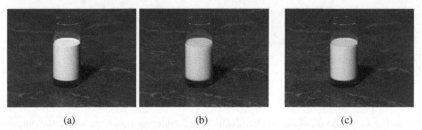

(a)   (b)   (c)

Figure 4.10 Rendered milk, using: (a) a BRDF approximation to the dipole model; (b) and (c) the dipole-based BSSRDF with measured parameters for skimmed and whole milk, respectively. (From [Jensen et al. 01b] © 2001 ACM, Inc. Included here by permission.)

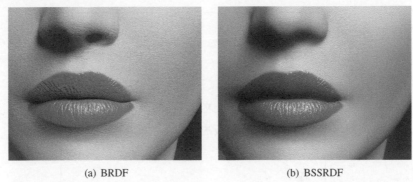

(a) BRDF   (b) BSSRDF

Figure 4.11   Images of a detailed human face model rendered with (a) a BRDF approximation to the dipole model; (b) the dipole-based BSSRDF model with measured parameters for human skin. (From [Jensen and Buhler 02] © 2002 ACM, Inc. Included here by permission.) (See Color Plate II.)

in other ways. Consequently, ray tracing is not needed to employ the diffuse BSSRDF model. This allowed it to be incorporated in a variety of rendering systems, including those used in motion picture production. The elimination of ray tracing is also advantageous for implementation in hardware shaders. A paper by Xuejun Hao, Thomas Baby, and Amitabh Varshney shows how the dipole model can be approximated with polynomials, and the integration over the surface precomputed so that evaluation requires relatively little computation at run time [Hao et al. 03].

4.3.4   Fast Translucency

A year after the publication of the dipole BSSRDF model, Jensen and Juan Buhler published a paper entitled "A Rapid Hierarchical Rendering Technique for Translucent Materials" [Jensen and Buhler 02]. What is meant by a "translucent material" is not well defined as technical term, but it generally refers to a medium that exhibits a high degree of scattering with strong forward bias in the scattering direction. That is, most of the scattering comes in the form of deflection of light paths, so that the single scattered light tends to propagate in the same general direction. In computer graphics "translucent" often implies that scattering becomes more isotropic after multiple scattering events, i.e., becomes diffuse. Marble, milk, and human skin (the materials studied in the 2001 BSSRDF paper) are examples of translucent materials.

Jensen and Buhler's "fast translucency" paper begins by examining Monte Carlo simulations of scattering in translucent materials. Figure 4.12 contains plots

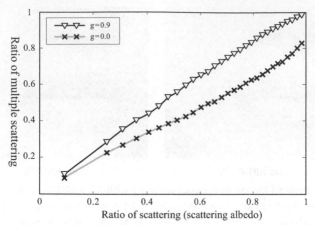

Figure 4.12   Importance of multiple scattering. The effect of multiple scattering dominates as the scattering albedo approaches 1, whether the scattering is isotropic or has a strong forward bias. (From [Jensen and Buhler 02] © 2002 ACM, Inc. Included here by permission.)

of the simulation results for a medium with isotropic scattering ($g = 0.0$) and a medium with strong forward scattering ($g = 0.9$) as a function of the scattering albedo. The vertical axis is the ratio of light from multiple scattering to the total exitant light. The plots shows that multiple scattering becomes more dominant with increasing albedo in both cases. In the anisotropic case, multiple scattering dominates entirely as the albedo approaches 1. From this the authors concluded that multiple scattering was the important effect in materials exhibiting a high degree of scattering, and they proceeded to develop an efficient algorithm targeting only multiple scattering.

As described in Section 4.3.3, rendering with the dipole-based diffuse BSSRDF model requires evaluation of R_d at many surface points spread out around

Figure 4.13   Sample point distribution for precomputed irradiance. (From [Jensen and Buhler 02] © 2002 ACM, Inc. Included here by permission.)

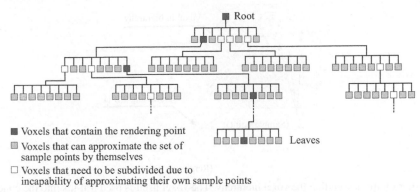

Figure 4.14   Hierarchy of voxels used in the "fast translucency" algorithm. The root voxel contains the entire object; the leaf voxels contain a single sample point. Parent voxels contain the aggregate values of the child voxels.

each "rendering" point at which the irradiance is needed. Some of these samples can be reused at nearby rendering points. The algorithm proposed in Jensen and Buhler's fast translucency paper does this: it first performs uniform, dense sampling over the surface, and then computes the irradiance at these points (see Figure 4.13). These precomputed irradiance values are reused during rendering.

As described in Section 4.3.3, sample points far away from an evaluation point have exponentially decreasing influence on the value of the dipole-based diffuse BSSRDF. Accordingly, the algorithm arranges the precomputed values in a hierarchy of increasingly small regions. The smallest regions contain the actual sample points. Larger regions are built from the smaller regions; the value of a larger region is the sum of the values in the smaller regions it contains. The hierarchy is traversed at each evaluation point in a manner that uses the aggregate value in the larger regions where the sample points are less significant.

The hierarchy is constructed from voxels. The voxel at the top level in the hierarchy corresponds to the entire object. Each voxel stores its position (the centroid of the voxel) and total irradiance (the sum of the sample values inside the voxel). Figure 4.14 illustrates the voxel hierarchy as a simple tree structure, although other data structures such as a kd-tree can also be used. The hierarchy is traversed at each evaluation point in order to adaptively use the precomputed sample points. How far away the voxel is from the evaluation point determines the level of the voxel to be used: near the sample point the finest level is used; further away, the summed value in a larger voxel suffices. Figure 4.15 illustrates how the voxel in the hierarchy level is chosen. If all the sample points in a voxel are inside a certain solid angle measured from the evaluation point, i.e., if $\Delta\omega$

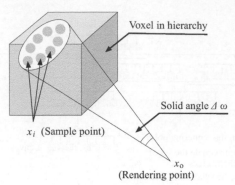

Figure 4.15   Criterion for descending the voxel hierarchy. The voxel itself is used if it fits into the cone
of a fixed solid angle, otherwise the algorithm descends into the subvoxels.

in Figure 4.15 is smaller than a particular threshold, the voxel is not considered
close to the evaluation point and the aggregate value is used. Otherwise, the test is
applied again at each subvoxel, and the process stops when the subvoxel is small
enough, or the finest level is reached. The voxels at the finest level contain a single
sample point.

Figure 4.16 contains images of a marble "Utah teapot" rendered with the
BSSRDF model. The left image was rendered using the basic sampling proce-
dure; the right image was rendered using the voxel hierarchy. Although the two
images are almost indistinguishable, the rendering times vary significantly: the
left image required 18 minutes to render; the right image, only seven seconds.

The fast translucency algorithm was developed in cooperation with PDI after
the publication of the original BSSRDF model, so the paper includes various en-
hancements that reflect the needs of movie production. For example, the dipole-
based multiple scattering model uses the parameters σ_a and σ_s' to specify the

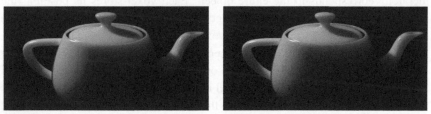

Figure 4.16   Comparison between a BSSRDF-based rendering (left) and a rendering using the "fast
translucency" algorithm (right). (From [Jensen and Buhler 02] © 2002 ACM, Inc. Included here by permission.)

absorption and scattering. However, these parameters are unintuitive and proved quite difficult for artists to use. So the authors replaced these physical parameters with two that are more convenient: there is one parameter for diffuse color and another for the translucency of the object. The diffuse color is actually a kind of average diffuse albedo, defined by the integral

$$\rho_d = 2\pi \int_0^\infty R_d(r)r\,dr = \frac{\alpha'}{2}\left(1 + e^{-\frac{4}{3}A\sqrt{3(1-\alpha')}}\right)e^{-\sqrt{3(1-\alpha')}}, \qquad (4.14)$$

where R_d is the multiple scattering reflectance defined in Equation (4.13). This diffuse albedo ρ_d is essentially the integral of the multiple scattering reflectance over the entire surface, assuming the object is uniformly illuminated by light of constant radiance coming from all directions. Given ρ_d, Equation (4.14) can be solved for $\alpha' = \sigma_a/\sigma_s'$. The translucency parameter is the mean free path l_d of light in the medium. As mentioned previously, $l_d = 1/\sigma_{tr}$. The values of σ_a and σ_s' can be determined from α and σ_{tr}:

$$\sigma_t' = \frac{\sigma_{tr}}{\sqrt{3(1-\alpha')}}, \qquad \sigma_s' = \sigma'\sigma_t', \qquad \sigma_a = \sigma_t' - \sigma_s'.$$

The parameters ρ_d and l_d were later used to control the variation in subsurface scattering across a surface using a form of a texture map known as an *albedo map*. This technique is now widely utilized in movie production.

4.3.5 The Multipole Model

The dipole model assumes the scattering medium is homogeneous and extends infinitely deep below the surface. This assumption is sufficient for some objects, but it breaks down for many real objects because they are not homogeneous or they are simply too thin. Some natural objects, such as plant leaves and human skin, can be regarded as having several thin (somewhat) homogeneous layers (Figure 4.4). The ordinary dipole model does not apply in this case, but the concept of using positive and negative virtual point sources does. Craig Donner and Henrik Wann Jensen developed a *multipole* method that extends the dipole model to subsurface scattering of multilayered objects [Donner and Jensen 05].

The core of the dipole BSSRDF model is the function $R_d(r)$ of Equation (4.13), which gives the ratio of light exiting the surface after multiple scattering to the incident light. There is only one interface, the surface of the scattering medium, and the virtual sources are arranged to satisfy the boundary condition that the net inward flux at the surface is zero. In a thin slab or multilayered structure however, there is an interface between each layer, and the transmittance of light through the layers has to be taken into account. Furthermore, appropriate boundary conditions at all the interfaces have to be satisfied simultaneously.

Thin slab approximation. Consider first the generalization of the dipole model to a thin strip of width d. This introduces a second interface at the plane $z = d$. (The coordinate system used for the multipole model has the plane $z = 0$ at the surface of the object, with the positive z-axis pointing into the object.) As in the dipole model, the boundary condition at the top surface is that the net inward flux is zero:

$$\int_{\Omega_+} L_d(r, \vec{\omega})(-\vec{n} \cdot \vec{\omega}) \, d\vec{\omega} = F_{dr} \int_{\Omega_-} L_d(r, \vec{\omega})(\vec{n} \cdot \vec{\omega}) \, d\vec{\omega} \qquad \text{at } z = 0,$$

(this is essentially the same as Equation 4.8 above). The condition at the lower interface is similar,

$$\int_{\Omega_-} L_d(r, \vec{\omega})(\vec{n} \cdot \vec{\omega}) d\vec{\omega} = F_{dr} \int_{\Omega_+} L_d(r, \vec{\omega})(-\vec{n} \cdot \vec{\omega}) d\vec{\omega} \qquad \text{at } z = d.$$

These reduce to the corresponding partial differential equations in the fluence $\phi(r)$:

$$\phi(r) - \frac{2A}{3\sigma_t'} \cdot \frac{\partial \phi(r)}{\partial z} \;=\; 0 \qquad \text{at } z = 0, \tag{4.15}$$

$$\phi(r) + \frac{2A}{3\sigma_t'} \cdot \frac{\partial \phi(r)}{\partial z} \;=\; 0 \qquad \text{at } z = d, \tag{4.16}$$

where $A = (1 + F_{dr})/(1 - F_{dr})$ as in Equation (4.10).

The condition at the upper boundary can be satisfied, approximately, as in the dipole model by placing virtual positive and negative point light sources so that the energy balances at the plane $z = -z_b$. This is illustrated in Figure 4.17; the dashed line marked A is at $-z_b$, and the two sources are positioned at $z_{v,0}$ and $z_{r,0}$. The positive and negative sources are thus placed on opposite sides of the plane at a distance $1/\sigma_{tr}$, the length of one mean free path. Note that this only works if the thickness d of the slab is larger than the mean free path.

Satisfying the boundary condition at the lower interface ($z = d$) requires a third virtual point source, a negative source placed so that the energy balances at $z = z_b + d$. That is, the third source is placed at $z_{v,1}$, which is $z_{r,0}$ mirrored about the dashed line B in Figure 4.17. Unfortunately, the presence of this new source breaks the boundary condition at the top surface. This is repaired by adding another positive source at $z_{r,-1}$, which is the mirror image of the bottom source in the plane $z = -z_b$ (the dashed line A in the figure). Yet another positive source mirrored in the plane $z = z_b + d$ has to be added to counteract this new positive source (at $z_{r,-1}$ in the figure). Then a new negative source has to be added (at $z_{v,-1}$ in the figure) and so the process goes.

An infinite number of sources is theoretically necessary to satisfy the boundary conditions. However, the contribution of each source decreases exponentially

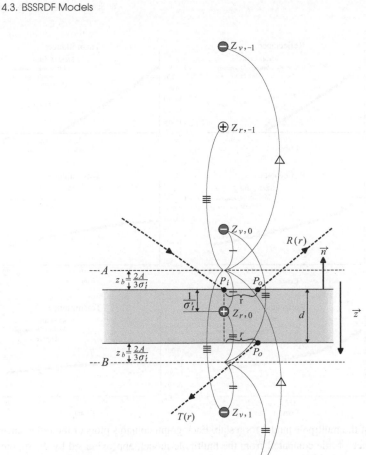

Figure 4.17   The multipole model for a homogeneous slab. Infinitely many positive and negative sources are needed to properly satisfy the boundary conditions, but a few suffice in practice.

with distance, so a finite number of sources provides a sufficient approximation. (The boundary conditions of Equations (4.15) and (4.16) are themselves approximations to the true diffuse boundary condition.) In practice, ten pairs of virtual point light sources usually gives a sufficient approximation, although thinner regions generally require more sources. The diffuse reflectance computed from these sources is known as a *multipole approximation* to diffuse multiple scattering in a thin slab.

The diffuse reflectance profile $R(r)$, the ratio of the radiant exitance at the top surface to the incident flux, is computed by summing the contributions of each

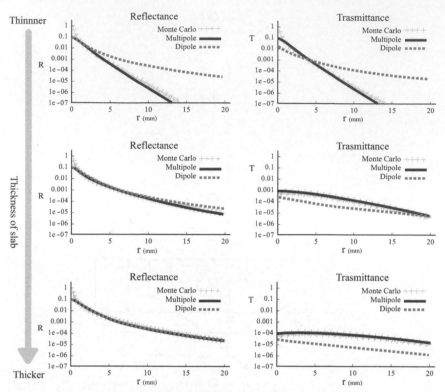

Figure 4.18   Verification of the multipole model for a slab. Each graph contains plots of the reflectance or transmittance profile computed from the multipole model, approximated by the dipole model, and computed using a Monte Carlo simulation. The thickness of the slab increases from top to bottom. (From [Donner and Jensen 05] © 2005 ACM, Inc. Included here by permission.)

of the sources just as in the dipole model (Equation (4.13)). For a thin slab, the ratio of the radiant exitance at the bottom surface to the incident flux is the diffuse *transmittance profile* $T(r)$. Figure 4.18 contains plots of $R(r)$ and $T(r)$ for slabs of widths varying from 2 to 20 times the length of one mean free path. Each plot also contains the corresponding dipole approximation and a Monte Carlo simulation of the multiple scattering inside the slab. These plots show a good match between the multipole approximation and the Monte Carlo simulation, although the approximation is better for thicker slabs. In contrast, the dipole reflectance matches the simulation poorly when the slab is thin, and the dipole transmittance does not match well for any thickness.

Figure 4.19 shows images of a back-lit parchment rendered using (left to right) the dipole model, the multipole model, and a Monte Carlo simulation. The visible

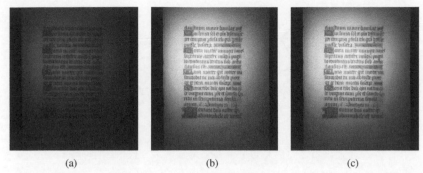

(a)   (b)   (c)

Figure 4.19 Rendering of a parchment using (a) the dipole model, (b) the multipole model and (c) a Monte Carlo simulation. (From [Donner and Jensen 05] © 2005 ACM, Inc. Included here by permission.)

light comes from light transmitted through the parchment, which is a fairly thin material compared to the mean free path. Not surprisingly, the dipole model fails to capture the essential lighting in the image. In contrast, the differences in the images rendered using the multipole model and the Monte Carlo simulation are hardly noticeable.

Handling multiple layers. The multipole model is derived for an infinite slab. Parchment is one example of a real object for which a thin slab is a good model. As described earlier in the section, some natural materials are better modeled by several thin layers. The multipole model does not immediately apply in this case. Simply stacking several thin layers and applying a multipole model to each does not work, because the light reaching the second layer is diffused by the first. The dipole and models are derived for a thin beam of light hitting the surface at a specific point. Applying them to diffuse incident light requires integrating the multipole model over the surface, as if there is a separate differential multipole at each surface point. The reflectance and transmittance profiles for combined layers are therefore quite complicated. Donner and Jensen employ Fourier transforms, a technique commonly used in signal and image processing, efficiently construct multilayer reflectance and transmittance profiles.

The transmittance of a slab can be interpreted as a kind of filter for the incoming flux. The transmittance of light through two slabs amounts to applying the filter of the second slab to the result of the incident flux filtered by the first slab. The net effect of two filters is determined by the *convolution* of the filters, which is a function whose value at a point x is the result of integrating one filter shifted by x against the other without a shift. For example, the net transmit-

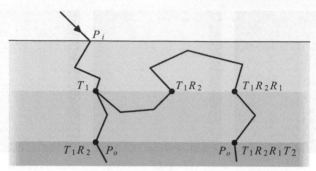

Figure 4.20   A multilayered model. Light scattering between layers is a significant complication.

tance for transmittance functions $T_1(r)$ and $T_2(r)$ is

$$T_1 * T_2(x,y) = \int_{-\infty}^{\infty} \int_{-\infty}^{\infty} T_1\left(\sqrt{x'^2+y'^2}\right) T_2\left(\sqrt{(x-x')^2+(y-y')^2}\right) dx' dy'.$$
(4.17)

Note that $T_1 * T_2(x,y)$ is a function of the position (x,y), as is the integral on the
right side of Equation (4.17). This dependence on position is omitted hereafter.

The convolution $T_1 * T_2$ is not quite the same as the transmittance function
of two adjacent layers, because it does not account for scattering between the
layers. For example, some of the light transmitted through layer 1 into layer 2 is
scattered back into layer 1, and some of that light is scattered back into layer 2,
where some of it gets transmitted (Figure 4.20). Light can scatter between layers
like this arbitrarily many times. The actual transmittance function T_{12} for two
layers is therefore the infinite series

$$T_{12} = T_1 * T_2 + T_1 * R_2 * R_1 * T_2 + T_1 * R_2 * R_1 * R_2 * R_1 * T_2 + \cdots. \qquad (4.18)$$

Considering that each convolution function is a double integral, Equation (4.18)
involves a lot of computation even when the series is truncated to just a few terms.

Fortunately, there is a shortcut. The *convolution theorem* states that the convolution of two functions can be computed from the product of their Fourier transforms. The Fourier transform of T_{12} is therefore

$$\mathcal{T}_{12} = \mathcal{T}_1 \mathcal{T}_2 + \mathcal{T}_1 \mathcal{R}_2 \mathcal{R}_1 \mathcal{T}_2 + \mathcal{T}_1 \mathcal{R}_2 \mathcal{R}_1 \mathcal{R}_2 \mathcal{R}_1 \mathcal{T}_2 + \cdots$$

where $\mathcal{T}$ and $\mathcal{R}$ denote the Fourier transforms of T and R, respectively, and the
product indicates pointwise multiplication of the transformed functions. Rear-

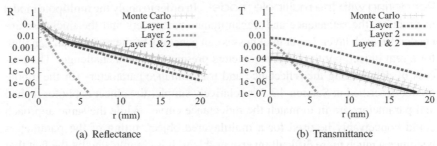

(a) Reflectance   (b) Transmittance

Figure 4.21   Verification of a two-layer model. The graphs show the (a) reflectance and (b) transmittance profiles for the combined layers compared with those of each separate layer, and the corresponding Monte Carlo simulations. (From [Donner and Jensen 05] © 2005 ACM, Inc. Included here by permission.)

ranging terms produces the formula

$$
\begin{aligned}
\mathcal{T}_{12} &= \mathcal{T}_1 \mathcal{T}_2 (1 + \mathcal{R}_2\mathcal{R}_1 + (\mathcal{R}_2\mathcal{R}_1)^2 + (\mathcal{R}_2\mathcal{R}_1)^3 + \cdots \\
&= \frac{\mathcal{T}_1 \mathcal{T}_2}{1 - \mathcal{R}_2\mathcal{R}_1}.
\end{aligned}
\tag{4.19}
$$

The inverse Fourier transform of the right side of (4.19) provides the transmittance function of the combination of the two layers.

The total diffuse reflectance of adjacent layers 1 and 2, which must account for light scattered between the two layers, can be computed similarly. The Fourier transform of the effective reflectance R_{12} is

$$
\mathcal{R}_{12} = \mathcal{R}_1 + \frac{\mathcal{R}_1\mathcal{R}_2\mathcal{T}_1}{1 - \mathcal{R}_2\mathcal{R}_1}.
\tag{4.20}
$$

Repeatedly applying the formulas of (4.19) and (4.20) produces the effective diffuse reflectance and transmittance profiles for multiple layers.

Figure 4.21 contains plots of the reflectance and transmittance profiles as a function of distance for a specific material. The material consists of an upper layer exhibiting little scattering over a thinner highly scattering lower layer. Each graph contains plots of the convolved multipole model for two adjacent layers, those of the individual layers, and the corresponding profiles derived from a Monte Carlo simulation. The graphs show a close match between the convolved model and the Monte Carlo simulation for both the reflectance and the transmittance. In particular, the convolved multipole model appears to work well for small values of r, i.e., where the the entry point of the incident light is close to the exit point.

Rendering with the multipole model. In order to apply the multipole model in practice, the reflectance and transmittance parameters and the thickness are needed for each layer. Layer thicknesses can generally be measured easily enough for a real object, but the other parameters present more of a challenge. The process of determining the reflectance and transmittance parameters for the dipole model described in Section 4.3.3 is relatively simple: the object is photographed and parameters are fit to match the reflectance curve. While the same approach could conceivably be used for a multilayered object, fitting of the parameters becomes a much more difficult inverse problem. It is complicated by the fact that the photograph provides only the convolution of the reflectance of the multiple layers, and in general it is not possible to deconvolve them. Faithfully measuring a real object requires examining each layer separately. Even so, measurements for the dipole model may not be immediately applicable to the multipole model because the dipole model tries to match the general appearance of subsurface scattering.

Another problem with the multipole model is that it assumes the layers are homogeneous. This is not true of many real objects, including plant leaves and human skin. The most visually significant variation occurs across the surface rather than beneath it—freckles and moles on skin, and patterns seen on plant leaves are examples. Existing measurements typically represent the average of the parameters over the surface. In the case of a single layer, the parameters at each position can be determined from the diffuse reflectance of the object based on the diffuse albedo of Equation (4.14). But this is more difficult for multilayer materials. Furthermore, the positional dependence of reflectance and transmittance acts as a kind of filter, and therefore must be included in the convolutions above. Donner and Jensen employ a simpler approach that uses an ordinary albedo map at the top surface. The same approach was used in the fast translucency paper, and is analogous to a texture map used in surface rendering wherein the reflected light is multiplied by the position dependent texture map value. The albedo map is convolved with the final diffuse reflectance and transmittance functions as illustrated in Figure 4.22. While this is not physically accurate, it has the effect of blurring the albedo map in a visually plausible manner.

The multipole model is derived under the assumption that all the interfaces (surfaces) are perfectly smooth. But real objects have rough surfaces. Donner and Jensen use the the microfacet-based BRDF model developed by Torrance and Sparrow (see Chapter 8) to model surface roughness. This changes the boundary conditions of Equations (4.15) and (4.16): the diffuse Fresnel reflectance F_{dr} has to be replaced by an average diffuse reflectance ρ_d, which is computed by numerically integrating the BRDF function. Surface BRDF rendering without subsurface scattering normally assumes that light not reflected is absorbed by the surface and

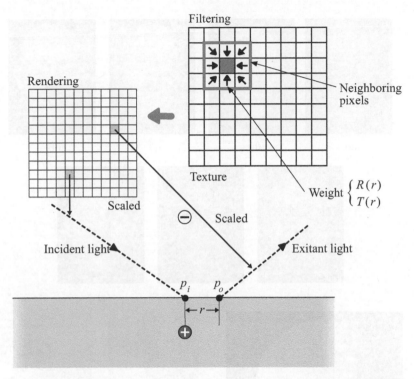

Figure 4.22   An albedo map works like a texture map, except that it is convolved with the reflectance profile. This acts as a filter.

therefore is lost. However, this unreflected light becomes the incident light for subsurface scattering. The authors use a complementary average diffuse BRDF to determine the amount of light entering the surface.

The rendered images of human skin are a compelling result of Donner and Jensen's 2005 paper. In the paper, skin is modeled as a three-layered medium consisting of the epidermis, the upper dermis, and the bloody dermis. The first two layers are highly scattering and quite thin; the bottom layer is treated as being infinitely deep and exhibits a much lower degree of scattering. Figure 4.23(a)–(e) illustrates each reflectance and transmittance profile as a shading of a human head model. Note that the transmittance is more significant than the reflectance (the bloody dermis layer has no transmittance, as it is infinitely deep). The three layers are convolved as described above to form the multilayer diffuse reflectance profile, which is shown in Figure 4.23(g). An illustration of the BRDF used to model the surface roughness of human skin is contained in Figure 4.23(f).

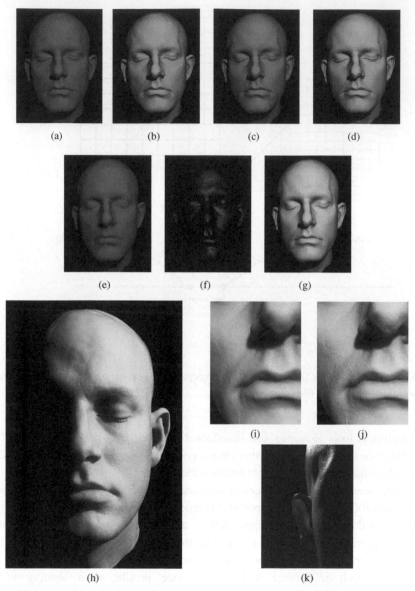

Figure 4.23 Multilayer model of human skin. (a) Epidermis reflectance. (b) Epidermis transmittance. (c) Upper dermis reflectance. (d) Upper dermis transmittance. (e) Bloody dermis reflectance. (f) Surface roughness. (g) Multilayer reflectance. (h) Application of the albedo map. (controlling parameters using albedo map). (i) Dipole model close-up. (j) Multilayer model close-up. (k) Back-lit close-up of the right ear. (From [Donner and Jensen 05] © 2005 ACM, Inc. Included here by permission.) (See Color Plate III.)

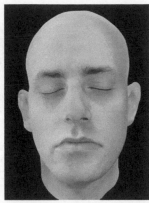

Figure 4.24   Albedo map for the human head model. (From [Donner and Jensen 05] © 2005 ACM, Inc. Included here by permission.) (See Color Plate IV.)

Human skin is not homogeneous; its density and reflectance properties vary across its surface. This is caused in part by variations in the thickness of the dermal layers, but also depends on the concentration of various pigments. The head model shown in Figure 4.23 was obtained through a high-resolution digital scan. An albedo map for the model was captured from a photograph of the person's face taken under uniform illumination (Figure 4.24). The color variation in the final image comes from the albedo map convolved with the reflectance function as described above.[2]

Figure ?? shows an image of the human head model rendered with the multipole model constructed for human skin combined with the albedo map derived from Figure 4.24. The rendering includes specular highlights from the BRDF model. Specular reflection is generally regarded as a surface-level effect and is handled independently from subsurface scattering. Figure 4.24(i) and (j) contain close-ups of the face rendered using a dipole approximation and the multilayer model. The effect of scattering in the epidermis is clearly visible in the multilayer model image. In contrast, the dipole model rendering looks overly translucent—it looks more like a wax model of a human head. Translucency is an important effect in the appearance of human skin, as the back-lit image of Figure 4.24(k) shows.

---

[2]The most significant pigment in human skin is *melanin*; different amounts of this pigment is the primary cause of differences in skin color. The particular individual who served as the model for the 2005 paper apparently has a low concentration of melanin. Although this helps illustrate the effectiveness of the multipole model, Figure 4.24 is certainly not representative of human skin color. Donner has since developed a more general human skin model that better handles variation in melanin concentration [Donner et al. 08].

(a) BRDF   (b) BSSRDF

Figure 4.25   Test images for the BSSRDF shader developed at ILM. (a) An image rendered with the
BRDF shader. (b) The same image rendered with the dipole-based BSSRDF shader. (Courtesy of Christophe Hery ©Industrial Light & Magic.) (See Color Plate V.)

4.3.6   BSSRDF Models in Motion Picture Production

The greatest demand for subsurface scattering in movie production comes from
the need for realistic skin rendering of CG characters. The computational cost of
physically based subsurface scattering had prevented it from being used in movies
until the early 2000s. The dipole-based BSSRDF model developed by Jensen and
his colleagues was really the first model simple enough yet sufficiently accurate to
meet the demands of the motion picture industry. This model was first considered
during production of *Star Wars Episode II: Attack of the Clones* [Lucas 02], in
a scene where a CG character and an actor hug each other. In this scene, the
actor was temporarily replaced by a CG digital double. The intention was to
use the dipole BSSRDF model to render the skin of the actor. Christophe Hery
implemented the model as a RenderMan shader at ILM. Test images with and
without the BSSRDF shader are shown in Figure 4.25. However, its use was
postponed because of stability concerns and time constraints. The implementation
was later used in the film *Harry Potter and the Chamber of Secrets* ; the BSSRDF
model was used to render a CG character named Dobby [Columbus 02].

Hery's RenderMan BSSRDF shader was implemented using a depth buffer,
as the ray-tracing capabilities of RenderMan were not well developed at the time.
As noted earlier, the dipole-based BSSRDF model does not require ray tracing.
To compute the exitance at a point p on an object, sample points are chosen by
taking points near p on the tangent plane at p (which is presumably a reasonable
approximation to the surface at p) and projecting those onto the surface. If the
light source is visible from a sample point, the exitance at p for the sample point
is computed using the diffuse BSSRDF formula of Equation (4.13). If the light
is not visible from a sample point, the sample point is replaced by a point on the
opposite side of the object (perpendicular to the tangent plane). The computation
is repeated for each sample point, and the sum of these results gives the exitance

at point p due to multiple scattering. The "fast translucency" algorithm, which employs sampling as preprocessing, nearly doubled the computation speed. The "fast translucency" paper by Jensen and Buhler also describes a way of using a specular reflection to approximate single scattering, so the multiple scattering model by itself sufficiently handles subsurface light transport.

The BSSRDF shader at ILM faced a great turning point during the production of *Lemony Snicket's A Series of Unfortunate Events* [Silberling 04]. The biggest challenge for ILM in this film was to replace the face of a real baby with CG. The BSSRDF shader used to render the Dobby character in the Harry Potter film used only direct lighting. While this worked well for that imaginary character, it was found to be insufficient for the scene with the human baby's skin. The problem was that the omission of global illumination (indirect lighting) resulted in inadequate photorealism. However, the BSSRDF model was developed for a single incident light direction. Including indirect illumination requires repeating the scattering computation for a collection of indirect samples. Unfortunately, the computation is expensive and the number of samples needed is large. To reduce the number of samples, the researchers employed a scheme where the incident flux (or irradiance) is stored at surface sample points and the actual incident light is computed from interpolating these samples. This approach is similar to the irradiance caching techniques described in Chapter 2.

Interpolation is well suited to multiple scattering computations, because the models are based on the assumption that multiple scattering is a diffusion process. This causes incident light to be blurred, so a certain amount of noise in the representation of the incident light tends to be smoothed out by subsurface scattering. This means that the incident irradiance at each sample point does not need to be computed very accurately, so a simple interpolation method suffices. Accounting for indirect illumination for subsurface scattering produced a greater improvement in the photorealism of the rendered images than the staff at ILM expected. It also showed the importance of accurate incident light for the dipole multiple scattering model.

Another innovation that came about during the production of *Lemony Snicket's A Series of Unfortunate Events* was to provide the artists more intuitive parameters to control multiple scattering. The dipole model depends on the diffuse scattering and absorption coefficients σ_s' and σ_a, which represent how much diffused light is scattered or absorbed. As described earlier, these are not particularly intuitive. Before the work on the baby's skin the parameters for scattering in skin (Table 4.1) were treated by the BSSRDF shader as constant across the entire skin. This proved inadequate for the baby's face; the effect of multiple scattering needed to vary with position, and the control of this needed to be based on both physical and artistic considerations. The diffuse reflectance and mean free path that Jensen and Buhler suggested in the "fast translucency" paper were a good choice, as they correspond roughly to the surface color and the translucency, respectively. A larger mean free path implies more transparency.

Hery extended this approach to control positionally dependent multiple scattering using textures [Hery 05]. Representing the diffuse reflectance and mean free path parameters in textures is straightforward to implement: at each sample point, the scattering computation proceeds with the parameter values obtained from the textures. However, the fact that these parameters are more intuitive does not mean that they correspond directly to the final appearance of the rendered object. In movie production, the process of modeling subsurface scattering often starts with a photograph of the live actor or detailed model of the character (known as a *maquette*) taken under uniform illumination. The goal of photo-realistic rendering is to match the scattering characteristics of the actual object, although there is also flexibility for artistic control. Adjusting the parameters to match the photograph is a tedious process of trial and error. Hery showed how the scattering parameters can be estimated directly from a photographic record as an inverse process. The mean free path $l_d = 1/\sigma_{tr}$ is obtained from a measured value of σ_{tr}, i.e., from Table 4.1. This parameter is set to be uniform over the whole object. Next, texture maps from the photograph are constructed for the object. The geometric model typically consists of micropolygons (polygons smaller than screen pixels in the final image), so the image is sampled and interpolated at the resolution appropriate for the micropolygons. The diffuse albedo parameters are determined as described in Section 4.3.4. The result is an albedo map for the object that can be artistically adjusted according to the particular production needs. The object is then rendered with the finished albedo map. This combination of physical accuracy and artistic control is a compelling advantage of the texture-based technique.

After the invention of the texture-based scattering parameter control, use of the BSSRDF shader spread rapidly at ILM and it was soon utilized in various other projects. Examples of its use include the skin of Yoda and the growing plants in the movie *Star Wars Episode III: Revenge of the Sith* [Lucas 05], the sea spray in *Poseidon* [Petersen 06], and the skin of Davy Jones in *Pirates of the Caribbean: Dead Man's Chest* [Verbinski 06]. Various creative efforts were employed to construct albedo maps and to represent the incident light according to the particular needs of each situation.

The BSSRDF shader at ILM has been extended to more general multilayer objects. Donner and Jensen's multipole model was not practical for production work because the parameters cannot be determined from photographs or albedo maps by direct inversion of the model formulas. One of the biggest problems was how to create a multilayer model that could be controlled intuitively by the artists.

Hery figured out a way to do this, and the implemented shader has been used in production since the film *The Spiderwick Chronicles*.

Regarding future work, Hery notes that it would be desirable to enable the dynamic control of the realism adaptively. As mentioned above, ILM improved the efficiency of the subsurface scattering shader by employing Jensen and Buhler's "fast translucency" method. However, movie production involves animation: the scene objects move between frames. It is problematic that the parts of the scene where realism is desired often changes according to the animation of the objects and the camera position. Precomputation, such as that employed in the fast translucency algorithm, may become useless within a few frames. What is needed is a way to adaptively improve efficiency based on the factors that affect the final visual quality the most. The solution to this problem will likely need ideas from both practitioners and academic researchers.

Hery also mentions that even when subsurface scattering is implemented correctly "something is still missing." For example, when GI was included to compensate for the lacking realism of the baby's skin, Hery found that the absence of skin microstructure was a significant missing element. Consequently, vellus hair (peach fuzz) was added. In Hery's opinion, missing details like this reveal unnatural visual qualities that audiences may notice without being aware of the actual cause. Discovering such missing qualities and learning how to compensate for them is what currently fuels the competition to enhance the simulated appearance of skin. Novel techniques in movie production arise from the tireless curiosity of the minds involved; higher quality images come only from endless trials.

4.4   Recent Progress in Subsurface Scattering

Another significant accomplishment in subsurface scattering was published in the 2007 paper entitled *Efficient Rendering of Human Skin* by Eugene d'Eon, David Luebke and Eric Enderton [d'Eon et al. 07]. Regarding multiple scattering as a kind of filter of the incident light led the authors to investigate whether a simple Gaussian filter could be used in place of the multipole reflectance profiles. A Gaussian filter has the form

$$G(r,v) = \frac{1}{\sqrt{2\pi v}} e^{-r^2/2v}, \tag{4.21}$$

where r is the distance from the point of incidence and v is the Gaussian *variance* or width. Gaussian filters are fast to compute, and have the additional property that the Fourier transform of a Gaussian is itself a Gaussian. This makes Gaussian reflectance and transmission profiles ideal for multilayer materials because the

Fourier transforms used in combining layers come essentially for free. d'Eon and his collaborators discovered that a single Gaussian function could not reproduce the realism of the multipole or even the dipole model. So the next step was to try summing multiple Gaussians of varying width. They found that a sum of as few as six Gaussians could adequately approximate the diffusion profiles of the multipole model. Their model also uses a more precise convolution expression for combining layers that depends on the direction of light propagation:

$$T_{12}^+ = T_1^+ * T_2^+ + T_1^+ * R_2^+ * R_1^- * T_2^+ + T_1^+ * R_2^+ * R_1^- * R_2^+ * R_1^- * T_2^+ + \cdots \quad (4.22)$$

where the "+" and "−" superscripts indicate direction. The model is amenable to implementation in graphics hardware. The authors' implementation was able to render a human head model at rates as high as 60 frames per second.

In 2008 Craig Donner, Tim Weyrich, Eugene d'Eon, Ravi Ramamoorthi and Szymon Rusinkiewicz published an enhanced multilayer model for subsurface scattering in human skin [Donner et al. 08]. The model includes a number of things the multipole model does not. For example, each layer has its own set of spatially varying reflectance parameters, and it also accounts for absorption at the interface between layers. The parameters are chosen from physical measurements computed from a series of photographs. The photographs are taken by a calibrated camera through a variety of filters, including a cross-polarization filter to eliminate unwanted glossy reflection. The measurements are then fit to the model. A notable advantage of the model is that it allows for greater flexibility in controlling skin parameters, e.g., the amount of melanin.

The representation of the effects of subsurface scattering by combining a single scattering model with a diffuse multiple scattering model became popular after the publication of the dipole-based BSSRDF model. However, it is based on the assumption that multiple scattering is diffuse. The diffusion approximation is after all only an approximation, and it only applies to materials exhibiting a high degree of scattering. The researchers who developed the diffusion-based models understood that subsurface scattering can also be important in materials in which the diffuse assumption breaks down. Donner et al. proposed a more generic BSSRDF model for homogeneous materials in the paper "An Empirical BSSRDF model" [Donner et al. 09] that neither splits scattering into single and multiple components nor relies on the diffusion approximation. The model employs a fairly simple analytic function of six parameters, although there may be many sets of such parameters for a single material. The parameters are determined by running a large scale particle simulation in the scattering medium. The exitant light distribution for the material is then examined for the distinct features corresponding to each parameter, e.g., anisotropy, peak direction, lobe shape and asymmetry, etc. Although the work is still in its early stages, it shows that the dipole model is not the only practical option for modeling multiple scattering even in homogeneous materials.

Image-based approaches offer another possibility for representing the effects of subsurface scattering. As is described in Chapter 5, image-based rendering starts with an acquired image that already contains effects such as subsurface scattering. However, an image-based approach does not provide a model for scattering, because there are no parameters to control so there is no direct way to adjust the scattering to achieve the desired effects. The recent paper "SubEdit: A Representation for Editing Measured Heterogeneous Subsurface Scattering" by Ying Song, Xin Tong, Fabio Pellacini, and Pieter Peers [Song et al. 09] suggests one interesting way around this. The idea is to decouple the nonlocal scattering effects from the local properties and allow them to be edited. The results seem promising and may lead to a general image-based subsurface scattering model.

It is typical in computer graphics for the first incarnation of a new technique or innovation to be aimed at something specific. Generalization comes in a second stage, after the new technique is widely applied and its advantages and limitations are better understood. It could be said that the progress of subsurface scattering is now beginning this second stage.

II

Image-Based Approaches

The rendering methods introduced in Part I reproduce the appearance of objects based on the physics of light transport. In the 1990s, a new approach to photorealistic rendering emerged that attempted to recover the appearance of objects directly from photographs. This has come to be known as an *image-based* approach to rendering. The philosophy of image-based rendering is this: because photographs already include the effects created by real-world light interaction, that information extracted from photographs can be substituted in place of physically based computations. Image-based techniques have in fact been very successful in improving both the efficiently and fidelity of photorealistic rendering.

It was not until after the emergence of image-based rendering methods that the potential was realized beyond photorealistic rendering. For example, the lighting and shadowing in a photograph contains information about shape and location as well as the reflection character of the photographed objects. While the problem of extracting such information from photographs is old and well studied, computer graphics has provided a rich source of applications for existing techniques as well as opportunities for further development.

In Part II, some representative image-based techniques are examined along with their practical application.

5

Image-Based Rendering

In the broadest sense, *image-based rendering* (IBR) refers to any rendering method that depends on existing images. However, in recent years, the term has come to refer to the particular problem of recovering the appearance of an object or environment from an arbitrary viewpoint using a collection of acquired images. These images might be rendered images themselves, but usually they come from photographs. One application of IBR is the creation of virtual walk-throughs of real environments. Another is to accelerate production of animated films by creating "in-between" frames from fully rendered frames, which is useful when full rendering is costly. This chapter introduces the fundamental concepts of image-based rendering and then describes some representative IBR techniques.

5.1 Stereo

Recovering 3D models from photographs is a form of *photogrammetry*, which is the general practice of determining geometry from photographs. Photogrammetry predates computer graphics; in fact, it is almost as old as photography itself. The process of obtaining 3D coordinates of an object from a combination of photographs taken from different viewpoints is known as *stereophotogrammetry*.[1] A fundamental result in stereophotogrammetry was proved by E. Kruppa in 1913: two different perspective images of five distinct points is sufficient to determine

---

[1] Although the term "stereo" often brings to mind "two" of something, it actually comes from the Greek *stereós*, meaning "solid." As a prefix, "stereo" implies "three-dimensional" or "having depth." For example, "stereophonic" audio indicates the spatial quality of the sound is reproduced, not that there are two channels. Likewise, "stereoscopic" vision refers to the notion of seeing depth; "binocular" implies two eyes or two images.

the relative position and orientation of the two viewpoints and also the 3D coordinates of the five points (in some arbitrary coordinate system). However, this theorem assumes the images come from an ideal perspective projection, which real cameras do not provide. Photogrammetry in general has been actively studied in other disciplines, such as computer vision. The process of stereophotogrammetry consists of the following three steps: camera calibration stereo correspondence, and stereo reconstruction.

5.1.1 Camera Calibration

The precise details of how a particular camera forms a 2D image of a 3D scene depends on two things: how incoming light paths are focused by the camera optics, and how the incident radiance is recorded in the image. The former is most relevant in stereo geometry reconstruction; the latter is of interest when the camera is used for physical light measurement. How 3D points are transformed to points on the 2D camera sensor plane can be modeled as a mathematical projection. Ultimately stereo reconstruction depends on the inverse of this projection. The projection is determined by the internal optics of the camera as well as its position and orientation in space with respect to the scene. The camera optics, e.g., the position of the sensor with respect to the lens and the optical properties of the lenses, are *intrinsic parameters* of the camera. The *extrinsic parameters* describe where the camera is located in space and where it is pointed.

What exactly the intrinsic parameters are depends on the projection model. Generally, intrinsic camera parameters include the focal length of the lens, the size of the aperture (f-stop), and the field of view. More detailed information such as the error between the center of projection and the center of the sensor plane, lens aberration, etc., may also be needed for more precise reconstruction. The general process of determining the intrinsic parameters is known as *camera calibration*. Most commonly, calibration is done by capturing a series of images of a known target.

A simple pinhole camera consists of a closed box with photosensitive film placed on the inside of one side and a small "pinhole" aperture punched in the center of the opposite side. Mathematically the pinhole aperture is assumed to be a single point, so each point on the film records the radiance of the light ray coming from the direction of the aperture. The pinhole camera projection is the standard perspective projection (Figure 5.1(a)). A lens camera uses a system of lenses to focus incoming light onto the film plane. An ideal lens camera focuses light rays coming from a specific *focal plane* in space onto the film plane so that each point on the film plane corresponds to a unique point on the focal plane. The focal plane thus appears perfectly in focus in the image. The position of the focal plane

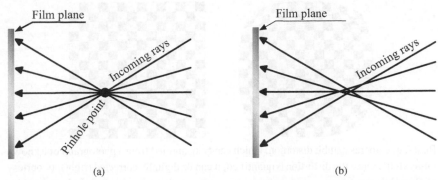

(a)   (b)

Figure 5.1   A camera directs light rays onto a film plane. (a) In a pinhole camera, all rays go through the pinhole aperture. (b) A lens camera focuses light so that rays from a focal plane in the scene converge on the film plane; rays from elsewhere do not converge, which results in blurring. (Courtesy of Paul Debevec.)

is related to the distance from the lens to the film plane; "focusing" the camera amounts to changing this distance. Light from points away from the focal plane is spread out on the film, so objects off the focal plane appear blurred. The blurring increases with distance from the focal plane. The distance at which objects start to appear noticeably out of focus is known as the *depth of field* and is controlled by the size of a circular aperture inside the lens. As the aperture size approaches zero, the lens camera approaches a pinhole camera in which everything appears in focus (Figure 5.1(b)).

A pinhole camera projects straight lines in the scene to straight lines on the film plane, as does the basic perspective projection. In an ideal lens camera model, straight lines on the focal plane are imaged as straight lines on the film plane. However, real cameras do not have ideal lenses. The ideal lens is typically approximated most closely near the center of the film plane. The image becomes more distorted further away from the center. The effects of distortion can be significant enough to affect the results of stereo reconstruction. Most camera distortion depends only on the distance from the center, and is therefore known as *radial distortion*. The distortion of a particular camera is typically measured by capturing an image of a known target such as a checkerboard. The distortion can be determined by comparing the image to the original target (Figure 5.2 (left)). A polynomial approximation to the radial distortion is often used in practice. Once its coefficients are determined, the distortion in each image captured by the camera can be corrected by applying the polynomial function to the image (Figure 5.2 (right)). The remaining intrinsic camera parameters can be determined from images corrected for distortion.

Figure 5.2   Real lens cameras exhibit distortion, which can be quantified from a photograph of a known
              target (left). Once the distortion is quantified, it can be digitally corrected (right). (Courtesy
              of Paul Debevec.)

5.1.2 Stereo Correspondence

Stereo correspondence is the process of finding corresponding points in images
captured from different viewpoints. This was once done manually by finding specific reference points in the photographs. An approach better suited to computer
processing is to attach special uniquely colored tags at strategic points on the
scene objects. The corresponding image pixels are then matched by color. However, this does require that the tags be placed on the objects before they are photographed. The general stereo correspondence problem assumes nothing about
the images, other than that they were captured from nearby viewpoints.

Suppose I_0 is a digitized image captured from one viewpoint, and I_1 is a secondary image captured from a nearby viewpoint. A pixel at (x, y) in the primary
image I_0 corresponds to a point on some scene object (actually, a small region
around the point on the object). The problem is to find the pixel in the secondary
image I_1 that corresponds to the same point on the same object. A naive approach
is to simply search the secondary image I_1 for a pixel having the same color as
the pixel at (x, y) in I_0. The problem, though, is that pixel colors of corresponding
points may not be quite the same, due to imaging issues such as lighting variation,
noise, blurring, etc. Furthermore, the point imaged at the pixel (x, y) might be hidden by another object in the secondary image. A search based on a kind of local
averaging is used instead, which works under the assumption that the neighborhood of pixels near (x, y) in I_0 corresponds to a pixel neighborhood in I_1, offset
by a vector (dx, dy). The neighborhoods match best when the sum of the squares
of the pixel differences,

$$E(dx, dy) = \sum_{k=x-w_x}^{x+w_x} \sum_{l=y-w_y}^{y+w_y} (I_1(k+dx, l+dy) - I_0(k, l))^2, \qquad (5.1)$$

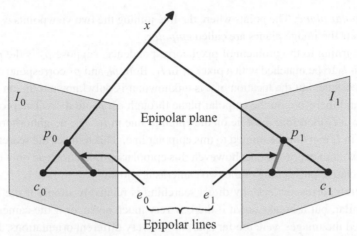

Epipolar plane

I_0

I_1

p_0

p_1

c_0

c_1

e_0 e_1

Epipolar lines

Figure 5.3 Epipolar geometry for two images of a scene. A point p_0 on either image plane lies on a unique epipolar plane through the two viewpoints c_0 and c_1. The intersection of this plane with the image planes I_0 and I_1 are epipolar lines. Any point in the scene that projects to p_0 must project to a point p_1 on the epipolar line in I_1.

is smallest. The neighborhood is a rectangular region of width $2w_x + 1$ by $2w_y + 1$ centered at (x, y) in I_0 and $(x + dx, y + dy)$ in I_1. The minimum is taken over all (dx, dy) under the restriction that the search points stay inside image I_1. This neighborhood search assumes that the scale and orientation of the images are essentially the same. If one image is rotated with respect to the other, the search also has to include rotations of the neighborhood.

The neighborhood search can be made more efficient by employing *epipolar geometry*. Normally the film plane of a camera is behind the focal point (i.e., the aperture) of the camera. The image can, however, be regarded as lying on a virtual image plane in front of the focal point. This arrangement is essentially the same as the virtual camera setup used in computer graphics rendering: the focal point is the "eye" point, the size and position of the image rectangle controls the field of view, and the perpendicular to the virtual image plane provides the "gaze" direction. Figure 5.3 illustrates this for two separate virtual cameras, each of which is aimed at the point labeled x. In this context, the camera focal point is often called the "viewpoint," the "eye point," or the "center of projection;" they are labeled c_0 and c_1 in Figure 5.3. Each point on the ray from the viewpoint c_0 through x projects to the point p_0 in image I_0, but the same points project to a line in I_1 from the viewpoint c_1 of the other camera. This line is an *epipolar line*. The ray from c_1 to x likewise projects to a single point p_1 in I_1, and to an epipolar line in I_0. The plane containing the point x and the focal points c_0 and c_1 is known as an *epipolar plane*. The points where the line joining the two viewpoints c_0 and c_1 intersects the image planes are called *epipoles*.

Returning to the problem of pixel correspondence, suppose p_o is the pixel at (x, y) in I_0 to be matched with a pixel p_1 in I_1. Both p_0 and p_1 correspond to point x in the scene, but the location of x is unknown; it is only known to lie on the ray $\overrightarrow{c_0 p_0}$, and therefore on the epipolar plane through c_0, p_0, and c_1. The projection p_1 of x in I_1 therefore must lie on the epipolar line in I_1. The neighborhood pixel search in I_1 can thus be limited to this epipolar line. This reduces the search space from two dimensions to one; however, this epipolar optimization can only be used if the relative positioning of the two cameras is known.

Stereo correspondence by direct searching is relatively simple if the images are similar, but it breaks down if there is very much noise, or if the cameras that captured the images were too far apart or had very different orientations. In such cases manual intervention is likely necessary. Automatic pixel correspondence in general is still regarded as a difficult problem, even when extensive searching is applied.

5.1.3 Optical Flow

One situation where the primary and secondary images are likely to be similar enough for automated stereo correspondence arises when the images are successive frames in a movie or animation. However, the differences in the images may come from the motion of the objects between frames as well as motion of the camera, so the epipolar approach does not necessarily apply. The general problem of tracking corresponding points between frames is called *optical flow*.

Optical flow has been extensively studied in computer vision; Beauchemin and Barron present a survey of optical flow algorithms [Beauchemin and Barron 95]. The basic problem is to construct a vector field on the primary image I_0, in which the vector at each point points to the corresponding point in a secondary image I_1. This vector field is called the *2D motion field*, and optical flow is sometimes referred to as the computation of *image velocity*. The actual motion field can be very complicated; in fact, it is not even defined for points that become visible or invisible between images. The general optical flow problem is to find an approximation to the true motion field.

For a rasterized image the motion field becomes a discrete vector field, a vector function $\vec{d}(x, y)$ of each pixel: if $\vec{d}(x, y) = (dx, dy)$, pixel (x, y) in I_0 corresponds approximately to pixel $(x + dx, y + dy)$ in I_1 (Figure 5.4). One way of defining the optical flow vector $\vec{d}(x, y)$ is to minimize the square of the pixel difference in a neighborhood of fixed size as in Equation (5.1). That is, the value of dx and dy for a particular pixel (x, y) are chosen so that $E(dx, dy)$ is minimized.

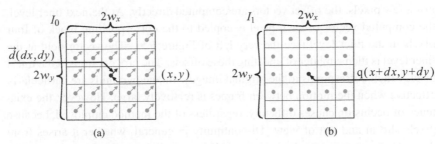

Figure 5.4   Corresponding neighborhoods in (a) the primary image and (b) the secondary image.

The correction vector computation thus reduces to a least squares problem that can be solved by standard methods. Other approaches use image gradients or higher-order approximations to how the pixels actually change.

An *image pyramid* method can be employed to improve optical flow computation. The original images are repeatedly downsampled to create a sequence of images of decreasing size that can be thought of as a kind of pyramid (Figure 5.5). Much like the construction of a mip map (Chapter 3), each pixel is the average of a block of four pixels at the previous level. Each image in the sequence therefore has half the resolution of the previous image. A pyramid is constructed for both images I_0 and I_1. The offset vector field computation is applied at each level of the pyramid starting at the top. At the top level, where the image has been reduced to

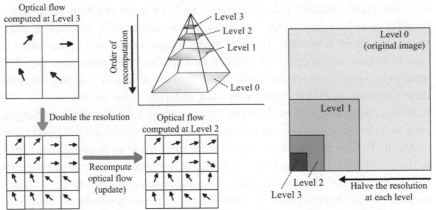

Figure 5.5   Optical flow can be made more efficient and stable with an image pyramid constructed by repeatedly downsampling the image by a factor of two (right). The optical flow is determined first at the top level, and the result is replicated on the pixels in the next level (left) which are then recomputed or refined.

just a few pixels, the offset vectors are computed directly. At the next finer level, the computed vector of each pixel is copied to the corresponding block of four pixels in the finer level (see the very left of Figure 5.5). The vector field at the finer level is then a matter of updating these offsets. The process stops at the finest level, which corresponds to the original images. Image pyramids are particularly effective when the motion between frames is relatively large. However, the existence of occlusion causes difficulty, regardless of the method employed, because pixels slip in and out of view. Discontinuity in general, whether it arises from discontinuous motion or discontinuous changes in lighting, is a serious problem for optical flow computation.

Optical flow determination has a number of applications. Video compression is one. If the optical flow changes little between several sequential frames, the middle frames can be reconstructed by interpolating pixels from the offset vectors of neighboring frames, so the middle frames need not be stored. Some contemporary high-end digital television systems do something similar, employing a kind of inverse of this approach to create smoother motion. These televisions are capable of displaying frames at a higher rate than video frames are delivered. Approximate frames in between true frames can be constructed by interpolating the motion field. Inserting such frames can cause motion to appear smoother, although the effectiveness of this technique depends on the nature of the video.

5.1.4   Refined Version of Stereo Correspondence

Methods for stereo correspondence traditionally assume that the images are similar. The paper entitled "Video Matching" by Peter Sand and Seth Teller introduced a technique that works for images having substantially different appearances [Sand and Teller 04]. The goal of the research described in this paper is how to obtain correspondences between two similar video sequences captured separately, albeit from similar viewpoints. Two sequences of a similar environment captured at different times may have differences for several reasons: the lighting conditions might be different, the scene may have some minor changes, such as added or removed elements, and the camera positions are not likely to be identical. The two images at the top of Figure 5.6 provide an example. The teapot in the left image is missing from right image; furthermore, the camera position has changed slightly between images. A human observer might see these images as quite similar, but the variation in the individual pixels is significant enough to cause trouble for automatic pixel correspondence.

Sand and Teller's approach to image correspondence considers two separate aspects: a measure of pixel matching consistency, and a measure of motion consistency. Pixel matching is done in a manner similar to the basic stereo correspon-

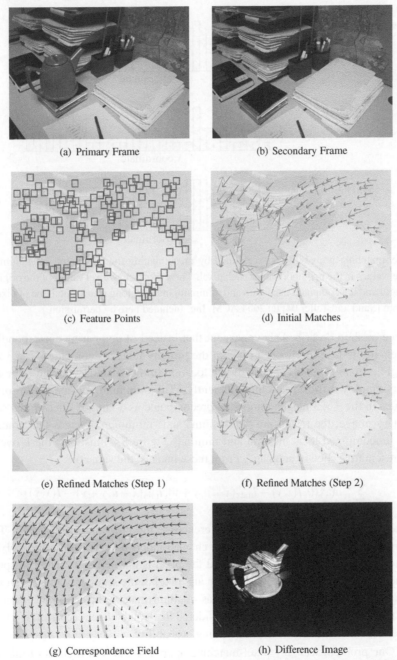

(a) Primary Frame (b) Secondary Frame

(c) Feature Points (d) Initial Matches

(e) Refined Matches (Step 1) (f) Refined Matches (Step 2)

(g) Correspondence Field (h) Difference Image

Figure 5.6   Update of the offset fields. (From [Sand and Teller 04] © 2004 ACM, Inc. Included here by permission.)

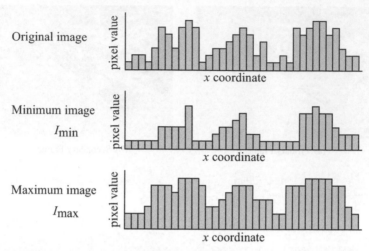

Figure 5.7   Pixel-matching probability is accelerated by precomputing the maximum and minimum
pixel values in the neighborhood at each pixel. These plots show pixel values of the original
images and the computed maximum and minimum images along a horizontal line of pixels.
(From [Sand and Teller 04] © 2004 ACM, Inc. Included here by permission.)

dence method described above, except that instead of comparing corresponding
pixels in the neighborhood, a pixel in the primary image is compared to a 3×3
neighborhood of pixels at a candidate location in the secondary image. The authors employ a trick to do this efficiently. The minimum and maximum pixel
values in the 3×3 neighborhood are precomputed as a kind of filter on the secondary image; the results are "maximum" and "minimum" images that contain
the precomputed local maxima and minima. Figure 5.7 illustrates these over a
representative slice of an image. From these images, the value of

$$\sum_{(x,y) \in R} \max(0, I(x,y) - I_{\max}(x+u, y+v), I_{\min}(x+u, y+v) - I(x,y))$$

instead of the square of the pixel differences is minimized over all (u,v). The
computation is repeated for each color channel independently. From this a pixel-
matching probability is computed, and the pixel is omitted from the correspondence if it is deemed unlikely to match any pixel in the secondary image. Doing
this makes the algorithm more robust, as small mismatches have limited effect on
the final matching. If the match is considered likely, the offset vector (u,v) of the
pixel is recorded along with the matching probability.

   One problem with any pixel-matching approach arises in regions of the image where there is little variation between pixel values, i.e., in areas of uniform
color. The file folder on the right in the images of Figure 5.6 is a good example;

pixel matching is of little use in this region. Such areas can be avoided by using a form of *feature extraction*: pixel matching is limited to parts of the image where there is notable variation in neighboring pixels, e.g., at corners and edges. Figure 5.6(c) shows the regions that result from the feature extraction method employed by the authors. Limiting the pixel matching to these regions helps avoids mismatches. Part (d) of the figure shows the corresponding offset vectors, colored by probability. The vectors shown in lighter gray have lower pixel matching probability.

The second part of the algorithm, the motion consistency estimation, considers how well the offset vectors match between neighboring pixels. This information is used to construct a smooth final correspondence vector field. When the offset vectors match well between pixels in a region, it can be expected that the average offset vector is a good representation of the general optical flow. One thing that might be done is to fit the offset vectors to a global projective transformation between the two images, which would correspond to the different camera positions. However, the images are not assumed to be corrected for camera distortion, so the authors use a more general technique. The approach fits a locally smooth function to the offset vectors using a method known as *locally weighted linear regression*. The pixel-match probability serves as the weight for the offsets: vectors for which the pixel-match probability is highest are given the most weight.

The authors employ an iterative approach to computing the final correspondence vector field. The initial matches are smoothed by the regression, and then the pixel-matching probabilities are recomputed from these smoothed vectors (other techniques from computer vision are applied in the process). Figure 5.6(e) shows the result. Repeating this process has the effect of improving the correspondence field and removing the incorrect offset vectors (Figure 5.6(f)), so the process is repeated until no more improvement results. At this point, the final correspondence field can be constructed (Figure 5.6(g)). The difference between the actual secondary image and the estimated image computed by extrapolating the correspondence field is shown in Figure 5.6. The pixels are darkest where they match. As expected, no matches are found for pixels on the teapot.

5.1.5   Stereo Reconstruction

As described previously, stereo correspondence is the problem of matching points between images. Once points are matched, the difference in their positions can be used to approximate the 3D position of the point in the scene to which they correspond. This is the problem of *stereo reconstruction*. The basic problem is to find the 3D coordinates of a point x in an environment that projects to point $\bar{x}_1$ and

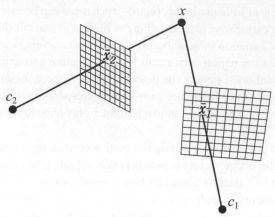

Figure 5.8   Stereo reconstruction is the problem of computing the 3D spatial coordinates of a point x
that projects to points $\bar{x}_1$ and $\bar{x}_2$ in two separate images.

$\bar{x}_2$ in two different images. Figure 5.8 illustrates; note the connection to epipolar
geometry.

Stereo reconstruction requires extrinsic camera parameters, i.e., the position
and orientation of the cameras when the images were captured. In Figure 5.8,
c_1 and c_2 are the viewpoints of each camera. The position and orientation of the
image planes are expressed in terms of transformation matrices P_1 and P_2, which
map the 2D image coordinates to 3D coordinates in the environment. The point x
satisfies

$$x = c_1 + t_1 P_1 \bar{x}_1 = c_2 + t_2 P_2 \bar{x}_2, \tag{5.2}$$

where t_1 and t_2 are the unknown parameters. Equation (5.2) is actually a system
of three equations, one for each coordinate. This system is overdetermined, as it
has only two variables. Solutions t_1 and t_2 for any two of the equations would
ideally be the same; however, the system is likely to have no exact solution due to
uncertainties in the coordinates. That is, the lines cannot be expected to intersect
exactly. Values of t_1 and t_2 are chosen to minimize the overall error, usually in a
least squares sense.

In practice, stereo reconstruction is applied to a collection of points, such as
a set of feature points in a real scene. The goal is to reconstruct (or create) an
underlying model by estimating the vertex coordinates. This requires minimizing
the error in the estimation over all the points, which can be formulated as a large
least squares system. But depending on the assumptions of the particular problem,
it may not be a linear system, in which case nonlinear optimization techniques

have to be applied. Generally the accuracy of the recovered coordinates increases with the number of images from different viewpoints, but so does the size of the optimization problem. One arrangement often used is to place the camera along orthogonal axes, at the front, back, left, right, and top of the object or model. The scale of the model can be determined if the camera focal lengths or distances between the camera positions is known.

5.2   Image Warping

The term "image-based rendering" was originally used in CG to describe any technique of generating a new image from existing images. Texture mapping and environment mapping,[2] could both be regarded as image-based techniques in that sense. In contemporary usage, "image-based rendering" (IBR) now refers to specific techniques of rendering from acquired image data. Section 5.3 covers this in detail. The term *image warping* is now used for general structural image manipulation. Texture and environment mapping can be classified as image warping, as can image reprojection. But the term more commonly refers to things like *morphing*, in which one image is continuously transformed into another in a way that makes it appear that an object in the image is changing its structure. Stereo correspondence and reconstruction came into the field of computer graphics from other disciplines, e.g., computer vision and photography, while image warping came out of CG itself. Combining image warping with stereo reconstruction allows photographs to be used directly for rendering.

In the 1990s, a technique of rendering from an arbitrary viewpoint by interpolating multiple existing images came into use as an image-warping technique. The 1993 paper "View Interpolation for Image Synthesis" by Shenchang Eric Chen and Lance Williams presented a method for rendering a scene using a collection of images captured from a fixed set of viewpoints in space [Chen and Williams 93]. The QuickTime VR developed by Apple Inc. is based on the technique introduced in the paper. The method uses an image-interpolation technique based on image morphing that allows rendering from an arbitrary viewpoint. Images from nearby capture points are morphed into each other; the interpolated image comes from the partially morphed image. It does, however, require "range data" so that the depth of each pixel in each image is known. That is, the underlying geometry of the model has to be known or at least approximated. Visibility is handled with a depth buffer based on pixel depth in the images. Although not published, considerable research into this approach was done during

---

[2]Environment mapping is a kind of texture mapping in which the texture is applied to surfaces "at infinity." This is discussed in greater depth in Chapter 7

this period. The common feature of the techniques developed was that the pixels were selected out of the image data set by depth.

These view-interpolation techniques assume that the depth of existing images is precomputed or already known. The problem of rendering from general photographs that have no range data remained unsolved. In the middle of the 1990s, CG researchers began to use stereo reconstruction to assign appropriate depths to images in the absence of range information. The method of recovering depth by using a form of stereo reconstruction is called *depth from stereo*. With depth from stereo, a collection of images can be re-rendered at an arbitrary viewpoint without any a priori knowledge of the underlying geometry. Doing this has come to be known as image-based rendering (IBR). An early IBR technique was developed in 1994 at INRIA, the French national laboratory [Laveau and Faugeras 94]. Basically, the technique works using stereo correspondence, but the depth is determined by measuring the "disparity" (distortion) between the primary image and a secondary image. The underlying geometry never needs to be constructed explicitly.

In 1995, Leonard McMillan and Gary Bishop published the paper "Plenoptic Modeling" [McMillan and Bishop 95] in which they argued that image based rendering ultimately amounts to determining the *plenoptic function*.[3] The plenoptic function gives the spectral radiance at each point in space, in each direction, at each point in time. It is therefore a function of seven variables: $P(x, y, z, \theta, \phi, \lambda, t)$, assuming an underlying coordinate system. The plenoptic function is an abstract construct; ultimately much of photorealistic rendering can be formulated as computing values of the plenoptic function. McMillan and Bishop's 1995 paper did not try to actually reconstruct the plenoptic function, rather it cast image-based rendering in the framework of computing a slice of the plenoptic function. The particular depth from stereo method employed in the paper uses cylindrical projections of panoramic images to represent the plenoptic function at specific points in space. Rendering from an arbitrary viewpoint is accomplished by warping these images. The environment is assumed to be static, so there is no variation in the images over time.

5.3   Image-Based Modeling and Rendering

In 1996, Paul E. Debevec, Camillo J. Taylor, and Jitendra Malik published "Modeling and Rendering Architecture from Photographs: A Hybrid Geometry- and

---

[3]The term "plenoptic function" was coined by vision researchers Adelson and Bergen [Adelson and Bergen 91]. The term is a combination of the Latin *plenus*, meaning "full" or "complete," and the Greek *optikos*, meaning "of sight."

Image-based Approach," which systematized existing image-based rendering techniques into something known as *image-based modeling and rendering* [Debevec et al. 96]. The pipeline of image-based modeling and rendering is intuitive and efficient, so the technology quickly spread into the production of movies and music videos. Debevec himself was excited to apply this technology in film making.

5.3.1 Origin of Image-Based Modeling and Rendering

Debevec said that his motivation for the 1996 paper was to create an animation of flying around the clock tower at the University of California, Berkeley, where he was studying at the time. Because of this, the paper introduces tools geared toward creating an animation. Debevec included the animation in a short film he directed called *The Campanile Movie* [Debevec 97] that was included in the Electronic Theater at SIGGRAPH (*Campanile* is the name of the clock tower at Berkeley). The following year, students who contributed to the creation of the short film participated in applying image-based rendering to the production of the movie *The Matrix*.

5.3.2 Pipeline of Image-Based Modeling and Rendering

The process of the rendering method presented in the 1996 paper by Debevec, Taylor, and Malik consists of a three-stage process, or pipeline, described as follows.

Stage 1. Photogrammetric modeling: Recovering approximate 3D models The goal of this stage is to construct an approximate architectural model of the scene from the captured photographs. This is not automated—it requires a fair amount of trial and error by a human using specialized software. This software assists the user in constructing the model and matching it to the images. The model at this stage is assumed to be fairly simple, consisting of simple geometric primitives. Primitives are parametrized polyhedral "blocks" arranged in a hierarchical structure maintained by the software. The parameters of the blocks, which are values such as the height and width, etc., are variables that can be linked together and constrained in a way that facilitates matching the model to the captured images.

The user starts by marking the edges in the captured images corresponding to edges in the rough model, then creates the model and lays out the parameters. Then the software does the work of stereo reconstruction, and projects the reconstructed model onto the image. The user then makes any adjustments and performs another reconstruction, and repeats the process as necessary. Figure 5.9 illustrates the process: part (a) shows the lines marked by the user, part (b) shows

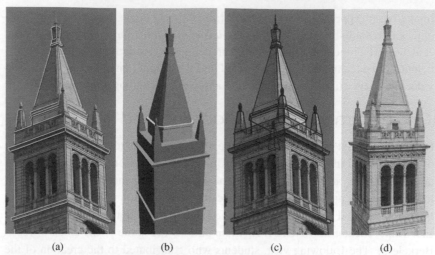

(a)   (b)   (c)   (d)

Figure 5.9   Recovering an architectural model. (a) The user starts by marking lines in the images that
corresponds to edges of the rough model, which is shown in (b). The accuracy of the
model is checked by projecting the captured image onto the model. (d) A rendering of the
completed model with view-dependent texture maps. (From [Debevec et al. 96].)

the recovered model, and part (c) shows the projection onto the image. Only one
of the lower pinnacles has been marked; the model geometry assures that it is
replicated properly at the other three corners.

The reconstruction algorithm described in the paper works by matching the
model edges to corresponding observed edges in the images, which have been
manually selected by the user. Figure 5.10(a) illustrates the projection of a 3D
scene edge projected onto the image plane of a captured image. The line containing the projected edge is the intersection of the image plane with the plane
through the 3D line and the camera viewpoint. The camera coordinate system is
represented by a rotation matrix R and a translation vector $\vec{t}$; if $\vec{v}$ is the direction
vector of the 3D line and $\vec{d}$ is any point on the line, then the normal vector to the
plane is

$$\vec{m} = R(\vec{v} \times (\vec{d} - \vec{t})). \tag{5.3}$$

The reconstruction works by choosing parameters to simultaneously minimize
the disparity of all the predicted model edges and the corresponding observed
edges. Figure 5.10(b) shows how this error is computed in an image plane. The
model edge is projected onto the image plane, and the the error is the integral
of the distance between the edge line and the observed edge over the length of
the observed edge. The camera parameters R and t are not known, so these are

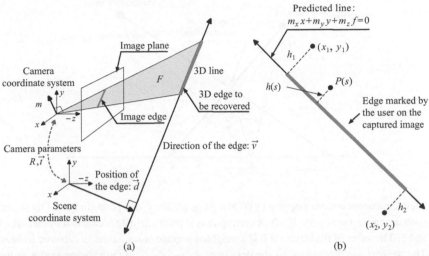

Figure 5.10 Stereo reconstruction based on lines. (a) A line in the scene is specified by a direction vector $\vec{v}$ and an off vector $\vec{d}$ in scene (world) coordinates, and it projects to a line on an image plane. (b) A line predicted by the model is compared to the observed line in the image plane. (After [Debevec et al. 96].)

included in the parameter set of the error optimization. The optimization problem is nonlinear. The numeric algorithm employed requires a good initial estimate for it to converge to the proper local minimum. The authors describe a method for finding an initial estimate that works by first estimating the camera rotation parameters. Equation (5.3) implies the constraints,

$$m^T R \vec{v} = 0, \tag{5.4}$$
$$m^T R(\vec{d} - \vec{t}) = 0. \tag{5.5}$$

Horizontal and vertical edges have a known orientation $\vec{v}$. If there are enough of these, as there probably are in any real architectural model, a least squares minimization of Equation (5.4) over all such edges provides a good estimate of all the camera rotations. Once these are computed, the camera translations and remaining parameters are estimated by minimizing Equation (5.5). These estimates serve as the initial guess for the numeric optimizer. Nonlinear optimization is not easy, and gets harder with more parameters. For this reason, it is important that the model at this stage is fairly simple. Geometric details are added to this initial rough model in the final stage.

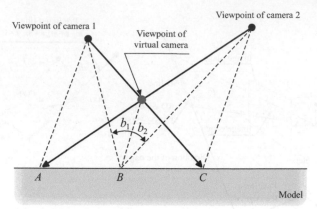

Figure 5.11   View-dependent texture mapping (VDTM). At an arbitrary viewpoint (indicated by the arrow) the camera sees point B, which corresponds to points in images captured by cameras 1 and 2. The value of the texture at B is a weighted average of the values in captured images. The weights are determined by the deviations b_1 and b_2 from the viewing angles of the captured images. (After [Debevec et al. 96].)

Stage 2. View-dependent texture mapping (VDTM): Mapping the captured images to the recovered model.

The ultimate goal is to re-render the model from an arbitrary viewpoint. It is assumed that the images are captured under approximately the same lighting conditions. However, the surfaces of the object being modeled are not likely to exhibit purely Lambertian reflectance, so their appearance depends on the view direction. The authors apply a *view-dependent texture mapping* approach to account for this. Figure 5.11 illustrates the concept. The pixel value seen by a virtual camera is interpolated from the corresponding pixels in nearby captured images as a weighted average. The weights are inversely proportional to the angles between the virtual view direction and the corresponding capture view directions. Figure 5.9(d) shows the model rendered with the view-dependent texture applied; capturing an image from this high viewpoint would be difficult.

Stage 3. Model-based stereo: Adding detail to the 3D model using image warping

The basic model constructed in the first stage is only a rough approximation to the underlying architecture model. As explained above, this simplifies fitting the parameters. However, the finer details of the model are important—rendering using the rough model cannot be expected to look right. For example, the rough model of the bell tower uses a single block for the section containing the bells: the arches and pillars and the inside elements are not included in the rough model.

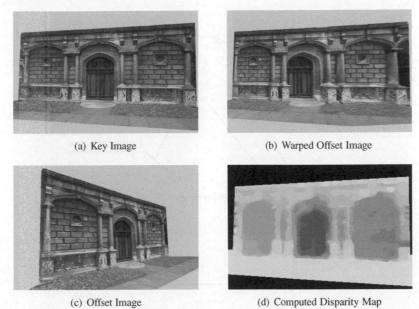

(a) Key Image (b) Warped Offset Image

(c) Offset Image (d) Computed Disparity Map

Figure 5.12 Model-based stereo. Fine detail is added to the model from two original captured images, (a) a key image and (b) an offset image. (c) The offset image is "warped" onto the rough model from the viewpoint of the key image. (d) The depth is computed using the disparity between the key image and the warped offset image. (From [Debevec et al. 96].)

Adding the detail is an application of basic stereo reconstruction. As described previously, stereo reconstruction works using the disparity (pixel offsets) between a key (primary) image and a secondary image. If the images are very different, it may not be possible to find pixel offsets between the two images. The images of the architectural objects are typically captured from viewpoints that are far apart, which means the images are not likely to be similar enough for the basic methods of stereo reconstruction. The authors get around this by working with the disparity between an original acquired key image and a virtual secondary image. This secondary image has the same viewpoint as the key image, but is constructed by projecting an image captured from a different viewpoint, known as the "offset image," onto the rough model rendered from the viewpoint of the key image (see Figure 5.12). Depth from stereo techniques can then be applied to the disparity between the key image and this virtual secondary image. The "depth" in this case is actually the offset of the detail from the surface of the model. The authors call this method *model-based stereo*.

Figure 5.13 illustrates the basic geometry of the model-based stereo technique. Epipolar geometry is applied; the two viewpoints are the positions of the camera

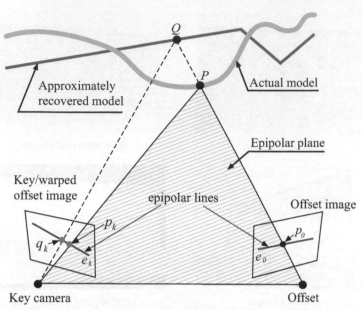

Figure 5.13   Pixel correspondence is determined in model-based stereo by searching the warped offset image along the epipolar line in the key image. (After [Debevec et al. 96].)

used for the key image, and that used for the offset image. A point P in the scene is contained in a unique epipolar plane through the two viewpoints. Suppose p_k is the pixel in the key image corresponding to P. Normally the pixel p_o corresponding to p_k in the offset image is found by searched along the epipolar line (the intersection of the epipolar plane through P and the image plane of the offset image). In model-based stereo, however, the corresponding pixel is contained in the warped offset image, which is formed by projecting the offset image onto the model from the position of the offset camera (P is projected onto Q in Figure 5.13) and that image is then projected back to the image plane of the key image. The pixel q_k that corresponds to p_k therefore lies in on the epipolar line in the warped offset image, which is the same as that of the key image.

The final rendering is performed by image warping. The recovery of the full 3D model and view-dependent texture mapping are performed before the final rendering in order to enhance the accuracy and efficiency of rendering. However, it is pointed out that these processes by themselves are not sufficient to create an image that looks accurate. Possibly because of this, the process of recovering a 3D model from photographs and then performing rendering after mapping the captured images, which were used for the recovery, became the definition of image-based modeling and rendering.

5.3.3 IBR in Movies

As previously mentioned, an notable early use of image-based rendering in movie production was in the "Bullet Time Shots" scene in the movie *The Matrix* [Wachowski and Wachowski 99]. George Borshukov, who was in charge of technical design in *The Matrix*, earned his PhD degree in computer science at the University of California, Berkeley. He became familiar with image-based rendering through his involvement with the production of Debevec's short film *The Campanile Movie*. In the "Bullet Time Shots" scene of *The Matrix* the camera swings around the main character 360 degrees while the character moves in extreme slow motion. The character was not created with CG; photographs were captured by cameras placed in a circle around a live actor. The cameras were set to capture the images in sequence around the circle, with a slight time delay between adjacent cameras in order to capture the motion of the actor. Assigning each sequential image to a frame in the animation creates the appearance of a camera sweeping around a slowly moving character. Image-based rendering was then used to create in-between frames for the appearance of smoothness. The objects in the background were recovered separately, as it was difficult to capture the background using the circular camera arrangement.

IBR had been used in the entertainment industry prior to *The Matrix*. The 1995 music video *Like a Rolling Stone* [Gondry 95], directed by Michel Gondry, shows characters frozen in midair produced using IBR (Figure 5.14). It is said that this music video provided inspiration for the "Bullet Time Shots" scene in *The Matrix*. The visual effects for the *Like a Rolling Stone* video were handled by the French/American digital effects company BUF Compangie. Researchers at BUF had been developing tools for stereophotogrammetry since the 1980s, even before IBR was actively studied in mainstream computer graphics. These tools were developed to reconstruct a 3D model of an object from a collection of photographs captured from different viewpoints. The captured photographs were also used to create the texture to be mapped onto the reconstructed 3D model in the rendering process. This work represented an early version of image-based modeling and rendering.

During a visit to BUF Compagnie in France, Michel Gondry became interested in how the IBR tools under development there could be used in actual film production. Gondry wanted to create a scene where a camera whizzes through a room filled with people frozen in mid-motion. The engineers at BUF did a test with Gondry himself as the subject. Using two synchronized still cameras, they captured a pair of photographs where he was jumping in the air surrounded by buildings. Then they demonstrated that, once the 3D environment was reconstructed, it became possible to create a scene where a virtual computer camera

Figure 5.14   Frozen in air in *Like a Rolling Stone*. (© 1995 Partizan Midi Minuit. All Rights
Reserved.) (See Color Plate VI.)

turned around the "frozen-in-air" Michel Gondry. This was precisely the solution
he was looking for, so he decided to use the technology in the *Like a Rolling Stone*
video.

After the work on "Like a Rolling Stone," BUF created various artistic effects in Hollywood films using IBR technology. BUF extended their IBR tool set
to the problem of performance capture in the movie *Arthur and the Minimoys*,
directed by Luc Besson [Besson 06]. Even though it was a CG animation film,
Besson wanted to do the direction using real actors. At the time, translating an
actor's performance into 3D animation data was typically done using an optical
motion capture system. However BUF used a different approach. They captured
the live actor's performance from many different angles using a set of carefully
placed calibrated cameras (Figure 5.15). A set of "multiview" photographs are
thus captured for each frame. The 3D pose of the actor in every frame of the
multiview sequence can be recovered using stereophotogrammetry. This capturing method later came to be known as "video motion capture." A great advantage
of video motion capture is the increased freedom for both the actors and the surrounding environment. Since 2008, its use in major Hollywood movie production
has quickly spread. At SIGGRAPH 2008, several papers were presented that pro-

Figure 5.15   Multiview video camera capture for *Arthur and the Minimoys*. (© 2006 EuropaCorp and
BUF Company.) (See Color Plate VII.)

posed different ideas for improving the accuracy and efficiency of video motion
capture [Vlasic et al. 08, de Aguiar et al. 08, Bradley et al. 08].

5.4   The Light Field

Two papers presented at SIGGRAPH 1996 introduced a new approach to image-
based rendering: "The Lumigraph" [Gortler et al. 96] authored by Steven J.
Gortler, Radek Grzeszczuk, Richard Szeliski, and Michael F. Cohen, and "Light
Field Rendering" by Marc Levoy and Pat Hanrahan [Levoy and Hanrahan 96].
Before these papers were published, IBR techniques used a collection of 2D images to store the acquired photographic images. Renderings from an arbitrary
viewpoint were constructed through interpolation or warping of these images.
Both the 1996 papers introduced essentially the same idea: to convert the acquired images to a radiance function of position and direction in an environment,
i.e., to construct the plenoptic function. In the absence of participating media,
this reduces to a 4D function on lines in space. Gortler and his coauthors call this

function the *lumigraph*; Levoy and Hanrahan call it the *light field*. The latter is used here.[4]

The light field is a general representation not limited to IBR, and has been used in other areas of CG rendering (see Sections 8.2 and 10.5). In fact, a new research field of *computational photography* [Raskar and Tumbin 09] was inspired largely by the light field. One drawback of the light field, though, is that it requires a lot of space—representing the light field for a scene of medium complexity can require gigabytes of storage. To mitigate this, compression schemes were investigated in the original papers.

5.4.1 Definition of the Light Field

As noted earlier, the plenoptic function describes the optical character of an environment by providing the radiance in every direction at each point in space, at each wavelength of light and each instant of time. The function thus has seven parameters; however, assuming a static scene and using a typical three-channel color representation reduces this to a 5D function $P(x,y,z,s,t)$ where s and t are the viewing direction parameters (Figure 5.16(a)). Another dimensional reduction results from assuming there is no participating medium, which means that the radiance is constant along line segments in space. The plenoptic function thus reduces to a radiance function of position and direction on object surfaces, which could be stored as part of the geometric model. However, the authors wanted a representation independent of geometry, so they instead considered the plenoptic function as a function on lines in space. The *light field* (lumigraph) formally refers to this function, although the term is also used for the 5D function and other variants. An image of the environment from an arbitrary viewpoint is a 2D slice of this function.

The light field is represented as a large collection of samples on lines in space. How these lines are represented is critical to the success of the representation. Both papers use the same general approach to parametrize lines: given two fixed planes, a line is uniquely represented by the coordinates (u,v) in one plane, and (s,t) in the other (Figure 5.16(b)). Intuitively, u and v might be regarded as the positional parameters, and s and t the directional parameters for each (u,v), but the view position can be arbitrary and neither plane is necessarily an "image" plane. Levoy and Hanrahan refer to the collection of lines between these two planes, limited to $0 \leq u,v,s,t \leq 1$, as a *light slab*. A light slab is thus the set of all lines between points in two rectangles (or general quadrilaterals) in space.

---

[4]Although both terms refer to essentially the same thing, and the papers are considered to be equally excellent, "light field" seems to be the name that has stuck. The term "light field" was actually coined in a 1936 paper by Alexander Gershun, referring to what is now called the vector irradiance.

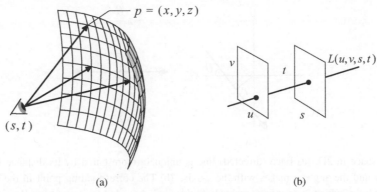

(a)   (b)

Figure 5.16   Basic concept of the light field. (a) The plenoptic function contains the radiance in each
viewing direction, parameterized by s and t, at each point (x, y, z) in space. (b) The light
field is a function on lines in space, lines are parameterized by the plane coordinates of their
intersection with two distinct planes. The set of all lines through two rectangles is called a
light slab. ((a) After [McMillan and Bishop 95]; (b) After [Levoy and Hanrahan 96].)

The light field for a light slab is represented as a collection of 2D images, with
one image for each discrete (u, v) parameter.

5.4.2   Construction of a Light Field

Constructing the light field for a virtual environment is relatively simple: the
samples for a light slab can be computed by tracing rays along the corresponding
lines. However, the light field does have to be prefiltered in the 4D line space
to avoid aliasing. This filtering has the side effect of introducing a blurring in
depth, but as happens, this ends up being desirable. Constructing the light field
from digitized photographs is much more difficult, as it requires a large number
of photographs, camera calibration, precise knowledge of the camera positions,
and a way to resample the images to match the light slab parametrization.

For a particular object or environment, constructing the light field starts by
choosing the light slabs. A single light slab cannot capture all directions of light
coming off an object, so more than one slab may be necessary to adequately
represent the light field. However, the light field of a single slab might be enough
if the set of views it represents is sufficient for the particular application. Gortler
and his collaborators proposed using light slabs based on the faces of a cube.
Other arrangements are possible, and may in fact be necessary. One or both of the
planes can even be placed "at infinity" to facilitate rendering orthographic views.

The distribution of directions for a slab is best illustrated using a 2D simplification; the "Light Field Rendering" paper includes several such illustrations.

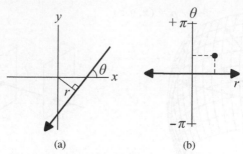

(a)   (b)

Figure 5.17   Line space in 2D. (a) Each (directed) line is uniquely represented by its distance to the
origin and the angle it makes with the x-axis. (b) The corresponding point in the space
of 2D lines, which is an infinite strip along the r-axis bounded by $\pm\pi$. (After [Levoy and
Hanrahan 96].)

The light field is a function on the space of lines. A 2D line in the plane can
be uniquely represented with two parameters: the distance r to the origin and
the angle θ the line makes with the x-axis (Figure 5.17(a)). So 2D lines are in
one-to-one correspondence with points in the infinite strip of the $r\theta$-plane, with
$-\pi < \theta \leq \pi$ (Figure 5.17(b)). This is a 2D "line space." The pair of planes of a
light slab reduce to a pair of line segments in the 2D case; a 2D light slab consists
of all lines through each segment in the pair. Figure 5.18(a) shows the set of lines
resulting from a discrete number of parameter samples in one 2D light slab. The
points in line space (the $r\theta$-plane) corresponding to these lines in 2D are shown
Figure 5.18(b). The distribution is not very uniform. Figure 5.18(c) and (d) shows
a collection of four different 2D light slabs, arranged to cover a square, and the
corresponding sample distribution in line space. A 3D version of this arrangement
was used to represent the light field of a small toy lion in Levoy and Hanrahan's
paper.

The storage required for the samples is proportional to the fourth power of the
number of samples in each parameter (although the parameters are not discretized
in the same way). Consequently, the storage requirements for a light field get very
large. For example, the toy-lion model light field required 402 MB. However, the
data has a fair amount of coherency and is therefore amenable to compression.
Levoy and Hanrahan used a two-stage compression algorithm. In the first stage,
the light slabs are tiled into "vectors" of data. These are then quantized into a
smaller set of representative vectors and coded using a lossy compression algorithm that facilitates fast lookup of compressed vectors via a "codebook." Each
tile thus reduces to an index known as a "codeword" into the quantized vectors in
the codebook. This stage of the compression reduces the storage requirements to

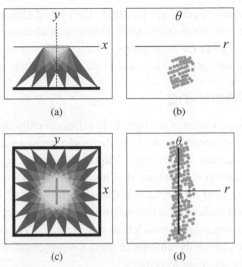

Figure 5.18   Sampling rays in a 2D light slab. (a) Six samples in each of the two lines corresponds to a reasonably dense sampling in 2D line space, shown in (b). (c) An arrangement of four slabs covers the square fairly well, as shown in (d). (After [Levoy and Hanrahan 96].)

about 16 MB. In the second stage, the codebook and the collection of indices are then compressed together using Lempel-Ziv compression (the algorithm used in "gzip") . This second stage reduces the toy-lion data to 3.4 MB.

5.4.3   Light Field Rendering

Light field rendering is the process of creating an image of the scene represented by the light field as it appears from an arbitrary viewpoint. Conceptually, rendering an image from a light field amounts to taking a 2D slice of the 4D data, but in practice it is more complicated. Before the light field can be used, it has to be uncompressed; only the second compression stage needs to be undone. Given a virtual camera, the value of pixel (x, y) on the image plane is the radiance carried along the line through that pixel to the viewpoint. This line has coordinates (u, v, s, t) in the line space of an appropriate light slab, so the value can simply be looked up in the light field. This requires determining the appropriate light slab if there is more than one. If there is no appropriate slab, then the pixel cannot be rendered.

Of course, as with any table lookup, the value for the exact parameter set (u, v, s, t) is not likely to exist in the table. Therefore the value must be interpolated from nearby values. The method of interpolation is critical to the quality of the resulting image, as poor interpolation will result in aliasing artifacts.

Various interpolation schemes are possible. Levoy and Hanrahan experimented with several, and concluded that a quadralinear (simultaneous) interpolation in all four parameters gives the best results. However, they note that that the faster method of bilinear interpolation in u and v only is sometimes sufficient.

5.4.4 Light Field Mapping

The geometry independence of the light field is theoretically interesting, but there are good reasons to represent view-dependent radiance as a surface function. Efficiency is one. The paper "Light Field Mapping" [Chen et al. 02], by Wei-Chao Chen, Jean-Yves Bouguet, Michael H. Chu, and Radek Grzeszczuk presents a surface-based light field representation that is well suited to the graphics hardware pipeline. Each surface is partitioned into triangles. Rather than construct the light field function separately on each triangle, which can result in discontinuities at the triangle boundaries, the authors propose a representation that uses sampled light field values at the triangle vertices.

The vertex light field functions are spread across the surface triangles using bilinear interpolation, also known as barycentric interpolation, in the same way vertex colors are interpolated across triangles. The surface triangle light field is thus a weighted average of the vertex functions. The weights can be expressed as function of position on a triangle: the function Λ^{v_j} is the barycentric weight of vertex v_j; its value is 1 at v_j and ramps down to 0 on the ring of triangles adjacent to v_j. Exactly three such functions are nonzero on the interior of a given triangle (the weighting functions of the vertices of the triangle) and they sum to 1 across the triangle. Figure 5.19 illustrates this. The resulting interpolation is continuous, but has discontinuities in the first derivative.

Barycentric interpolation was not new when the "Light Field Mapping" paper was published, although it had not been applied to partitioning surface light fields before. The *surface light field* is a function of four parameters: $f(r, s, \theta, \phi)$, where r and s provide the position on the surface; θ and ϕ, the direction. The light field function for vertex v_j is "partitioned" from f via the formula

$$f^{v_j}(r, s, \theta, \phi) = \Lambda^{v_j}_{\triangle_t} f(r, s, \theta, \phi),$$

which therefore remains a function of four variables. Representing such functions requires a lot of storage as the earlier light field research had discovered. So the authors approximated the functions as a sum of products of a pair of two-parameter functions,

$$f^{v_j}(r, s, \theta, \phi) \approx \sum_{k=1}^{K} g_k^{v_j}(r, s) h_k^{v_j}(\theta, \phi),$$

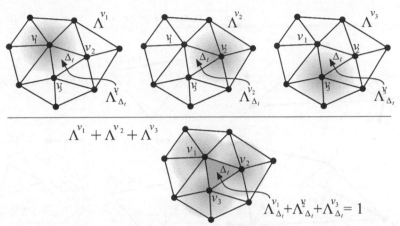

Figure 5.19   Basis (weighting) functions for spreading a vertex light field across adjacent triangles. Top row: there is one basis function Λ^{v_j} for each vertex. The value of a basis function, which is shown in gray (darkest gray is 1, white is 0), has a value of 1 at the vertex and ramps down to zero at the far edge of each adjacent triangle in the ring. Bottom: the weighting functions for the three vertices of triangle $\triangle_t$ sum to 1 across the triangle. (From [Chen et al. 02] © 2002 ACM, Inc. Included here by permission.)

of position and direction. This kind of variable separation is a standard technique and had already been applied to surface reflectance functions [Fournier 95, Kautz and McCool 99]. The primary contribution of the paper came in the method the authors proposed for the approximations.

The authors actually propose two approximation methods, both of which use matrix factorization applied to a collection of samples of each vertex light field function. One method employs *principal component analysis* (PCA) to find, in a manner of speaking, the best basis for the matrix. The result is a sequence of samples that approximate the function in the sense that the contributions decrease, so a limited number of terms provides a useful approximation. However, the resulting sample values can be negative. The authors point out that this complicates a hardware implementation. In contrast, *nonnegative matrix factorization* (NMF) requires all the terms to be used, but the sample values are all nonnegative. In either case, the light field function $f^{\triangle_t}$ over triangle $\triangle_t$ is a discrete approximation of the form

$$f^{\triangle_t}[r_p, s_p, \theta_q, \phi_q] = \sum_{j=1}^{3} g_{\triangle_t}^{v_j}[r_p, s_p] h^{v_j}[\theta_q, \phi_q].$$

The "functions" g and h are actually 2D arrays of values, i.e., textures, that the authors describe as a *surface map* and a *view map*, respectively.

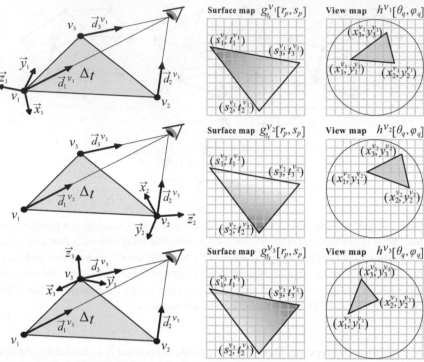

Figure 5.20   Surface maps and view maps for a surface light field. Being vertex based, there is one term
for each triangle vertex. The spatial value for a term in the approximation is stored in a
texture map called a "surface map" (middle column), obtained from the surface coordinates
(r, s) at the evaluation point. The directional value is obtained by projecting the view
direction in the local coordinate system at a vertex (the axes are labeled $\bar{x}_i$, $\bar{y}_i$, $\bar{z}_i$) and the
value is obtained from the "view map" texture (right column). (From [Chen et al. 02]
© 2002 ACM, Inc. Included here by permission.)

The surface light field is rendered over each triangle by looking up values in
the surface and view maps for the vertices of the triangle, as illustrated in Figure 5.20. The left column of this figure shows the (view-dependent) rendering
geometry; the surface and view maps are shown in the middle and right columns,
respectively, corresponding to the particular vertex in the left column. The surface map is a straightforward texture map lookup: the position on the triangle is
converted to texture coordinates and the value of g is obtained from the matching
texel. Lookup in the view map is slightly more complicated. Unlike the surface
map, which stores the value of g directly as a function of position, the view map
gives the value of h at the vertex. The view direction at the vertex is computed

in the local coordinate system of the vertex, and is projected via an orthographic projection onto the texture coordinate plane (the circles in Figure 5.20 are the bounds of this projection). The surface map and view map values are multiplied directly; the surface map includes the value of the weighting function (which is shown as a gradation in Figure 5.20), so the result can be added directly to the accumulated sum for the triangle. These computations can all be done efficiently on a GPU.

The surface representation of the light field presented in the 2002 "Light Field Mapping" paper performs particularly well on objects having intricate surface geometry detail, but does have some drawbacks. The construction of the surface and view maps, i.e., the construction of the vertex function approximations, requires a huge number of radiance samples. Furthermore, the representation of the maps requires less storage than the spatial light field, but it takes up significant space nonetheless.

5.4.5   Light Field Photography

In 2005, Ren Ng and his colleagues at Stanford University published two papers that introduced a new connection of the light field to photography. "Light Field Photography with a Hand-held Plenoptic Camera," a technical report written by Ng, Levoy, and Hanrahan along with Mathieu Brédif, Gene Duval, and Mark Horowitz, describes a digital camera modified with a microlens array that can capture a portion of the light field in a single exposure. The authors show how the acquired light field can be used to digitally refocus an image. The paper "Fourier Slice Photography," presented at SIGGRAPH 2005, contains a mathematical framework for imaging from the light field [Ng 05]. The main result is a new theorem that relates an image as a slice of the 4D Fourier transform of the light field.

The light incident on the surface of the main lens of a camera is a light field: at each point on the lens, radiance from a set of ray directions enters the lens. The set of directions is further limited by the aperture, and the rays are refracted by the optics in the lens system, but each point on the sensor plane ultimately receives radiance from a set of directions. The set of light rays reaching the sensor plane is called the *in-camera light field*. Figure 5.21 illustrates the concept. A point (x, y) on the sensor plane receives radiance from a set of points parameterized by (u, v) on the main lens, although this correspondence depends on the optics and focus state of the camera. If F is the distance from the lens plane to the sensor plane, the radiance at (x, y) from point (u, v) is denoted by $L_F(x, y, u, v)$. Because of other optical elements, including the aperture stop, there may not be a light

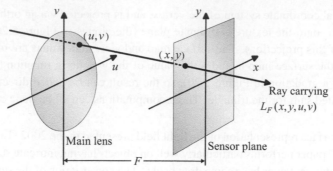

Figure 5.21   The in-camera light field. A point (x,y) on the sensor plane gets radiance from points on
the main lens parameterized by (s,t). (After [Ng et al. 05] © 2005 ACM, Inc. Included
here by permission.)

path from an arbitrary point (u,v) on the lens to an arbitrary (x,y), in which case
$L_f(x,y,u,v) = 0$.

The pixel value of the image formed inside a digital camera at a sensor photosite is ideally proportional to the time-integrated flux across the pixel photosite.
For sufficiently small pixels, the flux is essentially just the irradiance, which is
computed by integrating the incident radiance. Irradiance is obtained by integrating the incident radiance over the hemisphere of directions (See Equation (1.5)).
In camera computations it is more sensible to integrate across the lens, which requires a change of variables to the lens parameters u and v analogous to the surface
integral transformation applied in the rendering equation (Equation (2.4)).

The actual integration depends on a number of intrinsic camera parameters,
as well as some extra geometry terms. However, under appropriate assumptions
the photosite irradiance can be approximated by

$$E_F(x,y) = \frac{1}{F^2} \iint L_F(x,y,u,v)A(u,v)\cos^4\theta\,du\,dv. \qquad (5.6)$$

Here $A(u,v)$ is an "aperture" function that models the camera aperture: its value is
0 if the point (u,v) on the lens is outside the aperture, and 1 otherwise. The angle
θ is the angle of incidence measured at the sensor surface; the fourth power comes
from the change of variables. When a sensor pixel corresponds to a *focused* point
in the scene, the irradiance comes from the radiance leaving that point in the scene
(located on the plane of focus in the scene). Assuming the radiance L_F is constant
over the pixel, the irradiance E_F on a focused pixel reduces in this case to

$$E_F = \frac{\pi}{4}\left(\frac{d}{F}\right)^2\cos^4\theta\,L_F,$$

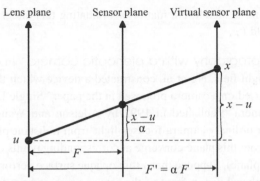

Figure 5.22 Digital refocusing involves moving the sensor plane with respect to the lens, just as a real camera would be focused. (For clarity, the planes are shown in only one dimension.) Refocusing on a virtual sensor plane a factor of α further away from the lens than the original sensor plane moves the ray intersection a factor of α away from the perpendicular. (After [Ng et al. 05] © 2005 ACM, Inc. Included here by permission.)

where d is the diameter of the camera aperture. The value L_F is known as the *scene radiance* of the pixel.

The cosine factor is sometimes absorbed into L_F, or, in the case of a sufficiently small field of view, regarded as constant and then factored out of the integral. The aperture function can likewise be absorbed into L_F, in which case Equation (5.6) reduces to just

$$E_F(x,y) = \frac{1}{F^2} \iint L_F(x,y,u,v)\, du\, dv, \qquad (5.7)$$

and E_F thus becomes directly proportional to L_F.

Now suppose that the camera focus is changed, which amounts to changing the distance F between the lens and sensor plane as illustrated in Figure 5.22. The new position of the sensor plane, which is called the "virtual sensor plane" in Figure 5.22, is placed at distance $F' = \alpha F$. The new light field $L_{F'}$ on the sensor plane at F' becomes a "sheared" version of the original sensor plane light field:

$$L_{F'}(u,v,x,y) = L_F\left(\left(1-\frac{1}{\alpha}\right)u + \frac{x}{\alpha},\ \left(1-\frac{1}{\alpha}\right)v + \frac{y}{\alpha},\ u,\ v \right). \qquad (5.8)$$

The photosite irradiance (pixel value) is then given by substituting Equation (5.8) into Equation (5.7):

$$E_{F'}(x,y) = \frac{1}{\alpha^2 F^2} \iint L_F\left(\left(1-\frac{1}{\alpha}\right)u + \frac{x}{\alpha},\ \left(1-\frac{1}{\alpha}\right)v + \frac{y}{\alpha},\ u,\ v \right) du\, dv. \qquad (5.9)$$

Digital refocusing is therefore a matter of evaluating this integral, given the in-camera light field L_F.

Light field photography with a plenoptic camera. In order to capture the in-camera light field, Ng et al. constructed a device which they call a "light field camera" based on a camera proposed in the paper "Single Lens Stereo with a Plenoptic Camera" published in 1992 by Adelson and Wang [Adelson and Wang 92].[5] An ordinary camera focuses light from a distant plane of focus so that light rays from this plane converge at corresponding points on the sensor array (or the film plane). Suppose that a thin opaque surface perforated by an array of pinholes is placed just in front of the sensor array, and the image is focused onto this surface instead. Each pinhole spreads out the convergent light onto the sensor plane in the form of a disc-shaped image, which represents what can be seen through the pinhole. The sensor plane image then records these images into a single image, which looks like an array of small images of the scene, each captured from a slightly different viewpoint. Judiciously placing the pinhole surface maximizes the sizes of these images so that they just touch each other.

The light field camera described by Ng and his collaborators uses this principle, except that an array of microlenses is used in place of a pinhole surface.[6] In the light field camera, the image is focused on the microlens array and each microlens creates a small sharp image of what is seen through the lens on the sensor array. The image, called a "microlens image," is recorded by a group of pixels corresponding to the microlens. The image captured by the light field camera therefore has the appearance of a collection of small images of the object, each with a field of view several times larger than that corresponding to the original group of pixels (Figure 5.23).

Each microimage contains a small 2D slice of the in-camera light field. The pinhole model helps illustrate why. The microlens array is placed where the sensor array would be in an ordinary camera, so the (x, y) parameters correspond to

---

[5]The idea of "plenoptic" photography has a long history, which can trace its roots back more than a century to the "integral photography" method pioneered by M. G. Lippmann [Lippmann 08]. Adelson and Wang's incorporates a single main lens along with an array of small lens-like elements placed at the sensor plane. This arrangement allows for the simultaneous capture of a set of images corresponding to shifted views of a scene seen through subregions of the main lens. Their work includes a method they call "single lens stereo" for reconstruction based on the parallax of the captured images. The light field camera constructed by Ng et al. had a design similar to Adelson and Wang's, but the microlens array was more precisely constructed and was moved away from the sensor plane.

[6]Cameras with similar microlens arrays had been used before for similar purposes. The 2001 paper "3-D computer graphics based on integral photography" by T. Naemura, T. Yoshida, and H. Harashima [Naemura et al. 01] is representative of this work. The system described in the paper enables interactive recovery and display of objects from an arbitrary viewpoint. The light field camera developed by Ng et al. was novel in the sense that it was designed specifically for capturing the in-camera light field, and its primary purpose was to study digital refocusing.

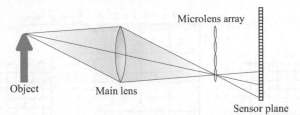

Figure 5.23   Schematic diagram of a camera with a microlens array. The image is focused on the microlens plane, and each microlens spreads out the incident rays by direction onto a microimage on the sensor plane. (After [Ng et al. 05] © 2005 ACM, Inc. Included here by permission.)

microlens surface points. Consider the microlens centered at at (x_m, y_m). The sensor pixel at point (u', v') on the corresponding microlens image records the radiance from the line joining the center of the pixel and the center of the microlens. Consequently, the parameters (u', v') correspond to lens parameters (u, v), and the microlens image therefore records samples of $L_F(x_m, y_m, u, v)$. The number of pixels in each microimage thus corresponds to the directional sampling density; the number of microlenses, to the position sampling density. The prototype described by the authors has an array of 296×296 microlenses, each corresponding to a microimage about 13 pixels wide (the correspondence between the lenses and the pixels need not be precise). Digital refocusing can be applied using Equation (5.9) with L_F interpolated and resampled appropriately.

There is, however, a better way of performing digital refocusing that employs an alternate interpretation of the light field camera image. A pixel in a microimage corresponds to a small cone of light that can be regarded as coming from a small virtual aperture on the lens—something like a pinhole on the lens. By nature of the projection, corresponding pixels in each microimage get light from nearly the same virtual aperture. Collecting all these pixels (there is one for each microlens) into a separate image produces a *subaperture image* (Figure 5.24). There is one subaperture image for each microimage pixel, and each shows the object from a slightly different perspective. Because the effective aperture is small, each subaperture image appears sharp, i.e., has essentially infinite depth of field. This sharpening ability is an important characteristic of the light field camera, although subaperture images have only the resolution of the microlens array. As it happens, the value of L_F in the integrand of Equation (5.9) is just a scaled and shifted version of a subaperture image, so refocusing amounts to summing shifted and scaled subaperture images over the entire lens.

The "Light Field Camera" paper presents experimental validation of the capturing and refocusing technique, and verifies that the refocus performance does

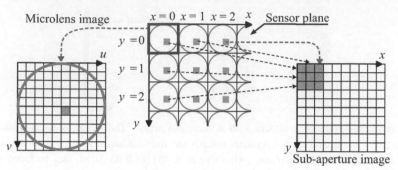

Figure 5.24   A subaperture image. A pixel (shaded) in a microlens image corresponds to what is seen through a small virtual aperture on the lens. Collecting the corresponding pixel in each microimage, which sees the same virtual aperture, produces a subaperture image. The image is smaller than the sensor image, as there is only one pixel for each microlens.

depend on the sampling rate of the light field. In particular the refocusing sharpness and the range of possible refocusing depths are linearly proportional to the directional resolution. However, the method depends on a number of approximating assumptions, and the lack of a reference solution made it difficult to quantify the accuracy of the light field and the error in the rendered images.

Fourier slice photography. Ng developed a mathematical framework for light field presented in the paper "Fourier Slice Photography" that provided a theoretical foundation for light field imaging [Ng 05]. The main result of the paper is a theorem called the *Fourier slice photography theorem*, which provides a method for creating images from a light field in the Fourier domain. The theorem is based on a generalization of a known theorem, the *Fourier slice theorem* that relates two kinds of dimensional reductions of functions. To make this more precise, suppose F is a real-valued function of n real variables. An *integral projection* of F is obtained by integrating F over some of its variables, which results in a function of m variables. For example, the integral in Equation (5.7) that determines the irradiance at a sensor pixel is an integral projection:

$$E_F(x,y) = \iint L_F(x,y,u,v)\, du\, dv \qquad (5.10)$$

(this is one reason the $\cos^4\theta$ factor and the aperture functions are omitted or absorbed into L_F). A *slice* is another kind of dimensional reduction obtained by fixing some of the variables of a multivariate function. An example of a slice of a function is the radiance distribution $L_F(x_m, y_m, u, v)$ of the image of a microlens at (x_m, y_m). The Fourier slice theorem states that the Fourier transform of an

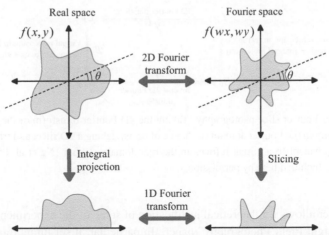

Figure 5.25 The Fourier slice theorem. Projecting in real space corresponds to slicing in Fourier space. A rotation by θ applied before the projection is matched by the same rotation in Fourier space before the slice is taken.

integral transform of a function is a slice of the Fourier transform of the function. In contrast to integral projections, which involve multiple integration, slices are almost trivial to compute—there lies the benefit of the Fourier slice theorem.

Integral projections and slices can be generalized to include a linear transformation of the variables, which is also known as a *change of basis*. This does not affect the validity of the Fourier slice theorem because the Fourier transform is itself linear, meaning it "passes through" linear transformations. Figure 5.25 illustrates the Fourier slice theorem in this more general context: the projection and slice are both applied after the coordinates are rotated by θ. The refocusing transformation implied in Equation (5.9) is in fact a linear transformation of the light field parameters:

$$(x, y, u, v) \mapsto \left(\left(1 - \frac{1}{\alpha} \right) u + \frac{1}{\alpha} x, \; \left(1 - \frac{1}{\alpha} \right) v + \frac{1}{\alpha} y, \; u, \; v \right). \qquad (5.11)$$

Consequently, the process of refocusing an image from an in-camera light field can be formulated as the integral projection (Equation (5.10)) of the light field after a linear transformation of the parameters (Equation (5.11)). By the Fourier slice theorem, the Fourier transform of a refocused image is a 2D slice of the 4D Fourier transform of the in-camera light field. This, combined with the particular transformations involved, is the Fourier slice photography theorem.

Analysis of sampling and image quality is mathematically simpler in the Fourier domain. The mathematical framework of the "Fourier Slice Photogra-

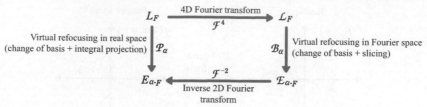

Figure 5.26   Diagram of Fourier slice photography. Taking the 4D Fourier transform of the light field, transforming in the Fourier domain (a change of basis), taking a 2D slice, and transforming back is equivalent to a virtual refocus in the real domain. (After [Ng et al. 05] © 2005 ACM, Inc. Included here by permission.)

phy" paper allows for theoretical justification of some of the experimental results in the "Light Field Photography" paper. In particular, it set limits on the available range of exact refocusing and proved that the sharpness increases linearly with the directional sampling rate. The analysis also shows that "the digitally refocused photograph is a 2D (low-pass) filtered version of the exact photograph" which gives a proof for the observation that refocused photograph is less noisy. In summary, the paper answered the question of what quality could be expected from refocused images of acquired light fields.

The Fourier slice photography theorem leads to a more efficient digital refocusing algorithm (in the sense of being faster and less dependent on the sampling rate of the light field) called *Fourier slice digital refocusing*. As illustrated in Figure 5.26, the Fourier transform of a 4D light field is computed first, and then the operations for refocusing (application of the shear and the 2D slice) are performed in the Fourier domain. The inverse transform of the result is the final image. Another feature of this approach is that the Fourier transform of the 4D light field, which is the costliest part, only has to be computed once for as many different refocuses as desired.

Figure 5.27 contains images of the digital refocusing process using the Fourier transform. The first row shows the light field as captured by the light field camera. Closeups are included at the right. The second row shows the Fourier transform of the light field, arranged into a 2D image similar to the way the light field is stored in the 2D light field image. The third row contains slices of the 4D transform data, after the shear transformation is applied for each of three refocusing arrangements; from left to right $\alpha > 1$, $\alpha = 1$, $\alpha < 1$. (Note that the Fourier transform images do not correspond very well to the actual images, although they are interesting to look at.) The bottom two rows show refocused images. The images in the second lowest row are the inverse transforms of the 2D Fourier transform slices shown in the images above. The images in the bottom

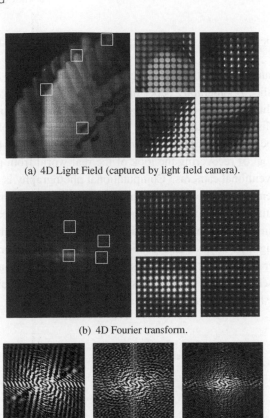

(a) 4D Light Field (captured by light field camera).

(b) 4D Fourier transform.

(c) Change of basis and 2D slicing in 4D Fourier domain (each image represents a different degree of refocusing).

(d) Inverse 2D Fourier transform.

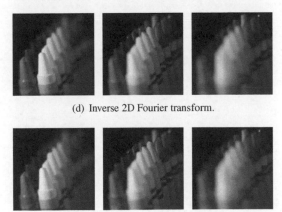

(e) Refocus computed by direct integration.

Figure 5.27   Fourier slice digital refocusing. (From [Ng et al. 05] © 2005 ACM, Inc. Included here by permission.)

row were rendered by direct integration of Equation (5.9) and are provided for comparison.

It can certainly be said that the light field photography work of Ng et al. and Ng's Fourier slice photography paper opened the door to a new range of applications for light fields, and reinvigorated research in the area. In fact, these papers were published about the time that the new research field of *computational photography* began to get off the ground. The original image-based technologies had the goal of recovering the look of the real-world from photographs acquired by conventional cameras. Computational photography is concerned with the development of new devices to capture and record photographic data in a manner best suited to the particular purpose. Ng's two papers greatly inspired research in this area. Various practical methods that attempt to extend the possibility of in-camera light fields have emerged in computational photography [Georgeiv et al. 06] [Veeraraghavan et al. 07] [Raskar et al. 08] [Liang et al. 08] [Lanman et al. 08] [Hirsch et al. 09]. It could be said that the emergence of computational photography ushered the light field into a new practical era.

6

High Dynamic Range Imaging

6.1 Response Curves and HDR Imaging

The main purpose of image-based rendering is to reproduce the real world faithfully and with photorealism. However, film and digital cameras are intrinsically limited in their ability to capture real world radiance values. In imagery, the range of reproducible light intensity is limited by the characteristics of the film or sensor array: if there is not enough light, nothing gets recorded; if there is too much, the film or sensor saturates. The minimum and maximum values that can be recoded by a device is known as the *dynamic range* of the device. A photograph of a scene that has a greater range of radiance values than the dynamic range of the camera—as real scenes often do—cannot faithfully capture the lighting in the scene. When using these images in rendering in techniques such as IBR, it can substantially influence the appearance of the resulting images. This is why it became necessary to capture a greater range of radiance values than is possible with an ordinary camera. This process is called *high dynamic range* (HDR) imaging.

6.1.1 Response Curves

As described in Chapter 5, a pixel in the sensor of a digital camera records the incident irradiance integrated over the time it is exposed. This value is called the *exposure*. If the scene is static, the irradiance is constant and the exposure is simply the product of the irradiance and the amount of time the shutter is open:

$$X = E\Delta t. \tag{6.1}$$

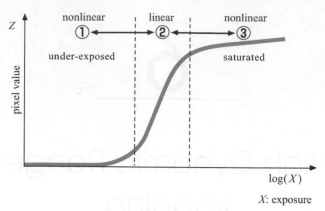

Figure 6.1   A hypothetical response curve for an electronic sensor. Exposure values in the region labeled "1" are too low to be recorded; values in region "3" cause the senor to saturate and record the maximum value regardless of the exposure. In region "2", the sensor records a value approximately proportional to the exposure, so it is known as the *linear* or *working* range of the device. Region 1, the left part of the sigmoid shape, is typically ignored in recovering the response of a particular device. (After [Debevec and Malik 97].)

The irradiance E reaching a sensor pixel is affected by a number of factors, such as attenuation in the lens and other imperfections in the optical system. That aside, the sensor pixel does not record the precise exposure value due to physical limitations of the sensor as well as processing by the camera. It is very difficult to model all these processes accurately. Instead, the conversion from ideal scene radiance values to pixel values is modeled as a function of the pixel exposure. This function (or its graph) is known as the *response curve* of the device (Figure 6.1). The discussion here refers to digital cameras, but the same principles apply to film cameras. The difference is that film does not have discrete pixels. Exposure at a point refers to the irradiance on a small neighborhood of a point on the film. The response curve of a film camera is really the response curve of the particular film with which it is loaded.

The response curve is usually treated separately for each color channel. The exposure X is the horizontal axis, the pixel value Z the vertical axis. For historical reasons response curves are usually plotted on logarithmic axes. When the exposure is close to zero, the response curve is nearly zero. (The sensor pixels in digital cameras never really report zero exposure values due to a physical effect called *dark current* in the sensor array.) When the exposure reaches a level high enough to be accurately recorded, the response curve grows rapidly and the graph becomes almost a straight line. When the exposure is too large, the sensor pixel saturates and the pixel records the maximum value it can record. The range of exposures in the middle section of the response curve is known as the *linear range* or *working range* of the device. Ideally the recorded value is directly proportional to the exposure. In practice however, there is some variation. Outside the linear range, the pixels cannot be expected to faithfully represent scene radiance values. The dynamic range is therefore limited to the middle range in practice.

Under normal shooting conditions, a photographer tries to set the exposure time (the shutter speed) and the lens aperture so that the exposure values corresponding to the scene radiance values fall within the linear range of the camera. But in many scenes, particularly those in direct sunlight, the range of values in the scene exceeds the dynamic range of the camera. Photographers often divide the apparent brightness in a scene into three conceptual ranges: *shadows, midtones (photographic brightness range)*, and *highlights*. The camera is normally set to capture the mid-tones, and detail is expected to be lost in the shadows and highlights. One approach to faithfully capturing a greater dynamic range is to take a collection of photographs of increasing exposure time, a process known as *bracketing* the exposure. A collection of bracketed images can be digitally combined into a single image of a higher dynamic range, but doing this accurately requires precise knowledge of the camera response curve.

6.1.2   HDR Response Curve

The paper "Recovering High Dynamic Range Radiance Maps from Photographs" by Debevec and Jitendra Malik provides a simple, effective method for constructing a high dynamic range image from a collection of photographs [Debevec and Malik 97]. The motivation for the work came from Debevec's short film *The Campanile Movie*, described in Chapter 5. Debevec had originally intended to shoot the movie on a clear day, but the clock faces in direct sunlight were so much brighter than the clock faces in shadow that the photographs could not simultaneously capture the appearance of both. Setting the exposure time to capture the sunlit faces caused the shadowed faces to come out too dark; using a long enough exposure time to capture the shadowed faces made the sunlit faces appear "blown out." He found an easy way of getting around this problem: he simply shot *The Campanile Movie* on a cloudy day. But his interest in high dynamic range imaging was piqued.

Extending the effective dynamic range of photographs and prints is an old problem in photography. By the time Debevec became interested in the problem, a number of methods to create a linear response curve from of wide range of brightnesses existed in the computer vision literature. Debevec was particularly interested in a method for recovering a linear response from digital camera images proposed in a 1995 paper by Steve Mann and Rosalind W. Picard [Mann and

Picard 95]. Starting from this work, he was able to develop a more robust method for reconstructing the response curve. The method, which is described in the next subsection, was implemented and released as open source software known as HDR Shop. This helped bring high dynamic range imaging to mainstream computer graphics.

6.1.3   Recovering the Response Curve

The ultimate goal of Debevec's work was to construct an image in which each pixel contains absolute real-world irradiance values rather than just the pixel exposures. The value of a pixel then represents the actual radiance carried along a ray coming off a (focused) object in the original scene. He described such an image as a *high dynamic range radiance map*. The process of constructing an HDR radiance map begins with a collection of photographs of the same scene shot at different exposures. The first step is to reconstruct the response curve of the camera or film used to capture the images, which is the function f defined by

$$Z = f(X) = f(E \triangle t). \tag{6.2}$$

The inverse of f maps pixel values to actual exposures, and from these the irradiance can be recovered if the exposure time Δt is known. Rather than try to reconstruct the response curve for each individual image, Debevec and Malik's method performs a simultaneous global fit to all the images. The result is called the *high dynamic range response curve*.

The input to the algorithm is a collection of P digitized images of the same scene photographed under the same conditions and same camera settings except for the shutter speed, which is varied over almost all speeds available. Then N representative pixels are chosen, and the pixel values of these N pixels are selected over all the images; Z_{ij} denotes the value of pixel i in the image exposed for time Δt_j. The goal is to approximate the general response function f, or rather, its inverse. This is best done logarithmically. Taking the natural logarithm of both sides of Equation (6.2) (the Z values are never zero, by choice), we get

$$g(Z) = f^{-1}(Z) = \ln E + \ln \Delta t, \tag{6.3}$$

where g is the unknown inverse response function. Note that the right-hand side of Equation (6.3) is not a direct function of the variable Z, so this equation does not provide a formula for g—it only gives the relationship between values of g and the irradiance E, the other unknown.

Because the pixel values are discrete, the inverse function g has a finite domain running over the possible integer pixel values $Z_{\min}, \ldots, Z_{\max}$ (the process is repeated for each color channel). Consequently, g is entirely determined by its value on an array of integer pixel values. Replacing $g(Z)$ with the array value $g[Z]$ and applying Equation (6.3) to each pixel sample Z_{ij},

$$g[Z_{ij}] = \ln E_i + \ln \Delta t_j \tag{6.4}$$

produces a system of equations that runs over the i and j indices. Here the E_i and the $g[Z]$ values are the unknowns. If enough pixel samples are chosen, the Z_{ij} can be expected to cover most of the pixel values. However, some of the Z_{ij} will be repeated, and this results in more than one equation for $g[Z_{ij}]$. The system of equations is therefore overdetermined. A solution that minimizes the error in a weighted least squares sense is used: the values of $g[Z]$ and E_i are chosen to minimize

$$\sum_{i=1}^{N} \sum_{j=1}^{P} \left(\omega(Z_{ij}) \left(g[Z_{ij}] - \ln E_i - \ln \Delta t_j \right) \right)^2$$
$$+ \quad \lambda \sum_{z=Z_{\min}+1}^{Z_{\max}-1} \left(\omega(z) g[z-1] - 2g[z] + g[z+1] \right)^2. \tag{6.5}$$

The second term in the objective function in Equation (6.5) is a smoothness constraint in the form of a discrete approximation to the second derivative of g. The λ coefficient is a constant value that specifies the relative importance of this smoothness constraint, and can be varied depending on the amount of noise in the data. The weighting function $\omega(z)$ is included to limit the effects of pixel values outside the linear range. A continuous weighting function is employed that weights pixel values at the middle of the range most heavily:

$$\omega(z) = \begin{cases} z - Z_{\min} & \text{for } z \leq \frac{1}{2}(Z_{\min} + Z_{\max}), \\ Z_{\max} - z & \text{for } z > \frac{1}{2}(Z_{\min} + Z_{\max}). \end{cases}$$

The minimization results in the array of response function values $g[Z]$ and recovered exposure values E_i. Figure 6.2 contains plots of the sample values before and after they have been fit to the response curve. In this figure, there are five images and three pixel values ($P = 5, N = 3$), corresponding pixels have the same marker. In Figure 6.2(a), each pixel is assumed to have unit irradiance E_i so the values of different pixels are spread out. Figure 6.2(b) shows the true recovered values. Figure 6.3 shows a recovered response curve and how it matches the samples it was constructed to fit.

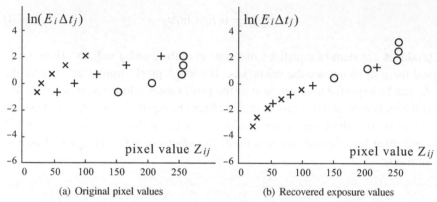

(a) Original pixel values   (b) Recovered exposure values

Figure 6.2   Images of increasing exposure are used to reconstruct the response curve. (a) Plots of pixel values from the original images. The different marks correspond to different pixels; values across five images are plotted. (b) The corresponding recovered exposure values computed from the reconstructed response curve. (After [Debevec and Malik 97].)

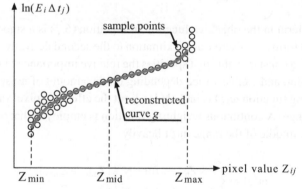

Figure 6.3   Response curve recovery: the response curve is fit to pixel values in the linear range, weighted by how close they are to the middle of the range. (After [Debevec and Malik 97].)

6.1.4   HDRI and the Radiance Map

Given the recovered inverse response function g, the next step is to construct the radiance map, which amounts to computing the values of E for each pixel. The values of E_i for the pixel samples are recovered in the process of minimizing Equation (6.5), but it is better to recompute each E_i using the reconstructed response function g. From Equation (6.4),

$$\ln E_i = g[Z_{ij}] - \ln \Delta t_j.$$

A more robust method is to recompute E_i as the weighted average of the pixel values Z_{ij} in all the images:

$$\ln E_i = \frac{\sum_{j=1}^{p} \omega(Z_{ij})(g[Z_{ij}] - \ln \Delta t_j)}{\sum_{j=1}^{p} \omega(Z_{ij})}.$$

Doing it this way has several advantages. Summing over all the images reduces noise in the images, and using the weighted average ensures that the pixel values near the middle of the range are weighted most heavily. Also, the summation can be taken over more images than were used to reconstruct g, which is likely to produce a better average.

Formally, the *radiance map* is the set of radiance values L_i that represent the actual radiance received at pixel i, which is related to the irradiance E_i by Equation (5.6). Assuming the radiance is constant over the pixel, and omitting the term $\cos^4 \theta$ (which is eliminated by the optics of some cameras anyway), L_i becomes proportional to E_i. Actually, E_i represents the physical sensor irradiance only up to an unknown constant factor. For many rendering purposes this constant is not important, because the pixel values are eventually mapped to the middle range of a device anyway. However, some applications may need the true radiometric values. The constant associated with the absolute irradiance (and radiance) comes from the "speed" of the film. Formulas relating the film speed to the film response are sometimes available, either from the film manufacturer or from other literature. Most high-end digital cameras provide the effective film speed in standard (ASA or ISO) format so the same formulas can be applied.[1]

A radiance map constructed by Debevec and Malik's method is one form of a *high dynamic range (HDR) image*. Sometimes "HDR image" is shortened to just "HDRI," but this is more often applied to the process of high dynamic range *imaging*. Debevec used the term "HDRI" specifically for images of unlimited brightness range, but just about any image having a higher dynamic range than what is produced by a conventional camera can properly be called a "high dynamic range" image.

---

[1]Commercial digital cameras normally apply a correction curve as a postprocess to the captured pixel values. This complicates the recovery of the HDR response curve. At the present time, only high-end single-lens reflex digital cameras provide the unaltered sensor output.

6.1.5   Tone Mapping: Displaying HDR Images

Acquiring an HDR image is, in some sense, only part of the battle. The problem of how to display a HDR image on a low dynamic range display remains. This process is known as *tone mapping*, a term that came out of photography. Strictly speaking, tone mapping refers to mapping the density of a developed negative to the density of a finished print (print density is known as "tone"). The problem is not trivial, as photographic film typically has a much higher dynamic range than print media. In computer graphics, tone mapping generally refers to the process of reducing the dynamic range of an image while preserving detail in visually important parts of the image. Tone mapping is an active research field in itself. Because it has an artistic aspect, there is no "best" way to do it. Debevec and Malik enlisted the help of Greg Ward for the problem of tone mapping their captured HDR images. Figure 6.4 illustrates some of the results of rendering a particular HDR image captured inside of a church. Figure 6.4(a) shows a linearly mapped image, which displays only a small fraction of the dynamic range (the YCC encoding used for generating the image does perform a limited amount of dynamic range reduction). Figures 6.4(b) and (c) contain tone-mapped results; part (c) includes some perception-based adjustments, including the simulation of

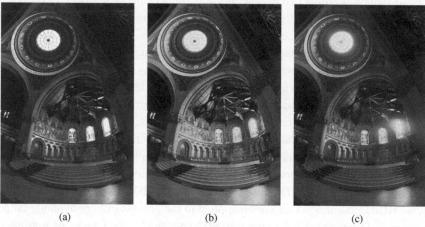

(a)   (b)   (c)

Figure 6.4   A high dynamic range image of the inside of a church. Displaying the image becomes a challenge, as it has a greater range than the display medium. (a) HDR converted to Kodak's PhotoCD output, which uses YCC encoding. (b) Tone-mapped HDR image. (c) Tone-mapped HDR image with modifications to simulate human perception. Note the glare around the bright windows. The tone mapping algorithm used for these images is described in [Ward Larson et al. 97]. (From [Debevec and Malik 97] © 1997 ACM, Inc. Included here by permission.) (See Color Plate VIII.)

glare. The tone mapping algorithm used for these images is described in the paper "A Visibility Matching Tone Reproduction Operator for High Dynamic Range Scenes" by Ward, Holly Rushmeier, and Christine Piatko [Ward Larson et al. 97].

In 2002, a new tone mapping method was presented in the paper "Photographic Tone Reproduction for Digital Images" by Erik Reinhard, Michael M. Stark, Peter Shirley, and James Ferwerda [Reinhard et al. 02]. The method described in this paper applied photographic concepts to tone mapping, including the *zone system*, which is a way of maintaining consistency from exposure to print originally developed by photographers Ansel Adams and Fred Archer. In 2003, Helge Seetzen, Lorne A. Whitehead, and Greg Ward published a description of a high dynamic range display device that could display HDR images directly [Seetzen et al. 03]. An improved version was described in the paper "High Dynamic Range Display Systems" by the same authors and several others [Seetzen et al. 04]. The device uses a low resolution LED grid that acts as a backlight for a high resolution LCD panel, and is capable of reading and displaying HDR file formats.

In 2009, the paper "Modeling Human Color Perception under Extended Luminance Levels" by Min H. Kim, Tim Weyrich and Jan Kautz presented a new model for color perception [Kim et al. 09]. As the title suggests, the model covers a wide range of brightness levels. The authors conducted psychophysical measurement of human color perception under extended real-world luminance levels. Based on the analysis of the data, they proposed a new color appearance model and cast HDR imaging into the model. The results were compelling enough to remind the CG community of the importance of human color adaptation.

6.1.6 The Effect of Motion-Blur

An interesting ancillary application of HDR imaging is the simulation of motion blur that results from spinning or moving the camera during the exposure. The effect is quite simple to create: the image is just filtered in the direction of the blurring, which Figure 6.5(b) illustrates. The image in part (a) was captured by actually spinning the camera, part (b) shows the filtering technique applied to one of the original captured images, and part (c) shows the result of filtering the actual HDR image. In the absence of high dynamic range data, the filtering cannot reproduce the light trails of the windows.

6.2 HDR File Formats

Image files for computer graphics traditionally used a three or four channel (RGB or RGBA) format, with 8 bits per channel. Each color is therefore limited to

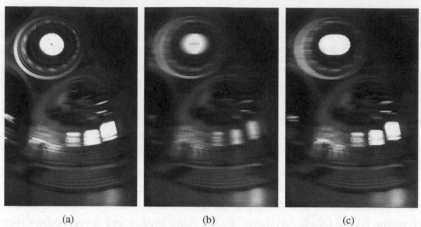

(a)   (b)   (c)

Figure 6.5   Motion-blur resulting from spinning the camera. (a) An real photograph; the photographer rotated the camera during the exposure. (b) Simulated motion blur using a conventional photograph. Note the bright windows are not properly spread along the direction of motion. (c) Simulated motion blur using an HDR image. The simulated motion does not quite match the real motion of the camera. (From [Debevec and Malik 97] © 1997 ACM, Inc. Included here by permission.)

an integer value of 0–255. This format is not sufficient to store an HDR image; it simply does not provide the necessary range. A specialized *HDR file format* is needed to store HDR images. The simple solution, using more bits per channel for the HDR format , has the problem of requiring too much space: two or three three times as many bits per pixel would be needed to store an image with a moderately high range of pixel values. This is not a very efficient representation, because each value does not have that much precision—the extra space is only needed to store the general magnitude of the value, so each channel would have a lot of zero or otherwise useless bits. A better approach would be to use a floating-point format for each channel, but that requires even more space (normally 32 bits per channel) and again there is the issue of unnecessarily high precision.

6.2.1 The Origin of the HDR File Format

Debevec did not have to look very far to find a file format capable of storing his HDR images. Ward already had developed a file format for HDR images through his work with the RADIANCE rendering system. Photorealistic rendering attempts to model real world illumination, and because real world illumination has a high dynamic range, so do the rendered images. The problem of tone mapping and storage of high dynamic range images was well studied in this context.

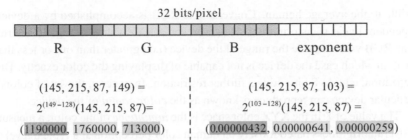

Figure 6.6   Arrangement of values in a pixel used in the 32-bit RGBE HDR image format (top), and examples illustrating the meaning of the fields (bottom). (After images courtesy of Greg Ward.)

Debevec's work was different in that it was concerned with the problem of reconstructing HDR images from a set of captured images. Ward's format for storing HDR images uses the usual three-byte RGB value along with an extra *exponent* channel that scales the overall magnitude of the value by a power of 2. The exponent channel is an 8-bit integer stored as a *biased* value: if e is the stored value, the actual integer has the value $e - 128$. The possible range of exponents is thus -128 through 127, which corresponds to a range of about $10^{\pm 38}$. This vastly exceeds the needs of real world HDR images. This format is known as the *RGBE* file format and is a standard part of the RADIANCE system (Figure 6.6).

6.2.2   Human Perception and Image Formats

Representing color in terms of red, green, and blue color components has some limitations. Notably, it has no independent meaning beyond providing the values for an RGB display device. Different devices may have different color characteristics, so the actual color displayed from an RGB representation varies by the device. This is not necessarily a problem for much of computer graphics, because the human visual system is not very sensitive to absolute colors, just as it is not very sensitive to absolute brightness. However, in some applications precise color reproduction is essential, and this requires a *device-independent color* representation.

Measurement and representation of color is part of *colorimetry*, a subfield of color science in general. Color science and colorimetry predate computer graphics. The CIE, the Commission Internationale de l'Eclairage (the International Commission on Illumination) created the standard XYZ color space in 1931. Colors in this space are represented by a set of three *tristimulus* components, X, Y, and Z, which are computed by integrating the spectrum of the color against three standard illuminant curves. The XYZ color space includes the full gamut of colors visible to the average human. Conversion to RGB is accomplished by a device-dependent linear transformation. However, some XYZ values can get converted to an RGB value outside the range of the device (i.e., greater than one or less than zero), in which case the device is not capable of displaying the color exactly. Discretization, e.g., to 8 bits, adds a further restriction. In general, the set of colors a particular device can reproduce is known as the *color gamut* of the device.

The value of Y in the XYZ color space is the *luminance* of the color, a measure of overall brightness based loosely on human color perception at a typical level of brightness adaptation. At the same radiometric radiance level, green light appears somewhat brighter than red light, and significantly brighter than blue or violet light. The luminance is often used in conversion from color to grayscale. The X and Z components of an XYZ color record the color information; the values $x = X/(X+Y+Z)$ and $y = Y/(X+Y+Z)$ are the *chromaticity* values (coordinates) of the color. The chromaticity values x and y are invariant under a linear scaling of the color, so they represent, in some sense the "hue" of the color independent of the brightness. However chromaticity is not uniform in the way humans perceive color: how much x and y have to change in order for a human observer to notice a difference in the color depends on the particular values of x and y. For example, a slight change of values may make a noticeable difference in the blue range, but the same change is hardly noticeable in the green range. This is relevant to image storage, because it implies that greater precision is needed to accurately represent blues than greens.

In 1976, the CIE adopted another color space, the Luv space, that is closer to being perceptually uniform. The coordinates, properly written as L^*, u^*, and v^* (the $*$ superscript is sometimes omitted), vary in approximately the same manner as human perceive changes in color. The variable L represents the overall apparent brightness or lightness of the color, while u and v are adjusted chromaticity values. In this context, the values are sometimes called by the more general name of *chrominance* values. Ideally, a small change in any of the Luv coordinates corresponds to a similar apparent change in color. The values are determined from X, Y, and Z through a nonlinear relationship. Figure 6.7 illustrates a *chromaticity diagram* in Luv space. Here, L is fixed, at $L = 1$ and the diagram shows how the color varies as a function of u and v. The outer region contains all the colors visible to the human eye, while the inner triangular region is the gamut of a representative RGB color display device.

After he had some experience with the RGBE format, Ward began to see the advantages of a file format that contained a device-independent representation of pixel values. Human vision is much more sensitive to brightness (luminance) than chromaticity, and brightness covers a wider range. More precisely, human perception of brightness is roughly logarithmic: repeatedly doubling the luminance

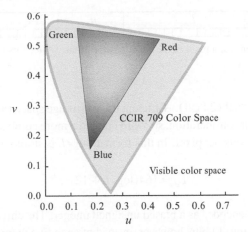

Figure 6.7   A slice of the CIE Luv color space ($L = 1$). The inside triangle is the color gamut of the CCIR 709 color space, which is used in Kodak's PhotoCD format. (After images courtesy of Greg Ward.)

tends to look like a series of uniform steps in brightness. In contrast, human color response is closer to being linear, so u and v are unaltered in the format. For his new format, Ward decided to use a variant of the Luv color space, in which the L value is replaced by its base-two logarithm. Storing the logarithm of L in the pixel representation accomplishes essentially the same thing as the "exponent" in the RGBE format, and it better matches human perceptual response to brightness. Tone mapping was another reason he chose to use the logarithm of L. Tone mapping typically works with the luminance rather than the color channels; in fact, some operators use the logarithm of the luminance directly. Using the Luv space in the file format not only facilitates tone mapping computation, it mitigates possible precision loss that might be incurred in color space conversion. Ward's new HDR file format, known as LogLuv, has found widespread use, and is now part of the TIFF specification. The format has two variants.

LogLuv format (32 bit).   An Luv pixel is packed into 32 bits by using 16 bits to store $\log_2 L$, and 8 bits each to store u and v. The values are all represented as fixed-point integers. While u and v are never negative, $\log_2 L$ needs a sign bit. Figure 6.8 illustrates how the bits are allocated. The first bit is the sign of $\log_2 L$, the next 15 bit are its absolute value, the next 8 bits store u, and the last 8 bits store v. The "e" subscript indicates the fixed-point representation. This format provides a better representation than the 32 bit RGBE format, even though it uses the same amount of storage per pixel.

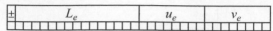

Figure 6.8   Storage arrangement for a pixel in 32 bit LogLuv format. (After images courtesy of Greg
               Ward.)

LogLuv file format (24 bit). Efficient use of storage space (and network band-
width) is always a consideration, so Ward created a more compact LogLuv format
that uses only 24 bits per pixel. In this format, $\log_2 L$ is stored as a 10-bit integer,
computed from

$$L_e = \lfloor 64(\log_2 L + 12) \rfloor,$$

i.e., the integer is encoded as a biased unsigned integer. The chrominance values u
and v are packed into 14 bits; however, instead of encoding them into two separate
7-bit integers, the 14 bits contain a single integer index in an implicit map of
actual u and v values. Figure 6.9 illustrates the format. The bottom part of the
figure shows the u, v map. This map has to be searched for the actual values,
which does require extra computation. As is often the case with data formats,
there is a trade-off between computation and storage.

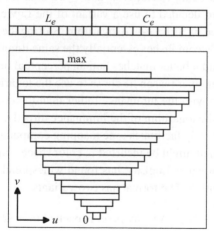

Figure 6.9   The 24 bit LogLuv format stores an index C_e (top) into a table of u and v values (bottom).
               Decoding requires searching the table. (After images courtesy of Greg Ward.)

6.2.3   A New HDR file format

Another HDR file format called OpenEXR was released by Industrial Light &
Magic in 2002. Although it is not really a lightweight file format, it does have the

advantage of offering more precision than the LogLuv formats.[2] The OpenEXR format is very flexible. While RGBE and LogLuv are limited to three color channels, OpenEXR allows for arbitrary many channels. These extra channels can be used for any number of things, such as compositing or general transparency. Another notable feature is the use of a 16-bit *half-precision* floating-point number format. Ordinary floating-point numbers use either 32 bits (single precision) or 64 bits (double precision). The 16-bit half-precision format allows negative numbers, which may be needed by some color space representations. Furthermore, some GPUs support half-precision floating-point computations so the OpenEXR format meshes well with graphics hardware.

A drawback of OpenEXR is its complexity; however, ILM released a set of software tools for working with the format along with the specification. The specification and tools were released under an open source license, which has encouraged the widespread use of OpenEXR outside ILM.

6.3 HDR Video

Since 2003, adapting HDR imaging to video has become more prevalent. This section introduces some representative work in early HDR video capture that inspired a substantial body of work in recent years.

6.3.1 Video and HDR Images

The method of Debevec and Malik described in Section 6.1 requires a precise knowledge of the exposure times used to capture the images in order to reconstruct the HDR response function.[3] The assumption is that the aperture setting of the lens was the same for all the images. Exposure control in video cameras is more easily done by changing the aperture size, especially if changes need to be made during filming. Image noise also tends to be higher in video shots, and this disrupts the measurements of the pixel exposures across images. In the paper "Radiometric Self Calibration," Tomoo Mitsunaga and Shree K. Nayar presented a new method for recovering the response curve of a camera using only rough estimates of the camera parameters [Mitsunaga and Nayar 99].

---

[2]For storing $\log_2 L$, the OpenEXR format has a higher precision than the 24-bit LogLuv, but lower precision than the 32-bit LogLuv format. OpenEXR achieves a 0.1% quantization precision, whereas 32-bit LogLuv has 0.3% steps.

[3]The authors were so concerned about accurate exposure times, they were not convinced the shutter speeds provided by the camera were sufficiently precise. So they made audio recordings of the shutter being released at each speed and then determined the actual speeds by analyzing sounds from the recording.

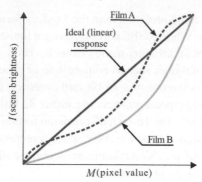

Figure 6.10   Radiometric response functions of two kinds of films. Neither matches the ideal linear response function very closely. (From [Mitsunaga and Nayar 99] © 2009 IEEE.)

The physical process of camera imaging was described in Chapter 5. The camera lens focuses scene radiance L onto each pixel, which produces an irradiance E on the pixel. The time-integrated irradiance during the time Δt that the shutter is open is the ideal exposure $I;$[4] assuming the irradiance is constant over the exposure time, $I = E\Delta t$. An ideal camera records the exposure exactly; however, the relationship between exposure and a pixel value is governed by the response function of the camera. The biggest challenge in HDR imaging is the reconstruction of the camera response curve. Figure 6.10 contains plots of the response functions of two different kinds of film, compared to the ideal linear response of an ideal camera.

The scene radiance L at a particular point on the image plane of an ideal camera is related to the ideal pixel exposure $I = E\Delta t$ according to the formula given in Equation (5.4.5). The formula can be rearranged as

$$I = \underbrace{\left(\frac{\cos^4 \theta}{F^2} \right)}_{k} \underbrace{\left(\frac{\pi d^2}{4} \Delta t \right)}_{e} L,$$

where F is the distance from the sensor plane to the lens and d is the aperture diameter. The value of k is constant for each pixel, as long as the camera is not refocused; e is a function of the aperture size and the exposure time. This refactoring $I = keL$ thus combines the essential two variables that affect exposure, the aperture size and the exposure time, into a single variable e. If M is the recorded value of a pixel, Mitsunaga and Nayar model the inverse response function as a

---

[4]In Section 6.1, X was used to denote the ideal exposure; I is used here to match the notation of Mitsunaga and Nayar's paper. The paper also uses M for the pixel values rather than Z.

univariate polynomial in the pixel value,

$$I = f(M) = \sum_{n=0}^{N} c_n M^n.$$

Only the coefficients need to be determined in order to model the response function. There is no theoretical reason to believe that camera response functions are polynomials; however, the model is justifiable because *any* function can be uniformly approximated by a polynomial.

The authors describe their method to compute the polynomial coefficients as *radiometric self-calibration* The process works on a sequence of $q = 1, 2, \ldots, Q$ images, each taken from the same vantage point under the same lighting conditions. It is assumed that the only variation is in the exposure time and the aperture size. If the pixels are indexed by p, $M_{p,q}$ and $I_{p,q}$ denote the pixel value and ideal exposure, respectively, of pixel p in image q. Suppose the ratio $R_q = e_q/e_{q+1}$ between two images q and $q + 1$ in the image is known. Then, for each pixel p,

$$R_2 = \frac{I_{p,q}}{I_{p,q+1}} = \frac{f(M_{p,q})}{f(M_{p,q+1})},$$

and therefore

$$\sum_{n=0}^{N} c_n M_{p,q}^n = R_q \sum_{n=0}^{N} c_n M_{p,q+1}^n. \tag{6.6}$$

Equation (6.6) is a system of linear equations in c_n and R_q over all the pixels p. With a known value of R_q, this system is an overdetermined linear system; a solution that minimizes the error in the least squares sense is used. This amounts to minimizing a system of quadratic equations, which can be done exactly by setting the derivatives with respect to the variables c_n to zero and solving the resulting system of linear equations. An extra constraint is applied so that the response curve of the maximum pixel value is normalized.

In practice, the ratios R_q are not known, but they can be estimated by taking the ratio of pixel values in the middle range. Mitsunaga and Nayar employ an iterative method. It starts with an approximation to each R_q, computes the polynomial coefficients, then constructs a new value of R_q using the approximation to f. The value of R_q is computed from the values of I using the polynomial approximation to f. The process is repeated until the computed error term is sufficiently small, or stops changing. More precisely, each iteration starts with an approximation $R_q^{(k-1)}$, computes the polynomial coefficients $c_n^{(k)}$, then updates R_q from

$$R_q^{(k)} = \sum_p \frac{\sum_{n=0}^{N} c_n^{(k)} M_{p,q}^n}{\sum_{n=0}^{N} c_n^{(k)} M_{p,q+1}^n}.$$

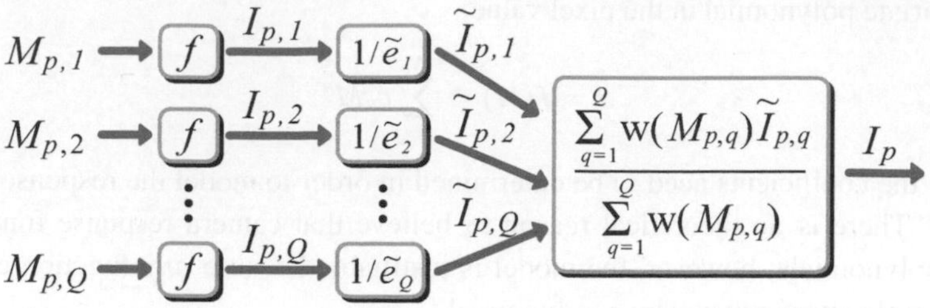

$$M_{p,1} \rightarrow \boxed{f} \xrightarrow{I_{p,1}} \boxed{1/\widetilde{e}_1} \xrightarrow{\widetilde{I}_{p,1}}$$

$$M_{p,2} \rightarrow \boxed{f} \xrightarrow{I_{p,2}} \boxed{1/\widetilde{e}_2} \xrightarrow{\widetilde{I}_{p,2}} \boxed{\dfrac{\sum\limits_{q=1}^{Q} \mathrm{w}(M_{p,q})\widetilde{I}_{p,q}}{\sum\limits_{q=1}^{Q} \mathrm{w}(M_{p,q})}} \xrightarrow{I_p}$$

$$M_{p,Q} \rightarrow \boxed{f} \xrightarrow{I_{p,Q}} \boxed{1/\widetilde{e}_Q} \xrightarrow{\widetilde{I}_{p,Q}}$$

Figure 6.11   Flowchart for radiometric self-calibration. (From [Mitsunaga and Nayar 99] © 2009 IEEE.)

The authors tested the method on synthetic images with an appropriate amount of noise deliberately added. They found that using $N = 10$ (i.e., 11 polynomial coefficients) gives sufficiently accurate results, and fewer than 10 iterations are needed to determine the final values. Figure 6.11 illustrates the conceptual process of each iteration ($\widetilde{I}$ is used in place of $f^{(n)}(M)$ in the figure). Mitsunaga and Nayar's self-calibration algorithm does not need exposure time information to accurately reproduce the response curve. Furthermore, noise can be reduced by employing a time averaging of pixel values for images in a video sequence. Also, because the solution method solves a system of linear equations rather than employing a nonlinear optimizer, the algorithm is very fast. A drawback, however, is that the polynomial model requires increasingly many coefficients as the dynamic range increases, and therefore cannot cover an unbounded range. Debevec and Malik's method does not have this limitation. Nonetheless, the self-calibration algorithm has been shown to work very well in practical cases, except for those having an extremely large dynamic range.

6.3.2   HDR Video Capture and Display

In 2003, Sing Bing Kang, Matthew Uyttendaele, Simon Winder, and Richard Szeliski presented the paper "High Dynamic Range Video" [Kang et al. 03]. This paper describes a general method of generating an HDR video from a sequence of frames captured with different exposures. The basic idea is to capture the sequence of frames using a wide range of exposure times. Each frame in the sequence therefore has a significantly different exposure than the previous frame. Widely varying the exposure times between frames results in a set of images having a much greater dynamic range than could be captured with a conventional digital video camera (Figure 6.12). The problem, though, is that the images change between frames. The methods described so far in this chapter all assume a static environment, so they do not apply to HDR video capture. The steps in the al-

Figure 6.12   High dynamic range video of a driving scene. Top row: input video with alternating short
and long exposures. Bottom row: high dynamic range video (tone-mapped). (From [Kang
et al. 03] © 2003 ACM, Inc. Included here by permission.) (See Color Plate IX.)

gorithm described in the "High Dynamic Range Video" paper are described as
follows.

1. Video capture. The authors used a specialized digital camera to capture
the image sequence. The camera had a programmable control unit that allowed a
tethered computer to control the exposure in real time. The video is shot so that
dark and bright regions of the scene are exposed in rapid succession. The actual
range of exposures is adjusted dynamically to optimize effective capture. This
works much like the "auto-bracketing" feature available on many contemporary
digital still cameras: the camera determines the average scene brightness and then
captures a series of images with exposure times less than and greater than the
computed optimal exposure. In capturing video, these differently exposed images
are separate frames in the video sequence.

2. Frame registration. Ultimately the captured images are collected into an
HDR video sequence, but this is complicated by the fact that the images are not
static. The camera used by the authors captured 15 frames per second, so there is
enough time between frames for the images to change appreciably. However, the
frame rate is fast enough that sequential frames are likely to be similar enough
to apply an automatic optical flow algorithm (see Chapter 5). However, the basic
search methods for pixel correspondence do not directly apply, because corresponding pixel values vary widely between frames. At the same time, the difference in these values is needed to construct the HDR radiance map. The authors
describe an image correspondence method they call *HDR stitching*.

The HDR stitching algorithm works by constructing warped intermediate images between captured frames. This requires matching of corresponding pixels

between the frames, which in this context is called *image registration*. Optical flow is applied to register adjacent images, but before this can be done the pixel brightness values have to be matched. This is accomplished by synthetically boosting the exposure of the image with the shorter exposure time to match the exposure time of the other image. These exposure times are known because the camera tags each captured image with exposure information, including the exposure time, and the camera is radiometrically calibrated.

The HDR stitching for one frame, called the *current frame*, depends on the adjacent frames, called the *previous* and *next* frames. From these frames, three warped images are constructed: a *previous-to-current* image, a *next-to-current* frame, and a bidirectional image, which is interpolated from the previous and next frames and then warped to the current frame. The two unidirectionally warped images are constructed using optical flow in one direction; the previous (or next) frame is registered to the current frame and then warped toward the current frame. The registration is done using a method similar to the pyramid-based optical flow algorithm described in Chapter 5.

The process of creating the bidirectionally warped image is considerably more complicated. It begins by constructing an image C' by interpolating the previous and next frames at the midpoint between them. That is, the previous and next frames are both warped toward the current frame and the results are averaged into C'. The optical flow for this computation also uses a pyramid approach, but the motion estimate uses linear transformations and translations, and the local correction is symmetric. Ideally, the resulting interpolated image C' would match the current frame exactly; however, the motion estimation process is not perfect, and even if it were, there is still the issue of camera shaking between frames. The difference between C' and the current frame actually provides a measure of the consistency of camera motion, as it is constructed assuming constant velocity between captured frames.

The optical flow used to construct C' is improved by applying the correction necessary to match C' to the current frame. This additional registration step uses a hierarchical version of optical flow estimation, in which the motion model in each region is a projective (perspective) transformation. This is a more constrained version of optical flow estimation. The constraint is necessary to reduce the possibility of erroneous warping due to low contrast and saturated pixels. All three interpolated images can be regarded as "stabilized" versions of the current frame.

3. HDR recovery. All three interpolated images are used to recover the HDR content of the current frame along with the current frame image itself. The camera is radiometrically calibrated, so the pixels in all of these images can be converted

to radiance. The final recovered HDR value is a weighted average of the radiance values of the corresponding pixels across the images. The weights are based on the reliability of the radiance values. Pixels that have very low contrast or are close to being saturated are deemed to be less reliable, so they are given lower weights. The weights themselves come from a continuous reliability estimation function.

If a pixel in the current frame is considered reliable, i.e., is not too dim or saturated, its HDR value is computed without the bidirectionally warped image. That image is only used to fill in regions of the current frame where the pixel values are too low or considered saturated—the registration used to construct the previous-to-current and next-to-current images is not reliable in this case. The final HDR video is obtained by repeating the frame registration and HDR recovery for each frame in the captured video sequence.

4. Tone mapping. Displaying the high dynamic range video on a low dynamic range display requires tone mapping. Compared to still images, the tone mapping problem for video has the extra challenge of temporal coherence: if the tone mapping operator varies between frames—as some certainly would—the results will appear uneven. Flickering of individual pixels is one example of the kind of artifact that could result. The authors found that the tone mapping algorithm developed by Reinhard et al. [Reinhard et al. 02] worked well when it was adapted to video.

7

Image-Based Lighting

7.1   The Basics of Image-Based Lighting

In the production of special effects for live action films, objects created with CG
are composited with real life video frames that contain the background and sometimes live actors. In order to perform this compositing without noticeable visual
inconsistencies, there is a need to recreate, as accurately as possible, the lighting
of the real scene and to render the CG objects using this lighting. One method is to
capture images of a white polystyrene or metallic sphere positioned in the scene
where the CG object would be and perform CG lighting based on the captured
images. However, this requires a lot of trial and error and provides a limited measurement of the scene lighting. More accurate—and more automatic—methods
were needed. It can be said that the awareness of this issue led to the concep-
tion and practical application of *image-based lighting* (IBL), in which lighting is
reconstructed directly from photographs of the original environment.

7.1.1   The Birth of IBL

As mentioned earlier, Paul Debevec became interested in high dynamic range
imaging during his work on the *The Campanile Movie* [Debevec 97]; however,
HDR was not the only issue that troubled him during the creation of that film.
Debevec's goal of photorealistically rendering computer-generated objects within
real environments required the CG objects to be illuminated by the lighting captured from the environments. The lighting information used in image-based rendering was combined with the object textures. What was needed was a way to
separate the lighting information from the general appearance of objects using
the captured images.

The problem of accurately capturing images covering a wide range of brightnesses, and the problem of recovering the lighting information from environment images were originally treated as separate problems. While working on *The Campanile Movie*, Debevec had a vague idea of treating the background image as a source of lighting. After developing a method to create HDR images, he turned to the problem of recovering lighting information from real-life background images.

Debevec thought of performing global illumination calculations by treating the pixels in the HDR background image as light sources scattered around the background of the CG environment. Trying this out required a good set of GI rendering tools. Luckily, Greg Ward, whom Debevec came to know through his work on HDR images, had already added functionality to the RADIANCE system that could perform GI using environment maps. Debevec proceeded to develop his rendering system using this idea and created the first test images in RADIANCE. Although Ward had doubts about whether Debevec's idea could be realized, they were both pleasantly surprised by the results.

The method used to create these test images was presented at SIGGRAPH in the paper "Rendering Synthetic Objects into Real Scenes" [Debevec 98]. However, the term "image-based lighting" was never actually used in the paper. The term was first coined when Debevec's series of animated films were shown in Germany using the title "Image-Based Modeling, Rendering and Lighting." Debevec took a great liking to the phrase "image-based lighting" and used it in subsequent publications and presentations. Before long, the term "IBL" became well established in the CG field.

7.1.2   The Basic Process of IBL

Figure 7.1 illustrates the basic process described in Debevec's "Rendering Synthetic Objects into Real Scenes" paper. The "real scene" in this figure is a table with some real objects. The goal is to add a CG object (on the tabletop) to a photograph of this scene so that it looks like a part of the original scene. The steps are outlined as follows.

1. The scene is photographed; the CG object will be composited into this image (Figure 7.1(a)).

2. The lighting of the environment is obtained at the point where the CG object is to be placed. This is done by photographing a *light probe*, which is a mirrored sphere placed in the environment where the CG object will go. The light probe is photographed from several viewpoints, each using a range of exposure times (Figure 7.1(b)).

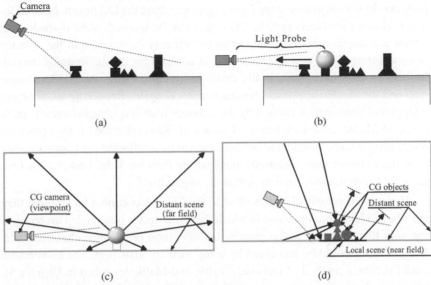

Figure 7.1   The basic process of capturing a real environment map for IBL. (After [Debevec 98] © 1998 ACM, Inc. Included here by permisiion.)

3. An omnidirectional HDR radiance map is constructed from the light probe images. The images from each viewpoint are first converted to an HDR image using Debevec and Malik's technique (see Chapter 6), then these HDR images are stitched together into an HDR radiance map of the environment as it appears from the center of the sphere (Figure 7.1(c)).

4. A model of the local environment is constructed. The model only needs to include the part of the environment close to the CG object. This model is used to simulate *near-field* illumination effects such as interreflection and shadowing. The surface reflectance properties of local objects need to be known, but only approximately (Figure 7.1(d)).

5. The CG object is added to the local model and rendered using the captured radiance map as the source of illumination.

6. The rendered object is composited into the photograph from Step 1.

The illumination recovery thus has two elements: the radiance map of the environment, which represents the *far-field* illumination, and the construction of the local model for near field effects. The local model is also needed to include shadows of the CG object in the scene. The local model construction is comparatively more difficult than obtaining the radiance map from the light problem.

If objects in the environment are far enough away from the CG object, interreflection between the objects and the CG object can be ignored. And if shadowing effects are also considered unimportant (which may be the case in the absence of concentrated light sources) then there is no need for the environment model. In this case, all the lighting in the environment comes from the HDR radiance map and the rendering process becomes much simpler. Rendering a CG object with global illumination using only the radiance map is a straightforward application of Monte Carlo path tracing (Chapter 2). Rays reflected off the object are not directly traced; instead, the radiance carried by a reflected ray comes directly from the radiance map. Interreflections within the object do, however, involve secondary path tracing, but only within the object itself.

However, if near-field effects close to the CG object cannot be ignored, they must be modeled into the scene in which the CG object is rendered. This requires not only the geometry of the objects, but also their reflectance characteristics. The geometry could be recovered by using methods IBR (e.g., the architecture model recovery method of Debevec Taylor, and Malik described in Chapter 5), but recovering reflectance was a much more difficult problem. Debevec therefore made the simplifying assumption that nearby scene objects had Lambertian surfaces. The method starts by estimating the scene object albedos, then refining the estimates by rendering the CG object and comparing the result in the composite image. Although this may seem unscientific, the goal of the work was to create plausible results so this approach is reasonable. In fact, such ad hoc adjustments to improve visual quality are common in production (and research) computer graphics—sometimes rendered images lack an aesthetic quality that can only be added by human intervention. Nevertheless, the problem of recovering reflectance characteristics from captured images remained unsolved.

7.2 Environment Maps and IBL

The basic process introduced in Debevec's "Rendering Synthetic Objects into Real Scenes" paper has been refined for use in more practical situations. In recent years the method of using HDR environment maps as the light source for rendering computation has become the main method of IBL. Interest in general environment map research has been part of this trend. Originally, environment maps were used as a special kind of texture map. However, in modern research they are being used for lighting in GI computation. This section introduces the use of environment maps in this more modern context, and explores their relationship with IBR in general.

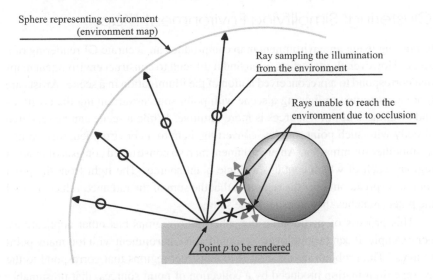

Figure 7.2   GI computation using an environment map.

7.2.1   IBL Using HDR Environment Maps

An HDR radiance map recovered from Debevec's light probe images provides the incoming radiance from each direction at the center of the probe. But it could also be regarded as coming from a distant point on a very large sphere that encompasses the whole environment. In this sense, the radiance map is a kind of HDR environment map. The interpretation is useful, as environment maps are well established in basic rendering; in fact, environment map lookup is commonly available in graphics hardware so that it can be employed in GPU shaders.

Figure 7.2 illustrates how an environment map is used in rendering a simple scene consisting of a sphere sitting on a block. Rendering a point p on the surface of the block including global illumination can be accomplished by Monte Carlo ray tracing (see Chapter 2). Rays are sampled in directions on the hemisphere of directions above the surface at p. A ray that is unoccluded in the environment hits the environment sphere, and the radiance carried along the ray thus comes directly from the environment map. If the ray in a particular direction hits another object, the GI computation has to be done at the point of intersection with that object. That computation is done the same way, by sampling over the environment. The method does not strictly need to use an HDR environment map, but the dynamic range of illumination in a real environment is usually much larger than can be stored in an ordinary texture map. Low dynamic range environment maps have limited use as illumination sources.

7.2.2 Clustering: Simplifying Environment Maps

Rendering using an environment map can produce an accurate GI rendering of a scene. However, digital artists often find it difficult to construct environment maps that correspond to a preconceived notion of the illumination in a scene. Artists are more accustomed to lighting a scene with point sources; arranging the positions and brightness of point sources is more intuitive. While a scene can be rendered directly with such point sources, converting them to an environment map results in smoother illumination. An environment map so constructed consists of disjoint regions, each of which contains a single point source. The light from the point source is spread out over the region so that the sum of the radiance values over all the pixels matches the intensity of the source.

This process of partitioning the sphere into regions has other applications. For example, it can be employed to simplify an environment with too many point sources. The problem in this case is to construct regions that correspond to the average illumination produced by a collection of point sources, that presumably have similar intensity. The illumination in the region is an average of the sources it contains, or perhaps is that of one representative source in the region. This process is known as *clustering*. The illumination produced by a cluster region can be regarded as that of a single point source at the center of the region. Each pixel of a digitized environment map, such as one obtained using the light probe method described, can be regarded as a point source. Clustering can be applied to reduce all these pixels to a few representative point sources, or *samples* as they may be called in this context.

Clustering points on the sphere can be accomplished using the k-means algorithm. In this algorithm, the number of clusters is determined at the outset. If there are to be N cluster regions, a preliminary set of regions is created based on N randomly chosen samples $U_1, U_2, \ldots, U_N$. The regions form a partition of the sphere known as a *Voronoi diagram*: all points on the sphere inside the region containing U_i are closer to U_i than any other of the randomly chosen points. Figure 7.3 shows part of three such regions for sample points labeled U_1, U_2, and U_3. Note that the regions are bounded by line segments midway between neighboring sample points. Each preliminary region thus contains one of the N randomly chosen sample points as well as any number of remaining points. The next step is to update the regions to better match the points as a whole. The centroid (average position) of all the points contained in each region is computed (Figure 7.4), and the regions are reconstructed using the centroids instead of the original N sample points. This step is repeated until the regions converge. The name "k-means" refers to the notion that a collection of points is represented by k averages (means).

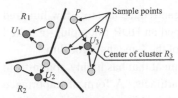

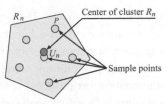

Figure 7.3   Dividing sample points into clusters   Figure 7.4   Updating the cluster center points
via the k-means algorithm.   for the next iteration of the k-means
algorithm.

Applying the k-means algorithm to partitioning the sphere based on a set of point sources has a major drawback. The partitioning is done by distance from the point sources—the intensity of the sources is not considered. Consequently, the regions for the most important light sources are treated the same as the regions for sources of lesser importance. If the point sources have roughly the same intensity, this is not a problem. However, cinema lighting (real and virtual) is typically done with different kinds of lights: *key lights* are used for the primary illumination of scene elements; *fill lights* are added to reduce shadows and change the contrast. Fill lights normally have lower intensity than key lights, and there are typically many more of them. An environment constructed using the k-means algorithm is not likely to provide a good representation of key and fill lights.

7.2.3   Sampling an Environment Map

When an HDR environment map is used for scene illumination, it often contains all the illumination sources, including the lights. Sampling via ray tracing over the hemisphere therefore suffers from the same problems described in Chapter 2: a large number of samples is necessary to ensure that enough randomly chosen rays hit the light sources and other bright spots. The problem is more general in environment maps, and also more complicated, because the bright parts of the map are not necessarily known in advance. The church image shown in Figure 6.4 is a good example. In that environment, most of the illumination comes from the windows. In this particular environment, the windows are fairly broad, but other environments might have smaller concentrated sources that have little chance of being hit by a random sample. Some way of ensuring that bright parts of a high dynamic range environment map are properly sampled is therefore necessary.

The k-means algorithm provides on way of doing this. Each pixel in an environment map can be regarded as a point source, i.e., a point sample on the sphere. The k-means algorithm can be applied to cluster these samples into a collection of fewer representative samples. For example, a typical HDR environment map has several million pixels. The k-means algorithm can reduce this to a few hundred representative clusters. Jonathan Cohen developed an HDR Shop plug-in called LightGen that does this using weighted version of the k-means algorithm.[1]

Simply put, uniform sampling of an environment that has highly nonuniform illumination (as most do) is likely to result in artifacts. A form of importance sampling is therefore necessary for efficient sampling. The paper "Structured Importance Sampling of Environment Maps" by Sameer Agarwal, Ravi Ramamoorthi, Serge Belongie, and Henrik Wann Jensen presents one method of importance sampling using a spherical partition of the environment map [Agarwal et al. 03]. The partitions, called *strata* in the paper, essentially represent a set of directional light sources that approximate the illumination of the environment. The k-means algorithm described previously does something similar; however, the method described in the paper produces a better set of samples and also arranges them in a hierarchy for more effective rendering.[2]

The process of constructing the samples first divides the environment map into sections or "layers" of similar brightness. Boundaries of these layers resemble the contour lines on a topographic map (Figure 7.3(a)). These layers are then partitioned into disjoint "strata," each of which will contain one sample. The number of strata (samples) is determined using a measure of importance that balances the relative area with the relative brightness. This is based on the function

$$\Gamma(L, \Delta\omega) = L^a \Delta\omega^b, \tag{7.1}$$

in which L is the radiance (brightness) and $\Delta\omega$ is the total solid angle of the region, i.e., the spherical area of the region. The relative importance of area and brightness are controlled by adjustable parameters a and b. For example, if $a = 0$ and $b = 1$, then the importance sampling is driven only by area. As described previously, this parameter choice will underemphasize the importance of small light sources. On the other hand, if $a = 1$ and $b = 0$, sampling is driven entirely by brightness. The problem in this case comes in the improper representation of broad sections of dim pixels that collectively have a substantial contribution to illumination. The implementation in the paper actually uses $a = 1$ and $b = \frac{1}{4}$, and it also employs a modification to ensure $\Delta\omega$ does not become too small.

Splitting the map into layers to be sampled separately allows the sampling to be more dense in brighter layers, while at the same time ensuring that layers having the lowest brightness value are properly included. The stratification works on the connected components of the layers, starting with the brightest layer and

---

[1] http://gl.ict.usc.edu/HDRShop

[2] There are other sampling methods well suited for IBL using environment maps such as [Kollig and Keller 03] [Ostromoukhov et al. 04].

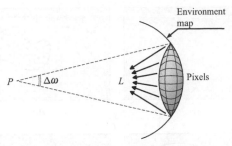

Figure 7.5   The solid angle $\Delta\omega$ of a group of pixels in the environment map as seen from a point p.

working toward the dimmest (this is where the hierarchy comes in). The number of samples in each layer is proportional to the value of Γ in each layer, where L and $\Delta\omega$ come from summing the value and solid angle (Figure 7.5) of all the pixels in the component (Equation 7.1). The collection of all these pixels is regarded as a set of point samples, and the goal is to cluster them into a collection of representative samples. The authors employ an algorithm known as the Hochbaum-Shmoys clustering algorithm, which uses a "farthest-first" approach. The first sample is chosen to be the brightest pixel in the region. Then the next choice is the point in the region farthest from this first sample. At each iteration, the next sample point is the point farthest away from all the samples chosen so far; i.e., the next sample is the point in the region having the largest minimum distance from all the other chosen samples.

Figure 7.6(b) shows the resulting set of samples and the corresponding strata for a component of the brightest layer. The strata for points near the edge of the component are clipped by the component boundary for clarity; they really extend further outward. The stratification process continues with the next layer (Figure7.6(c)). The sample points in the higher layer remain the same. The new sample points continue to be chosen using Hochbaum-Shmoys algorithm as if nothing changed. The only difference is that fewer samples per area are chosen at this layer, which results in a coarser sampling density. The process then continues with the next lower layer, and stops when the lowest layer has been stratified (Figure 7.6(d)). The sampling density is thus finest at the brightest parts of the environment map, and becomes progressively coarser as the brightness decreases.

Figure 7.7(a) contains rendering of a simple scene illuminated by the HDR environment map captured in an environment with highly nonuniform illumination and a number of bright illumination sources The multiple shadows in the image are cast by these various light sources and are basically correct, even though they look a bit strange out of context. Figure 7.7(b) shows close-ups of the rectangular areas in the scene in part (a). The images in the left column were rendered using

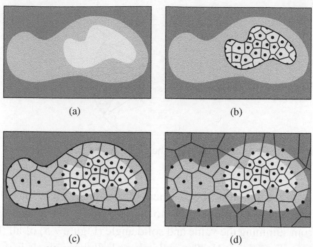

(a)   (b)

(c)   (d)

Figure 7.6   Clustering stages for structured importance sampling an environment map. (a) The map
              is partitioned into levels (areas) of similar brightness. (b–d) Each layer is partitioned into
              strata based on selected sample points, proceeding from the brightest to the dimmest levels
              layers. Note the samples are most dense in the brightest layer, and become more sparse
              in the dimmer layers. (From [Agarwal et al. 03] © 2003 ACM, Inc. Included here by
              permission.)

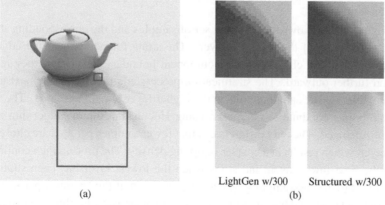

LightGen w/300   Structured w/300
(a)   (b)

Figure 7.7   Rendering using structured importance sampling, using 300 samples (point sources) to
              represent the environment map. (a) Image rendered using structured importance sampling.
              (b) Magnifications of the marked rectangles in (a). The images in the left column were
              rendered by LightGen and are included for comparison. LightGen employs the k-means
              algorithm; the discrete levels visible in the shadow are an artifact of poor sampling density
              in bright parts of the environment map. (From [Agarwal et al. 03] © 2003 ACM, Inc.
              Included here by permission.)

Plate I   Rendered image of fire. (From [Nguyen et al. 02] © 2002 ACM, Inc. Included here by permission.) (See Figure 3.18.)

(a) BRDF   (b) BSSRDF

Plate II   Images of a detailed human face model rendered with (a) a BRDF approximation to the dipole model; (b) the dipole-based BSSRDF model with measured parameters for human skin. (Image from [Jensen and Buhler 02] © 2002 ACM, Inc. Included here by permission.) (See Figure 4.11.)

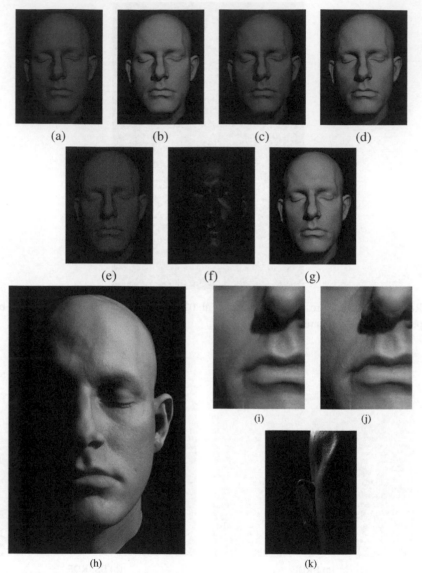

Plate III   Multilayer model of human skin. (a) Epidermis reflectance. (b) Epidermis transmittance. (c) Upper dermis reflectance. (d) Upper dermis transmittance. (e) Bloody dermis reflectance. (f) Surface roughness. (g) Multilayer reflectance. (h) Application of the albedo map. (controlling parameters using albedo map). (i) Dipole model close-up. (j) Multilayer model close-up. (k) Back-lit close-up of the right ear. (From [Donner and Jensen 05] © 2005 ACM, Inc. Included here by permission.) (See Figure 4.23.)

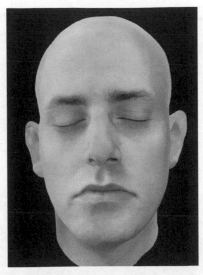

Plate IV   Albedo map for the human head model. (From [Donner and Jensen 05] © 2005 ACM, Inc. Included here by permission.) (See Figure 4.24.)

(a) BRDF   (b) BSSRDF

Plate V   Test images for the BSSRDF shader developed at ILM. (a) An image rendered with the BRDF shader, (b) The same image rendered with the dipole-based BSSRDF shader. (Courtesy of Christophe Hery © Industrial Light & Magic.) (See Figure 4.25.)

Plate VI   Frozen in air in *Like a Rolling Stone*. (© 1995 Partizan Midi Minuit. All Rights Reserved.)
(See Figure 5.14.)

Plate VII   Multiview video camera capture for *Arthur and the Minimoys*. (© 2006 EuropaCorp and
BUF Company.) (See Figure 5.15.)

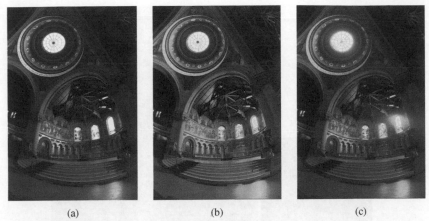

(a)   (b)   (c)

Plate VIII   A high dynamic range image of the inside of a church. Displaying the image becomes a challenge, as it has a greater range than the display medium. (a) HDR converted to Kodak's PhotoCD output, which uses YCC encoding. (b) Tone-mapped HDR image. (c) Tone-mapped HDR image with modifications to simulate human perception. Note the glare around the bright windows. The tone mapping algorithm used for these images is described in [Ward Larson et al. 97]. (From [Debevec and Malik 97] © 1997 ACM, Inc. Included here by permission.) (See Figure 6.4.)

Plate IX   High dynamic range video of a driving scene. Top row: input video with alternating short and long exposures. Bottom row: high dynamic range video (tone-mapped). (From [Kang et al. 03] © 2003 ACM, Inc. Included here by permission.) (See Figure 6.12.)

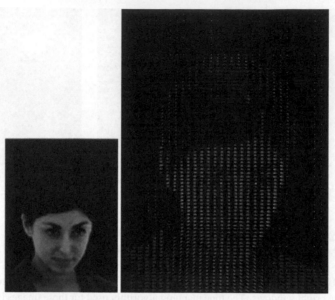

Plate X   All the reflectance images captured from the light stage spotlights can be tiled into a single texture image (right). A captured image is shown on the left. (Courtesy of Paul Debevec.) (See Figure 8.27.)

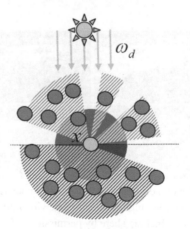

Plate XI   A cluster of hair has a density factor giving the approximate number of hairs per area of a cross section. The red areas affect global scattering; the blue areas cause local backscattering. (From [Zinke et al. 08] © 2008 ACM, Inc. Included here by permission.) (See Figure 8.65.)

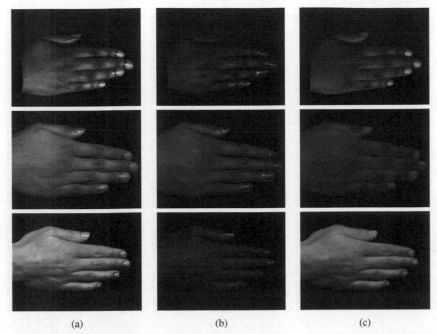

(a)	(b)	(c)

Plate XII   Separation of direct and indirect lighting in human hands. (a) Original captured image. (b) Separated direct illumination. (c) Separated indirect light; most of this comes from subsurface scattering. Evidently, subsurface scattering decreases with increasing skin pigmentation. (Courtesy of Shree K. Nayar, Columbia University.) (See Figure 8.49.)

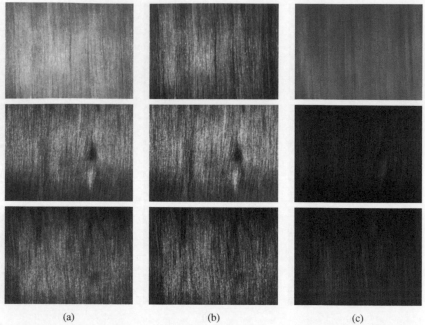

(a)　　　　　　　(b)　　　　　　　(c)

Plate XIII   Separation of direct and indirect lighting in human hair. (a) Original captured images.
(b) Separated direct illumination (c) Separated indirect illumination, including multiple
scattering. The color of light hair is almost entirely determined by scattering in the fibers.
(Courtesy of Shree K. Nayar, Columbia University.) (See Figure 8.50.)

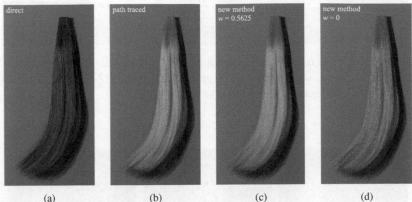

(a)	(b)	(c)	(d)

Plate XIV Renderings of light hair using volumetric multiple scattering. The model is rendered (a) with direct lighting only (there is essentially no color), (b) using path tracing, for a reference image, (c) using the volumetric particle simulation method, and (d) assuming the scattering is isotropic. Note that the forward scattering assumption is necessary to reproduce the color. (From [Moon and Marschner 06] © 2006 ACM, Inc. Included here by permission.) (See Figure 8.59.)

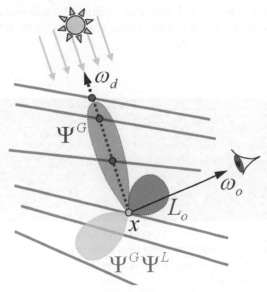

Plate XV The basic concept of dual scattering method is to split the scattering into the *global scattering* of light from the light source and the *local scattering* within a local cluster of hair fibers. (From [Zinke et al. 08] © 2008 ACM, Inc. Included here by permission.) (See Figure 8.64.)

Plate XVI Effect of the density factor. Normal human hair ranges from 0.6 to 0.8. Lower density means less scattering, which makes the hair appear darker. (From [Zinke et al. 08] © 2008 ACM, Inc. Included here by permission.) (See Figure 8.66.)

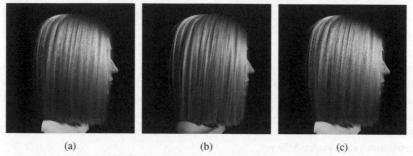

(a)   (b)   (c)

Plate XVII Comparison of rendering methods using the dual scattering approximation: (a) path tracing, for reference (7.8 hours); (b) offline dual scattering (5.2 minutes); (c) real-time dual scattering (14 frames per second). (From [Zinke et al. 08] © 2008 ACM, Inc. Included here by permission.) (See Figure 8.67.)

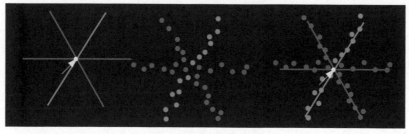

vspace*4pt

Plate XVIII The recentering correction works by fitting lines to the ribbon sample points, and using the best intersection of the lines. (From [Jakob et al. 09] © 2009 ACM, Inc. Included here by permission.) (See Figure 8.73.)

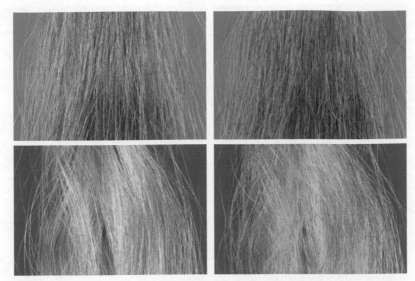

Plate XIX   Rendered images of reconstructed hair geometry (right), giving a "ground truth" comparison to captured images (left). (From [Jakob et al. 09] © 2009 ACM, Inc. Included here by permission.) (See Figure 8.74.)

Plate XX   Rendered result under different simulated lighting conditions. (© 2009 Arno Zinke, GfaR mbH.) (See Figure 8.80.)

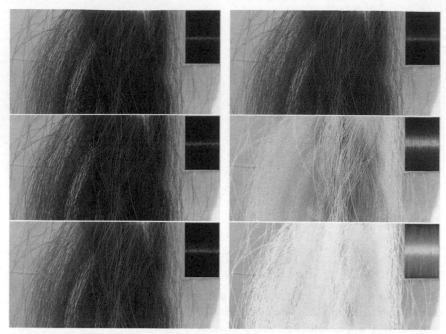

Plate XXI   Rendered images of the hair geometry reconstructed by the method of Wenzel Jakob et al. using the image-based hair reflectance model. (© Arno Zinke, GfaR mbH.) (See Figure 8.81.)

Plate XXII   Real-time rendering results using exit transfer matrices containing subsurface scattering. (From [Sloan et al. 03a] © 2003 ACM, Inc. Included here by permission.) (See Figure 10.15.)

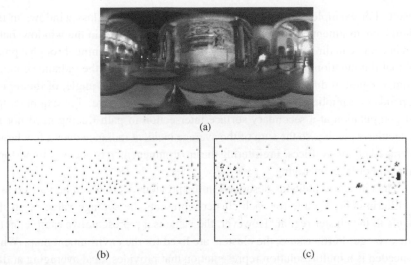

Figure 7.8   Distribution of samples (point light source) resulting from (b) the k-means algorithm, and (c) structured importance sampling. The corresponding environment map is shown in (a). The k-means algorithm does not place enough samples across the very bright window at the far right of the map, which is the primary source of light. (From [Agarwal et al. 03] © 2003 ACM, Inc. Included here by permission.)

samples constructed by the weighted k-means algorithm (via LightGen); those in the right column were rendered using the structured importance sampling algorithm. Both used the same number of samples (300) to represent the environment map. The banding effect visible in the k-means images is a result of the sudden appearance of samples representing the bright lights, which occurs because not enough samples were used for those parts of the environment map. Figure 7.8(b) and (c) illustrate the distribution of sample points generated by the weighted k-means algorithm and the stratified importance sampling algorithm, respectively, compared to the environment map itself shown in Figure 7.8(a). The k-means algorithm fails to concentrate samples in the bright windows, which results in the banding artifacts. The authors point out that in addition to producing better results with the same number of samples, their algorithm requires much less preprocessing time than is needed for the k-means algorithm.

7.2.4   Environment Maps and Prefiltering

Another problem that arises with point sampling HDR environment maps comes in capturing "high frequency" detail. If the environment map has a lot of detail, a small variation in a sampling direction can produce a large difference in the result. For example, a sample point on one of the stained glass windows in the church environment of Figure 6.4 might hit a lead separator in the window, but a slight change in direction gets the value of direct sunlight coming through a pane. Global illumination computation really needs an average of the radiance coming from a region of directions on the sphere. The size, or solid angle, of the region depends on sampling density and also the particular purpose. For example, the GI computation at a secondary surface intersection in path tracing need not be particularly precise, so the sum of the average incident radiance over a few larger averaged regions suffices. Prefiltering the environment map is one way to perform this kind of local averaging.

The clustering methods described in the previous section can be viewed as a prefiltering: the sample for each cluster represents the average value of all the pixels in the cluster region. However, the value is a representative sample, not a true average. Furthermore, the clusters are fixed for the environment map. What is needed is a multiresolution representation that provides local averaging at different scales. The image pyramid method used in optical flow and mip mapping for rendering antialised textures are examples of multiresolution techniques.

An environment map is a radiance function defined on the sphere. An established method for approximating functions on the sphere uses *spherical harmonics*. Spherical harmonics are a generalization of linear harmonics to the sphere. The term "harmonic" arises from music. A musical tone produced by an instrument at a particular frequency, the *fundamental frequency*, actually consists of a series of vibrations at integer multiples of the fundamental frequency, which are known as *harmonics* or *overtones*. Any pure tone can be reproduced as a sum of weighted harmonics. This corresponds to the mathematical notion of a *Fourier series* of a periodic function.

A function $L(\theta, \phi)$ on the unit sphere can be represented in an analogous manner as sum of spherical harmonic (SH) basis functions:

$$L(\theta, \phi) = \sum_{l=0}^{\infty} \sum_{m=-l}^{+l} L_{l,m} Y_l^m(\theta, \phi), \qquad (7.2)$$

where each coefficient $L_{l,m}$ is computed by integrating $L(\theta, \phi)$ against the corresponding basis function $Y_{l,m}(\theta, \phi)$ over the sphere:

$$L_{l,m} = \int_0^\pi \int_0^{2\pi} L(\theta, \phi) Y_l^m(\theta, \phi) \sin\theta \, d\phi \, d\theta. \qquad (7.3)$$

The same letter "L" is used here for both the function and the SH coefficients to disambiguate coefficient sets for different function, e.g., radiance L and irradiance E. Figure 7.9 illustrates the coordinate system used for SH expansions. Note that θ is measured from the positive z-axis, while ϕ is the "longitude" coordinate.

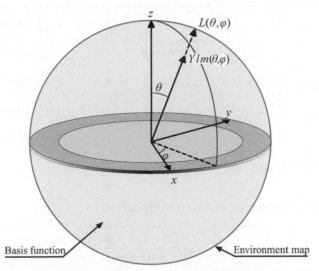

Figure 7.9   Approximation of an environment map using spherical harmonic basis functions.

The spherical harmonic basis functions Y_l^m, which are defined below, are complex functions on the sphere. For each $l = 0, 1, \ldots$ there is a basis function for each $m = -l, \ldots, l$. The SH basis functions are an *orthonormal basis*, which means

$$\int_0^\pi \int_0^{2\pi} Y_l^m(\theta, \phi) Y_{l'}^{m'*}(\theta, \phi) \sin\theta \, d\phi \, d\theta = \begin{cases} 1 & \text{if } l = l' \text{ and } m = m', \\ 0 & \text{otherwise,} \end{cases} \quad (7.4)$$

where the * superscript means complex conjugation. The formula for the coefficients $L_{l,m}$ given in Equation (7.3) depends on this property.[3]

Spherical harmonic basis functions. The spherical harmonic basis functions Y_l^m are defined for each $l = 0, 1, \ldots$ and for each $m = -l, -l+1, \ldots, l$ by

$$Y_l^m(\theta, \phi) = K_l^m P_l^{|m|}(\cos\theta)(\cos m\phi + i \sin m\phi), \qquad -l \le m \le l$$

---

[3] Functions on the sphere form a general vector space; i.e., each function on the sphere is a "vector" in this space. Integration of one function against another on the sphere is the "dot product" for this space. The SH basis functions are analogous to the unit direction vectors in 3D space. Equation (7.4) essentially states that the SH basis functions are mutually orthogonal (the dot product of two vectors is zero if, and only if, the vectors are orthogonal). The fact that the dot product of a basis function with itself is 1 means that the basis functions are "unit vectors."

		$Y_{2,-2} = \sqrt{\frac{15}{16\pi}} \sin^2\theta \cos 2\phi$
	$Y_{1,-1} = -\sqrt{\frac{3}{4\pi}} \sin\theta \cos\phi$	$Y_{2,-1} = -\sqrt{\frac{15}{4\pi}} \sin\theta \cos\theta \cos\phi$
$Y_{0,0} = \sqrt{\frac{1}{4\pi}}$	$Y_{1,0} = \sqrt{\frac{3}{4\pi}} \cos\theta$	$Y_{2,0} = \sqrt{\frac{5}{16\pi}} (3\cos^2\theta - 1)$
	$Y_{1,1} = -\sqrt{\frac{3}{4\pi}} \sin\theta \sin\phi$	$Y_{2,1} = -\sqrt{\frac{15}{4\pi}} \sin\theta \cos\theta \sin\phi$
		$Y_{2,2} = \sqrt{\frac{15}{16\pi}} \sin^2\theta \sin 2\phi$

Table 7.1   Real spherical harmonics for $l = 0, 1, 2$.

where K_l^m is a normalizing factor, typically defined by

$$K_k^m = \sqrt{\frac{(2l+1)(l-|m|)!}{4\pi(l+|m|)!}}$$

although there are other definitions.[4] The $P_l^m(x)$ are the *associated Legendre polynomials*. There is no direct formula for the coefficients of these polynomials. They can be defined in several ways, such as,

$$P_l^m(x) = \frac{(-1)^m}{2^l l!} (1-x^2)^{m/2} \frac{d^{l+m}}{dx^{l+m}} (x^2-1)^l \qquad -l \le m \le l;$$

however, the recurrence formula

$$P_{l+1}^m(x) = \frac{(2l+1)xP_l^m(x) - (l+m)P_{l-1}^m(x)}{(l-m+1)}$$

is often used in practice.

When applied to real-valued functions, a "real form" of the basis functions Y_l^m can be used instead. These *real spherical harmonics* are

$$Y_{l,m} = \begin{cases} \sqrt{2}\,\text{Re}(Y_l^m) & = \sqrt{2}K_l^m \cos(m\phi)P_l^m(\cos\theta), & m > 0, \\ \sqrt{2}\,\text{Im}(Y_l^m) & = \sqrt{2}K_l^m \sin(-m\phi)P_l^{-m}(\cos\theta), & m < 0, \\ Y_l^0 & = K_l^0 P_l^0(\cos\theta), & m = 0, \end{cases}$$

and are distinguished from the complex versions by putting both indices in the subscript. Table 7.1 contains the first few real SH basis functions.

Spherical harmonic expansions of environment maps. An expression of the form Equation (7.2) is known as a *spherical harmonic expansion*. In practice, the series is usually limited to a finite number of terms, in which case the

---

[4]Sometimes the 4π term is omitted, and an extra sign term $(-1)^m$ is sometimes added.

expansion becomes a linear combination of SH basis functions. One advantage is that mathematical operations such as differentiation and integration of the expanded function reduce to the operation on the SH basis functions, and because these are independent of the function L, the operation can be done without any knowledge of the function L. How many terms to include in an approximation depends on the particular situation. The index l is known as the *degree* of the basis function $Y_{l,m}$. There are $2l + 1$ SH basis functions of degree l. The degree also indicates the frequency of the basis functions: for a particular l, the basis functions oscillate l times around the sphere (loosely speaking). This formalizes the notion of "frequency" of detail in an environment map, as the minimum degree l required for an SH approximation to faithfully represent the map.

An expansion up to degree l simply cannot capture detail that changes faster than the oscillation of the basis functions. Terms up to twice the frequency of the pixel resolution have to be included to capture pixel-level detail in a general environment map. That is, about four times as many coefficients as there are pixels are needed to properly represent pixel-level detail. The primary use of SH expansions is to capture the general slowly varying behavior of the function. For an environment map, a low-frequency SH approximation is a kind of filtering of the map. The first basis function $Y_{0,0}$ is actually constant, so the corresponding coefficient $L_{0,0}$ is the average value of the map. The basis functions for $l = 1$ go through one period around the sphere, so they represent something like a local average per octant. The set of coefficients at degree l thus captures the general change at that frequency. A slowly changing approximation to an environment map can be useful in some situations, such as the approximation of diffuse lighting. The spherical harmonic expansion of an environment map is thus a kind of multiresolution prefiltering of the map.

At the other end of the spectrum, a discontinuity is, in some sense, an infinitely fast change. A finite SH expansion cannot capture a discontinuity—the infinite SH series is needed for this. Unfortunately a convergence problem occurs with a finite SH approximation at a discontinuity. At a "jump" discontinuity, a finite approximation exhibits an oscillation at the frequency of the maximum degree of the expansion. A useful analogy to this effect is a sudden strike of a bell: the result is a decaying audible vibration. Oscillatory artifacts in approximations in general are thus known as *ringing*. Spherical harmonic approximations often exhibit ringing; the severity of the effect depends on the application.

7.2.5 Irradiance Environment Map

Because increasing the degree of a spherical harmonic expansion results in a quadratic increase in the number of coefficients, the computational load gets heavy for high-degree expansions. On the other hand, limiting the number of terms also limits the accuracy of the expansion. Ramamoorthi and Hanrahan found one application in which a remarkably low-degree SH representation is sufficient. As they demonstrate in their paper "An Efficient Representation for Irradiance Environment Maps" nine SH terms are sufficient for a useful approximate the irradiance produced by an environment map [Ramamoorthi and Hanrahan 01a].

As described in Chapter 1, light incident on a Lambertian (diffusely reflecting) surface is reflected equally in all directions. Reflected radiance from a Lambertian surface is therefore dependent only on the surface irradiance—the direction of incident illumination is unimportant. (This property of diffuse reflection is often exploited in rendering, as discussed in Chapter 2.) Ramamoorthi and Hanrahan looked to spherical harmonics to approximate surface irradiance. The surface irradiance at a point is the integral of the cosine-weighted incident radiance. From Equation (1.6),

$$E(\vec{n}) = \int_{\Omega(\vec{n})} L(\vec{\omega}) \cos\theta \, d\vec{\omega} \qquad (7.5)$$

where $\vec{n}$ is the surface normal, and $\Omega(\vec{n})$ is the hemisphere above the surface; it is expressed as a function of $\vec{n}$ to emphasize that it depends on the surface normal.

Now consider the SH expansion of the incident radiance

$$L(\theta, \phi) = \sum_{l=0}^{\infty} \sum_{m=-l}^{+l} L_{l,m} Y_{l,m}(\theta, \phi).$$

If L comes from an environment map, then the coefficients $L_{l,m}$ can be precomputed. The goal is to find the coefficients $E_{l,m}$ for the expansion of the surface irradiance. This is complicated by the surface itself—radiance from below the surface does not contribute to the irradiance. Assuming for the moment that E and L are expanded in the same spherical coordinate system, Equation (7.5) can be extended to an integral over the entire sphere by adding a geometric "clipping" term $A(\theta) = \max(\cos\theta, 0)$:

$$E(\vec{n}) = \int_{\Omega_{4\pi}} L(\vec{\omega}) A(\theta) \, d\vec{\omega}. \qquad (7.6)$$

Substituting the SH expansions of L and A into Equation (7.6) produces an expression that can be integrated to obtain the SH coefficients $E_{l,m}$ for the irradiance.

Were it not for the orthonormal property of the SH coefficients, the nested double infinite summation that results from the substitution would be of little practical use. However, expanding the sums results in a collection of terms of the form

$$L_{l,m}A_{l',m'}Y_{l,m}(\theta,\phi)Y_{l',m'}(\theta,\phi),$$

which, by virtue of Equation (7.4), are zero unless $l = l'$ and $m = m'$. Furthermore, the nonzero terms reduce to just $L_{l,m}A_{l',m'}$. In other words, integration of a product of SH expansions amounts to summing the products of their coefficients. This property is used extensively in the precomputed radiance transfer methods described in Chapter 10. For the surface irradiance problem, the SH coefficients for the clipping term $A(\theta)$, which does not depend on ϕ, are only nonzero if $m = 0$. Consequently,

$$A(\theta) = \sum_{l=0}^{\infty} A_l Y_{l,m}(\theta,\phi)$$

($SHlm(\theta,\phi)$ does not actually depend on ϕ). The SH expansion of surface irradiance actually becomes

$$E(\theta,\phi) = \sum_{l=0}^{\infty} \sum_{m=-l}^{+l} \sqrt{\frac{4\pi}{2l+1}} A_l L_{l,m} Y_{l,m}(\theta,\phi). \qquad (7.7)$$

This is indeed a remarkable result, as it reduces integration of the environment map to a direct multiplication of SH coefficients.

The $L_{l,m}$ coefficients in Equation (7.7) can be precomputed for a particular environment map. The A_l coefficients depend only on l; Ramamoorthi and Hanrahan derived a direct formula for A_l in terms of l. Figure 7.10 shows a plot of the A_l as a function of l. Remarkably, the values drop to zero very quickly—only three terms are needed for a reasonable approximation. This means l can be limited to 2 in Equation (7.7), and the resulting irradiance approximation consists of only nine terms.

The derivation above assumes the irradiance is computed in the same global spherical coordinates (θ,ϕ), and the surface normal is implicitly assumed to have $\theta = 0$. In other words, the irradiance is computed for a specific surface, the "equator" plane of the global spherical coordinate system. Surfaces in the scene to be rendered have arbitrary surface normals. Suppose a scene surface has (unit) normal $\vec{n}$. The derivation above still applies, but in a local spherical coordinate system for which $\vec{n}$ is the "north pole." The clipping function $A(\theta)$ refers to this local coordinate system, so the values of A_l are unchanged. However, the radiance coefficients $L_{l,m}$ have to be recomputed for this local coordinate system, which would normally require filtering the environment map again. Doing this for each surface normal direction defeats the purpose.

Fortunately, there is a better way. The spherical coordinate systems each correspond to a rectangular coordinate system. This is illustrated in Figure 7.11, in

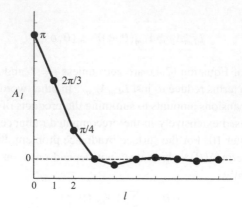

Figure 7.10   The SH coefficients for the clipping geometry term A drop to zero very quickly; the first three terms (through $l = 2$) provide a sufficient approximation. (Courtesy of Ravi Ramamoorthi.)

which the global coordinate axes are labeled x, y, and z; the local axes are labeled x', y', z' ($\vec{n}$ has the same direction as z'). The coordinate systems are related by a linear transformation. Each SH basis function $Y_{l,m}(\theta, \phi)$ is expressed in terms of sines and cosines of θ and ϕ, and can therefore be expressed as a polyno-

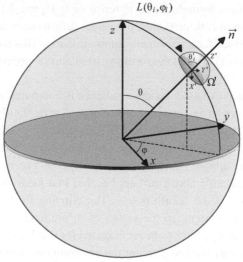

Figure 7.11   The SH approximation to the environment map radiance L is in a global coordinate system, with axes labeled x, y, and z. The irradiance needs a local coordinate system coincident with the surface normal $\vec{n}$. (After [Ramamoorthi and Hanrahan 01b].)

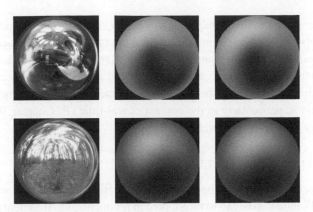

Figure 7.12   Irradiance environment maps. The left column shows the original HDR environment map rendered onto a sphere. The middle and right columns show the irradiance distribution, also rendered onto a sphere. The irradiance at each point is that produced on a surface that "looks up" at the corresponding point in the environment map at the left. The images in the middle column show the precisely computed irradiance; those at the left show the nine-term SH approximation. The differences are hardly noticeable. (From [Ramamoorthi and Hanrahan 01a] © 2001 ACM, Inc. Included here by permission.)

mial (of degree l) in three rectangular coordinates. Applying the linear coordinate transformation to this polynomial effects a change of coordinates. Because the degree l is limited to 2, the irradiance $E(\vec{n})$ can thus be expressed explicitly as a quadratic polynomial in x', y', and z' with coefficients in terms of the precomputed $L_{l,m}$ and A_l. Such polynomials are easily computed by hardware pixel shaders; in fact, $E(\vec{n})$ can be expressed as a 4×4 matrix multiplication—a highly optimized operation in graphics hardware.

Figure 7.12 illustrates results of Ramamoorthi and Hanrahan's method. The left column shows the original HDR environment maps used for the experiments. The middle column shows the irradiance computed by directly integrating the HDR environment map; the right column shows the result of the quadratic SH approximation. The irradiance $E(\vec{n})$ is a function of direction, so the results are displayed on a sphere to match the representation of the environment map. As noted in the paper, the average error is less than 1%, and the maximum error is under 5% for these images. (Under appropriate assumptions, the theoretical error is at most 9%.)

The primary goal of the method introduced in the "An Efficient Representation for Irradiance Environment Maps" paper was to make rendering using prefiltered environment maps more efficient, but the paper has had a wider impact. It had been known for many years that low frequency illumination, such as diffuse lighting, can be approximated using a small number of SH basis functions, but the actual number of SH basis functions needed to obtain a particular accuracy was never theoretically proven. Ramamoorthi and Hanrahan mathematically proved that SH basis functions up to the second degree can be used to accurately approximate irradiance. The paper influenced a renewed interest in the use of SH representations, particularly in the context of real-time GI. Chapter 10 describes some of this subsequent research.

7.2.6 Ambient Occlusion Maps

After the year 2000, rendering methods using HDR environment maps as the source of illumination began to be adopted in production environments, including movie production. However local effects including shadows and interreflections are difficult to incorporate into environment map rendering. At the time ray tracing was not used much in movie production, so the basic ray-tracing approach proposed by Debevec did not fit well into the movie production pipeline. Consequently, the notion of an *ambient occlusion map* was conceived to capture indirect illumination in environment map rendering [Landis 02].

Surface reflection in CG rendering has traditionally consisted of a specular component, a diffuse component, and a constant ambient term. The ambient term is an approximation to the general diffuse global illumination. It can be regarded as the average value of the environment map (perhaps after the areas correspond-

Figure 7.13   The ambient occlusion map used for rendering a B-25 Mitchell bomber model for the movie *Pearl Harbor*. The gray level represents the amount of ambient occlusion; the lightest areas see almost all the environment. (© 2001 Industrial Light & Magic. All Rights Reserved.)

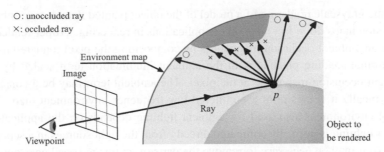

Figure 7.14   An ambient occlusion map is constructed at point p on a surface by casting rays, and counting rays that hit the environment map. (© Lucasfilm Ltd. Used with Permission.)

ing to the light sources have been removed). Conveniently, this is the first term $L_{0,0}$ in the SH expansion of the environment map. The ambient term has generally been treated as constant in the scene, but the idea of varying its value according to the local geometry has been used to increase realism. An *ambient occlusion map* is one way of doing this. This map specifies the attenuation of the ambient term at each surface point. This form of "attenuation" is a result of ambient light blockage by scene elements, and normally does not include light attenuation in the context of a participating medium.

Ambient occlusion maps are typically constructed for a single complex object, such as the airplane model in Figure 7.13. At each point on the surface, the value of the map records the cosine-weighted fraction of the environment map that is invisible from that point. More precisely, the value is the normalized irradiance at the surface point that would result from a constant environment map. This can be computed using a simplified form of Monte Carlo ray tracing that works by casting sample rays over the hemisphere of directions above the point (Figure 7.14). The summation is simpler than it is in ordinary MCRT. If a sample ray does not hit another point on the object, the direction of the ray represents an unoccluded path to the environment map. In this case the ray contribution is $\cos\theta$, where θ is the angle the ray makes with the surface normal. Otherwise the ray hits the object and therefore has no contribution. The *ambient occlusion* is the sum of all the ray contributions divided by the sum of $\cos\theta$ for all cast rays.

The image in Figure 7.13 illustrates the ambient occlusion map. Each point is shaded only by the ambient occlusion value, which is represented as a level of gray. Surface points that are nearly white have an ambient occlusion near 1, meaning that the point has a nearly unobstructed view of the environment. Darker points see less of the environment. Even though it is just an illustration of the ambient occlusion map, the image in Figure 7.13 might pass as an overexposed realistic grayscale rendering of a model of the object painted flat white. Ambient occlusion maps do in fact have other applications in rendering. Proper rendering using an ambient occlusion map works by compositing the pixel rendered using the normal shading pipeline with the ambient illumination term scaled by the ambient occlusion map value at the pixel. The ambient term may be a constant, but typically it comes from a prefiltered low frequency environment map. The actual environment map used for ambient lighting depends on the application. Direct lighting is normally computed directly from the light sources in a separate step, so it may be necessary to remove the parts of an image-based environment map that correspond to light sources before it is used in as an ambient illumination source.

The value obtained from an ambient environment map depends on the orientation of the surface. Looking up the illumination according to the surface normal does not work well, because it may not represent the primary direction of the incident illumination. For example, the lower part of the seat backs in the airplane cockpit in Figure 7.13 are illuminated mostly by light coming from the top windows, which comes at an angle well away from the surface normal. Another problem with getting the illumination from the direction of the surface normal is that a particularly bright spot in the environment can slip in and out of view of the surface normal. This can cause artifacts such as inappropriately hard shadows and generally incorrect illumination. The environment map lookup actually uses an average light direction vector instead of the surface normal. This vector is the average direction of all unoccluded rays obtained during the ray-casting computation in the construction of the map. In practice, the average light direction vector is stored as an offset of the surface normal, hence the name *bent normal* is sometimes used instead.[5] Figure 7.15 illustrates the bent normal.

Ambient occlusion maps were first used in the movie *Pearl Harbor* [Bay 01] (see Figure 7.13) and subsequently in *Jurassic Park 3*. ILM, which was in charge of the visual effects for these movies, previously used precomputed self occlusion by tracing rays in the direction of mirror reflection to test for occlusion. The results were used to compute specular reflection without tracing rays at render time. Ambient occlusion maps were created as a synthesis of this method and IBL environment maps. The greatest advantages of ambient occlusion maps lie in their ability to approximate visually important lighting without using ray tracing, and the compatibility with IBL in general. Their use quickly spread in major movie production after *Pearl Harbor*.

---

[5]An ambient occlusion map is typically stored as a four-channel (RGBA) texture map. The ambient occlusion value together with the three coordinates of the average light direction vector (bent normal) fill out a texel.

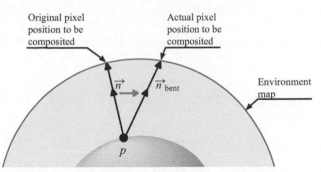

Figure 7.15   The ambient light at P comes from the ambient environment map, but from the direction of a "bent normal" that represents the average direction of incident ambient light. Using the bent normal instead of the surface normal also helps soften shadows.

The invention of ambient occlusion maps significantly increased the applicability of image-based lighting, and contributed to the widespread use of IBL in production rendering. It is not an exaggeration to say that IBL would not have become so popular in the entertainment field without ambient occlusion maps. Since 2008 however, rendering directly with ray tracing has become more prevalent in Hollywood movie production. This is a result of improvements in computing power and also a push for more realism. ILM developed a new physically based rendering pipeline for the film *Terminator Salvation* (2009), and since then, the use of ambient occlusion maps and some other IBL techniques have been replaced with more physically accurate ray-tracing methods. Nonetheless, ambient occlusion maps still have their place, as does image-based lighting in general. Both offer freedom and flexibility and apply to a wide variety of visual expressions. In tandem with the progress of GPU computation, it is expected that IBL will enter into a new stage in the entertainment industry.

Coalescence of Geometry-Based and Image-Based Approaches

The development of high dynamic range image-based methods has allowed photographs to be integrated into the traditional rendering pipeline as physically accurate sources of lighting. This has accelerated the coalescence of traditional rendering techniques (geometry-based approaches) and rendering techniques using photographs (image-based approaches).

One of the most significant aspects of this coalescence lies in the combination of geometry-based and image-based approaches to problems that are difficult or impossible to solve using either approach separately. Accurate rendering of real-world materials is a representative example. Geometry-based approaches render materials using mathematical approximations to the interaction of light with the environment. Highly accurate rendering, however, requires high computational cost. In contrast, rendering with photographic data captured from real objects can represent appearance characteristics that are extremely difficult to reproduce using only geometric models and mathematical simulation. A drawback, though, is that image-based approaches are often limited in terms of reproducing appearance under arbitrary lighting conditions and viewing directions. In many applications, such as movie production, limitations of this nature are not acceptable. An optimal combination of the two approaches is, of course, the ideal.

While geometry-based approaches are gradually moving from software to graphics hardware, which often allows for rendering at interactive rates, modern hardware is not advanced enough for all rendering tasks. Employing image-based methods is one way of speeding up software rendering; when these approaches can be modified to work in hardware, the speed improvement can be quite significant.

Geometry-based and image-based approaches have also coalesced for the task of interactive synthesis of realistic rendering of human beings, particularly of facial expressions.

8

Reconstruction of Reflectance

The appearance of an illuminated surface depends on how light is reflected from the surface. *Reflectance* in computer graphics sometimes has a specific meaning, such as the ratio of incident flux to radiance exitance, but the term is usually used in a broader sense to describe any model or function that describes how light is reflected. A general reflectance function quantifies the amount of incident light that is reflected from a surface. How light is reflected from a surface depends on the shape of the surface, the microscopic roughness of the surface, and the physical properties of the material at and below the surface itself. Various reflectance models take different kinds of surface properties into account. The simple bidirectional reflectance distribution function models (BRDFs) introduced in Chapter 1 really only consider surface roughness in a very approximate sense. The more complicated bidirectional subsurface scattering (BSSRDF) models described in Chapter 4 include transport in the material below the surface in the reflectance model. In this chapter, BRDF models, including physically based models, are examined in greater detail. Other ways of representing reflectance are considered, and methods for separating direct illumination from global (indirect) illumination are introduced. The chapter concludes with a particular problem of great recent interest in movie production: the modeling and rendering of hair.

8.1   BRDF Models

In Chapter 1, the *bidirectional reflectance distribution function* (BRDF) was introduced as one way of modeling surface reflection. A BRDF is a function that relates the amount of light incident on a surface from one direction to the amount of light reflected off the surface in another direction. A BRDF is thus a function of two directions; each direction can be represented by two spherical coordinates, so a BRDF is a function of four variables. If the reflectance varies across a surface, then two more variables are added, the parameters of the surface position. Although BRDFs do not include some physical phenomena, most notably, subsurface scattering, the reflectance character of many real-world surfaces can be approximated well by a specific BRDF.

The rendering equation described in Chapter 2 assumes surface reflection is governed entirely by the BRDF of the environment surfaces. Because the rendering equation was developed for photorealistic image synthesis, much research in the subject of global illumination has been devoted to better BRDF models. A number of notable models have been proposed since the 1980s. In this section, the history of the progress of BRDF models is explored, and some representative models are described. BRDF models for the simplest kinds of reflection are introduced first; ways of extending these to handle more complicated forms of reflection are then discussed. After that, more physically based models are introduced. Finally, the process of recovering BRDFs from photographs is investigated.

8.1.1   Modeling BRDFs

As described in Chapter 1, a BRDF is defined as the ratio of the reflected radiance in one direction to the irradiance of light incident from another direction. More precisely, for a particular direction $\vec{\omega}_i$ of incident light, and outgoing direction $\vec{\omega}_r$ of reflected light,

$$\text{BRDF}(\vec{\omega}_i, \vec{\omega}_r) = \frac{\text{radiance in } \vec{\omega}_r}{\text{irradiance from } \vec{\omega}_i}. \tag{8.1}$$

If, as in Figure 8.1, (θ_i, ϕ_i) are the spherical coordinates of the incident direction $\vec{\omega}_i$ in a local coordinate system, and (θ_r, ϕ_r) are that of the outgoing direction $\vec{\omega}_r$, the BRDF value is formally defined as

$$f_r(\theta_i, \phi_i, \theta_r, \phi_r) = \frac{L_r(\theta_r, \phi_r)}{L_i(\theta_i, \phi_i) \cos \theta_i \, d\vec{\omega}_i}, \tag{8.2}$$

where L_i and L_r are the incident and reflected radiance functions, respectively, and $d\vec{\omega}_i$ is a differential solid angle of the incident light. The angles θ_i and θ_r are known as *polar angles* or *colatitude* angles; ϕ_i and ϕ_r are *azimuthal angles* or *longitude* angles.

The definitions given in Equations (8.1) and (8.2) are abstract. In order to do any rendering with a BRDF, a concrete representation of the BRDF f_f is

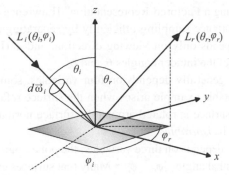

Figure 8.1   Coordinates for BRDFs.

needed. Such a function is called a *BRDF model*. As described in Chapter 1, a BRDF model must satisfy the conditions of bidirectionality and energy conservation. Bidirectionality requires that the value remains the same if the incident and reflected directions are interchanged. Energy conservation assures that no more light can be reflected out than comes in. The latter condition is surprisingly difficult to satisfy, and many models used in practice are not always energy conserving. There is also an implicit requirement that a BRDF be fairly simple (or at least easy to evaluate) because of the huge number of times the function is likely to be evaluated in rendering computations. Early BRDF models were designed with efficient rendering in mind, even though they were only used for direct lighting at the time. The ambient term was originally invented to approximate global illumination over the entire environment.

If a BRDF varies across a surface, it becomes a function of six variables as noted above. Although a few BRDF models do incorporate position dependence, for the most part they depend only on the two directions. Position-dependent reflection is typically handled with a surface texture map or something similar. Early BRDFs split the reflection into diffuse and specular parts. The diffuse part is independent of the outgoing direction, while the specular part measures the "spread" of light around the direction of mirror reflection. Recently, BRDF models have been proposed by representing the four-dimensional BRDF as a product of two-dimensional functions (akin to the separation of variables applied in the surface light field mapping of Chapter 5). In the paper "Interactive Rendering with Arbitrary BRDFs Using Separable Approximations," Jan Kautz and Michael D. McCool show how the 2D functions can be stored in texture maps and then combined at rendering time using operations available in graphics hardware [Kautz and McCool 99]. Jason Lawrence, Szymon Rusinkiewicz, and Ravi Ramamoorthi proposed a different kind of factorization in the paper "Efficient BRDF Importance Sampling Using a Factored Representation" [Lawrence et al. 04]. The method performs importance sampling efficiently by separating the BRDF into a 2D function that depends only on viewing direction, and a 1D function that depends on a function of the incident angles θ_i and ϕ_i.

Although a BRDF generally depends on four variables, some BRDFs contain redundancy. A notable example arises when the surface reflection does not change (much) as the surface is rotated around the surface normal. In this case, the reflection is said to be *isotropic*.[1]

An isotropic BRDF depends on three variables: the polar angles θ_i, θ_r and the difference of the azimuthal angles $|\phi_r - \phi_i|$.[2] Many real surfaces exhibit isotropic or nearly isotropic reflection. Plastic, polished metal, paper, human skin, and most painted surfaces are typical examples of isotropic surfaces. In contrast, some surface reflection is distinctly *anisotropic*. Surfaces that have an oriented surface roughness usually exhibit anisotropic reflection. Fine oriented scratches in brushed or milled metal cause reflection to vary with rotation: a brushed metal object looks entirely different, depending on whether the view direction aligns with the scratches or is perpendicular to them. Woven cloths also exhibit anisotropic reflection, as their appearance depends on the orientation of the woven threads.

8.1.2 Basic BRDF models

BRDFs for two special kinds of surface reflection, ideal diffuse reflection and ideal mirror reflection, were developed in Chapter 1 and are reviewed here. A Lambertian surface exhibits ideal diffuse reflection: incident illumination is reflected uniformly in all directions. The reflected radiance in any direction is proportional to the incident radiance, regardless of incident direction. The BRDF of a Lambertian surface is therefore a constant, given by

$$f_r = \frac{\rho_d(x)}{\pi},$$

where $\rho_d(x)$ is the albedo (Lambertian reflectance), the ratio of radiant exitance to the incident irradiance as defined in Equation (1.12). (The factor of $1/\pi$ comes in converting radiant exitance to radiance.) An ideal mirror surface reflects all the light coming from one direction to the direction of mirror reflection. The BRDF of a perfect mirror therefore acts as a Dirac δ, where the value of f_r is "infinity"

---

[1] The term *isotropic* is also used in the context of light scattering to mean that the scattering is uniform in all directions (see Chapter 3). The word is derived from the Greek *iso*, meaning "equal" and *tropos*, loosely meaning "turn." In general, "isotropic" refers to anything that stays constant under rotation.

[2] Recent research into isotropic BRDFs suggests that some can be adequately represented as a function of only *two* variables [Stark et al. 05, Edwards et al. 06].

when the incoming and outgoing directions are mirror reflections of each other, and zero elsewhere.

As described in Chapter 1, perfectly diffuse and perfect mirror surfaces do not really exist. Surfaces that are nearly Lambertian exhibit some directional dependence, just as some of the light reflected off a mirror deviates slightly from the ideal direction of reflection. For a general surface, the *specular direction* is defined as the direction that light would be reflected if the surface were a perfect mirror; in polar coordinates, the specular direction of (θ_i, ϕ_i) is simply $(\theta_i, \phi_i \pm \pi)$. The *specularity* of a surface depends on how broadly reflected light is distributed around the specular direction. At medium angles of incidence, the light reflected from typical specular surfaces is greatest at the specular direction, and falls off quickly as the outgoing vector moves away from the specular direction. The rate of this "falloff" is one measure of the specularity of a surface: shiny surfaces have a sharp falloff away from the specular direction; the falloff is more gradual for more dull surfaces.

The Phong model. Around 1973, Bui Tuong Phong proposed a simple model for specular falloff using an integer power of the cosine of the angle α that the outgoing direction vector makes with the specular direction [Phong 75]. The purpose was to add realism to renderings of 3D models. CG rendering was still in its infancy at the time. Scanline rendering of polygons was the predominant method (if not the only method) for rendering 3D surfaces. Henri Gouraud had developed the now ubiquitous technique of computing the lighting at the vertices of a polygon mesh, and continuously interpolating the computed vertex colors across a polygon during scanline rendering [Gouraud 71].[3] Phong extended this method to interpolate vertex normals, so that an approximate surface normal was available at each point on the polygon during scanline rendering. The object was usually assumed to be illuminated by a single directional light source. To render a point, the specular direction is computed according to the interpolated surface normal, and the specular deviation angle α between the reflected light direction and the direction to the eye is used to compute the specular falloff (Figure 8.2). The term *Phong shading* is often used to refer to the method of interpolating vertex normals as well as the cosine falloff model.

Figure 8.2 illustrates the angles used in Phong's reflection model. In the context of simple specular BRDF models, the incident direction is the direction of the

---

[3] At the time, frame buffers had yet to be realized; scanline rendering was usually done by rendering each individual pixel onto photosensitive film. A basic film recorder places a flat cathode ray tube (CRT)) screen against the film, and exposes a single pixel by illuminating the corresponding point on the screen for a fixed exposure time. Early rendering algorithms had to be sure not to record a pixel more than once, or it would appear twice as bright.

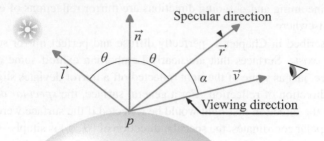

Figure 8.2   Geometry for the Phong model and general cosine lobe specular models. The specular
value depends on the angle α between the view direction and the reflected light direction.

light source, which is denoted by $\vec{l}$, the direction of specular reflection from the
light source is denoted by $\vec{r}$, and $\vec{v}$ denotes the viewing direction. The angle α is
the angle between $\vec{r}$ and $\vec{v}$. (In BRDF notation, $\vec{l}$ and $\vec{v}$ correspond to $\vec{\omega}_i$ and $\vec{\omega}_r$,
respectively.) Phong's original model included an ambient term and was not cast
in the BRDF framework. The actual Phong model is more properly called a "surface appearance model," or a "shading model." Expressed as a BRDF, Phong's
model is the sum of a diffuse and a specular term:

$$f_{\text{Phong}}(\vec{l},\vec{v}) = \frac{c_d}{\pi} + c_s (\cos\alpha)^n.$$

The specular reflection is thus controlled by two parameters: the *specular coefficient c_s* and the *specular exponent n*. In the original model, c_d/π and c_s had to
sum to less than one (minus the ambient term) so that the computed pixel value
stays in the proper range. As a general BRDF this is not necessary; however, the
value of the specular coefficient c_s has to be adjusted in order to conserve energy.
Applying the Phong model to a particular surface therefore amounts to selecting
the diffuse and specular coefficients, which is done for each color channel independently; normally the specular term has the same value for all the channels, so
the highlights appear white.

   One way of visualizing a BRDF model is to plot $f_r(\theta_i, \phi_i, \theta_r, \phi_r)$ as a function
of θ_r only, i.e., with the other three variables fixed. Normally such a diagram
has $\phi_r = \phi_i + \pi$ so that the incoming and outgoing directions are in the same
plane, which is known as the *plane of incidence*. Of course, this only shows a 1D
slice of the BRDF, but it is useful nonetheless to get an idea of the shape of the
function. Figure 8.3 illustrates such plots; Figure 8.3(a) shows the specular part
of the Phong model for various exponent values. The teardrop-shaped curves are
known as cosine *lobes*. Notice that the lobe becomes narrower as the exponent
n increases. As $n \to \infty$ the reflection approaches perfect mirror reflection. A

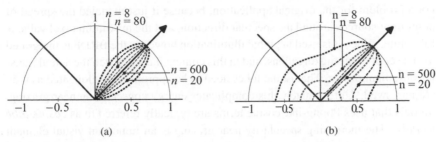

(a)   (b)

Figure 8.3   General cosine lobes. (a) The cosine lobe $\cos^n \alpha$ becomes more narrow as the exponent n
increases. (From [Lafortune et al. 97] © 1997 ACM, Inc. Included here by permission.)

larger n thus produces a narrower lobe and a more specular surface, so the specular
exponent n models how shiny the surface appears.[4] Figure 8.3(b) shows the effect
of adding the diffuse term.

Variants and improvements of the Phong model.   As BRDF, the Phong
model has some problems. One is that the lobes are symmetric about the specular
direction. This is reasonable near normal incidence, but the symmetric shape of
the lobe is unrealistic for more oblique incoming light. A particular interesting
area for BRDF models occurs as the angle of incidence approaches $90°$, i.e., when
the incident and reflected directions get close to the plane tangent to the surface.
This is called *grazing reflection*. Most real surfaces become more reflective at
grazing angles; in fact, some surfaces essentially become mirrors when viewed
from an angle nearly parallel to the surface (see Figure 8.4). The Phong model
fails to capture this behavior. Furthermore, the original Phong model fails to conserve energy; the Phong lobe needs to be increasingly scaled down toward grazing
in order to satisfy the energy conservation requirement. The scale of the lobes is
another issue with the Phong model. As the lobes get narrower, less light ends up
being reflected. Really the lobes need to get longer as they are narrowed. This was

Figure 8.4   Specularity often increases near grazing angles of reflection. (From [Lafortune et al. 97]
© 1997 ACM, Inc. Included here by permission.)

---

[4]The story is that after Phong got his model working, he and his colleagues at the University of
Utah went around the building pointing out the exponent of all the objects they could find.

not a problem for the original application, because it just modeled the spread of
point light sources around the specular direction, and the maximum pixel value is
full white. When it is used in global illumination however, the BRDF is integrated
over a set of outgoing directions, and in this context it must match the actual transfer of radiant power. That is, the lobes need to be appropriately elongated as they
are narrowed. Unfortunately this complicates energy conservation near grazing.
Models that uses Phong-like cosine terms are typically referred to as *cosine lobe
models*. The increasing specularity near grazing is an important visual element
that is missed when Phong models are applied to general surface reflection. Peter
Shirley, a pioneer in physically based rendering, had noted the importance (and
the absence) of an energy conserving Phong-like model that includes increasing
specularity at grazing. Michael Ashikhmin finally succeeded in constructing such
a model in 2000 [Ashikhmin and Shirley 00]. This model, which is now known
as the Ashikhmin-Shirley BRDF model, also includes an anisotropic extension.
(Phong's model was purely isotropic.)

One reason to base specular reflection on $\cos \alpha$ is that it can be computed
using simple vector operations:

$$\cos \alpha = 2(\vec{l} \cdot \vec{n})(\vec{v} \cdot \vec{n}) - (\vec{l} \cdot \vec{v}).$$

However, one disadvantage is that $\cos \alpha$ gets negative if the view direction and
the reflected direction are more than 90° apart. In practice, the cosine is clamped
to zero where it goes negative.

Another approach is to replace $\cos \alpha$ with $\cos \frac{\alpha}{2}$, as the value is never negative
for directions on the hemisphere. Jim Blinn proposed a different way of measur-
ing how far $\vec{v}$ is away from the specular direction using the angle between the
surface normal and the *half-vector* midway between the incoming and outgoing
directions. In symbols,

$$\vec{h} = \frac{\vec{l} + \vec{v}}{\|\vec{l} + \vec{v}\|}. \tag{8.3}$$

The half-vector $\vec{h}$ aligns with the surface normal if, and only if, the outgoing direction is the reflection of the incoming direction. Furthermore, $\vec{h}$ continuously
deviates from the normal as the outgoing direction deviates from the specular
direction. In Blinn's model, the cosine of the *half-angle* θ_h that the half-vector
$\vec{h}$ makes with the surface normal is used in place of the specular deviation angle α between the outgoing vector and the specular direction. As in the Phong
model, the specularity is controlled using the exponent m of $\cos^m \theta_h$. The value of
$\cos \theta_h$ is computed from the dot product of the half-vector and the surface normal:
$\cos \theta_h = \vec{h} \cdot \vec{n}$. Note that this depends on the normalization of $\vec{h}$ in Equation (8.3).

Near normal incidence, $\cos\theta_h \approx \cos\alpha$. That is, a half-angle lobe looks very much like a cosine lobe when the angles of incidence and reflection are small. However, $\cos\theta_h$ gets narrower in the azimuthal direction (i.e., as a function of ϕ) toward grazing in a way that better matches the apparent foreshortening of a surface viewed at an oblique angle. Another advantage is that $\cos\theta_h$ is always positive. A drawback, though, is that the computation of $\cos\theta_h$ requires normalizing the half-vector $\vec{h}$, and this results in an instability near grazing reflection, where $\vec{l}+\vec{v}$ can get arbitrarily small. The half-angle model is often used in place of the specular deviation angle α, because it does a better job simulating real surface reflectance. Many BRDF models that have what is described as a "Phong" term actually depend on $\cos\theta_h$ instead of $\cos\alpha$; the Ashikhmin-Shirley model is one example.[5]

Phong and the cosine lobe models, regardless of whether they use $\cos\alpha$ or $\cos\theta_h$, are really just heuristic approximations; they do not arise from any real physical properties of surfaces. Some observed reflection phenomena that have a known physical basis cannot be captured by Phong and Phong-like models. However, cosine lobes are suited to importance sampling because they are easily inverted. A number of extensions and modifications have been proposed over the years, some of which improve the physical basis of the model, others have concentrated on efficiency of computation. The Ashikhmin-Shirley model described above is an example of the former. An example of the latter is the Schlick model, which replaces the exponentiated cosine with rational functions that are faster to evaluate [Schlick 93]. Nevertheless, the basic Phong model remains in widespread use because it can successfully express realistic appearances using intuitive parameters. The notion of quantifying specularity in terms of a "specular exponent" has become permanently ingrained in at least two generations of CG professionals.

8.1.3   Off-Specular Reflection

The Phong model assumes that light is reflected the most strongly in the direction of the specular reflection. However, in the case of rough surfaces, the peak in the distribution of reflected light is not always in the specular direction. This is known as an *off-specular peak*, and is one example of the general phenomenon of *off-specular reflection*. Observed off-specular peaks become especially strong near grazing angles. Fresnel reflection is a primary cause of off-specular peaks

---

[5] Some authors described the Phong model with $\cos\alpha$ replaced by $\cos\theta_h$ as the "Blinn-Phong" model, but "Phong" is often applied to both. Blinn himself described the "Phong shading function" in terms of $\cos\theta_h$ as if it were part of Phong's original model; apparently he considered raising the cosine to an integer power the salient part of the Phong model.

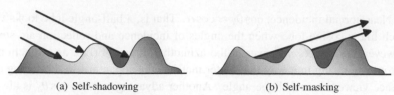

(a) Self-shadowing   (b) Self-masking

Figure 8.5   Local occlusion by nearby microgeometry elements has two forms: (a) self-shadowing is the blocking of incident light; (b) self-masking is the blocking of reflected light.

as well as general increasing specularity near grazing reflection. As described in Chapter 1, Fresnel reflection is derived by considering light as a wave instead of using the wave path approach of geometric optics. The term "Fresnel reflection" is often used more loosely to describe reflection effects dependent on the wave nature of light. In some contexts it is synonymous with increasing specularity near grazing.

Another factor regarding off-specular reflection is light occlusion due to roughness of the surface itself. Real surfaces that appear smooth to the unaided eye can be very rough at the microscopic level. For example, a typical billiard ball scaled to the size of the Earth would have mountains much higher than Mount Everst. The microscopic topography—the hills and valleys and crags and tors—are part of the surface *microgeometry*. Occlusion due to microgeometry can be split into two forms: *self-shadowing* stops light from hitting a particular microscopic surface point; *self-masking* blocks light reflected from a surface point (Figure 8.5). Local occlusion in general is most prominent near grazing reflection. Fresnel reflectance increases the amount of reflected light near grazing, while local occlusion reduces it. In this sense the effects partially cancel each other out; however the effect of Fresnel reflection dominates very close to grazing directions.

8.1.4 Microfacet-Based BRDF Models

Surface reflection has been studied in the field of optics since long before the invention of the digital computer. As early as 1924, physicists were modeling light reflection by treating the surface as if it were made of microscopic flat mirror-like surfaces, now known as *microfacets*. Much of this work, however, was limited to the plane of incidence. In 1967, Kenneth E. Torrance and E. M. Sparrow published a microfacet-based surface reflection model that better matched observed off-specular peaks [Torrance and Sparrow 67]. The model, now known as the Torrance-Sparrow reflectance model was actually developed in the context of modeling heat transfer, but it is a genuine BRDF model and is therefore applicable to rendering.

Figure 8.6   A surface can be approximated with very small facets called *microfacets*.

A microfacet model of a surface regards the microgeometry as a collection of mirror polygons (Figure 8.6). Because the facets are perfect mirrors, the only facets that reflect light (directly) from a particular incoming direction $\vec{l}$ to another outgoing direction $\vec{v}$ are those having normals that match the direction of the half-vector of the given directions $\vec{l}$ and $\vec{v}$ (Figure 8.7). The microfacets are not explicitly modeled; rather, the microgeometry is described in terms of the distribution of the microfacet surface normals. If the microfacets were explicitly modeled, there would be a finite number of microfacet directions and the probability of there being a microfacet exactly aligned to a particular half-vector would therefore be zero. The distribution is assumed to be continuous.

The BRDF value for a pair of directions $\vec{l}$ and $\vec{v}$ depends on the percentage of facets whose normals correspond to the half-vector. This is given by the distribution of microfacet surface normal directions. The distribution is governed by a function $D(\vec{h})$, which provides the fraction of all microfacets that align with the vector $\vec{h}$. The Torrance-Sparrow model assumes a Gaussian distribution based on the angle α between the vector $\vec{h}$ and the surface normal (Figure 8.7),

$$D(\theta_h) = b\,e^{-c^2\theta_h^2}.$$

Figure 8.8 shows a plot of a Gaussian distribution. The maximum value is at $\theta_h = 0$. A geometric interpretation is that microfacets are most likely to be nearly parallel to the macroscopic surface normal.

Because each microfacet is assumed to be a perfect mirror, Fresnel reflection applies. If L_i is radiance coming from the direction that makes an angle θ_i with

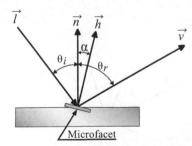

Figure 8.7   Reflection from a microfacet depends on the angle its surface normal makes with the macroscopic surface normal.

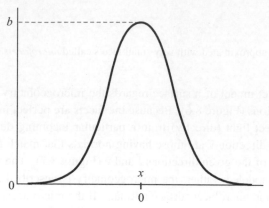

Figure 8.8   A Gaussian function $e^{-(cx)^2}$; the parameter c controls the width of the curve.

the microfacet normal, the reflected radiance from a microfacet is given by

$$\frac{L_i F(\theta_i)}{\pi \cos \theta_i}.$$

The formula for the Fresnel reflectance F is rather complicated. The original Torrance-Sparrow model uses the proper formula, but a simple approximation suffices, such as the approximation given by Christophe Schlick [Schlick 93]:

$$F(\theta) \approx F_0 + (1 - F_0)(1 - \cos \theta)^5.$$

Here F_0 is the Fresnel reflection at normal incidence ($\theta = 0$). (See Figure 8.9.) Fresnel reflection results in polarized light. Schlick's approximation does not include the effects of polarization, but polarized light is seldom considered in computer graphics. (Actually, the error incurred by ignoring polarization is greater than the error of Schlick's approximation.) The Fresnel term is wavelength depen-

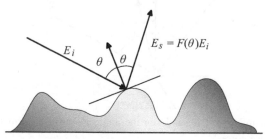

Figure 8.9   Fresnel reflection in the microgeometry.

dent, which means it has to be computed separately for different color channels. As noted in Chapter 1, materials that exhibit specular reflection can be broadly classified into either conductors (metals) or dielectrics. Generally, Fresnel reflection captures the intrinsic color of metals but not that of dielectrics.

The next thing to consider is self-occlusion. In terms of microfacets, self-occlusion can be more precisely defined: self-shadowing occurs when light that would be incident on one facet is blocked by another facet; self-masking occurs when light reflected off a facet is blocked by another facet (Figure 8.5). The Torrance-Sparrow model handles self-occlusion with a *geometric attenuation factor* denoted by G. This factor accounts for light not reaching the microfacet due to self-shadowing, and light not reflected from the facet due to self-masking. Blinn proposed the formula

$$G = \min \left(1, \frac{2(\vec{n} \cdot \vec{h})(\vec{n} \cdot \vec{v})}{(\vec{v} \cdot \vec{h})}, \frac{2(\vec{n} \cdot \vec{h})(\vec{n} \cdot \vec{l})}{(\vec{v} \cdot \vec{h})} \right) \tag{8.4}$$

for the geometric attenuation term in the paper "Models of Light Reflection for Computer Synthesized Pictures," which introduced microfacet models into computer graphics [Blinn 77]. The second term in Equation (8.4) is the effect of self-shadowing; the third is that of self-masking.

The full Torrance-Sparrow BRDF model is constructed from the product of the three effects described so far: the fraction $D(\theta_h)$ of microfacets aligned to the half-vector, the Fresnel reflectance $F(\theta_i)$, and the geometric attenuation factor G:

$$f_r = \frac{DGF}{\pi \cos \theta_i \cos \theta_r}$$

where θ_i and θ_r are measured from the microfacet normal.

While studying physically based surface reflection as a graduate student at Cornell University, Rob Cook came across the paper describing the Torrance-Sparrow model and found that Ken Torrance was actually working in the Mechanical Engineering department at Cornell at the time. Cook met with Torrance, and eventually developed an improved version of the Torrance-Sparrow model designed for realistic rendering. The primary modification was to replace the Gaussian microfacet distribution with a distribution based on the *Beckman function*,

$$D = \frac{e^{-[(\tan \beta)/m]^2}}{4m^2 \cos^4 \beta},$$

where β is the angle between the normal of a microfacet and the surface normal, and m is a parameter for the roughness of the surface. The model, which is now known as the Cook-Torrance BRDF model, was published in 1982 [Cook and Torrance 82] and found widespread use in the next decades.[6]

A later extension to the microfacet model, developed by Xiao D. He, Torrance, François X. Sillion, and Donald P. Greenberg, includes a directionally diffuse reflection term (the original model assumed a single diffuse term for the whole surface) and also handles wavelength-dependent local occlusion. This model, which is known as the He BRDF model or the He-Torrance BRDF model is considered one of the most complete analytical BRDF models for specular reflection developed to date. Other notable microfacet-based models are the Oren-Nayar BRDF model developed by Michael Oren and Shree Nayar [Oren and Nayar 94], which uses diffuse microfacets, and a very general model microfacet simulation developed by Michael Ashikhmin, Simon Premože, and Peter Shirley [Ashikhmin et al. 00].

8.1.5   Measured Data and BRDF Models

The Phong model has a simple formulation and is easy to apply, but it has has some serious limitations. On the other hand, microfacet-based models are not so practical. For example, the He-Torrance model is costly to evaluate, and the parameters are difficult to measure directly. Most other microfacet-based models have similar issues. The model proposed in the paper "Measuring and Modeling Anisotropic Reflection" by Greg Ward sought to balance physical accuracy and efficient, intuitive implementation [Ward 92]. This model is now known as the Ward BRDF model, and has the advantage of being based on parameters that can be determined by photographing real surfaces. Ward's model is empirical; the measure of its utility comes in the ability to reproduce measured reflectance. Its simplicity is also useful in Monte Carlo sampling. Moreover, the Ward model also handles anisotropic reflection.

Surface reflectance is normally done by directing a collimated thin beam of light onto a sample of the surface and recording the reflected radiance in another direction using a calibrated sensor. Varying the position of the light source and the position of the sensor captures a set of BRDF values. Of course, thousands of measurements may be necessary to properly represent the BRDF of a particular sample. A robotic device known as a *gonioreflectometer* automates the process. To fit the parameters to the Ward model, a real surface is photographed with sev-

---

[6]The work with Cook was the beginning of a long-term collaboration between Ken Torrance and the Program of Computer Graphics at Cornell University that lasted nearly 30 years. Torrance had a significant impact on early research into physically based rendering, much of which took place at Cornell in the 1980s. Many Cornell alumni and others who worked there credit him as a major influence in their own careers. Sadly, Ken died at the age of 69 while this book was in production. He will be greatly missed.

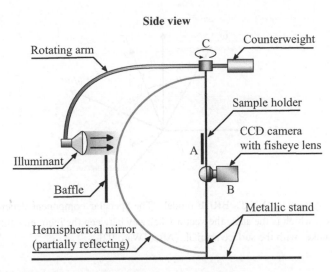

Side view

Rotating arm

Counterweight

C

Sample holder

CCD camera
with fisheye lens

Illuminant

A

Baffle

B

Metallic stand

Hemispherical mirror
(partially reflecting)

Figure 8.10   Greg Ward's apparatus for image-based measurement of BRDFs. (After [Ward 92].)

eral pairs of light directions and viewing directions. The photographs are digitized and pixel values are extracted to approximate the BRDF for the incoming and outgoing directions. The corresponding parameters to the model are obtained by minimizing the difference between the measured BRDF values and the values calculated using a simplified version of the model.

Ward also created a device for BRDF measurement. A surface sample is placed inside a partially reflecting hemispherical mirror, and a camera records light reflected from the object using a fisheye-lens camera that has a hemispherical field of view. The sample is illuminated from outside the hemispherical mirror, which has the benefit of reducing stray light inside the hemisphere. A rotating robotic arm controls the position of the light, and therefore the direction of the illumination; this is the only moving part of the device. (Figure 8.10). Light from the illumination source is reflected by the sample across the entire hemisphere. A single photograph of inside of the hemisphere captures the light reflected in nearly every direction. An entire "slice" of the BRDF is thus recorded in a single image. Varying the position of the light source captures the BRDF data for a representative collection of incident light directions. To calibrate the device, a set of photographs is taken with the sample replaced by a diffuse surface of known reflectance. The ratio of the values of corresponding pixels in the photograph of the sample with the reference photograph provides the actual BRDF value. This process is much more efficient than the typical process of measuring the reflectance value for each pair of directions separately, although it is generally

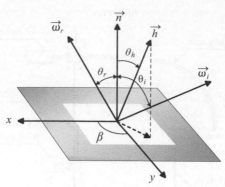

Figure 8.11   Coordinate system for Ward's BRDF model. The specular component depends on the half-angle θ_h, which is the angle the vector $\vec{h}$ halfway between the incoming and outgoing directions makes with the surface normal. (After [Ward 92].)

not as accurate. Also, the dynamic range of the measured BRDF is limited by the camera.

In the Ward model, the Fresnel reflectance and local occlusion terms are replaced with a single Gaussian function. The primary reason for this, according to Ward himself, is that the measurement apparatus was not capable of capturing measurements at angles low enough to accurately record these phenomena. Omitting these effects undermines the physical basis of the model; however, for many surfaces the increased reflectance due to Fresnel reflection is partially counteracted by the effects of self-occlusion. In any case, it makes the model simpler. The Ward model represents the ratio of reflected light by a Gaussian function of the tangent of the half-angle θ between the surface normal and the half-vector $\vec{h}$ (Figure 8.11):

$$\frac{1}{\sqrt{\cos \theta_i \cos \theta_r}} \frac{e^{-\tan^2 \theta_h / k^2}}{4\pi k^2}. \tag{8.5}$$

The coefficient k, which represents the falloff rate of the Gaussian function (the standard deviation, in statistics parlance), corresponds to the roughness of the surface and can be fit to the measured data (Figure 8.12).[7]

Equation (8.5) models isotropic reflection: rotating the incoming and outgoing vectors about the surface normal does not change BRDF value. In fact, the model depends only on the angle θ_h the half-vector makes with the surface normal. Ward extended the model to anisotropic reflection by adding a dependence on the angle β the half-vector makes with the coordinate axes (Figure 8.11). The anisotropic

---

[7] Arne Dür showed that omitting the square root in in Equation 8.5 provides a better normalization.

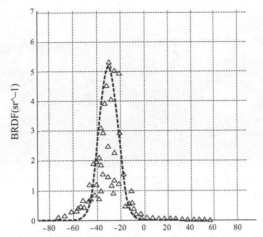

Figure 8.12   Fitting measured data to the Ward model. (From [Ward 92] © 1992 ACM, Inc. Included
here by permission.)

version of the model is given by

$$\frac{1}{\sqrt{\cos\theta_i \cos\theta_r}} \frac{\exp(-\tan^2\alpha(\cos^2\beta/k_x^2 + \sin^2\beta/k_y^2))}{4\pi k_x k_y}. \qquad (8.6)$$

The parameters k_x and k_y control the reflection character; they represent the falloff
in the x and y directions, respectively, and can be fit to the data captured by Ward's
measurement system. Note that when $k_x = k_y$, Equation (8.6) reduces to Equation (8.5). Applying an anisotropic reflection model requires choosing a coordinate system on the surface. The x-axis is typically aligned with the orientation of
the surface microgeometry, e.g., the scratch directions of brushed or milled metal,
or the grain direction in wood.

Figure 8.13 shows the results using the Ward model. The left image is the
captured photograph, the middle is the rendered result using the isotropic Ward
model, and the right is that using the anisotropic Ward model.

Ward's image-based approach to measuring BRDFs has some significant advantages over conventional gonioreflectometry measurement. Because each individual pixel in a captured image represents a measurement, a single image captures the equivalent of thousands (or millions) of measurements for a particular
light direction. Not only is this much less time intensive than acquiring each measurement directly, it results in a much denser sampling in the outgoing directions
than is practical from individual measurements. A set of measurements recorded
by a gonioreflectometer is usually too sparse for direct rendering, so some form
of interpolation between samples is needed. This is a difficult 4D "scattered data"

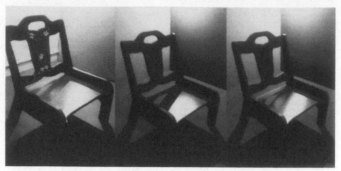

Figure 8.13   Images rendered using the Ward model. (From [Ward 92] © 1992 ACM, Inc. Included
here by permission.)

interpolation problem. The dense sampling of Ward's image-based measurement
system eliminates the need for interpolation in the outgoing direction, and greatly
simplifies it over incoming directions. A drawback, however, is that the measurement precision is limited by the dynamic range of the camera, and even further
by the fact that the measured values come from dividing by the reflectance of the
reference sample, which is measured separately. Spectral sensitivity is also an
issue, which in Ward's arrangement is limited to the three-channel output of the
digitized camera image. In contrast, sensors are available that have a much higher
dynamic range and greater spectral sensitivity.

The original goal of the work described in Ward's paper "Measuring and Modeling Anisotropic Reflection" was the construction of the measurement system.
However, he felt that a paper describing the measurement method alone would be
less useful without an accompanying BRDF model, so he formulated the model
a few weeks before the submission deadline. Ironically, the greatest impact of
the paper turned out to be the BRDF model rather than the measurement system. Ward himself never imagined the model would end up in such widespread
use.

8.1.6   Generalization of BRDF Models

Ward's BRDF model was unusual in that it was developed for the specific purpose
of fitting measured reflection; most other models were based either on a simple
heuristic like the Phong model, or derived from assumptions about the specific
surface, i.e., microfacet models. In the 1990s, new developments for accurately
measuring the BRDFs of real surfaces opened up possibilities for a different approach. Fitting parametric representations to the measured data made it possible
to represent various types of reflection using the same basic expressions.

The model proposed in the paper "Non-Linear Approximation of Reflectance Functions" by Eric P. F. Lafortune, Sing-Choong Foo, Kenneth E. Torrance, and Donald P. Greenberg is an example of this approach [Lafortune et al. 97]. This model, which has come to be known as the *Lafortune BRDF model*, combines multiple cosine lobes with different directions, sizes, and widths. It handles many characteristics of reflection.

A Lafortune BRDF consists of a sum of generalized cosine lobes, each of which is given by the matrix expression

$$S(\vec{\omega}_i, \vec{\omega}_r) = \left(\begin{bmatrix} \omega_{rx} \\ \omega_{ry} \\ \omega_{rz} \end{bmatrix}^T \begin{bmatrix} C_x & & \\ & C_y & \\ & & C_z \end{bmatrix} \begin{bmatrix} \omega_{ix} \\ \omega_{iy} \\ \omega_{iz} \end{bmatrix} \right)^n. \tag{8.7}$$

The diagonal elements C_x, C_y, and C_z are parameters that control the shape of the lobe; the value of the exponent n controls the specularity, just as in the Phong model. The actual Lafortune BRDF model uses a weighted sum of lobes having the form of Equation (8.7), with varying weights and exponent.

If C denotes the diagonal matrix, Equation (8.7) can be expressed as

$$S(\vec{\omega}_i, \vec{\omega}_r) = \vec{\omega}_i^T C \vec{\omega}_r = (C^T \vec{\omega}_i) \cdot \vec{\omega}_r,$$

(C is symmetric, so $C^T = C$). In other words, a Lafortune lobe can be expressed as the dot product of the incoming direction $\vec{\omega}_i$, transformed by C, with the outgoing vector $\vec{\omega}_r$. If C is the matrix that effects a reflection in the surface normal, then $(C^T \vec{\omega}_i)$ is the specular direction, and therefore $(C^T \vec{\omega}_i) \cdot \vec{\omega}_r = \cos \alpha$ as in the Phong model. In this sense, a Lafortune lobe is a proper generalization of a Phong lobe (Figure 8.14): in a manner of speaking, the diagonal elements C_x, C_y, and C_z specify a more general specular direction. With $C_x = C_y = -1$ and $C_z = 1$, the

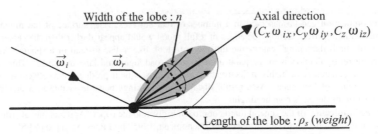

Figure 8.14   A specular lobe in the Lafortune. The lobe is defined in terms of the angle that the outgoing direction $\vec{\omega}_r$ makes with a general linear transformation of the incoming direction $\vec{\omega}_i$. A Phong lobe is a Lafortune lobe where the transformation is just the reflection in the surface normal.

matrix C represents the ordinary specular reflection. With $C_x = C_y = C_z = 1$, C becomes the identity matrix and the effective specular direction is just the incoming direction $\vec{\omega}_i$. In this case, the lobe models *retroreflection*, which is a property of some surfaces that reflect a significant amount of light back into the direction from which it came.[8] The values of C_x, C_y, and C_z cannot be arbitrarily chosen. For example, an isotropic surface requires that $C_x = C_y$. Lafortune and his coauthors suggested replacing the diagonal matrix with a more general 3×3 matrix to model anisotropic reflection.[9]

Figure 8.15(a) shows a series of images rendered from different viewpoints using the traditional cosine lobe model. In these images, the specular reflection on the surface of the desk disappears as the viewing direction gets more parallel to the surface. In reality, the opposite effect is observed: surfaces usually look more reflective at grazing angles. Figure 8.15(b) shows the same series rendered using the Lafortune model; the reflection toward grazing is more plausible.

The Lafortune BRDF model has been successful in representing many common types of reflection, including directionally diffuse reflection, general off-specular reflection, and retroreflection. Because the isotropic model specifies each lobe as a function of four parameters: C_x, C_y, C_z, and the exponent n; only three parameters are needed for an isotropic lobe, as $C_x = C_y$. The authors found that fitting these parameters to measured BRDF data obtained at the Cornell Light Measurement Laboratory resulted in a good match. One advantage of the multilobe nature of the Lafortune model is that more nodes can be added to better approximate the underlying data.[10] The simplicity of the Lafortune model makes it suitable for hardware rendering. The paper "Efficient Rendering of Spatial bidirectional Reflectance Distribution Functions" by David K. Mcallister, Anselmo Lastra, and Wolfgang Heidrich [Mcallister et al. 02] presents a GPU-based technique that stores the diagonal matrix elements and the exponent of each Lafortune lobe in the RGBA channels of a texture map texel. The textures then represent

---

[8]Retroreflection can be observed in a number of real surfaces. The surface of the moon is an example; without retroreflection, the edges of a full moon would appear darker than the center. This absence of "limb darkening" causes the full moon to look like a disc instead of a sphere. Another example of retroreflection is in the paint used in some road signs and lane markings. This special paint is impregnated with highly reflective tiny glass beads, which produce retroreflection even at very low angles of incidence. As a result, distant road markings become visible to a driver from retroreflection of the car's own headlights.

[9]Some justification of the general matrix approach is given in the paper "Applications of Irradiance Tensors to the Simulation of Non-Lambertian Phenomena, 1995" by James Arvo [Arvo 95].

[10]The simplicity of the Lafortune model is also a drawback: the small number of parameters limits the flexibility of the model. Subsequent research has shown that although the model fits measured data well in the plane of incidence, the lobes do not get sufficiently narrow in the azimuthal direction near grazing reflection [Ngan et al. 04, Stark et al. 05]. As a result, no sum of Lafortune lobes can accurately represent certain types of reflection.

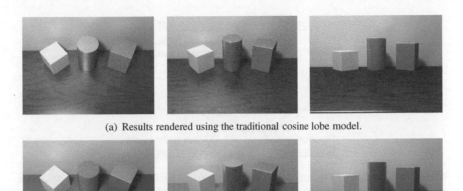

(a) Results rendered using the traditional cosine lobe model.

(b) Results rendered using the Lafortune BRDF.

Figure 8.15   Renderings of a simple scene viewed from increasing angles. (a) The cosine lobe model
fails to capture the expected increasing specularity near grazing reflection. (b) The Lafortune model is an improvement. (From [Lafortune et al. 97] © 1997 ACM, Inc. Included
here by permission.)

the variation of reflectance across a surface. The idea to render the surface with
varying reflectance can also be extended to "bidirectional texture map" rendering
as introduced in the next chapter.

8.1.7   Image-Based BRDFs

Advances in measurement devices.   Ward's image-based BRDF measurement method does not measure the BRDF values directly; the true BRDF values
are derived by comparing the image pixels with the those of a reference material.
The dynamic range of the camera and the relative measure of the reference material limit the range of measurements. This is a serious issue, because the range of
BRDF values can be very large, especially for specular surfaces. The emergence
of HDR imaging opened the door on better image-based measurement. One development was described in the paper "Image-Based Bidirectional Reflectance Distribution Function Measurement" by Stephen R. Marschner, Stephen H. Westin,
Eric P. F. Lafortune, and Kenneth E. Torrance [Marschner et al. 00]. Their approach extracts BRDF values from captured HDR images of surface samples.

Unlike earlier measurement systems, which use a flat surface sample, Marschner's method attaches a sample of the surface to be measured onto a curved
surface, such as a cylinder or sphere. The reflection property of the material is

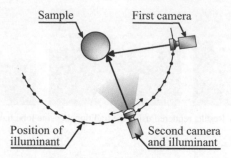

Figure 8.16   Marschner's apparatus for image-based measurement of BRDFs. The sample is placed on
the sphere at the center. The first camera records the reflectance, the second camera records
images used for reconstructing the positioning. (After [Marschner et al. 00].)

assumed to be uniform across the surface, a typical assumption in BRDF measurement. The advantage of the curved sample is that from a fixed viewpoint with
a fixed illumination direction, the incoming and outgoing directions vary across
the surface with the surface normal. Consequently, a single HDR image can capture BRDF measurements over a range of incoming and outgoing directions.

The measurement apparatus is illustrated in Figure 8.16. It consists of a fixed
primary camera, which records the HDR images, and a light source (illuminant)
that is attached to a rotating arm. The center of rotation of the arm is the center of
the sample, so the light source stays a fixed distance from the sample. A second
camera is included that moves with the light source. This second camera could be
used to measure retroreflection from the sample, but its purpose is to record the
position of the illuminant. As described in Chapter 5, a 3D model of an object
can be recovered using two photographs of the object taken from different viewpoints. On the other hand, if 3D coordinates of points on the object are known,
the positional relationship of the two viewpoints can be reconstructed from the
two photographs. In the BRDF measurement system, the primary camera is fixed.
The position of the light source is determined by the position of the second camera, which is determined by stereo reconstruction described in Chapter 5. The
background environment contains visible markers that serve as fiducial points in
an image captured by the second camera; the camera position can be recovered
from the locations of these markers in the image. Because the markers are designed for easy recognition by image processing software, the position recovery
is automatic. All that is needed to reconstruct the BRDF measurements is the
collection of images captured by both cameras.

Tracking the position of the light source using fiducial markers makes the
measurement process simpler. Without it, the position of the light source would
either have to be carefully controlled mechanically, as is done by conventional

gonioreflectometers, or separately recorded during image acquisition. It also allows more freedom of movement of the light source and makes the process more stable, as the camera positioning equipment need not be separately calibrated.

At each illuminant position, a sequence of photographs of varying exposure is captured by the primary camera, from which the HDR radiance map is reconstructed (see Chapter 5). Each pixel then contains the reflected radiance at a particular point on the sample. The corresponding direction with respect to the normal on the sample surface is determined by the known shape of the sample and the position of the pixel. Conceptually this amounts to tracing a hypothetical ray from the camera viewpoint through the pixel on a virtual image plane to the sphere on which the sample is affixed. The BRDF value is the ratio of the outgoing radiance to the irradiance of the incident illumination. A conventional image suffices for positioning; there is no need for an HDR image at the second camera. Like Ward's method, each pixel in the primary image serves as a sample of the BRDF, so the method provides a very dense sampling of the BRDF values in the outgoing direction.

BRDF models created with novel ideas. The value of a BRDF for an arbitrary pair of directions can be approximated by interpolating the measured BRDF data. As noted earlier, this is a difficult interpolation problem. Some mathematically sound interpolation methods result in unacceptable artifacts in the rendered images. Another problem is that measurement noise is propagated by interpolation. These issues have been one motivation for developing better BRDF models that can accurately represent observed BRDFs by smoothing out measured data. A paper entitled "A Data-Driven Reflectance Model" by Wojciech Matusik, Hanspeter Pfister, Matthew Brand, and Leonard McMillan [Matusik et al. 03] introduced a method of constructing general BRDF models directly from measured data. As in much of computer graphics, the "visual accuracy" is more important than numeric accuracy: representing the visually significant elements of a BRDF is more important than maintaining physically accurate values of the BRDF. The paper describes a method for extracting physically significant data from a general set of measured data in order to develop representative "basis" BRDFs. Arbitrary BRDFs can then be represented by a weighted sum of these basis functions. Since the basis functions are physically significant, the interpolation is more physically meaningful and hopefully less prone to noise.

To acquire measurements, the authors used a device similar to the one developed by Steve Marschner and his colleagues described above. Conventional BRDF measurements sample both the incoming angles in polar coordinates. A problem with this approach is that it is difficult to concentrate samples where they are important, such as at specular reflection. The method in the pa-

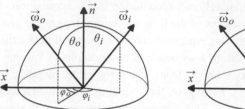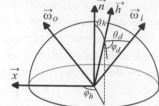

Figure 8.17   Parameterization used in image-based BRDFs. (From [Matusik et al. 03] © 2003 ACM, Inc. Included here by permission.)

per employs an alternative parameterization proposed by Szymon Rusinkiewicz [Rusinkiewicz 98] (Figure 8.17). This parameterization uses the half-angle θ_h, and measures the deviation of $\vec{\omega}_i$ from the half-vector with two parameters θ_d and ϕ_d. Specular reflection normally occurs when the half-angle is nearly zero, so the samples can be concentrated near $\theta_h = 0$. Sample points are taken at $1°$ intervals over θ_d and ϕ_d, and 90 nonuniformly spaced values of the half-angle θ_h most densely spaced near $\theta_h = 0$. The authors acquired BRDF measurements for a wide variety of surfaces. They started with 130 surface samples, but they ended up using only 103 after they excluded those that exhibited anisotropy or a notable positional dependence.

The approach taken in the paper was to regard all isotropic BRDFs as an abstract space; elements of this space are individual BRDFs. The idea was to find a general basis for this space. Because so many BRDF models depend on just a few parameters, it seemed reasonable to conclude that all observable BRDFs were part of a small subset of the full hypothetical BRDF space. A BRDF is represented as a vector of sample values, or the logarithm of the values. In the particular representation they employed, each sample has three color channels, so the vector representing a particular BRDF has $3 \times 90 \times 90 \times 360$ coordinates. The natural basis for this vector space has as many basis elements, so it is not very useful for a BRDF representation. A more representative basis was needed.

The *response matrix* is formed by placing the 103 measurement vectors in the rows of a matrix (Figure 8.18). The rows of the response matrix represent the variation in materials; the columns represent variation in the incoming and outgoing directions. This response matrix thus contains the reflectance for the discrete set of 103 samples. There are several techniques for approximating a response matrix as a linear combination of basis vectors. One such method known as *principal component analysis* (PCA) uses vectors of an associated matrix for the basis elements. PCA uses eigenvector analysis. Eigenvectors correspond to a set of representative incoming/outgoing direction pairs, and the most important

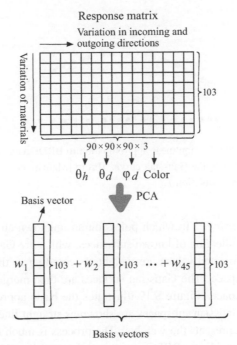

Figure 8.18   An approximate basis of the BRDF space is constructed using principal component analysis (PCA) to reduce the basis size from 103 to 45.

eigenvectors correspond to the largest eigenvalues. The authors found that 45 basis vectors (i.e., representative directions) were needed to accurately represent all their measurements (Figure 8.18).

The PCA approximation resulting in 45 basis functions is certainly useful, as it reduces the millions of samples to only 45 coefficients. However, that is a lot of parameters for a BRDF model, and each evaluation involves computing a linear combination of 45 vectors, each of which has 103 elements. Doing this for each BRDF evaluation gets expensive computationally. The authors point out a more serious theoretical concern: the subspace spanned by these basis vectors includes all the measured BRDFs, it also includes some BRDFs that are not physically plausible. Consequently, the actual useful BRDF subspace is a nonlinear subspace. Geometrically this means the subspace is a high-dimensional curved surface (properly, a *manifold*) in the 45-dimensional BRDF space. Constructing and representing this is no easy task. The technique described in the paper uses Gaussian functions to approximate the subspace; i.e., it represents a general BRDF as a collection of Gaussians. The method employed by the au-

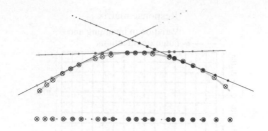

Figure 8.19   The process of "charting" a nonlinear approximation to BRDF data. Points in linear subspaces are projected onto the Gaussian curve. (From [Matusik et al. 03] © 2003 ACM,
Inc. Included here by permission.)

thors is called *charting*,[11] in which points on an unknown curved subspace are
projected onto a collection of known subspaces, which are Gaussian surfaces in
this case. The projected values are weighted according to their distance from
the unknown subspace. The Gaussian surfaces are then merged to approximate
the unknown subspace. Figure 8.19 illustrates the basic approach in the plane;
in this figure the Gaussian subspaces are shown as straight lines. The size of the
projected points represents the weights. The process is much more complicated
in the 45-dimensional linear BRDF space, and the actual method used by the authors is only sketched in the paper. The difficult part is selecting a minimal set of
Gaussians to cover the subspace.

The authors' experiments indicate that as few as 10 properly chosen Gaussian
surfaces is likely sufficient to represent the physically realizable BRDF subspace.
However, they employ a basis of 15 Gaussian to fit the measured data. They note
that this gives comparable approximation results to the 45 linear basis functions.
While this is a notable reduction, the real advantage of the nonlinear approximation is that it stays closer to the space of realizable BRDFs. As noted earlier, some
parts of the linear subspace correspond to implausible BRDFs. Figure 8.20 shows
an example: moving away from a point in the linear subspace results in a BRDF
that has a low value at the specular direction, which causes a specular highlight to
have a hole in the middle. In contrast, moving an equal distance on the nonlinear
subspace stays in the domain of plausible BRDFs.

Given the Gaussian basis, the next question is how to determine the weights
in order to represent a particular BRDF. Ultimately the authors wanted to provide
a BRDF designer with a set of intuitive controls, such as its "diffuseness" and
how "metallic" it appears. Ideally these controls should be independent of each
other. Unfortunately, the Gaussian bases are not very intuitive, so the authors de-

---

[11] Charting is described more fully in "Charting a Manifold" by Matthew Brand [Brand 03].

Figure 8.20   Differences between the BRDFs in the linear span of the PCA basis vectors and the Gaussian basis representation. A measured BRDF is shown at the left. In the center is an implausible BRDF from a nearby "point" in the linear span. The right image is a BRDF at a comparably close point in the Gaussian subspace; the BRDF is different, but still physically plausible. (From [Matusik et al. 03] © 2003 ACM, Inc. Included here by permission.)

veloped a method for searching the subspace for new traits in a way that maintains particular traits already specified by the user.

Although the image-based BRDF approach presented in the paper was more of a proof of concept than a fully developed BRDF generation system, it gained attention as an entirely new way of modeling BRDFs. In addition, while linear approximations had been used to approximate BRDFs for years, this was the first attempt at a representation of realizable BRDF as a nonlinear subspace of a general BRDF space. The work inspired research into other approaches that approximate reflection by mathematically analyzing sets of measured data. Much of this was concurrent with research into BTF rendering and relighting, which is described in the next chapter. Image-based BRDF models will likely play an important role not only in reconstructing real world surface reflectance, but also in improving analytical BRDF models.

In fact, the work has already provided insight into the effectiveness of existing analytical BRDF models. The authors' collection of measured BRDF data contains reflectances for a wide range of surfaces. Addy Ngan, Frédo Durand, and Wojciech Matusik used this data to test the effectiveness of many existing BRDF models in fitting real data. They presented the results in a SIGGRAPH technical sketch entitled "Experimental Validation of Analytical BRDF Models" and also in a technical paper published in the Eurographics Symposium on Rendering in 2005.

Existing BRDF models can be split into two basis types: those that use the specular deviation angle α between the view direction and the specular direction, and those that use the half-angle θ_h between the half-vector and the surface normal. The Phong model, general cosine lobe models, and the Lafortune model use the former; Blinn's model, Ward's model, the Ashikhmin-Shirley model, and most of the microfacet models use the latter. The conclusion was that models based on the half-angle θ_h clearly produce more accurate approximations across all the different surfaces.

8.2 The Reflectance Field

The methods described above allow for the recovery of BRDFs from photographs of surface samples under controlled lighting conditions. It is assumed that the pixel values of the captured images record the radiance directly reflected off the surface from the single illumination source. That is, global illumination effects such as indirect lighting are ignored. This is a reasonable assumption, because the photography is done in a closed laboratory environment with black matte walls or curtains that absorb stray light. The only light source is the surface illuminant. There is some stray light in the environment: interreflections between the surface sample and the camera and gantry device are probably the most significant source of this. But painting everything black minimizes these effects. Recovering BRDF data from photographs in an environment where there is significant global illumination is an entirely different problem—global illumination effects have to be separated from the direct reflection before the BRDF values can be obtained. This section introduces some approaches to performing this separation, and describes some other uses for the separation methods.

8.2.1 Inverse Global Illumination

Global illumination comes from three elements: the geometry of the scene, the reflectance properties of the scene objects, and the light sources in the scene. Methods described in Chapter 2 can be used to compute the GI solution for the scene, which gives the outgoing radiance at each point on each surface. The recovery of reflectance given the surface radiance along with the geometry and lighting of a scene is a formidable inverse problem. This is one form of an *inverse global illumination* problem. Figure 8.21 shows a schematic representation of the conceptual process. The paper entitled "Inverse Global Illumination" by Yizhou Yu, Paul E. Debevec, Jitendra Malik, and Tim Hawkins [Yu et al. 99], presents a method for approximating inverse GI that allows for the recovery of BRDF data from photographs in a general environment.

The method described in the paper attempts to reconstruct an approximate BRDF model for surfaces in a photographed scene. The dense sampling over many light and view directions used for more precise BRDF recovery methods is specifically avoided—the approach uses a minimum number of photographs. As illustrated in Figure 8.22, the angles the light and camera positions make with

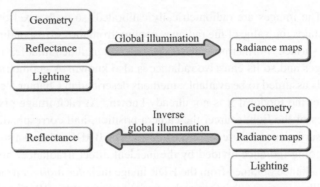

Figure 8.21   The basic concept of inverse global illumination. (After [Yu et al. 99].)

the surface normal (which correspond to the incoming and outgoing directions of the BRDF) varies over the surface. A single image thus captures a number of light and view directions even though the lighting and view (camera) positions are fixed. The BRDF parameters could be fit using the measurements obtained from a single image; however, the domain of incoming and outgoing angles is not usually large enough to adequately capture the BRDF over a broad enough domain of directions. A set of images from different viewpoints is therefore necessary in practice.

The input to the BRDF recovery method is a set of HDR images captured from a few representative viewpoints in the environment, and the goal is to match the parameters of a simple BRDF model to the recovered reflectance values. The authors use the Ward BRDF model, but note that other models could be used

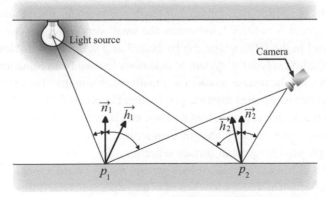

Figure 8.22   A single camera image captures a collection of different BRDF values because of the variation in local geometry. (After [Yu et al. 99].)

instead. The images are radiometrically calibrated, so each pixel of the HDR image contains the value of the radiance coming from the corresponding point on the object surface. Furthermore, the light source is included in at least one of the HDR images and so its emissive radiance is also known. A geometric model of the scene is assumed to be available; methods described in Chapter 5 can be used to construct the model if it is not already known. At each image pixel, the 3D coordinates of the light source, the camera position, and corresponding surface point and surface normal are therefore known. The BRDF value at a surface point is the outgoing radiance divided by the incident direct irradiance; however, the outgoing radiance obtained from the HDR image includes *indirect* irradiance due to global illumination. This has to be removed before the BRDF value can be computed. Unfortunately, standard methods for doing this requires knowledge of the BRDF of all the surfaces in the environment. Obtaining the BRDF is, in essence, an inverse GI problem.

If all the surfaces are Lambertian, the exitant radiance is proportional to the radiant exitance (radiosity) at the surface. In the radiosity method (see Chapter 2), the environment is divided into surface patches and the lighting is assumed to be constant over each patch. The reflectance of each patch can be determined from the final radiosity solution. The radiant exitance B_i from patch i satisfies

$$B_i = E_i + \rho_i \sum_j B_j F_{i,j}, \qquad (8.8)$$

where $F_{i,j}$ is the *form factor* between patch i and patch j, and represents the fraction of radiant power leaving patch i that hits patch j (or vice versa). The E_i term is the emission of the patch, and is zero unless the patch is a light source. In other words, the radiant exitance M_i of patch i is proportional to the sum of the radiant power received from all the other surface patches. The proportionality constant ρ_i is the diffuse reflectance (albedo) of patch i. Assuming for the moment that the environment is entirely Lambertian, the small surface region corresponding to each pixel in the HDR image can be treated as a surface patch. Normally the radiosity method solves the system of equations formed from Equation (8.8) for each patch i, but the inverse problem is actually much simpler. The exitance B_i (or E_I) of the patch is obtained from the pixel value. Equation (8.8) therefore has only one unknown ρ_i, and can be solved directly, independent of the other equations.

Of course, real surfaces are not Lambertian. The problem becomes much more complicated for general surface reflection. The diffuse reflectance term in Equation (8.8) has to be replaced by a general model (Ward's model) to recover specular reflectance. The approach used in the paper splits the diffuse component of the BRDF. Directionality plays an important role in recovering the specular components. Suppose a camera at C_v captures a patch P_i that has a notable spec-

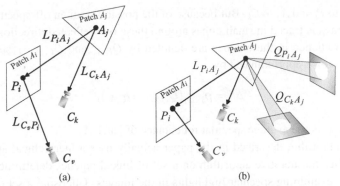

Figure 8.23   (a) The radiance $L_{P_iA_j}$ from patch A_j to point P_i on patch A_i is needed in the inverse GI problem but is not usually available. The radiance $L_{C_kA_j}$ captured by another camera C_k is an approximation. (b) To calculate ΔS, the reflectance of patch A_j is approximated by tracing incident light in a cone of directions around the specular directions. (After [Yu et al. 99].)

ular component. The specular reflectance depends on the radiance from all other patches. These values cannot be measured directly; the radiance L_{P_i,A_j} of light traveling from a particular patch A_j to patch P_i is only available if there happens to be an image from a camera placed directly between the patches. This is not likely, but there might be an image captured from a point that "sees" patch A_j from a similar viewing angle (see Figure 8.23). Suppose an image from a camera at a point C_k captures the radiance L_{C_k,A_j} from patch A_j. If A_j were Lambertian, the radiance values L_{P_i,A_j} and L_{C_k,A_j} would be equal. For a general surface, the radiance varies by a value denoted by ΔS:

$$L_{P_iA_j} = L_{C_kA_j} + \Delta S.$$

The values of ΔS are obtained iteratively, with each iteration improving the values.

The algorithm for recovering the specular reflectance starts by assuming $\Delta S = 0$. Incidentally, this does not mean the reflection is necessarily diffuse, it just means that the radiance values are close enough for an initial approximation. Assuming $\Delta S = 0$, the algorithm uses a nonlinear optimizer to approximate the BRDF parameters. From these, new values of ΔS are computed, and the BRDF parameters are estimated again using the updated ΔS values. The process continues until a termination condition is reached; the algorithm described in the paper stops after a fixed number of iterations. The key to the algorithm is the method used to approximate ΔS at each iteration. The value of ΔS is in essence the variation in the specular component. A simple approximation can be obtained by reversing the paths: i.e., tracing the rays in the mirror directions of the directions from A_j to P_i and A_j to C_k. But because of the possibility of an off-specular peak, a set of rays is traced in small cones around these two reflected directions. If the average radiance in these cones are denoted by Q_{P_i,A_j} and Q_{C_k,A_j}, respectively, then ΔS can be approximated by

$$\Delta S = \rho_{s(A_j)}(Q_{P_iA_j} - Q_{C_kA_j}),$$

where ρ_{s,A_j} is the average specular reflectance of patch A_j.

The algorithm described in the paper actually uses a hierarchical approach, and applies the iterative algorithm on a set of linked patches determined in advance by examining specular highlights in the images. Choosing a set of linked patches that properly represent the specular reflection is critical to the success of the algorithm. The average radiance values in the cones come from the direct recorded radiance values at the ray intersections. This amounts to a "one-bounce" approximation to ΔS. The authors note that path tracing could be employed to obtain a better approximation, but the one-bounce approximation is apparently sufficient.

Using a judiciously chosen set of sample patches (points), BRDF parameters can be recovered from even a fairly small number of captured HDR photographs. Because the BRDF parameters are recovered separately for each patch, spatially varying BRDFs can be captured as well. However, at least one of the images must capture a specular highlight of each patch for this method to work. Furthermore, since there is a need to accurately describe the interaction of light between patches to create the radiosity equation, the geometric model of the scene needs to be precise. In practice, these constraints make it difficult to apply the algorithm in a general environment. But if the geometry of an environment is accurately reconstructed, the method can be very useful.

8.2.2   Reflectance Field

The *light field* (or *lumigraph*) described in Chapter 5 records the 5D *plenoptic function*, the radiance at each point in space and each direction. The image of an object contained within the light field from any viewpoint can be reconstructed as a kind of slice of the light field. The light field representation is independent of the geometry of the object (although the detail of a light field image is limited by the sampling resolution of the representation). An analogous construct for surface reflectance was proposed in the paper entitled "Acquiring the Reflectance Field of a Human Face" by Paul E. Debevec, Tim Hawkins, Chris Tchou, Haarm-Pieter Duiker, Westley Sarokin, and Mark Sagar [Debevec et al. 00]. The *reflectance field*, as the construct is called, was developed for the purpose of representing light reflection from a human face.

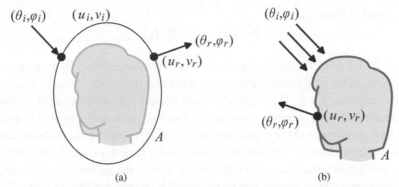

Figure 8.24   (a) The reflectance field is defined on a closed surface A surrounding the object. It gives
reflected radiance at a position (u_r, v_r) on the surface A in direction (θ_r, ϕ_r) from incident
light at position (u_i, v_i) and incident direction (θ_i, phi_i). (b) If the light source and viewpoint are sufficiently distant, the variation in incident position can be dropped, and the
surface A can be regarded as surface of the object. (From [Debevec et al. 00] © 2000
ACM, Inc. Included here by permission.)

The purpose of the reflectance field is to recover the appearance of an object
(a human face) from an arbitrary viewing direction under illumination from another arbitrary direction. It is constructed from photographs of each part of the
object taken from different viewpoints under different lighting conditions. The
reflectance field is an function of eight variables defined on a closed surface A,
such as a sphere or a cuboid, that encompasses the object (Figure 8.24(a)):

$$R(u_i, v_i, \theta_i, \phi_i;\ u_r, v_r, \theta_r, \phi_r).$$

The parameters are the position u_i, v_i and direction θ_i, ϕ_i of light incident on
the surface, and the position u_r, v_r and direction θ_r, ϕ_r of reflected radiance. The
reflectance field R can be regarded as a function of two 4D light fields: one for
incident light and one for the reflected light. If the surface A coincides with the
physical surface of the object, the reflectance field is equivalent to the BSSRDF
(equivalently, subsurface scattering can be expressed as a reflectance field.

In acquiring the reflectance field, the surface A can be thought of as being coincident with the object surface. The positions (u_i, v_i) and (u_r, v_r) can be regarded
as parameters on the object itself (Figure 8.24(b)). That is, the light source and
viewpoint are sufficiently far away that the light direction is essentially the same
from a point on the reflectance field surface and a corresponding point on the object surface. In fact, for a distant light source, the light direction can be taken as
constant across the entire object, in which case the reflectance field reduces to a

six-variable function

$$R'(\theta_i, \phi_i; u_r, v_r, \theta_r, \phi_r).$$

A BRDF models only the absolutely local reflection behavior at a single point. The reflectance field includes everything that happens from the point of incidence to the outgoing point. This includes near-field light interaction such as shadows, interreflection, and subsurface scattering. Once the reflectance field is acquired, the true appearance of the object from an arbitrary viewpoint and lighting direction can be accurately reproduced without having to perform any further rendering calculations. Because of the additivity of light,[12] the appearance of the object under several distant sources can be recovered by simply adding the images constructed for each separate source. In fact, the appearance under *any* incident light field (i.e., environment map) can be recovered by sampling the incident directions and treating each sample as a separate light source. In this context "adding" images refers to adding the radiance values directly; tone mapping or any other nonlinear correction must be applied only to the final image.

Acquiring the reflectance field for a fixed viewing direction is relatively simple because of the nature of the parameter set. For a fixed θ_r and ϕ_r, the radiance at a set of surface point samples u_r, v_r is recorded for a set of illumination directions θ_i and θ_r. However, if the viewing direction is allowed to vary, the acquisition of the reflectance field becomes more complicated. This is especially true for a human face. The reason for this is that small changes in the viewing direction can cause not-so-small changes in the appearance due to different parts of the object slipping in and out of visibility and a general lack of understanding of physical reflectance of a human face. In the "reflectance field" paper, the authors propose a method of first acquiring the reflectance field with the viewing direction fixed in the same direction as the camera, and then changing this reflectance field so that it is applicable to an arbitrary viewing direction.

8.2.3 The Light Stage

Debevec and his colleagues devised a measurement apparatus known as a *light stage* to acquire the reflectance field of an object by taking photographs from a sequence of different lighting directions. A light stage has white spotlights of equal brightness uniformly positioned on a spherical grid, all aimed at a subject sitting on a fixed chair in the center of the grid (Figure 8.25). The spotlights are

---

[12]Radiometric quantities are assumed to be additive, or linear, in all physical simulations; for example, the radiance reflected from a surface illuminated by two light sources is equal to the sum of the reflected radiance from the sources considered separately. However, human perception, camera and film response, and tone mapping are not generally additive: the sum of two tone mapped images is not the same as the tone mapped image of the sum of the original images.

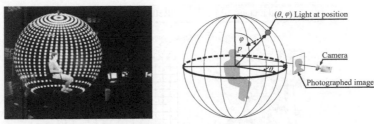

Figure 8.25   The light stage. (Left image courtesy of Paul Debevec.)

lit individually in sequence; a camera captures images of the the subject's face
illuminated by each spotlight. Several exposures are recorded, which are later
combined into an HDR image to represent the reflectance field for the incident
direction of the particular spotlight.[13]

Next, the collection of pixel values corresponding to a sample point on the
physical surface are extracted from each captured HDR image. The pixel values
are then arranged into a 2D array by the θ_i and ϕ_i values of the spotlight in the
HDR image from which they came, to create what is called a "reflectance function" in the paper. Figure 8.26 illustrates the process. A reflectance function is
essentially a slice of $R'(\theta_i, \phi_i; u_r, v_r, \theta_r, \phi_r)$ with u_r and v_r (the pixel locations)
as well as θ_r, ϕ_r (the camera position) fixed. A separate reflectance function is
defined for each of a set of fixed sample points on the physical surface. For each
sample point, the reflectance function expresses how the reflectance at that point
changes with different lighting directions.

The reflectance functions can be combined into a tiled mosaic texture map,
similar to an image produced by the light field camera described in Chapter 5,
although the arrangement is different. Each tile in this texture map contains the
reflectance function for a single pixel, and thus shows how the appearance of that
surface point changes with the position of the light source. Figure 8.27 shows a
reflectance function mosaic created for a face. The right side of Figure 8.27 shows
the combined tiled texture map; the left side shows the original image. Near the
center of each tile is the reflectance for the spotlight near the camera, so the values
there correspond to the front-lit image. This is why the face is discernable in a
kind of "fractured" form.

---

[13]The light stage has evolved since the reflectance field was first introduced in 2000. The system
described in the original paper actually used a single spotlight attached to a rotating arm. A video
camera recorded images as the spotlight rotated around the subject. Other devices for capturing and
displaying reflectance fields have since emerged. For example, a paper entitled "Towards Passive 6D
Reflectance Field Displays" by Martin Fuchs, Ramesh Raskar, Hans-Peter Seidel, and Hendrik P. A.
Lensch [Fuchs et al. 08] describes a prototype of a flat display that is view and illumination dependent.
It works by discretizing the incident light field using a lens array and modulating it with a coded
pattern.

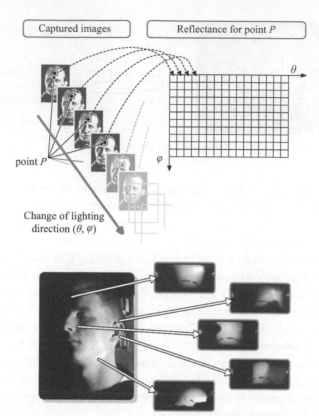

Figure 8.26   Some reflectance functions for a human face. Reflectance functions are 2D arrays of pixels formed by extracting the pixel at the same position from all the captured images (top). Each reflectance function shows how the reflectance at a single point on the surface changes with lighting direction (bottom). (Courtesy of Paul Debevec.)

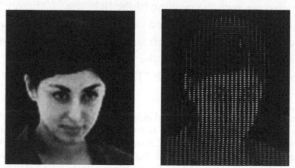

Figure 8.27   All the reflectance function images captured from the light stage spotlights can be tiled into a single texture image (right). A captured image is shown on the left. (Courtesy of Paul Debevec.) (See Color Plate X.)

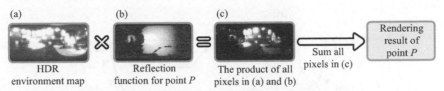

(a)   (b)   (c)

HDR environment map

Reflection function for point P

The product of all pixels in (a) and (b)

Sum all pixels in (c)

Rendering result of point P

Figure 8.28   Rendering using reflectance functions. (After [Debevec et al. 00].)

To render a point p on the surface of an object illuminated by a point light source in direction (θ_i, ϕ_i), the reflectance function pixel value is just multiplied by the radiance of the source. The corresponding pixels across the surface of the object so multiplied collectively produce an image of the object as if it were lit by the source. To render the point using an HDR environment map, each value in the reflectance function for p is multiplied by the value of the environment map from the corresponding direction (Figure 8.28). Pixels in an HDR environment map can be arranged to match the arrangement of θ_i and ϕ_i directions in each reflectance function, which simplifies this process, and also makes it more suitable for hardware implementation. The sampling density of the environment map may be much larger than the density of the spotlights, in which case the environment map pixels need to be downsampled so that pixels in the reflectance function match pixels in the filtered environment map. Just as pixels in the environment map can be regarded as point sources, a point source can be regarded as a pixel in the environment map. An environment map for a single point source has just one nonzero pixel—the one corresponding to the source. Regardless of the illumination, the reflectance field includes all the local interreflection, shadowing, and subsurface scattering. It is indeed remarkable that all these effects can be accounted for by simple multiplications.

8.2.4   Acquiring a Facial Reflectance Field

The method described in the previous subsection only works for a single viewpoint, i.e., a fixed θ_r and ϕ_r. In order to acquire the complete reflectance field, the process has be repeated for a set of different viewpoints. That is, the camera must be moved and another set of HDR images captured for each of the spotlights in the light stage. Unfortunately, the subject has to sit perfectly still throughout the entire acquisition process, which puts a practical limit on the number of camera positions. The density of viewpoints is much lower than the density of spotlights. The authors of the "reflectance field" paper refer to the process of interpolating viewpoints as "synthesizing" the reflectance field from an arbitrary viewing position. This process involves finding pixel correspondences between images:

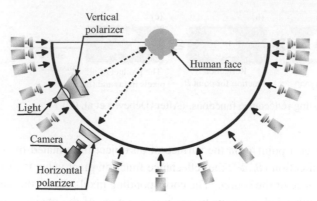

Figure 8.29   Measuring facial reflectance using linear polarizers. Putting a vertical polarizer on the light and a horizontal polarizer on the camera lens essentially removes the specular reflectance. (After [Debevec et al. 00].)

the pixels for each surface sample point (u_r, v_r) have to be matched across all the images. The relatively limited number of viewpoints complicates this process. Because there are fewer viewpoints, the images captured from neighboring viewpoints differ noticeably. As described in Chapter 5, automatic pixel correspondence depends on the images being fairly similar.

Another complication to the pixel correspondence is that the radiance values captured for a given (u_r, v_r) surface point are likely to differ dramatically, because a point will have a specular highlight from some viewpoints (and light directions) but not others. To mitigate this, the authors employ an approximate model of skin reflectance based on a (separate) set of captured images of a human forehead. The model splits the reflectance into a diffuse and a specular component. The specular component presumably comes from light reflected off the top surface of the top layer of skin. The diffuse component includes only light from subsurface scattering. The specular component is polarized, while the random subsurface scattering diffuses the polarization. Polarized light can be produced by placing a linear polarizer over the light source, and captured by placing a linear polarizer over the camera. How these two polarizers are oriented affects the image capture: if they are oriented in perpendicular directions, specular reflection gets filtered out; if they have parallel directions, it is accentuated. Capturing two sets of images for each lighting arrangement and viewpoint produces separate diffuse and specular reflectance maps. Figure 8.29 illustrates the arrangement.

From the collection of captured images using the polarizers, the next step is to construct a skin reflectance model. Figure 8.30(a) shows the rearranged specular and diffuse components of a single point on the subject's forehead. The

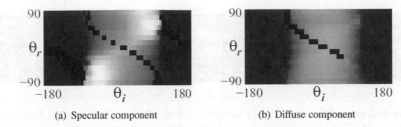

(a) Specular component   (b) Diffuse component

Figure 8.30   The captured specular and diffuse components as a function of the incoming and outgoing angles. The black pixels are holes in the measurements where the camera and light position overlap. (From [Debevec et al. 00] © 2000 ACM, Inc. Included here by permission.)

bright spots near the corners of the specular image correspond to reflection at grazing angles. This increasing specularity at low angles of incidence is common in real surfaces, and is partially caused by Fresnel reflection as described in the previous section. Here, the specular component is approximated using the Torrance-Sparrow microfacet model, which is capable of capturing the increasing specularity at grazing angles. The basic Torrance-Sparrow model assumes a Gaussian distribution of microfacets. The authors do not use this assumption; instead, they recover values of the distribution function directly from the acquired data.

What is regarded as the diffuse component in the human skin model includes subsurface scattering. The skin color in the measured diffuse reflection is not constant as it would be if the surface were perfectly Lambertian: a desaturation (loss of color) is observed as the angles θ_i and θ_r approach $90°$. That is, the diffuse color washes out to white at grazing angles. This effect is modeled using the function

$$f(\theta_i, \theta_r) = \alpha_0(\cos\theta_i \cos\theta_r) + \alpha_1(1 - \cos\theta_i \cos\theta_r) \qquad (8.9)$$

where α_o and α_1 are color parameters matched to the captured data. This function f serves as a replacement for the Lambertian term in the Torrance-Sparrow model. Note that it depends on both θ_i and θ_r; the Lambertian model depends only on θ_i.

Returning to the original problem of synthesizing (interpolating) the reflectance function for an arbitrary viewpoint, suppose the surface point (u, v) is fixed. The goal is to compute $R'(\theta_i, \phi_i; u, v, \theta_r, \phi_r)$ for arbitrary (θ_i, ϕ_i) and (θ_r, ϕ_r). This is done by synthesizing the diffuse and specular components separately, which requires separating the reflectance field into diffuse and specular components. The polarizing filter method is really not feasible for a complete light stage reflectance map, because it requires two separate sets of photographs and also the alignment of a polarizing filter on the camera would have to be changed for each

(a)   (b)   (c)

Figure 8.31   Separation of the diffuse and specular components in a reflectance function. (a) Reflectance
function. (b) Specular component. (c) Diffuse component. (From [Debevec et al. 00]
© 2000 ACM, Inc. Included here by permission.)

viewpoint and each spotlight. So the authors employ a different approach based
on the simplifying assumption that the diffuse reflection has the color of the surface, while the specular reflection has the color of the light. This is a reasonable
assumption for human skin, as it is basically a dielectric material—as noted previously, specular reflection from a dielectric usually does not capture the color of
the underlying surface. Each pixel can be roughly separated into a diffuse and
specular component based on this assumption. Figure 8.31 illustrates this separation: as the light color is white, the reflectance function (Figure 8.31(a)) is
first separated into the white specular component (Figure 8.31 (b)) and the diffuse
component, which contains the skin chromaticity (Figure 8.31 (c)).

Based on the preliminary separation, the surface normal direction at the surface point (u, v) can be estimated from the diffuse component: the light direction
is known, so the normal comes from fitting to a Lambertian "lobe." The two color
parameters α_0 and α_1 from Equation (8.9), which defines the modified diffuse
component, are fit using the approximate surface normal. From these parameters,
the diffuse component is separated again, this time more precisely, and the surface
normal is computed again from this more precise diffuse component.

From the separate diffuse and specular BRDF components, the surface normal, and the skin reflectance model, the reflectance field value R' can be synthesized for an arbitrary view direction. The diffuse and specular components are
constructed separately; the diffuse component comes from Equation (8.9). The
specular component is more difficult to compute. The process works by factoring
the Torrance-Sparrow BRDF model into a product of the separate Fresnel term F,
the geometry term G, and microfacet distribution. The first two, F and G, can be
computed analytically. As the Torrance-Sparrow model depends on the product
of all three terms, the distribution term can be estimated from the ratio of specular
reflectance values of two specular reflectance functions.

The reflectance function for an arbitrary viewing direction is synthesized by
separately synthesizing the diffuse and specular reflection functions, and adding

the corresponding pixel values. This completes the construction of the reflectance field for an arbitrary viewpoint and lighting direction. As previously mentioned, the reflectance field includes the effects of phenomena such as indirect illumination and subsurface scattering. It also includes shadowing, but a correction is necessary for shadows. The authors employ a thresholding method to determine if a point is in shadow: if the value of a pixel in the synthesized reflectance function falls below this threshold, the point is assumed to be in shadow.

The method described in the "reflectance field" paper assumes the object is static. It becomes difficult to calculate reflections using only the information from the reflectance field in cases where the original object changes shape, or if the reflections on the original object are partially occluded by another object that was not there at the time of capture. Reflectance fields also do not capture the change in reflectance due to a change in position of the object. These limits are overcome with techniques introduced in the next chapter.

8.2.5   A Reflectance Field for Variable Geometry

A drawback of the reflectance field is that it does not handle any changes in the shape of the object. One method of acquiring the reflectance of a deforming object would be to capture a new set of images with a light stage each time the object changes shape, thereby creating a new reflectance field from those images. However, this is obviously not an efficient (or practical) method. Even if the data were available, as it could be if the object were synthetically rendered, some way of parameterizing the deformation would be needed, and each deformation parameter adds another variable to the reflectance field function.

The assumption of a static model is particularly troublesome in modeling facial reflectance, because human faces are constantly changing. An efficient method of calculating the reflectance field for an animated face was introduced in the paper "Animatable Facial Reflectance fields" by Tim Hawkins, Andreas Wenger, Chris Tchou, Andrew Gardner, Fredrik Göransson, and Paul E. Debevec [Hawkins et al. 04]. The paper describes a scheme of obtaining the reflection for a face after it has changed shape, using the reflectance functions of the original shape. The method requires a precise model of the face geometry, which is obtained by placing fiducial marker dots on the subject's face. The authors used 300 dots, and captured light stage image sets for six different camera positions. The process was repeated for 60 different expressions. The dots in the image sets were then registered to produce a deformable triangulated model of the face.

The ultimate goal of the work was to produce a reflectance field model valid for arbitrary deformations and also arbitrary viewing directions. The underlying

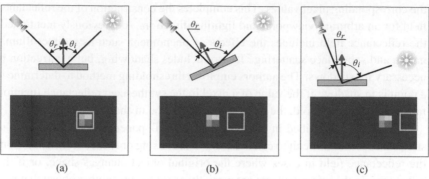

(a)   (b)   (c)

Figure 8.32   A simple deformation changes only the orientation of the surface normal (top parts). This amounts to a simple rotation of the reflectance function (bottom parts). The gray square shows the part of the reflectance function to which the deformed surface corresponds. (a) The original surface is oriented toward a specular highlight. (b) Rotating the surface moves away from the highlight. (c) In the coordinate system of the surface normal, the light and camera directions are what change in a deformation. (After [Hawkins et al. 04].)

geometric model is needed to approximate the surface of the face only to the precision needed for the reflectance field, and to represent arbitrary synthesized facial expressions. (A conventional rendering of the triangular model would not be at all realistic.) The true geometry is contained in the reflectance field in the form of reflectance functions from captured images.

In the original reflectance-field method described in the previous subsection, the geometry of an object surface depends only on the surface normal direction. As the normal direction changes due to a deformation, the lighting and view directions change with respect to the normal, even if the actual positions of the light and viewpoint remain the same. The top parts of Figure 8.32(a) and (b) show how these angles change as a surface element rotates. The reflection map can be sampled at the incident angles θ_i and view angle θ_r measured from the surface normal after the deformation. Alternatively, the coordinate system can be rotated so that the surface normal matches the predeformation (original) surface element (Figure 8.32(c)). The reflectance functions can be resampled directly, or approximated by simply rotating the predeformation reflectance function to match the deformed normal. The bottom parts of Figure 8.32(a) and (b) illustrate how the angles with respect to the deformed normal correspond to a different part of the predeformation reflectance map; part (c) shows the effect of the rotation. The square in this figure corresponds to the postdeformation reflectance map. In this particular case, the contents are dark because the deformation has moved the surface element away from the specular highlight.

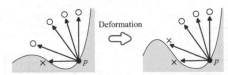

Figure 8.33   A more general deformation changes the local geometry, which affects occlusion.

Of course, deformation of the model involves an actual change in the geometry. This affects local interreflection and shadowing: a change in the local surface
geometry can change the visibility of the light sources (Figure 8.33). Resampling
the predeformation reflectance functions cannot capture this. However, because
there is a model for the geometry, shadow rays can be cast from the point to be
rendered over the hemisphere of directions using the deformed model. This technique was applied when the animatable reflectance field technique was used in
the movie *Spider Man 2*, as described next.

8.2.6   Use of the Light Stage in Movie Production

The method described in the "Animatable Facial Reflectance Fields" paper was
used in the movie *Spider Man 2* [Raimi 04] to calculate the reflectance of a face
that deformed due to animation. The texture of the faces of the Spider Man character and his enemy "Doctor Octopus" were reconstructed with the use of a light
stage. The person charged with this task was Mark Sagar, a coauthor of the paper "Acquiring the Reflectance Field of a Human Face" described above and an
expert in rendering faces.

The process of acquiring the reflectance of the faces was based on the method
in the above paper, but in *Spider Man 2*, there was a need to acquire the reflectance
for the entire surface of the head, including the sides and back. Images therefore
had to be captured from more viewing directions. Also, in the rendering system
used in movie production, rendering is performed by passing the shaders diffuse
and specular values. Consequently, the reflectance functions are separated into
diffuse and specular components (as they are in the methods described above) but
these components are not recombined; they are stored in separate texture maps.
The process from image capture to rendering consists of the following steps (see
also Figure 8.34).

1. A reflectance function for each point on the surface of the face is constructed from a set of images captured using the light stage.

2. The reflectance functions are split into diffuse and specular components;
   the surface normal direction of the point is recovered at the same time.

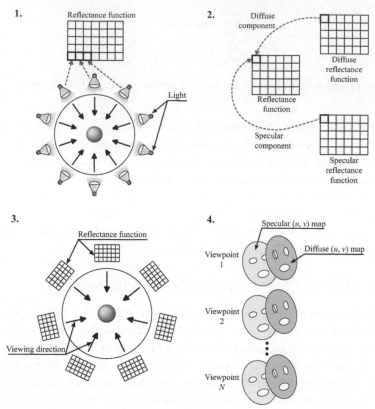

Figure 8.34   Steps in capturing face reflectance fields for *Spider Man 2* using a light stage.

(The normal direction is practically constant using any of the reflectance functions captured from different viewing directions).

3. The reflectance functions are densely resampled over the sphere of viewing directions; this simplifies the process of reflectance map lookup in varying surface direction.

4. The face is rendered using the reflectance maps and the environment map for the particular scene and animation frame. The diffuse and specular reflection extracted from the reflectance functions for pixels across the facial surface are stored in a (u,v) texture map for the face, which is referenced in computing the lighting using the environment map for the incident light.

A major challenge in the production of the movie was the efficient acquisition of the face reflectance fields—the actors' faces could not be recaptured with every

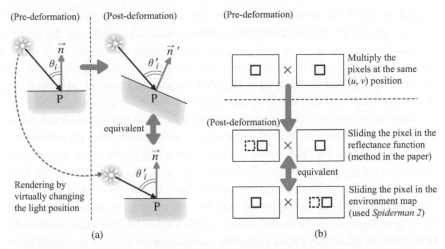

Figure 8.35   Rendering a reflectance field with an environment map amounts to multiplying the environment map with the appropriate slice of the reflectance function. A surface deformation has the effect of rotating the reflectance field, or, equivalently, rotating the environment map. In producing *Spider Man 2*, this rotation was approximated by a translation.

possible expression, and even if it were possible, the storage requirements would have been extreme. The method in the "Animatable Facial Reflectance Fields" paper employs a method of reusing sections of the face that do not change with certain deformations. The forehead, neck, and eyes are examples. The method, called "coherent expression culling" in the paper, not only reduces the storage requirements, it also reduces possible artifacts that may occur as the same nearly unchanged parts of the face are resampled.

The basic method used in *Spider Man 2* followed the method in the paper, but there were some differences. To render an image, the incident illumination is multiplied by the appropriate reflectance function, and the results are summed to produce the exitant radiance. The incident illumination is contained in an environment map. Rotating the environment map is equivalent to rotating a surface element (this is essentially what is done in Figure 8.32(c)). If the angle of rotation is not too large, the rotation can be approximated by simply translating or "sliding" the pixels in the environment map (Figure 8.35). This is faster than performing the rotation, and better suited to hardware rendering.

Rendering a point from a particular viewing direction on the postdeformation face is performed as follows. First, the reflectance map corresponding to the viewing direction with respect to the predeformation surface normal is located. Rendering is performed using this reflectance function with the environment map rotated to match the rotation induced by the deformation; as described in the previous paragraph, this rotation can be approximated by translating the pixels. To calculate the change in shadowing, rays are cast from the surface point in the postdeformation model in the direction of pixels in the reflectance function. If the cast ray is occluded, the pixel is excluded from the summation. In reality, the deformation also changes the local interreflection, but this is not considered.

Mark Sagar was of the opinion that reflectance field rendering had much room for improvement. Nonetheless, the results were more realistic than the production staff had expected. This reaffirmed the benefits of using image-based techniques, and expanded the potential use of the light stage in movie production. The next task would be to provide digital artists the flexibility to directly control the diffuse and specular components calculated from the reflectance functions. This would allow light stage data to be used in more creative ways. The light stage has already been used in other ways than capturing the reflectance field. One application in movie projects has been to fit parameters to shading models. Improvement in the speed of image capture has made this process easier for artists. Image-based geometry reconstruction (Chapter 5) is another potential application of a light stage.

8.3   Separation of Direct and Global Illumination

The term "global illumination" normally refers to all the lighting in an environment, including interreflection and scattering effects. As noted in Chapter 2, global illumination can be regarded as having two components: the direct component, which is caused by light from light sources reflecting directly from scene surfaces to the eye or camera, and the indirect component, which comes from multiple reflections. The indirect component is often called the "global component," especially in literature concerned with the separation of the two components. This convention is followed in the present chapter: "global" and "indirect" are often used interchangeably.[14]

The BRDF models introduced in this chapter often separate the reflection into diffuse and specular components. The face reflectance recovery methods described in the previous section do something similar; in fact, in the separation of the reflectance field into diffuse and specular components is the key to synthesizing reflectance functions for an arbitrary viewpoint. A related separation,

---

[14]To complicate matters further, the term "radiosity" is sometimes used to describe indirect lighting, especially from interreflection. This usage arose in the 1980s when the predominant (if not the only) method of computing global illumination was the radiosity method. In recent years this somewhat inaccurate use of "radiosity" has largely been replaced by the term "global illumination."

the splitting of illumination into direct and indirect lighting, is frequently used in global illumination computation. As described in Chapter 1, reasons for this come from the greater importance of direct lighting, and the greater difficulty of indirect lighting computation. However, the inverse process of splitting captured radiance into direct and indirect components remained an unsolved problem. The method of employing polarizing filters described previously does do a form of this separation, as the specular reflection comes from direct lighting, but this does not work for the diffuse reflection (which has a direct and indirect component). It also requires the use of polarized illumination and capture, which is not always possible. Had a more general method for image-based separation of direct and global illumination been available, it might have provided a more accurate way of acquiring the reflection field.

A flexible method for performing the direct/global split was presented in a paper entitled "Fast Separation of Direct and Global Components of a Scene using High Frequency Illumination" by Shree K. Nayar, Gurunandan Krishnan, Michael D. Grossberg, and Ramesh Raskar. Nayar, an expert in computer vision, has studied the problem of removing global illumination since the 1990s. The problem is fundamental in computer vision. A number of image-based methods described in this book so far have depended on how the pixel colors change with variations in lighting and surface orientation. The effects of indirect lighting complicates this substantially. A particularly difficult situation arises when the object is concave: indirect illumination is more prominent for such objects because of the orientation of the nearby surfaces (see Figure 8.38). If the shape recovery assumes all the lighting is direct, the extra interreflection increases the error in the recovered geometry.

8.3.1 Separation in the Lambertian Case

Nayar along with Katsushi Ikeuchi and Takeo Kanade developed a method that splits global illumination from direct lighting in the context of recovering geometry, which they described in a paper entitled "Shape from Interreflection" [Nayar et al. 91]. The method solves the separation problem for purely Lambertian surfaces. Starting with captured images, which naturally include GI, a preliminary geometric model is recovered by applying a basic photometric stereo algorithm. The GI solution for this preliminary model is an approximate solution to the real model; removing the indirect component from the original images and recovering the geometry again provides a better geometric model. This process is repeated until the model converges.

Figure 8.36 contains a flowchart of the iterative algorithm. At the outset, a collection of images of the object are captured under three separate illumination

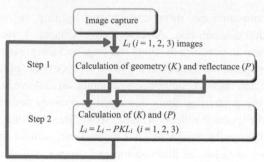

Figure 8.36 Recursive calculations to remove the effects of global illumination.   (After [Nayar et al. 91].)

sources. For definiteness, these are indexed by $i = 1, 2, 3$. In Step 1, the geometry of the object and the reflectance are recovered from the current set of images. A variant of the radiosity method is employed to remove the GI components at each interaction. The recovered geometry takes the form of a collection of m surface facets, and the radiosity solution is computed using these facets as the surface patches. The actual facets match the pixels directly: the facet corresponding to pixel j is the subset of the object surface that projects to pixel j on the sensor plane (assuming ideal focus, i.e., the pinhole camera model).

The coordinates of the facet vertices are recovered from the captured images using photometric stereo, from which the normal vector is derived. Because the surfaces are assumed to be Lambertian, the BRDF is constant, and the diffuse reflectance (albedo) of a facet is directly proportional to the cosine of the light direction. The computed normal $\vec{n}_j$ and reflectance ρ_j of facet j are recorded as part of the geometry. From these, a "geometry matrix" K is constructed, the elements $K_{j,k}$ correspond to the form factors between the facets: $K_{j,k}$ is the amount of radiant power leaving facet j that arrives at facet k. The radiosity equation cannot be applied directly, because none of the facets emit light and the solution would therefore be trivial (all the patches would be black). Instead, the "emission" term for each facet is taken to be the direct illumination—it is assumed the the light source is visible from each facet. Consequently, the surface radiance of patch i satisfies

$$L_j = L_j^1 + \rho_j \sum_k L_j K_{jk}, \qquad (8.10)$$

where L_j^1 denotes the direct (one-bounce) lighting, computed from the source intensity and the reflectance ρ_j of the facet. In matrix form, Equation (8.10) becomes

$$(I - PK)L = L^1, \qquad (8.11)$$

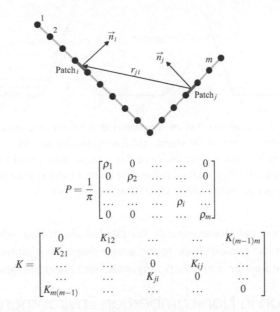

$$P = \frac{1}{\pi} \begin{bmatrix} \rho_1 & 0 & \cdots & \cdots & 0 \\ 0 & \rho_2 & \cdots & \cdots & 0 \\ \cdots & \cdots & \cdots & \cdots & \cdots \\ \cdots & \cdots & \cdots & \rho_i & \cdots \\ 0 & 0 & \cdots & \cdots & \rho_m \end{bmatrix}$$

$$K = \begin{bmatrix} 0 & K_{12} & \cdots & \cdots & K_{(m-1)m} \\ K_{21} & 0 & \cdots & \cdots & \cdots \\ \cdots & \cdots & 0 & K_{ij} & \cdots \\ \cdots & \cdots & K_{ji} & 0 & \cdots \\ K_{m(m-1)} & \cdots & \cdots & \cdots & 0 \end{bmatrix}$$

Figure 8.37   Recovering the geometry of a concave Lambertian object from captured images. The surface patches in the geometric model correspond to the pixels in the images. An initial guess provides the patch normals $\vec{n}$ and reflectances ρ, from which the form factors can be computed. The matrix P contains the reflectances; K contains the form factors. (After [Nayar et al. 91].)

where I is the identity matrix, P is the diagonal "reflectance" matrix of reflectances ρ_i, and K is the geometry matrix (see also Figure 8.37); L and L^1 are vectors of the radiance values arranged by facet index j.

In Step 2, the calculation to remove the effects of GI is performed. The radiosity solution is computed by solving the system of equations, which amounts to matrix inversion: $L = (I - PK)^{-1}L^1$. The indirect component is $L - L^1$, which is then subtracted from the pixel values. This is done for each of the three source images. Then the process starts over at Step 1 using the improved source images, and is repeated until the geometry converges.

The matrices K and P do not depend on the light direction. Therefore when Step 1 is applied to the original images, the recovered shape is the same regardless of the directions of the light sources as long as the object is concave and fully illumination. The authors called this the *pseudo shape*, and note that the pseudo shape appears more shallow than the true shape. Figure 8.38(a) and (b) show a cross section of an object and its pseudo shape, respectively. Because any concave Lambertian surface has a unique pseudo shape, it makes the iterative recovery

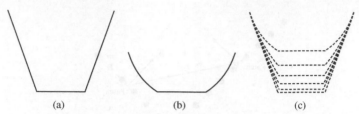

(a)   (b)   (c)

Figure 8.38   The effect global illumination has on reconstructed geometry of a concave Lambertian object. (a) A cross section of the object. (b) Reconstructing the object assuming all illumination is direct produces a pseudo shape that is incorrectly curved and more shallow than the real object. (c) Repeatedly removing the indirect lighting from the reconstructed geometry converges to the true shape. (After [Nayar et al. 91].)

of the true shape and albedo not only feasible but also robust—there is a single mapping from the pseudo shape to the actual shape, so a convergent iterative algorithm must find the actual shape. Figure 8.38(c) illustrates the convergence.

8.3.2   Separation in Non-Lambertian Environments

In a paper entitled "A Theory of Inverse Light Transport," Steven M. Seitz, Yasuyuki Matsushita, and Kiriakos N. Kutulakos present a method of extracting the effects due to direct illumination by multiplying the captured image with a matrix in a single pass [Seitz et al. 05]. By analyzing the light transport based on the rendering equation, it was proved in this paper that such a matrix exists regardless of the reflectance characteristics of the object. Furthermore, the 1991 paper by Nayar et al. depends on a precise geometric model of the object; the matrix in the 2005 paper can be created without such a model.

The method employs the remarkably simple idea of lighting an object with a precise beam of light so narrow that it hits only "one pixel" of the object. That is, given a camera position, the beam illuminates only the small area of the object captured by a single pixel in the image. In this scenario, the object is assumed to be contained in an entirely dark environment in which the light beam is the only source of light. If the object is convex and exhibits no appreciable subsurface scattering, all the light reflects away from the object so there is no indirect illumination. A captured image therefore has only one nonzero pixel, the pixel corresponding to the illuminated point. Conversely, if such an image of an arbitrary object has only one nonzero pixel, then there is no measurable indirect light. The authors call such an image an *impulse scattering function*.[15] If an im-

---

[15]The name "impulse" refers to the idea that the narrow light beam is essentially a Dirac δ illumination function; "impulse function" is another name for the Dirac δ often used in signal processing literature.

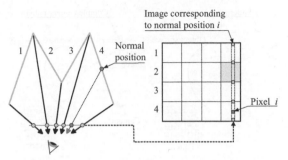

Figure 8.39   Matrix T accounts for the effects of global illumination. (After [Seitz et al. 05].)

pulse scatter function is captured for each separately lit pixel, and each image is arranged into a column vector, they collectively form the columns of a square matrix T. In the absence of indirect lighting, each impulse scatter function has only one nonzero value, which corresponds to the single lit pixel in the image. In this case, the collective matrix T is a diagonal matrix. Conversely, a diagonal matrix T implies there is no indirect lighting. Consequently, the process of removing the indirect component amounts to converting the impulse scattering function matrix T to a diagonal matrix. This casts the separation of direct lighting as the process of diagonalizing the matrix T. In the case of a purely Lambertian surface, the diagonal matrix is proportional to the reflectance matrix P in Equation (8.11) and diagonalization corresponds to the operation of removing the effects of indirect illumination in the 1991 paper. Figure 8.39 illustrates the idea.

8.3.3   A New Concept for Separation

The main result of the 2005 paper by Seitz et al., the existence of a matrix to remove the effects of indirect illumination regardless of the characteristics of the reflection of the object, certainly has theoretical importance. However, in order to apply the method in practice, the impulse scattering images would have to be physically obtained. While not impossible, it would require a precisely controlled collimated light source, and a huge number of captured images. Subsequent research concentrated on ways to reduce the number of images, and also on finding more practical capture methods. The 2006 paper "Fast Separation of Direct and Global Components of a Scene using High Frequency Illumination" by Nayar et al. mentioned above was a major advance on both fronts. This paper was also considered a landmark work in the nascent field of computational photography.

In computer vision, the main purpose of separating direct lighting from global illumination had been to improve the accuracy of geometry reconstruction. In contrast, Nayar's goal was to develop a method for re-rendering a captured im-

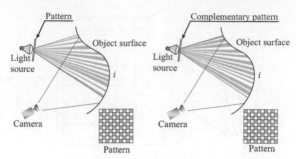

Figure 8.40   Image capture using binary checkerboard light patterns. Two images are captured, with opposite squares of the checkerboard lit. (After [Nayar et al. 91].)

age in two ways: one accounting for only direct lighting, and another including only indirect illumination. The reasoning was that having such images would be extremely useful in verifying existing reflectance models and rendering methods, and would also assist in creating new image-based techniques. Of course, the separate computation of direct lighting and global illumination was not new in computer graphics, but this separation in *captured* images showed the effects of direct and global illumination in real scenes for the first time.

Nayar's method described in the paper works with images of a scene captured under complementary "high frequency" patterns of incident light, e.g., a checkerboard pattern.[16] An image captured under such a pattern of light is said to be "partially lit;" the light source is called a "partial source." The basic process uses two partially lit images. The first photograph (image 1) is captured by placing a checkerboard filter between the light source and the scene (Figure 8.40 (left)). The second photograph (image 2) is captured with a checkerboard filter having the same frequency of squares, but with the dark and light squares interchanged (Figure 8.40 (right)). In either image, light coming from the unlit parts of the scene is entirely indirect. These unlit parts are complementary, so combining the unlit parts of the two images produces a complete image containing only indirect lighting.

Of course, finding the unlit parts of a captured image is a difficult problem in itself; doing it directly would require a precise geometric model of the scene, the position of the camera, and the orientation of the checkerboard filter. The point is that the two images contain the information needed for the separation of indirect lighting. The actual separation method does not try to combine the images directly. Conceptually, the scene objects are split into hypothetical surface patches.

---

[16]The "frequency" of the illumination is determined by the size of the checkerboard squares: the finer the black and white checks, the higher the frequency. In this context "frequency" refers to the illumination pattern, not the frequency of the light as an electromagnetic wave.

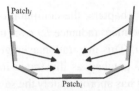

Patch$_j$

Patch$_i$

Figure 8.41   The checkerboard pattern illuminates patches unevenly, but the integral of incident radiance at patch i from patch j is about the same as if the illumination were evenly spread over patch j.

The collection of patches includes one patch for each pixel in the image, and also a separate collection of hypothetical patches for scene surfaces not visible from the camera. The basic idea is that the high frequency illumination is smoothed out by interreflections among the patches. As a result, the amount of global illumination in the first captured image (under the first checkerboard light pattern) is half of the full global illumination.

Rather than constructing a physical filter for the light source, the authors actually used a digital projector as a light source; the lighting pattern is created by projecting an image of fully lit or entirely unlit pixels. This allowed experimentation with a number of different lighting patterns, including various forms of the checkerboard filter. Normally, the lighting pattern has the same number of activated pixels as deactivated pixels, so that the light pattern and its complement have the same total radiant power. But this is not strictly necessary; the constant α represents the fraction of the area of the light source that is covered ($\alpha = \frac{1}{2}$ for the checkerboard patterns).

The paper uses a special notation for the radiance values of pixels in the captured images: the radiance of pixel i as captured by camera c is denoted by $L[c,i]$ in general; $L^+[c,i]$ and $L^-[c,i]$ denote the radiance values in the images with the basic checkerboard and its complement, respectively. A d subscript is added for the direct radiance, and a g subscript is added for the radiance from the global (indirect) component. The separation of direct and indirect components is concisely formalized in this notation:

$$L[c,i] = L_d[c,i] + L_g[c,i].$$

Further distinctions can be made: $L_{gd}[c,i]$ denotes two-bounce radiance (source to some patch j, to patch i, to the camera); $L_{gg}[c,i]$ denotes radiance from patch i after at least two previous bounces. These two values form a separation of the indirect radiance: $L_g[c,i] = L_{gd}[c,i] + L_{gg}[c,i]$. The relevance comes in considering the indirect component $L_g^+[c,i]$ in the first partially illuminated image.

As described in earlier chapters, the computation of $L_{gd}^+[c,i]$ involves integrating of the direct (one-bounce) radiance L_d over the hemisphere of directions above the surface of patch i. This integration averages out high frequency direct illumination over the scene patches, as illustrated in Figure 8.41. The integral over the partially lit patches has approximately the same value as the integral over the patches with the partial illumination spread evenly across the patches, i.e., as if the full illumination were reduced by the coverage factor α. That is,

$$L_{gd}^+[c,i] = \alpha L_{gd}[c,i], \tag{8.12}$$

and a similar argument shows the same approximation holds for the multiple bounce radiance, and therefore $L_g^+ = \alpha L_g$. In other words, the global component of a partially illuminated image is approximately equal to the global component of the fully illuminated image scaled by the fraction of the partial illumination.

Separation formulas. If pixel i is directly lit in the first partially illuminated image, then $L_d^+[c,i] = L_d[c,i]$ and it follows that

$$L^+[c,i] = L_d[c,i] + \alpha L_g[c,i], \tag{8.13}$$
$$L^-[c,i] = (1-\alpha)L_g[c,i]. \tag{8.14}$$

The left sides of these equations are the pixel values in the partially illuminated images, so the system can be solved for the two unknowns $L_d[c,i]$ and $L_g[c,i]$, which are the direct and global components of the illumination, respectively. Because of physical limitations of the projector, deactivated pixels do allow some light through. If this light has a fraction b of the power emitted by the active pixels, and $\alpha = \frac{1}{2}$, Equations (8.13) and (8.14) become

$$L^+[c,i] = L_d[c,i] + (1+b)\frac{L_g[c,i]}{2},$$
$$L^-[c,i] = bL_d[c,i] + (1+b)\frac{L_g[c,i]}{2},$$

which can likewise be solved for the direct radiance $L_d[c,i]$ and indirect (global) radiance $L_g[c,i]$. The simplicity of these formulas is truly remarkable.

Conditions for separation. The averaging assumption of indirect illumination depends on the high frequency nature of the lighting, and also assumes the reflectance is not extremely specular. If any of the surfaces were mirrors, a point on patch i might see a direct reflection of one of the checkerboard parts of the light, while a nearby point on the same patch did not. The separation theorem is not valid in this case. The proof of Equation (8.12) involves a frequency domain analysis, and requires that the BRDF has a lower frequency than the illumination pattern. In essence, this means that the BRDF lobes are at least as wide as the apparent angle of the checkerboard squares of the light source. For most scenes this is a reasonable assumption, but if the scene has strongly specular elements, separation cannot be performed. Of course, the frequency of the lighting pattern can always be increased to match the frequency of the BRDF, but the lighting frequency has to be well above the image pixel frequency because the separation depends on being able to discern lit and unlit pixels in the captured images.

Participating media and scattering. The derivation above omits volumetric scattering; i.e., there is no scattering of light between surface patches. However, an adjustment to the argument generalizes the result to scenes involving a participating medium. The effects of scattering can be separated into two types (Figure 8.42). The first effect is scattering between surface patches, which is part of GI computation and can be accomplished by integrating over rays incident at a surface point. The averaging assumption applies in this situation much as it does in the integration over patches, so the indirect component can be separated in the same way.

The second effect is the in-scattering toward the viewpoint (camera), which makes the participating medium itself visible. This is computed by integrating over each ray in the set of rays forming the line of sight of a pixel. For this computation it is helpful to (hypothetically) divide the scene volume into voxels corresponding to the squares of the checkerboard illumination. Each voxel is then either directly illuminated in full, or not directly illuminated at all. Each ray through a pixel can be expected to hit approximately a fraction α lit voxels, and

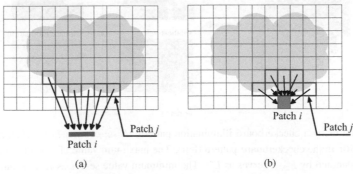

(a)   (b)

Figure 8.42   Effects of a scattering medium.

$1 - \alpha$ unlit voxels. Consequently, this second scattering effect can be separated in the same way as the other GI effects.

Practical separation. The separation of direct and global illumination is theoretically possible from the two captured images of the scene under checkerboard illumination described above. But complications arise in reality: digitally captured photographs have noise, and the projector does not produce a perfectly uniform radiance. These cause variation in the captured image pixel values that have nothing to do with global illumination. To solve this, a set of images is captured for each configuration by shifting the checkerboard pattern by small steps in each direction. Normally five steps are used, so there are 25 images captured in total. Instead of manually selecting the lit and unlit pixels in the image, $L^+[c,i]$ and $L^-[c,i]$ are approximated from the largest and smallest corresponding pixel values, respectively, in the 25 captured images (Figure 8.43).

Figure 8.44 shows some results of the separation method. The scene was constructed to include most of the global illumination effects considered in the paper. The bright area in the corner where the two walls meet is a result of diffuse interreflection. Specular interreflection occurs on the shiny object just under the curtain. The slab of marble at the bottom center of the scene exhibits significant subsurface scattering, as does the candle just behind it. The frosted glass container at the right has a translucent surface, and the glass at the left contains diluted milk that exhibits volumetric scattering. The scene in the bottom row is much simpler in content, but has trickier high frequency reflection. Figure 8.44(a) contain an

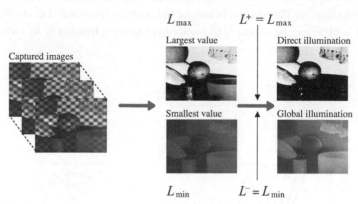

Figure 8.43   Separation using a checkerboard illumination pattern. A set of images are captured with slight shifts in the checkerboard pattern (left). The maximum value of a pixel in the set of images, denoted by $L_{\max}$, serves as L^+. The minimum value serves as L^-. (From [Nayar et al. 06] © 2006 ACM, Inc. Included here by permission.)

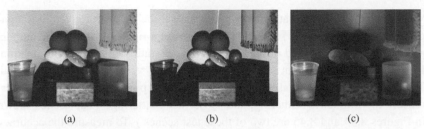

(a)   (b)   (c)

Figure 8.44   Separation results. (From [Nayar et al. 06] © 2006 ACM, Inc. Included here by permission.)

unaltered image of the scene captured under full illumination. Parts (b) and (c) contain the direct and global components separated using the checkerboard illumination. These images are an example of a "successful" separation: the computed direct and global images match expectations. In the image representing direct lighting (Figure 8.44(b)) the parts of the scene where global effects dominate— the glass of diluted milk, the translucent container, and the interreflection on the walls—are appropriately dark. In the global illumination image, those areas are the brightest. (The computed images in Figure 8.44 have been brightened somewhat for clarity.)

The corresponding set of images in Figure 8.45 show an example of "failed" separation. The scene consists of three diffuse walls and mirror sphere. The reflection off the sphere has (nearly) an infinitely high frequency: the specular lobe is nearly an infinitely narrow Dirac δ. The reflection off the sphere therefore does not smooth out the incident illumination—it reflects the checkerboard pattern onto the walls. Consequently, the value of $L_g^+[c, i]$ is not smooth enough for the approximation of Equation (8.12) to apply. In other words, the two-bounce illumination retains the high frequency pattern of the light. The checkerboard pattern is actually visible on the walls of the (incorrectly) computed direct and global images.

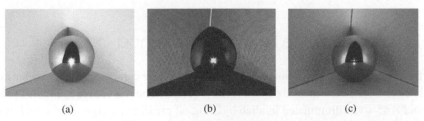

(a)   (b)   (c)

Figure 8.45   Separation results. (From [Nayar et al. 06] © 2006 ACM, Inc. Included here by permission.)

Verification. From a mathematical perspective, the argument given in the paper for the validity of the separation falls short of a rigorous proof. The authors point out that the method only estimates the separation of global illumination. It was therefore important to provide experimental verification of the method. The authors created several physical test scenes that prominently exhibited inter-reflection, volumetric scattering, and subsurface scattering. (The scenes shown in Figures 8.44 and 8.45 are two of these test scenes.) To measure the accuracy of the separation, they made an approximate direct measurement of the global component at several points in the scene. This was accomplished by fully illuminating the scene except for a small region in the immediate vicinity of the point to be measured, which is effected by deactivating small squares of pixels in the projector that illuminate the point. A captured image of the scene so illuminated therefore records only the global component at the point. A general separation method can be verified by comparing this directly measured global component to the computed global component. The authors experimented with the size of the deactivated square, and found that measurements taken from squares of 3×3 pixels to squares of 11×11 stayed within a 10% margin of error. One exception is a test point on the slab of marble, which exhibits a lot of subsurface scattering.

The authors ran several other sets of experiments. One set of experiments varied the light patterns, maintaining the frequency and the overall coverage at $\alpha = \frac{1}{2}$. Comparing the results of the separation over all the patterns showed little variation. Another set of experiments used a fixed-sized 6×6 square with varying pixel coverages. This tested the validity of the general approach, by comparing how the value of L_g^+ matches the theoretical approximation αL_g on which the separation is ultimately based. The results showed that this proportional relationship is generally valid for $0.1 \leq \alpha \leq 0.9$. The final experiment varied the frequency of the checkerboard lighting pattern. For square sizes from 3 to 16 pixels, the results varied little. However, with larger square sizes the illumination frequency falls below the frequency of the interreflections, in which case the method does not apply.

8.3.4   Extensions of the Separation Method

Depending on the light source, there are cases where capturing images under the checkerboard illumination pattern is not practical. The test scenes in Figures 8.44 and 8.45 were illuminated in a lab by a digital projector. Large scenes, and outdoor scenes in daylight simply cannot be illuminated in this way. However, high frequency illumination can be improvised. One way of doing this is to add an

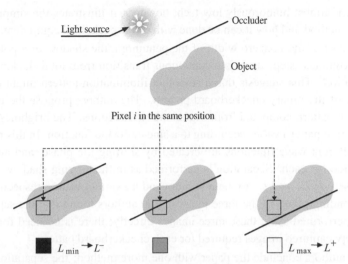

Figure 8.46 Moving a thin occluder over a scene while capturing images can provide high frequency illumination.

occluder, such as a long thin pole, to cast an appropriate shadow on the objects. Images are captured as the pole is incrementally moved in small steps across the scene. (The authors actually used a video camera and moved the pole across the image continuously.) The pixels are then compared across the images. The largest pixel value is taken as L^+; the smallest, as L^-. Figure 8.46 illustrates the idea.

The sun is an area light source, so it casts soft shadows. The umbra is the part of the shadow where the sun appears completely blocked; the penumbra is the part where the sun appears only partially blocked. The relative size of the umbra and penumbra depend on how far the pole is above the scene. If the pole is very close to the ground, the umbra is nearly the size of the pole and the penumbra is an almost unnoticeable narrow region around the umbra. As the pole gets higher off the ground the umbra narrows and the penumbra widens. Eventually the umbra disappears altogether and only the penumbra remains as a diffuse bright shadow. The frequency of the light pattern produced by the sun with the shadow of a pole thus decreases as the pole gets further from the scene. In order for the separation to work, the pole must be sufficiently close to the objects that each scene point is in the umbra in some captured image, and the penumbra is not too wide. An added constraint of course is that the pole itself does not block the scene objects. The idea that simply recording a movie of a pole being swept over an object gives enough information to separate the lighting into direct and indirect components may seem almost humorously low-tech; however, it illustrates the simplicity of Nayar's method and how it can be done with little specialized equipment.

Because of the nonzero width of the penumbra, the shadow of a pole is not a true brightness step: there is a continuous transition from total shadow to full illumination. This suggests that a smoother illumination pattern might be used in place of the binary checkerboard pattern. The authors propose the use of a wave-like pattern computed from trigonometric functions. The brightness of the illumination pattern varies according to a sine or cosine function. In this method, three different wave functions are created by shifting the phase, and an image is captured for each. Separation is performed as in the moving shadow method, i.e., by setting L^- and L^+ to the minimum and maximum values, respectively, of corresponding pixels in the three images. The authors found that the separation can be performed using these three images directly; there is no need for the 25 separately captured images required for each checkerboard pattern.

The authors conclude the paper with one more method: the separation of direct and global components using a *single* image. The method works by illuminating the scene with a high frequency binary pattern in the form of parallel strips a few pixels wide. Then the image is separated into square tiles, each of which is large enough to contain several cycles of the illumination pattern (Figure 8.47). These tiles form a kind of lower resolution version of the image; each tile is a "pixel" of the smaller image. But unlike the original pixels, the tiles contain high frequency lighting information. The maximum and minimum pixel values are averaged across the tile, and using these as the L^+ and L^- values allows the separation to be performed as usual. However, this only works if the detail of the object changes slowly enough to be considered approximately constant over each

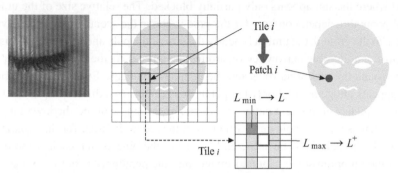

Figure 8.47   Separation using only one image can be accomplished by splitting the image into tiles and treating the tiles as individual pixels in a smaller image. (From [Nayar et al. 06] © 2006 ACM, Inc. Included here by permission.)

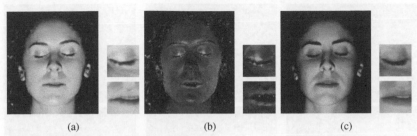

(a) (b) (c)

Figure 8.48   Results of single-image separation of a human face. (a) Direct illumination. (b) Indirect illumination. (c) Subsurface scattering in the skin. (From [Nayar et al. 06] © 2006 ACM, Inc. Included here by permission.)

tile. Otherwise the maximum and minimum values will measure to variation in the object radiance rather than response to high frequency lighting.

A drawback of the single-image method is that the separation is performed as if the tiles were the individual pixels, and this has the effect of producing lower resolution separated images. In other words, it is difficult to create high resolution results. One way around this is to interpolate the values of $L_{\min}$ and $L_{\max}$ between the tiles, which results in full resolution images. However, the authors advocate simply capturing the images at increased resolution, i.e., higher than is neededfor the particular application. Figure 8.48 shows the results of using this method to separate a human face into direct and global components. The global component includes subsurface scattering. These results reaffirm the importance of subsurface scattering in the appearance of human skin.

As mentioned earlier, the high frequency lighting technique developed by Nayar and his collaborators provided the opportunity to examine the effects of direct and indirect illumination in real objects. For example, Figure 8.49 shows the separation results of different human hands. The results indicate that the effect subsurface scattering has on the appearance of skin depends on the concentration of pigments. This is consistent with the subsurface scattering models developed by other researchers, as described in Chapter 4. As pigment concentration also varies in human hair, these results suggest that subsurface scattering is an important part of the appearance of hair. Figure 8.50 shows some examples of direct and global effects in hair.

The conceptual separation of local and global lighting effects were introduced in Chapter 1 and have been a frequent theme throughout this work. The introduction of new concepts, such as image based BRDFs and reflectance fields as well

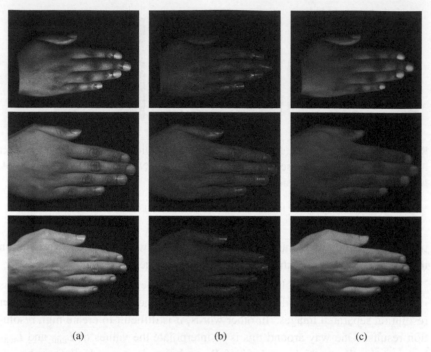

Figure 8.49   Separation of direct and indirect lighting in human hands. (a) Original captured image. (b) Separated direct illumination. (c) Separated indirect light; most of this comes from subsurface scattering. Evidently, subsurface scattering decreases with increasing skin pigmentation. (Courtesy of Shree K. Nayar, Columbia University.) (See Color Plate XII.)

separation of direct and global illumination!using high-frequency illumination!in human hands

as better surface reflection models, has expanded the idea of reflection to include more global effects. Methods of separating a captured image into the effects of direct illumination and the effects of global illumination will doubtlessly play an important role in creating more globally oriented reflectance models.

8.4 Reflectance of Hair

This chapter has explored the development of general reflectance models. The remainder of the chapter is devoted to the specific but very important problem of rendering human hair. The demand for photorealistic rendering of hair has existed since the earliest days of realistic CG rendering. Fundamental models of hair

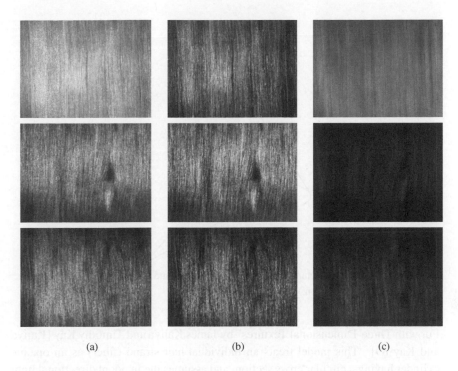

(a)   (b)   (c)

Figure 8.50   Separation of direct and indirect lighting in human hair. (a) Original captured images. (b) Separated direct illumination (c) Separated indirect illumination, including multiple scattering. The color of light hair is almost entirely determined by scattering in the fibers. (Courtesy of Shree K. Nayar, Columbia University.) (See Color Plate XIII.)

and hair rendering were established in the early days in CG. However, rendering hair is a computationally costly job because of the geometric complexity and the huge volume of data it involves. Modeling the tens of thousands of strands of hair on a typical human head is no easy task either. Consequently, progress in physically based hair rendering lagged somewhat behind other materials. Then in 2002 something of a revolution in the subject occurred.

The key to achieving realism in hair rendering is the accurate representation of light scattering. This has customarily been split into two problems: light scattering in individual strands of hair, and light scattering within a hair volume. The former is handled by a hair reflectance model; the latter is the more general process of hair rendering. This section covers models of single-strand hair reflection.

The oldest and most well known hair-reflectance model is the Kajiya-Kay hair-reflectance model, presented in the SIGGRAPH paper entitled "Rendering

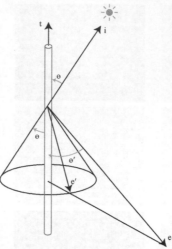

Figure 8.51   The Kajiya-Kay hair reflectance model. (From [Kajiya and Kay 89] © 1989 ACM, Inc.
Included here by permission.)

Fur with Three-Dimensional Textures" by James Kajiya and Timothy Kay [Kajiya
and Kay 89]. This model treats an individual hair strand (fiber) as an opaque
cylinder having a circular cross section, and assumes the incident directional light
is reflected to a cone (Figure 8.51). The corresponding highlight is modeled with
a Phong lobe. All the other reflection is approximated by a single diffuse term as
if the cylinder has a Lambertian component.

The Kajiya-Kay model is a phenomenological model that has no real physical
foundation. It merely captures the most obvious reflectance features of a single
hair fiber. Even so, it was a popular method of rendering hair for more than a
decade after its publication. However, as the level of expectation of realism in CG
rendering increased, limitations of the model became more problematic. From the
standpoint of visual effects, the most serious deficiency is the assumption that a
hair fiber is opaque—it does not account for light transmission or scattering. Real
hair, particularly light colored hair, is translucent; most of the color of blond hair
comes from transmission and scattering.

A model for reflectance that includes scattering was introduced in a paper entitled "Light Scattering from Human Hair Fibers" by Stephen R. Marschner, Henrik Wann Jensen, Mike Cammarano, Steve Worley, and Pat Hanrahan [Marschner
et al. 03]. The model, now known as the *Marschner model*, was the first hair reflectance model introduced in computer graphics that was based on actual
measurements of real human hair. The emergence of the Marschner model had a
substantial impact on subsequent hair-rendering research and visual effects ren-

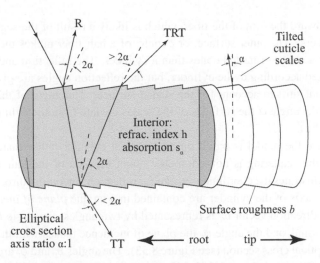

Figure 8.52 Basic geometry of the Marschner hair reflectance model. (From [Marschner et al. 03] © 2003 ACM, Inc. Included here by permission.)

dering. It sparked a rapid evolution of physically based hair-rendering technologies shortly after its publication.

Marschner became interested in the scattering properties of hair fibers while working at Microsoft Research. His colleagues there had been working on real-time rendering of fur based on the Kajiya-Kay model. A certain lack of realism in the results got Marschner thinking of ways to improve it.

Later he had the opportunity to collaborate with Pat Hanrahan and Henrik Wann Jensen at Stanford University, where he became convinced of the importance of a physically-based hair reflectance model. In their background research, he and his collaborators came across some relevant papers in the cosmetics literature that inspired the model published in the 2003 paper.

The Marschner model incorporates several ideas for rendering hair that were new at the time, but two aspects of the model particularly influenced subsequent research. The first is the notion of modeling hair fibers as colored dielectric cylinders having elliptical cross sections. The second is the representation of the scattering components. Light scattering in a dielectric cylinder has three strong components or modes, illustrated in Figure 8.52. The modes are named with a sequence of "R"s and "T"s; "R" stands for "reflection," "T," for "transmission." The "R" component is thus the first reflection of light off the surface of the hair fiber. The "TT" component represents the transmission of light through the hair fiber, and the "TRT" is the result of a single internal scattering event on the opposite side of the fiber. The authors note that the specular peak is shifted slightly toward the root of the fiber, which is likely a result of the scaled surface of hair fibers. The outer surface, or *cuticle*, of a hair fiber makes the fiber look more like a series of nested cones than a cylinder. The reflection and scattering is computed according to the cylinder, but the reflection angles are given a small longitudinal shift to account for the scaled surface. The angle of this shift depends on the angle α the surfaces of the scales deviate from the cylinder surface (Figure 8.52).

Because the model is based on an elliptical cylinder rather than a circular cylinder, the scattering is not symmetric about the axis of the hair fiber. Figure 8.53 illustrates the coordinate system for reflection. Incoming direction vector $\vec{\omega}_i$ and the axis of the cylinder are contained in a unique *plane of incidence*. An incoming direction vector $\vec{\omega}_i$ is represented by two angles: the angle θ_i from the surface normal, and the angle ϕ_r the plane of incidence makes with the long axis of the elliptical cross section (see Figure 8.53). The angles θ_r and ϕ_r are measured similarly. The scattering model is the sum of the R, TT, and TRT components, each of which can be expressed as the product of a function of θ_i and θ_r, and a function of $\theta_r - \theta_i$, ϕ_i, and ϕ_r:

$$S(\theta_i, \theta_r, \phi_i, \phi_r) = M_R(\theta_i, \theta_r) N_R(\theta, \phi_i, \phi_r)$$
$$+ M_{TT}(\theta_i, \theta_r) N_{TT}(\theta, \phi_i, \phi_r)$$
$$+ M_{TRT}(\theta_i, \theta_r) N_{TRT}(\theta, \phi_i, \phi_r). \qquad (8.15)$$

The functions M are called *longitudinal* functions, as they depend on the longitudinal angles θ_i and θ_r, both of which are measured according to the long axis of the cylinder. The functions N are *azimuthal* functions. Equation (8.15) thus

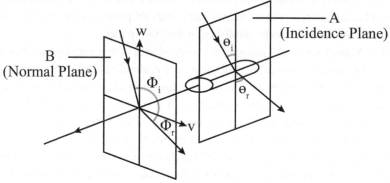

Figure 8.53   Angles used in the Marschner hair reflectance model. The plane of incidence contains the incident ray and is parallel to the axis of the cylinder and contains the incident light direction; the normal plane is perpendicular to the axis.

expresses the four-parameter reflectance function as a sum of products of two- and three-parameter functions. If the model is simplified to have a circular cross section, then the azimuthal dependence reduces to the difference $\phi_r - \phi_i$ of the azimuthal angles ϕ_i and ϕ_r. Therefore, $S(\theta_i, \theta_r, \phi_i, \phi_r)$ becomes an expression involving two-parameter functions, which can be precomputed and stored in a 2D table (i.e., a texture map).

The longitudinal functions M were fit to observations; the azimuthal functions N came from physical considerations. The M functions were found to be fairly close to the Kajiya-Kay model, although the specular highlight is shifted by the angle α of the cuticle scaled as described previously. In the final model, the M functions are a Gaussian functions centered at the half-angle between the incident and reflected directions, but shifted by a multiple of α according to the number of reflection and refraction events involved. The M_{TT} and M_{TRT} lobes are shifted towards the tip of the hair fiber, whereas the M_R is shifted toward the root.

Marschner and his colleagues were not the first to perform direct measurements of reflection in hair fibers (this had been done years earlier in the context of cosmetic science) but they were the first to perform full hemispherical measurements of hair reflection. They also recorded a special set of measurements by

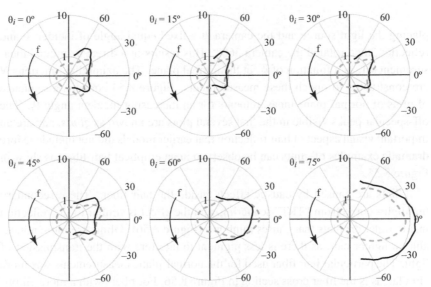

Figure 8.54 Plots of azimuthal measurements. For each fixed incident direction θ_i, a sensor is placed at the specular direction and rotated around the fiber. The plots show the off-specular peaks known as *glints* evolving toward the normal specular highlight as θ_i increases. (From [Marschner et al. 03] © 2003 ACM, Inc. Included here by permission.)

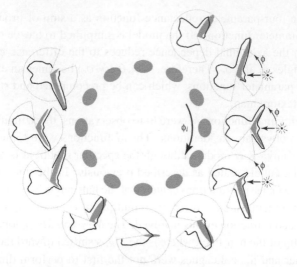

Figure 8.55   Scattering in the normal plane from an elliptical blond hair fiber. Illumination comes from
               the right. The dark lines show the measured reflectance; the gray regions illustrate the
               results of Monte Carlo simulation in the Marschner model. The glints are significant for
               this fiber. (From [Marschner et al. 03] © 2003 ACM, Inc. Included here by permission.)

placing the light source and the camera at a fixed equal angle of incidence and
reflection, then rotated the camera 360°. This results in a direct azimuthal measurement set, as a function of ϕ, in the normal plane. The azimuthal functions N
are constructed to match these measurements. Figure 8.54 contains a sequence
of plots of normal-plane measurements for an increasing incident angle θ_i. The
off-specular peaks visible in the first several plots are known as *glints*, and are an
important visual aspect of hair reflection that earlier models did not include. More
dramatic examples of glints can be observed in an elliptical hair fiber, as show in
Figure 8.55.

Glints are caused by caustic effects inside the hair fiber. These secondary
highlights come from "TRT" scattering, and the effect is similar to the reflection
inside water droplets that causes rainbows (Figure 8.56). Glints are more noticeable in lighter hair, as there is less pigment to interfere with the transmission of
light. The particular hair fiber used for the normal-plane measurements was more
circular, as is the fiber cross section in Figure 8.56. For fibers with a more elliptical cross section, which better models real hair, the strength and location of glints
depends on the orientation of the ellipse around the hair-fiber axis. This varies
significantly, especially in "curly" hair, which has a more elliptical cross section,
and is what gives a hair fiber its "distinctive sparkling appearance" according to

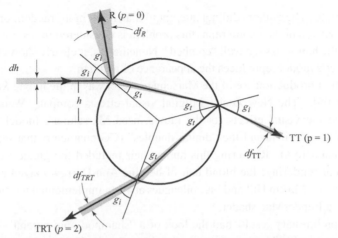

Figure 8.56   Light reflection and transmission of a hair fiber as viewed along the axis of the hair fiber. Although it is circular in this figure, the general model has an elliptical cross section. (From [Marschner et al. 03] © 2003 ACM, Inc. Included here by permission.)

the authors. Note that glints normally have the color of the hair, while the primary specular highlight has the color of the light.

A complete physical analysis of scattering from hair fiber is very complicated. Marschner's model is relatively simple, yet captures the physical characteristics essential to realistic rendering. Figure 8.57 shows rendering of a geometric model of human hair with the Kajiya-Kay model and the Marschner model compared to a photograph. The geometric model of the hair fibers used in these renderings is

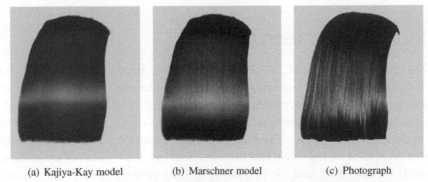

(a) Kajiya-Kay model   (b) Marschner model   (c) Photograph

Figure 8.57   Comparison of renderings using the Kajiya-Kay model, the Marschner model, and a photograph. (From [Marschner et al. 03] © 2003 ACM, Inc. Included here by permission.)

approximate. The authors did not attempt to match the more random orientation of fibers visible in the photograph (this problem is considered in Section 8.6). As a result, the hair looks too well "combed." Nonetheless, it clearly shows how well Marschner's model reproduces the appearance of real hair.

The first production use of the Marschner model was in the movie *King Kong* [Jackson 05]. The New Zealand digital visual effects company Weta Digital, which did the visual effects for the movie, used Marschner's model for King Kong's fur as well for all the "digital doubles" (CG characters that replace actual human actors). Rendering this human hair included the greatest challenge yet for hair rendering: the blond hair of heroine Ann Darrow played by actress Naomi Watts. Martin Hill and his colleagues at Weta implemented the Marschner model as a RenderMan shader.

The preliminary results had the look of a "shampoo commercial"—the hair looked too good. This was not such a problem for the human characters, but it was less suitable for Kong himself. He was, after all, a wild gorilla. A series of different implementations were required to get the desired look. In order to produce a dusty appearance, an analytic cylindrical diffuse model was layered on Marschner's model. In other cases, geometric debris was stuck between multiple hair strands to form clumps. Glossy highlights were added to produce the appearance of wetness. For shadowing within the fur, deep shadow maps (Section 3.3.8) were used in conjunction with volume occlusion maps, which work like ambient occlusion maps in volumes. The amount of occlusion is computed for each point in the fur in a reference pose, and this is stored as a 3D volume that can be accessed at render time to obtain the occlusion. The "bent normal" approach used in the ambient occlusion map (Section 7.2.6) was also employed. Later, Weta Digital developed a more physically accurate rendering pipeline that included the effects of multiple scattering.

8.5   Multiple Scattering in Hair

The primary characteristic of light colored hair is its translucency. As described in Chapter 4, multiple scattering is an important element of the appearance of translucent objects, so accounting for multiple scattering is necessary to realistically render light colored hair. The direct and indirect separation shown in Figure 8.50 affirms this. The Marschner model considers only reflection and transmission in an individual hair fiber. A "head" of hair consists of many thousands of hair fibers, and the interaction of light between them is not directly handled by Marschner's reflectance model. The images in Figures 8.57 were rendered by ray tracing a complex geometric model with each hair strand explicitly included as a geometric primitive. At an intersection with a hair fiber, the Marschner reflectance model was used to compute the surface radiance. The ray tracing accounted for occlusion but not multiple scattering between the hair fibers. Even so, this kind of explicit geometry is costly because of the sheer size. An alternative approach is to treat a head of hair as a volume rather than a collection of individual strands.

8.5.1   A Volumetric Approach

Earlier in the history of rendering, hair was regarded as a volume, or the surface of a volume. This idea predates computer graphics of course; artists seldom draw hair as a set of individual strands—they draw or paint it like a volume and add details to suggest the structure. In 2006, Jonathan T. Moon and Marschner presented a method for simulating multiple scattering in hair as a volume function in the paper "Simulating Multiple Scattering in Hair Using Photon Mapping Approach" [Moon and Marschner 06]. The paper begins with an analysis of the general characteristics of multiple scattering in a hair volume and then presents a simulation method that uses a particle simulation.

Figure 8.58 illustrates the scattering distribution from an individual blond hair strand. The "TT" component, which represents the transmitted light (see Figure 8.52), has the largest lobe. This matches intuition, because the translucency and lack of pigment in a light colored hair fiber can be expected to transmit a large amount of light. Stated in the language of volume scattering, light hair has a strong forward scattering component, and this means the directionality of light tends to be preserved as it travels through a volume of hair. Most of the work in subsurface scattering described in Chapter 4 depends on the diffusion approximation; it assumes that scattering causes directional light to spread out and thereby lose its directionality after a few scattering events. This assumption is not valid for scattering within a hair volume.

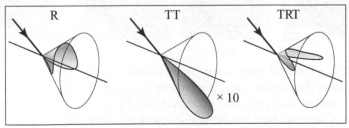

Figure 8.58   The three major modes of scattering from a single hair fiber of light-colored hair. (From [Moon and Marschner 06] © 2006 ACM, Inc. Included here by permission.)

The highly directional nature of the scattering and the varying density within a hair volume due to natural hair clumping make it difficult to approximate multiple scattering in a hair volume with simple formulas. So Moon and Marschner took a particle-simulation approach. The method they employed is based on the concept of a volume photon map (see Section 2.4), but the specific properties of scattering in hair necessitated some modifications to the method. The first major difference in Moon and Marschner's algorithm is that in the particle simulation phase, photons are deposited uniformly along the particle paths instead of at surface intersections. The other major difference is that because light scattering in hair volume is highly directional, the photon map is represented in a 5D space that includes direction instead of the usual 3D space. That is, in the nearest neighbors search for particle lookup, particles are "near" each other if they are close in spatial proximity and also have nearly the same direction. In the normal photon map method, closeness is only measured in spatial position.

Figure 8.59 shows the results of the particle simulation method compared to other methods of rendering a lock of hair. The image in part (a) was rendered using direct lighting only; without any scattering it looks black. The image in part (b) is a reference image rendered using path tracing. The image in part (c) was rendered using the volumetric particle simulation. Although it lacks some of the fine detail visible in the path-traced image, the overall appearance matches

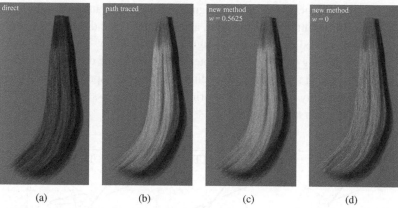

(a)   (b)   (c)   (d)

Figure 8.59   Renderings of light hair using volumetric multiple scattering. The model is rendered (a) with direct lighting only (there is essentially no color), (b) using path tracing, for a reference image, (c) using the volumetric particle simulation method, and (d) assuming the scattering is isotropic. Note that the forward scattering assumption is necessary to reproduce the color. (From [Moon and Marschner 06] © 2006 ACM, Inc. Included here by permission.) (See Color Plate XIV.)

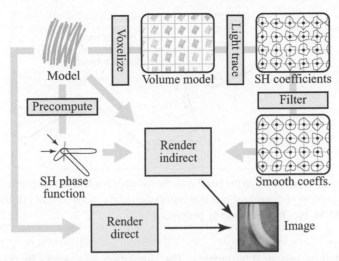

Figure 8.60   A schematic illustration of the spherical harmonics method of computing multiple scattering in hair.   (From [Moon et al. 08] © 2008 ACM, Inc. Included here by permission.)

very well. The image in part (d) was rendered with the volumetric method, but under the assumption that the scattering is isotropic. Without the strong forward scattering bias, the color washes out to a neutral gray. This illustrates the importance of the directionality of scattering in a hair volume.

The particle simulation approach in Moon and Marschner's 2006 paper can accurately simulate multiple scattering in hair, but it has the drawbacks of large storage requirements of the photon map and the computational cost of the particle simulation. In 2008, Moon, Bruce Walter, and Marschner presented a different approach in a paper entitled "Efficient Multiple Scattering in Hair Using Spherical Harmonics" [Moon et al. 08]. Figure 8.60 contains an outline of the method. As in many rendering algorithms, the rendering is split into direct and indirect illumination. The direct illumination is computed using ray tracing or any other suitable technique. The method of computing the indirect component is the novel part of the work.

The indirect illumination is computed using a two-pass method similar to the photon-mapping approach: the first pass is a simulation process that traces light paths, and the actual rendering is done in the second pass. In order to make the first pass (light tracing process) more efficient, the hair volume is voxelized. That is, a grid of voxels covering the hair volume is constructed so that each voxel in the voxel grid contains the average density and direction of the hair fibers in the voxel. Each voxel also stores a directionally dependent radiance distribution

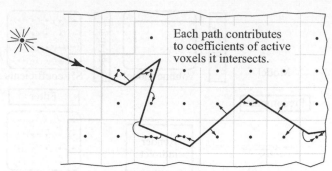

Figure 8.61   In tracing a light path through the voxel grid, the radiance is added to the spherical harmonics representation of directional radiance distribution of the voxel. (From [Moon et al. 08]
© 2008 ACM, Inc. Included here by permission.)

represented by spherical harmonics. The simulation pass works by tracing random rays from the light through the grid (Figure 8.61). Radiance is deposited
into each voxel the light path hits by projecting its value onto spherical harmonic
basis functions. The value is recorded as a *scattering matrix* representing the
scattering function of the hair; the values stored in the grid are therefore just
the SH coefficients (Section 7.2.5). After the lighting simulation is complete, the
SH coefficients are smoothed to reduce noise.

In the rendering phase (Figure 8.62), rays are traced from the eye. At the
intersection with a hair fiber, the scattered radiance is obtained from the SH representation in the voxel. The scattering at the fiber is computed by multiplying
the SH coefficients by the scattering matrix. Before this can be done, the SH co-

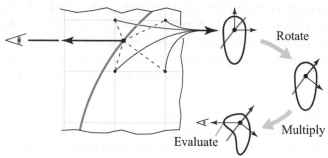

Figure 8.62   Rendering a point on a hair fiber using the spherical harmonics representation in the voxel
requires rotating the SH basis to the hair fiber axis direction. From there, the scattering
computation reduces to a matrix multiplication. (From [Moon et al. 08] © 2008 ACM,
Inc. Included here by permission.)

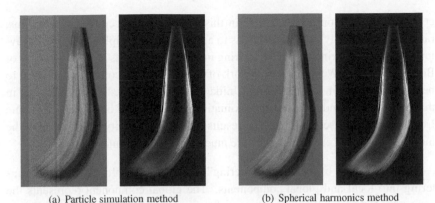

(a) Particle simulation method   (b) Spherical harmonics method

Figure 8.63   Comparison of image rendered using (a) the photon mapping method, and (b) the spherical harmonics method. The images on the right are lit from behind. (From [Moon et al. 08] © 2008 ACM, Inc. Included here by permission.)

ordinate system must be rotated to match the orientation of the fiber. This has to be done separately during the rendering phase, because each voxel may contain many fibers, so the SH coordinate system is left in the "neutral" coordinate system of the grid.[17]

Using spherical harmonics in this way reduces the computation of the scattering integral (see Section 3.3.2) to a simple matrix multiplication. As a result, the process is much faster than the volumetric photon mapping and dramatically faster than a brute-force path-tracing approach. Figure 8.63 contains a pair of images, one lit from the front, and one lit from the back, rendered with the photon map method described in the 2006 paper and the corresponding images rendered using the spherical harmonics approach. The images are practically indistinguishable, but the SH implementation runs about 10 times faster.

Martin Hill and his colleagues at Weta Digital began implementing these two-pass methods for rendering hair starting in 2007. They established an efficient GI rendering pipeline based on the concept of precomputed radiance transfer (see Section 10.5), which they applied to the production of the movie *Avatar*.

8.5.2 An Analytical Approach.

In 2008, another method for efficiently rendering multiple scattering in hair was presented in the paper "Dual Scattering Approximation for Fast Multiple Scattering in Hair" by Arno Zinke, Cem Yuksel, Andreas Weber, and John Keyser [Zinke

---

[17]The details of the scattering matrix and its relationship to spherical harmonic basis functions is covered in Section 10.2.2.

et al. 08]. The approach described in this paper does not employ simulations; rather, it analytically derives functions to approximate multiple scattering behavior. Arno was working on light scattering in general filaments at the University of Bonn [Zinke and Weber 07]. The work of Marschner and colleagues led him to become interested in hair rendering. Unlike the typical "hacks" sometimes used in the visual effects industry, the approximations of Zinke and his colleagues come from physically based insights. The results have visual quality comparable to the methods described earlier, but they are much faster to compute.

The basic idea of the "dual scattering" method is to split the multiple scattering into local and global components. The global component represents the amount of light from the source that reaches a particular point in the hair volume. It is computed by approximating the overall density of the hair volume and computing the scattering along a single light path to the source, which the authors call a *shadow path*. The global multiple-scattering component depends primarily on forward scattered light; backward scattering is treated as part of the attenuation. In contrast, the local multiple-scattering component comes from all multiple scattering within a neighborhood of a particular hair fiber, which normally includes several other nearby fibers. The primary constituent of local multiple scattering is backscattering from these nearby hair fibers. The total multiple scattering, as a function of position and incident and scattering directions, is a sum of the global

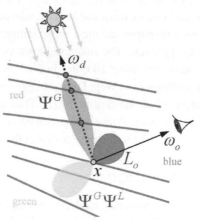

Figure 8.64   The basic concept of dual scattering method is to split the scattering into the *global scattering* of light from the light source and the *local scattering* within a local cluster of hair fibers. (From [Zinke et al. 08] © 2008 ACM, Inc. Included here by permission.) (See Color Plate XV.)

scattering function Ψ^G and the further local scattering function Ψ^L:

$$\Psi(x, \vec{\omega}_i, \vec{\omega}_s) = \Psi^G(x, \vec{\omega}_i, \vec{\omega}_s) + \Psi^G(x, \vec{\omega}_i, \vec{\omega}_s)\Psi^L(x, \vec{\omega}_i, \vec{\omega}_s).$$

That is, the local scattering applies to the light reaching the point after the effects of global scattering. Figure 8.64 illustrates the two scattering functions and the total scattering as colored lobes.

The global scattering function is approximated by a product of the total transmittance along the shadow path, and a "spread" function that indicates how multiple scattering spreads out the radiance according to direction. Both are computed as if the shadow path intersects a certain number of hair fibers. The transmittance component is computed according to Marschner's (single) scattering model for the hair fiber. The spread component is modeled using a narrow Gaussian distribution function of direction. The local scattering is computed by modeling the backscattering from hair fibers in the local hair "cluster." Unlike the global component, which is determined by a single light path, the local component includes a collection of local paths that end up back at the particular hair fiber. This includes single-bounce and multiple-bounce light paths. Because the local multiple scattering is concerned with backscattering, only paths that can hit a particular fiber through one or more backscattering events are considered.

The reflection model uses an estimate of the density of hair fibers instead of

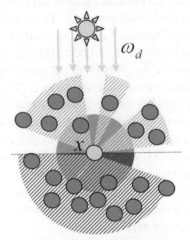

Figure 8.65 A cluster of hair has a density factor giving the approximate number of hairs per area of a cross section. The red areas affect global scattering; the blue areas cause local backscattering. (From [Zinke et al. 08] © 2008 ACM, Inc. Included here by permission.) (See Color Plate XI.)

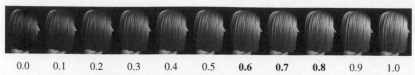

| 0.0 | 0.1 | 0.2 | 0.3 | 0.4 | 0.5 | **0.6** | **0.7** | **0.8** | 0.9 | 1.0 |

Figure 8.66   Effect of the density factor. Normal human hair ranges from 0.6 to 0.8. Lower density means less scattering, which makes the hair appear darker. (From [Zinke et al. 08] © 2008 ACM, Inc. Included here by permission.) (See Color Plate XVI.)

a geometric model of the hair volume. Figure 8.65 illustrates the density of hair fibers in a cross section of a hair cluster. The shaded areas indicate the angular regions for which multiple scattering is possible. Two separate density factors are used: d_f represents the density of fibers along the shadow path from the light source (shown in the red hatched region in the figure); d_b represents the density of fibers in the local hair cluster from which backscattering is possible (in the blue hatched region in the figure). Values of the density factors d_f and d_b for human hair range from about 0.6 to 0.8; both were fixed at 0.7 for most of the examples in the paper. Figure 8.66 illustrates the effect of changing these values. At values near zero, there is little multiple scattering, which causes the hair to appear much darker as explained in the previous section.

To render a point in a hair volume using the method, the incident light, attenuated by the global multiple scattering function, is integrated over the incident directions. This includes unoccluded incident light, the reflection of which is computed directly from the Marschner model. There are several ways this might be done. A ray-"shooting" approach simply casts rays from the evaluation point and counts intersection with other hair fibers. If there are none, the Marschner model is applied. Otherwise the global forward-scattering function is computed for the number of intersections as described above. While this can be done as part of the rendering process, a more efficient method is to precompute this attenuation along all shadow paths, and store the results in a volumetric data structure for subsequent lookup during rendering. This process employs *deep opacity maps* [Yuksel and Keyser 08], which can be implemented on a GPU if the hair volume is approximated by a collection of layers. Figure 8.67 contains a comparison of results. Part (a) of the figure is rendered using brute-force path tracing, Part (b) is rendered using the dual scattering approach with ray shooting, Part (c) is a snapshot of the hardware implementation.

The conceptual separation of global and local multiple scattering certainly has theoretical importance, as it creates the opportunity to use different approaches for approximating the two effects independently. However, its primary impact has been the method for fast rendering of hair volumes with accuracy comparable

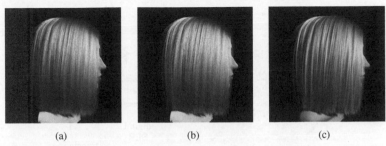

(a)   (b)   (c)

Figure 8.67   Comparison of rendering methods using the dual scattering approximation: (a) path tracing, for reference (7.8 hours); (b) offline dual scattering (5.2 minutes); (c) real-time dual scattering (14 frames per second). (From [Zinke et al. 08] © 2008 ACM, Inc. Included here by permission.) (See Color Plate XVII.)

to path tracing. This method came into practical use quickly after its publication. The first use of this method in entertainment works was in Disney's film *Tangled* (2010) [Sadeghi et al. 10]. Hair rendering was once considered a very specific rendering problem; however, the volumetric approaches definitely have a kind of general applicability that makes them likely to be applicable in rendering other materials.

8.6   Recovering Details of Hair

It was shown in the papers described above that a good physically based hair reflectance model, such as the Marschner model, coupled with a multiple scattering rendering method is necessary to reproduce the appearance of real human hair. However, this alone did not satisfy the demand for realistic rendering of hair. Even with the refined hair reflection methods described in the previous section, rendered results still seemed to lack a certain realism. This was especially noticeable in applications for which the local detail was most important, such as in movie close-ups. So the next problem was to improve the geometric model of the individual strands. This kind of incremental pursuit of realism has been common in the history of computer graphics. Another force driving the improvement in hair models was the increasing prevalence of ray tracing in production rendering that began around the year 2008. This generated more interest in the geometric details of hair. In 2009, two methods emerged that largely met these new demands for better geometry control while maintaining accurate color. Both methods employed an image-based approach—they recovered the geometry of hair from captured data of real hair.

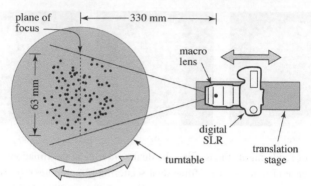

Figure 8.68   Measurement setup for capturing hair geometry. (From [Jakob et al. 09] © 2009 ACM, Inc. Included here by permission.)

8.6.1   A Fiber-Based Approach to Modeling Hair

A major advance in realistic geometric modeling of hair was presented in a paper entitled "Capturing Hair Assemblies Fiber by Fiber" by Wenzel Jakob, Jonathan T. Moon, and Steve Marschner [Jakob et al. 09]. In this paper, the authors point out that the local structure of hair strongly affects its appearance, but the existing hair modeling methods did not accurately reproduce such local structure. The typical method for generating detail in hair geometry was to randomly perturb the local arrangement of hair fibers in an ad hoc fashion. For example, guide curves can be created for the general structure of the particular hair arrangement, with individual fibers added along the curve offset by a small random amount. However, Jakob and his coauthors realized that in order to model the structure of hair, it was necessary to understand how real hair fibers are arranged. The paper thus begins by describing a method for precisely capturing the geometric details of real hair.

Capturing the small-scale structure of a lock of hair depends on the ability to reliably distinguish the individual hairs. The authors devised a method to do this using captured images from a set of viewpoints around the hair-lock sample. The apparatus is illustrated in Figure 8.68. A sample of hair is suspended from a turntable, then images of the sample are captured by a still camera that can be translated along the view direction of the camera. The camera is equipped with a macro lens having a wide aperture, so the depth of field is shallow. That is, only the hair strands near the plane of focus are discernible; the others are blurred. The turntable is rotated incrementally. At each orientation of the turntable, the camera captures a set of images as it is swept along the optical axis. This has the effect of moving the plane of focus. As a result, every photograph in a sweep provides information about a cross section of the hair sample. After combining

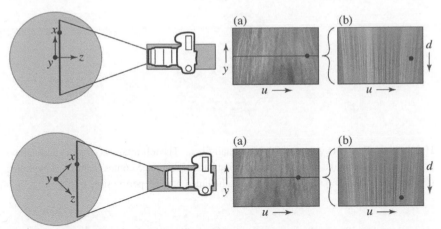

Figure 8.69   Overview of capturing process. At each position of the turntable, the camera is shifted so the plane of focus shifts through the image. The images labeled (a) are captured photographs; those labeled (b) are the result of combing in the row marked in black from all camera shifts. (From [Jakob et al. 09] © 2009 ACM, Inc. Included here by permission.)

all photographs in a sweep, the result would ideally be a complete volumetric model of the hair. This approach is not practical, however, because many hairs are not visible from a particular direction. Also, individual fibers are often in focus in several adjacent photographs, which makes it it difficult to determine their depth precisely. Both issues can be resolved by using multiple sweeps at different orientations of the turntable, which provides multiple observations of the clearly focused hair fibers from different camera angles.

Figure 8.69 illustrates two different camera positions and turntable orientations and the resulting images. The hair-fiber geometry is represented in a global (x, y, z)-coordinate system chosen such that the y-axis coincides with the rotational axis. The plane of focus in a captured image is a plane parallel to y but rotated by the angle θ of the turntable and displaced by a distance d according to the translation of the camera. A pixel in a captured image is given by coordinates (u, y), where u is the horizontal position in the plane of focus. The global (x, y, z)-coordinates of a focused pixel at position (u, y) in an image can be obtained by rotating (u, y) by θ and translating by d. Figure 8.69(a) shows a pair of captured images. Part (b) of the figure contains images constructed by stacking u-slices for a fixed y (shown at the left) for varying values of the camera distance d.

Figure 8.69 illustrates two different camera positions and turntable orientations and the resulting images. The images in part (a) are the captured images for the geometry shown at the left. Each captured image is processed using a *ridge*

Figure 8.70   Hair "ribbons" in a 3D volume of detected hair fibers. The left image is from a single viewpoint; the middle image is from two viewpoints; the right image comes from 24 viewpoints.
(From [Jakob et al. 09] © 2009 ACM, Inc. Included here by permission.)

detection algorithm to locate the focused hair fibers in the image.[18] This process
takes a large number of filters (the paper uses rotated oblong filters known as *Ga-
bor filters*) at various rotation angles and determines which most closely matches
the image around each pixel. If the match is close enough at a particular pixel,
it is likely that the pixel contains a hair fiber having the matching orientation.
The position of the match is recorded into a 3D volume representing a portion of
the hair fiber.

The ridge-detection algorithm provides a precise 2D position in the image.
The depth value however, which comes from the camera position of the particular
image, is much less certain. The images in part (b) of Figure 8.69 are formed
by sweeping the one-pixel slice of the captured images (indicated by the line in
part (a)) over all the camera positions. The individual hair fibers come into and
out of focus as the distance varies, but despite the very shallow depth of field,
each fiber appears in focus in several adjacent images. Consequently, the feature-
detection algorithm will find the fiber at several depth positions, and the detected
hair in the volume will appear as a 3D extrusion, i.e., is more like a "ribbon" than
a hair fiber. Figure 8.70 illustrates the resulting hair volume for a camera sweep
at one orientation.

The hair fibers could be reconstructed by chaining the centers of the ribbons in
the 3D volume, but the authors propose a more robust algorithm that leverages the
multiple viewpoint capture method. From different viewpoints, the same hair fiber
is matched to similar ribbons having different orientations. Figure 8.71 illustrates
the idea. The actual hair fiber is the intersection of the set of ribbons. There
is normally one ribbon for each rotation angle θ, but occlusion of hair fibers in
the sample can cause the set of ribbons to be smaller. Having the redundancy of

---

[18]Similar feature-detection algorithms are common in CG applications, and are fundamental in
computer vision. One example of ridge detection is the matching of fingerprints.

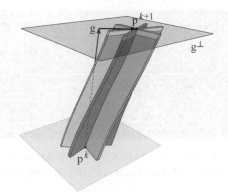

Figure 8.71   The fiber-growing algorithm estimates the direction $\vec{g}$ of the hair fiber, which lies at the intersection of the ribbons from p^k. The next point p^{k+1} is found in the cross section of the plane $g^\perp$ perpendicular to $\vec{g}$. (From [Jakob et al. 09] © 2009 ACM, Inc. Included here by permission.)

many viewpoints makes the fitting process less sensitive to local occlusion. In Figure 8.71 only three orientations (ribbons) are shown for clarity.

The 3D curve representing the hair fiber is constructed incrementally, using a set of small line segments to approximate the curve. The authors call the method a "fiber-growing" algorithm (but the algorithm does not simulate the growth of the hair as it developed from the hair follicle). The fiber-growing algorithm is a standard predictor/corrector method: at each iteration, the direction to the next point is predicted from the local geometry and then corrected to a better match for use in the next iteration. Without the correction step, the prediction error would likely increase with each iteration, causing the computed segments to drift away from the actual fiber curve.

The prediction step starts with a point in space and estimates the direction of the next point on the fiber. Just as the 3D curve can be locally approximated by a line, each ribbon can be locally approximated by a plane. The intersection of all the ribbon planes provides the direction of the fiber segment. However, due to measurement errors, it is not possible to determine this direction exactly. Determining this information from the intersection of the planes is a overdetermined problem. A least squares solution is extracted using the *singular value decomposition* (SVD), which is described more fully in Section 9.3.2. In a nutshell, the SVD factors a matrix into a product $U\Sigma V$ where Σ is a diagonal matrix of *singular values*. The SVD is applied to the matrix having the normal vectors $\vec{n}_i$ of the ribbons as its rows, and the vector in the third row of the V matrix is the estimated direction (Figure 8.72). This vector is the "most orthogonal" to the set of planes and thus is the best direction estimate. Denoting the predicted direction vector by $\vec{g}$, the

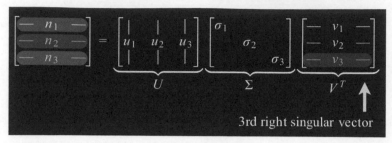

Figure 8.72   Direction estimation. The direction $\vec{g}$ is taken from the third row of the right vector in the singular value decomposition. (From [Jakob et al. 09] © 2009 ACM, Inc. Included here by permission.)

next predicted point is the current point p_k plus $h\vec{g}$, where h is the *step size* of the iteration.

Because it is just an estimate, the computed next point is likely to be slightly off the intersection of the ribbons (see Figure 8.71). The correction step "recenters" this point to the best approximation to the intersection of the ribbons in the plane $g^{\perp}$ perpendicular to the predicted direction $\vec{g}$. To compute this recentering, points on the ribbons are projected onto $g^{\perp}$, and lines in the plane are fit to the projected points. This forms a star-shaped set of lines as shown in Figure 8.73, the center of which is taken as the recentered point. Again, the intersection of the lines is overdetermined and not likely to be precise, so a least squares solution is employed for the best fit.

The algorithm for a single fiber terminates when the "grown" fiber runs out of data or exceeds the bounds of the sample. Repeating the algorithm until no ribbons remain, or the remaining ribbon data is not useful, resolves many visible hair fibers. But it may leave holes due to occlusion; hair fibers at the center of

Figure 8.73   The recentering correction works by fitting lines to the ribbon sample points, and using the best intersection of the lines. (From [Jakob et al. 09] © 2009 ACM, Inc. Included here by permission.) (See Color Plate XVIII.)

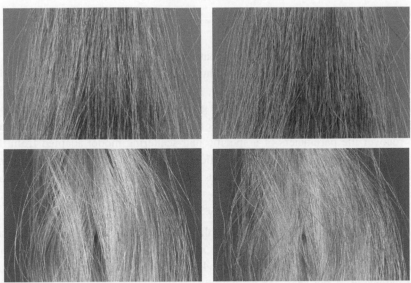

Figure 8.74   Rendered images of reconstructed hair geometry (right), giving a "ground truth" comparison to captured images (left). (From [Jakob et al. 09] © 2009 ACM, Inc. Included here by permission.) (See Color Plate XIX.)

the sample might be invisible to the camera from any of the positions. Even though fibers are not directly visible, they can affect the appearance of the hair volume through multiple scattering. Consequently, the authors propose a method for artificially generating hair fibers in the empty regions. The method uses a scheme to extrapolate already existing hair directions to the empty regions. The method is only briefly sketched in the paper, and the authors point out that in the case of a dense hair cluster (such as tightly braided hair) other approaches may be more suitable. Specifically, the infill generation method in the paper "Hair Photobooth" [Paris et al. 08] could be employed instead.

Figure 8.74 compares rendered images of the reconstructed model (right) to actual captured images (left). The images were rendered using the particle simulation approach of Moon et al. described in Section 8.5.1. The accuracy of the recovered geometry is remarkable. The "fiber by fiber" approach is a major advance in capturing fine detail of hair, and clearly shows the importance of fiber-level detail in realistic hair rendering. Data produced by this method can be expected to impact hair rendering technology in the immediate future.

8.6.2 Acquisition of Hair Color

A method to better reproduce the apparent color of real hair was proposed in the paper "A Practical Approach for Photometric Acquisition of Hair Color" by Arno Zinke, Martin Rump, Tomás Lay, Andreas Weber, Anton Andriyenko, and Reinhard Klein [Zinke et al. 09]. The goal of the work presented in this paper was to improve the realism of the color of rendered hair. The authors attempted to recover the parameters of a specific hair-scattering model adapted from the Marschner model by measuring the reflectance of actual macroscopic hair samples. The approach is similar to methods for recovering BRDF model parameters from measured data (see Section 8.1.5).

However, practical measurement of reflectance from individual hair strands is difficult. Moreover, it has been established that multiple scattering in the hair volume has more of an impact on the appearance of hair than scattering from individual hair fibers. The approach taken by Zinke and his collaborators was an extension of the approach of the "dual scattering" paper, in which the local scattering was approximated by a local cluster of hair. Instead of measuring the reflectance of individual hair strands, the authors adapted the approach to measure the reflectance of hair clusters as a BRDF. The parameters of the hair fiber scattering function can be obtained by fitting the hair cluster BRDF to measured data.

To obtain measurements, a "wisp" of hair is tightly coiled around a cylinder, and an image is captured of the cylinder so that its axis is parallel to the horizontal image axis (Figure 8.75). The light source is a flash unit attached to the camera. Because of the curvature of the cylinder, fibers in the coil are seen from a variety of different longitudinal angles. That is, the variation in incoming and outgoing angles is primarily in the plane of the axis of the hair fiber. Consequently, different points in the image capture the reflected radiance from hair fibers at different longitudinal angles with respect to the light. A single image thus simultaneously captures a set of longitudinal reflectance measurements. The fibers are also spread out horizontally over the surface of the cylinder, so different azimuthal angles are captured as well. However, the variation is not as large because the cylinder is flat in that direction, so this variation is ignored.

The appearance of hair largely depends on the appearance of the specular highlights. One of the most important features of the Marschner model is the separation of reflectance into longitudinal and azimuthal components. The color shift arises from the longitudinal component, so the measurement setup captures the angular dependence in the more important direction. The azimuthal variation

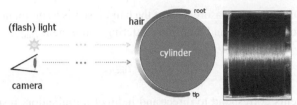

Figure 8.75   Setup for measuring reflectance from a "wisp" of hair fibers. (After [Zinke et al. 09].)

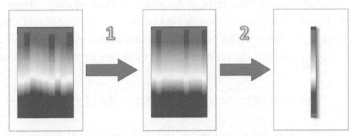

Figure 8.76   Preprocessing to reduce the variance in the fibers. The pixel columns are shifted vertically into alignment (step "1"), after which the average highlight can be determined (step "2"). (After [Zinke et al. 09].)

is primarily a result of asymmetry in the cross section of the hair fibers.

The hair strands wrapped around the cylinder should ideally be parallel, but in reality they are not perfectly aligned. This results in variations in the specular highlights visible in the captured image in Figure 8.75. The highlights look as if a small random vertical shift has been applied at each hair fiber. These shifts are evened out as a preprocess; Figure 8.76 illustrates how this works. After the images are registered and the camera is calibrated, the variation in the apparent highlight shifts are averaged so that the BRDF parameters can be fit. Figure 8.77 shows step "1" in Figure 8.76 in more detail. This step averages the highlight position across the cylinder; the second image in the sequence shows the average highlight spread out across the cylinder. Next, the pixel columns are individually shifted vertically to match the average highlight. The arrows on the third image in Figure 8.77 indicate these shifts, which results in the more even highlights at the right.

The BRDF fit to the measurement of the hair cluster is a summation of a single scattering component f_{dir} and multiple scattering component f_{indir}:

$$f_{\text{fit}} = f_{\text{dir}} + f_{\text{indir}}.$$

The components correspond to direct and indirect illumination, respectively, as the subscripts indicate. Basically, f_{dir} comes from the Marschner model, and f_{indir} comes from the local multiple scattering function in the "dual scattering" model described in Section 8.5.2. However, the goal of better reproduction of measured data required an extra diffuse term to be added to both models. These diffuse terms approximate some more complicated scattering effects not included in the original models, such as "TRRT" and off-specular scattering. The single scattering (direct) component of the reflectance is a modified version of the Marschner model,

$$f_{\text{dir}} = (1-d) \cdot \left(s_{\text{R}} \cdot f_{\text{R}} + f_{\text{TT}} + \tilde{N}_{\text{TRT}} \cdot M_{\text{TRT}} \right) + d \cdot \frac{r_d}{\pi^2}, \qquad (8.16)$$

where d is the magnitude of the diffuse component. The multiple scattering component f_{indir} comes from the local backscattering model.

Besides the elimination of the azimuthal dependence, Equation (8.16) employs two other modifications. One is the extra scaling parameter s_{R} of the R (simple reflection) term. This controls the relative importance of the R component compared to the TRT and TT components. This scaling parameter can be thought of as a way of accounting for azimuthally dependent properties, which are not directly measured. In the Marschner model (Equation (8.15)), the R term is the product of a longitudinal factor M_R and an azimuthal factor $N_R(\theta, \phi_i, \phi_r)$. The variation in N_R is primarily a result of noncircular cross sections of the hair fibers. The value of the scaling parameter s_R represents an average value of N_R. The azimuthal dependence is more significant in the TRT component. For this, the authors explicitly average the azimuthal factor N_{TRT} over the azimuthal direc-

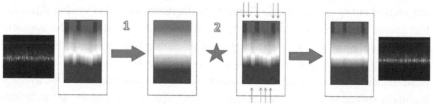

Figure 8.77   Details in the vertical shifting: an average pixel column is computed (step "1" here) then the individual vertical columns are shifted to match the average. A real data set (i.e., a photograph) is shown before (left) and after (right) the alignment. (After [Zinke et al. 09].)

Figure 8.78   Comparison of images rendered using the recovered parameters (top row) to the corresponding captured images (bottom row). The rendered images have a darker background. (From [Zinke et al. 09] © 2009 ACM, Inc. Included here by permission.)

tions:

$$\tilde{N}_{\text{TRT}} = \frac{s}{\pi} \int_{-\pi/2}^{\pi/2} N_{TRT}(\phi_i, \theta_i, \phi_r, \theta_r)\, d\phi_i$$

for use in Equation (8.16). The extra parameter s is used in the fitting process.

The BRDF parameter fitting involves a collection of parameters, including the diffuse magnitude d, the R scaling parameter s_R, and the N_{TRT} scaling parameter s. The fitting process minimizes the error of the fit over all the parameters. Because the reflectance model is nonlinear, a search algorithm is employed to find the minimum error. Unfortunately, nonlinear optimization of this form is not easy. Most methods employ a searching approach, but a common problem is that the search algorithm can converge to a local minimum rather than the global minimum of the best fit. The authors use an approach known as *simulated annealing*, which is a probabilistic model for global optimization.

Figure 8.78 compares captured photographs, from which the BRDF parameters are fit, and the results of rendering a comparable geometric hair model using the recovered parameters. Although the geometric model is not very precise (so the shifting in specular highlights on different fibers does not match the photographs) the hair color is faithfully reproduced. Figure 8.79 contains a similar comparison, except that the view direction is different from that used in the image capture. Figure 8.80 contains renderings under different lighting environments. Figure 8.81 shows some results of rendering the reconstructed geometric model described in the 2009 paper by Jakob, Moon, and Marschner. The rendering was done using Monte Carlo path tracing, the most accurate rendering method available.

The method of fitting the BRDF in the paper by Zinke et al. fits both the single and multiple scattering components in a single pass. Another possible approach, which might provide more insight into this split, might be to use the high frequency lighting separation method described by Nayar et al. in the 2006 paper described earlier (see Figure 8.50). Separation into direct and indirect illumination is essentially the same as the splitting of scattering into single and multiple components in hair. The single scattering is, in essence, the effect of direct lighting. However, the separation would have to be performed in terms of the hair volume—the direct reflectance from hair fibers has higher frequency than the checkerboard light pattern.

Another interesting connection is the link between hair color and hair geometry. As has been noted several times, the local arrangement of hair fibers substantially affects the appearance of color. It seems reasonable that a good color model could assist in the reconstruction of hair geometry. Because the optical features of hair, particularly highlights, are closely related to the orientation and curvature of the hair, exploiting the relationship between geometry and color could increase the accuracy of measurements and the realism of the rendered results.

8.6.3 Further Directions

As previously mentioned, "hair" is commonly visualized as a volume, mainly concentrating on large-scale structures. However the methods introduced in this section concentrate on the small-scale structures, and this has successfully led to a higher level of realism. From a practical standpoint, it can be said that these techniques are still in an early stage. But current demand for realistic hair rendering is likely to push this work into a more practical stage in the near future. Even now, the potential of this work is clear. For example, very little was known about the characteristics of the local structure of hair fibers until these recent publications. The data that these methods provide can be used to revise existing methods for hair modeling. Furthermore, the importance of the link between geometry and color is interesting from a theoretical standpoint. The importance of local microgeometry in realistic rendering has already been noted; hair rendering reaffirms the significance of this connection. However, it is still difficult to leverage this

Figure 8.79   Comparison of images rendered using the recovered parameters (top row) to photographs (bottom row). In this case, the photographs have different view directions than those used for the parameter fitting. The rendered results still match quite well. (© Arno Zinke, GfaR mbH.)

Figure 8.80   Rendered images under different simulated lighting conditions. (© Arno Zinke, GfaR mbH.) (See Color Plate XX.)

kind of local geometric structure in a practical manner for production rendering.

One critical aspect of hair rendering that has been omitted entirely in this discussion is the issue of hair dynamics—hair fibers move around in reality. In the visual effects area, it is still difficult to make the appearance of hair believable in digital doubles. At the present time this is done by hand with specialized tools. The method of capturing local hair structure could be very useful for this. However, there is still the problem of animating a geometric hair model. This remains a problem because of the complex interaction between hair fibers as they move. Factors as diverse as hairspray to static electricity to local airflow all affect the animation of hair. In summary, it can be said that closer links between the three components—geometry, color, and dynamics—may well bring the next level of realism to hair rendering.

Until recently, hair rendering relied on established existing methods. Once researchers started looking to modern physically based methodologies the field evolved very quickly. It is not an exaggeration to say that the research in hair rendering from 2003 to 2009 was the equivalent of more than a decade of research in other areas. Another remarkable phenomenon is how soon after its publication a new method has been implemented and adapted in practical rendering. In turn, this resulted in further advances in the research side. This is an ideal process for advancement in any field.

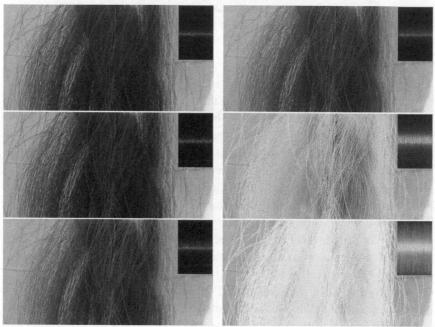

Figure 8.81   Rendered images of the hair geometry reconstructed by the method of Wenzel Jakob et al. using the image-based hair reflectance model. (© Arno Zinke, GfaR mbH.) (See Color Plate XXI.)

9

Bidirectional Texture Function

The appearance of an object depends on the response of the light reflected from its surface to the eye of the observer. For the purposes of photorealistic rendering, surface reflection was typically regarded at two levels: the *macrostructure* of an object refers to the basic visual geometry; the *microstructure* is the microscopic detail that affects light reflection, e.g., surface roughness and microgeometry, but the detail itself is not actually visible. The representative example is the combination of BRDFs and global illumination: BRDF models depend (implicitly, at least) on the microscopic detail of the surfaces; global illumination simulates light transport at the macroscopic scale.

The distinction between macrostructure and microstructure is made because they involve different approximation techniques. A middle level of detail, called the *mesostructure*, can also be separated. Mesostructures include fine structural detail that is visible, but the individual features are not large enough to affect global illumination directly. Examples of mesostructure include wood grain, detail in cloth, plaster, brush strokes, etc. Traditionally, microstructure is handled by the BRDF, and mesostructures are modeled by bump maps and displacement maps.

A *bidirectional texture function* (BTF) is a way of representing mesostructure using an image-based approach. It represents the changes in reflectance over a small area using a pixel array or general set of textures. In practice, the textures are photographs acquired under multiple viewing and lighting directions. A BTF predicts all the effects caused by mesostructure without explicitly modeling the actual geometry of the surface. Moreover, as the BTF is an image-based approach, it also includes local illumination effects such as interreflections, subsurface scattering, and shadowing. Incorporating BTFs in rendering can assist in efficient photorealistic rendering of complex materials.

The use of BTFs in production rendering is still in its early stages. However, since 2008, the use of physically based BRDF models along with physically based rendering techniques such as global illumination and ray tracing have become more prevalent, even in movie production. As previously mentioned, BTFs are considered useful in combination with physically based BRDF models and in other image-based approaches. BTFs are expected to play an important role in future rendering techniques. This chapter introduces the basic concept of BTFs and provides background on the progress of rendering techniques that use them.

9.1   Origin of BTFs

The idea of a bidirectional texture function originated in the paper entitled "Reflectance and Texture of Real-World Surfaces" by Kristin J. Dana, Bram van Ginneken, Shree K. Nayar and Jan J. Koenderink [Dana et al. 99]. This paper introduced the BTF as a new representation for surface reflectance that reproduced surface appearance more realistically than existing methods. Figure 9.1 illustrates the effect of changing the view or lighting direction on the appearance of a surface. The small pits and bumps on the surface exhibit shadowing and interreflection, which changes with the direction of the light. The local mesostructure also causes the appearance to change with viewing direction, as shown in Figure 9.2.

A *bidirectional texture function* is defined as a function of the lighting direction, the viewing direction, and the surface position. The BTF is thus a function of six variables: if θ_i, ϕ_i, represent the light direction in the local surface coordinate system, θ_r, ϕ_r represent the viewing direction, and x, y represent the position on

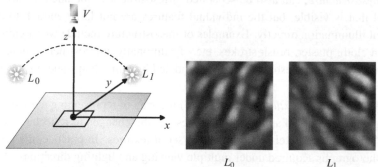

Figure 9.1   Variation of the appearance of a small area with changing light source direction. (From [Tong et al. 02] © 2002 ACM, Inc. Included here by permission.)

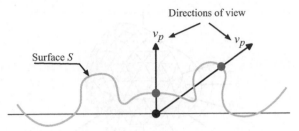

Figure 9.2   Variation of the appearance of a small area depends on the viewing direction, particularly when the surface is rough at the level of the mesostructure.

the surface, the BTF is denoted by

$$T(\theta_r, \phi_r, x, y, \theta_i, \phi_i) \tag{9.1}$$

(see Figure 9.3). A BTF is usually defined on a small representative region on a surface, and represents the spatially varying appearance of the surface from all lighting and viewing directions. In practice, a BTF is represented by a set of images, known as the BTF data or BTF data set, acquired by capturing the small area of the surface using different lighting and viewing directions. The process is similar to a method of obtaining BRDF measurements of a surface; however, the BRDF values are determined by averaging the pixels over each image, while the salient part of the BTF data consists of the actual pixels.

The image-based reflectance measurement techniques described in Chapter 8 all work by capturing images from different lighting and view directions; the sample itself remained fixed. The BTF acquisition method described by Dana et al. works by rotating the sample. The camera is placed at a fixed set of positions, and the light source is fixed throughout the process. The camera positions lie on a plane at increments of $22.5°$ from the light source. Images are captured at each camera position with the sample rotated by a robotic manipulator to a set of

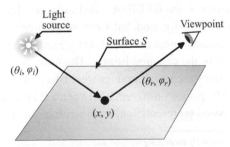

Figure 9.3   Geometry for the definition of a BTF texture function.

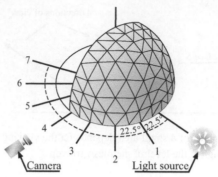

Figure 9.4   Arrangement for capturing BTF data. (After [Dana et al. 99].)

specific surface orientations. Figure 9.4 illustrates the arrangement; the vertices
on the triangulated quarter-sphere shown in the figure are the positions to which
the surface normals are rotated.

The measurement system is calibrated by replacing the surface sample with a
reference target of known reflectance. The target actually has a number of reference patches, each having a specific reflectance. The radiance reflected from each
patch is recorded by a calibrated photometer. This data is used as a reference to
correct the pixel values of the captured textures. Strictly speaking, the incident
irradiance from the light source varies over the position of a surface sample, as
does the direction to the light source. However, if the source is far enough away,
these variations are not significant and the illumination can therefore be regarded
as constant across the surface sample.

The authors took measurements of a number of different surface materials and
the data was made publicly available.[1] This data has contributed to widespread
use of BTFs and had substantial impact of further research in the subject.

9.1.1   BTFs and Spatially Varying BRDFs

As described in Chapter 8, the BRDF of a surface generally varies by position;
however, BRDFs are normally modeled for a single point. This is why basic
image-based BRDF measurement of a small surface sample averages the recorded
values over all pixels in the captured image. The term *spatially varying BRDF*
(SVBRDF) is sometimes used to disambiguate a BRDF that has a specific positional dependence. The primary difference between a BTF and a SVBRDF is that
a BTF is an image-based representation, and therefore includes local shadowing

---

[1]The BTF database created by measuring various materials in this way, is made publicly available
at http://www1.cs.columbia.edu/CAVE/curat; the database is used for verification of BTF theories.

and interreflection and also subsurface scattering. A SVBRDF normally does not include these effects; they are computed during the rendering process.

Before BTF synthesis was conceived, there were attempts at capturing variation in reflectance with changing position within a small area using SVBRDFs. The paper "Efficient Rendering of Spatial Bidirectional Reflectance Distribution Functions" by David K. Mcallister, Anselmo Lastra, and Wolfgang Heidrich is said to be the representative work in the subject [Mcallister et al. 02]. The method described in this paper captures images of a small area of a surface sample with varying lighting and viewing directions (in a manner similar to the way BTF data is acquired). A set of BRDF values is obtained from these images, and the Lafortune model is fit to each point on the sample surface. The authors describe a hardware implementation that stores the Lafortune parameters in textures, and employs a GPU shader to perform the rendering. The method presented in this paper was a forerunner to later developments in hardware BTF rendering.

9.2   BTF Synthesis

A BTF represents the interaction of the light mesostructure of a surface on a small area of the surface. This small area is assumed to be a rectangular planar patch. The original BTF paper by Dana et al. concentrated on the measurement process and the application to BRDF measurements. The authors suggested how BTFs could be used in image synthesis, by tiling the BTF of the small sample across larger surface in an environment. But they also note some potential problems. One is the issue of seams between adjoining tiles, which would have to be covered or smoothed in some visually plausible way. There is also the potential problem of the repeated pattern being noticed by human observers, and this would affect the realism of the rendering. Another is the problem of interpolating the BTF data for arbitrary lighting and view directions. This kind of interpolation has come to be known as *BTF synthesis*, as it involves synthesizing a new image for an arbitrary viewpoint. (The term "view synthesis" is used elsewhere, e.g., in the interpolation of light stage images.) In the case of BTFs, proper synthesis involves more than just interpolation; it requires recovery of the local mesostructure.

BTF synthesis can be viewed as a generalization of *texture synthesis*. The earliest implementations of texture mapping used a small texture map that was replicated across a surface. In order for this to work, the texture map has to be constructed so that the seams between the copies are not very noticeable. It was not long before researchers looked for ways of doing this automatically, which led to the more general problem of nonuniformly replicating the content of a small texture map into a larger map that *looks* like the same texture image. This is the general problem of texture synthesis, although this term also refers to the related problem replicating texture content to fill holes in images. BTF synthesis is more difficult, for the reasons noted in the previous paragraph, but some of the ideas are the same.

9.2.1 Origin of BTF Synthesis

The first practical BTF synthesis method was described in the paper "Synthesizing Bidirectional Texture Function for Real-World Surface" by Xinguo Liu, Yizhou Yu, and Heung-Yeung Shum [Liu et al. 01]. The method starts by assuming that the surface mesostructure of the BTF sample can be approximated by a height field above a planar reference surface. That is, the surface is represented by a height function above a reference plane. This approximation is valid if the surface is such that the line parallel to the reference surface normal hits the mesostructure surface only once. If the mesostructure has the equivalent of caves or overhangs, it cannot be represented by a height field. Some real surfaces, such as pile fabrics (e.g., velvet and shag carpet) cannot be accurately approximated by a height field, but many surfaces can. The authors represent a height field on a regular grid on the reference plane, which is coincident with the xy-plane, and store the height z as a value of the grid cell (Figure 9.5).

Recovering the height field from the captured BTF images is one of the biggest challenges in BTF synthesis. Liu and his colleagues used a technique for determining *height from shading* [Leclerc and Bobick 91], a variant of the general *shape-from-shading* problem that arises in computer vision. The height from shading method recovers the height field $z(i, j)$ directly rather than in terms of surface normals and surface patch coordinates. The method actually computes

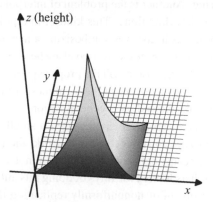

Figure 9.5   A height field as a surface function.

the finite differences of neighboring points on the height field, from which the actual z values can be readily reconstructed. The process minimizes a kind of energy function that quantifies how the reflection of the reconstructed surface differs from ideal diffuse reflection. The error expression is

$$E = \sum_{i,j} \left[\alpha \left(\rho R(p_{ij}, q_{ij}) - I(i,j) \right)^2 + \lambda \left(u_{ij}^2 + v_{ij}^2 \right) \right], \tag{9.2}$$

where p_{ij} and q_{ij} are the first-order finite differences of the height field; z_{ij}, u_{ij}, and v_{ij} are the second-order finite differences; $R(p_{ij}, q_{ij})$ is the computed Lambertian irradiance; and $I(i,j)$ is the pixel value.[2] The first term in the summand of Equation (9.2) is the difference between ideal Lambertian reflection and the captured pixel values; the second is a smoothness constraint. The parameters α and λ provide the relative weights of these terms. The value ρ is the Lambertian reflectance (albedo) of the surface.

The original height-from-shading algorithm assumes the surface is Lambertian, has a constant albedo, and only a single image is considered. In the BTF synthesis problem, the surface need not be Lambertian (the problem is much less interesting if it is), the reflectance varies over the surface sample, and instead of a single image, a collection of images is employed to reconstruct the geometry. The authors therefore employed a modified version of the algorithm better suited to the BTF images. Their approach starts with a few registered and aligned images of the surface sample. Each point of the height-field grid therefore has several pixel values $I_k(i,j)$ where k runs over the input images (only a few captured images having similar lighting/viewing directions are used for geometry recovery). The pixel values corresponding to a given point are not all the same: depending on the view and light directions, the point may be in shadow or show a specular highlight. The values needs to be de-emphasized in these cases, so the authors employ a weighting function $\eta_k(i,j)$ determined by classifying the pixel as being in shadow or having a highlight. The first term in Equation (9.2) therefore becomes

$$\alpha \sum_{k} \eta_k(i,j) \left(\rho_{ij} R_k(p_{ij}, q_{ij}) - I_k(i,j) \right)^2, \tag{9.3}$$

where ρ_{ij} is the position-dependent albedo. Another smoothing term also needs to be added to the formula for E to smooth the albedo values. Regarding geometric smoothing, one other modification is necessary. Because the height field may

---

[2]These finite differences are the *central* differences of the height field, defined by $p_{ij} = \left(z_{i+1,j} - z_{i-1,j} \right)/2$ and $q_{ij} = \left(z_{i,j+1} - z_{i,j-1} \right)/2$. That is, p and q are the differences of the heights at adjacent points in the horizontal and vertical directions, respectively. The second-order finite differences are defined analogously: $u_{ij} = \left(z_{i+1,j} - 2z_{i,j} + z_{i-1,j} \right)$ and $v_{ij} = \left(z_{i,j+1} - 2z_{i,j} + z_{i,j-1} \right)$.

have sharp changes, the geometry smoothing term $u_{ij}^2 + v_{ij}^2$ is given a position-dependent weighting function that de-emphasizes the value at points near an apparent discontinuity. This ensures that the reconstructed height field preserves the important discontinuities, i.e., is not too smooth.

The reconstructed height field corresponds to the small surface sample of the BTF data. This is not large enough to use by itself, so it must be expanded. As noted above, tiling the surface with the height field of the small sample will not be visibly plausible because of the obvious repetition of the sample. Instead, a basic 2D texture-synthesis algorithm applied to the height field after it has been converted to a grayscale image; the gray value is a function of the height. This results in a general synthesized height field for the entire surface; however, it is not suitable for direct use in BTF synthesis. Imprecision in the geometry reconstruction is propagated by the texture-synthesis algorithm. Height fields reconstructed from different viewpoints cannot be expected to have the same geometry, so the synthesized height fields will vary significantly. The BTF synthesis works by matching features of a synthesized texture with a captured image having a similar lighting/viewing directions.

Conceptually, the synthesis algorithm works by combining the important features of the reference image with the geometry of the template image. To perform the BTF synthesis at a desired viewpoint and lighting direction, the authors create a "template" image by rendering the synthesized height field with shadows from the given lighting/viewing direction. Next, they find a "reference" image in the captured image data set that has a similar orientation. The first step is to warp the reference image to the given viewpoint. If the reference image is sufficiently close to the desired lighting/viewing direction, this can be done using a simple projective transformation. Otherwise it becomes a more difficult structural morphing problem, because the apparent light direction has to be appropriately adjusted. The authors describe an algorithm for this in the paper, which is valuable in itself from a practical standpoint, as it provides a kind of direct BTF sample interpolation.

The process of combining the template image and the reference image amounts to replicating detail from the reference image into the template image. The method works by selecting blocks of pixels from the reference image and distributing them over the template image. The blocks are chosen according to a measure of importance: blocks that have the most significant detail are copied first, then blocks of less visual importance are copied. The template image is of course much larger than the reference image, so each block needs to be copied multiple times. When there are no spaces in the synthesized image large enough to accommodate a full block, smaller blocks are copied that can overlap with existing blocks. Finally, a 2D texture-synthesis algorithm is applied to fill in the remaining holes.

The 2001 paper by Liu et al. was significant in that it described the first use of BTF synthesis for actual rendering. Also the algorithm for constructing the reference image is useful in itself, as it provides a method for obtaining a usable BTF sample from a sparse set of captured BTF images. However, the synthesis method described in the paper has some limitations. For example, the geometry of the BTF is limited by the height-field representation. Also it did not consider mapping the BTF over surfaces having complex geometry. These problems are solved by the method introduced in the next section.

9.2.2 3D Textons

The notion of a *texton* was proposed by neuroscientist Béla Julesz in 1981 as a kind of elementary "atom" of human texture perception. According to Julesz's *Texton Theory*, textons are "the putative units of pre-attentive human texture perception." The idea is that a few simple visual structures known as textons (elements such as crosses, bars, and terminators) together with orientation indicators, provide a kind of basis for image recognition. Textons were only loosely defined until 2001, when Thomas Leung and Jitendra Malik formalized the notion of 2D and 3D textons in the paper entitled "Representing and Recognizing the Visual Appearance of Materials using Three-dimensional Textons" [Leung and Malik 01].

Textons come about from analyzing the results of filtering a pixel in a texture image by a "bank" of filters. Leung and Malik's filter bank had 48 filters in total, including elongated Gaussian filters, simple scaling filters, and phase-shifting filters. The filter response of a pixel is the collection of results of applying each filter to the pixel; this is a 48-dimensional vector in Leung and Malik's work. Of course, there is a great deal of redundancy in the filter-response vectors, which can be reduced by clustering the set of filter-response vectors. The k-means algorithm can be employed (see Section 7.2.2) to cluster the filter-response vectors for all the pixels in 48-dimensional space. All the vectors in a cluster are regarded as being essentially the same. The center of each cluster is the texton; the filter-response vector for the cluster is the *appearance vector*.

Three-dimensional textons are a generalization to textured surfaces that have notable geometric mesostructure. Mesostructures were originally defined as "local structures in the scale that human eyes can perceive," so in capturing filter responses at this scale, similar responses may be clustered together and considered the same response. The idea of 3D textons is that rough understanding of how responses are distributed in a small area, rather than considering differences in response, enables more efficient representation of the characteristics of the surface.

Images at different
viewing and
lighting directions

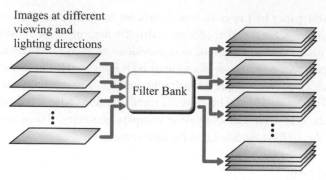

Filter Bank

Figure 9.6   Filtering of BTF data to construct textons. Each filter is applied to each image (left), which multiplies the data (right). (After [Leung and Malik 01].)

Because the variation in lighting and viewing direction affects the local appearance of a surface, the filter response is more complicated in the 3D case. The texton creation starts with a set of images captured under different lighting/viewing directions, i.e., a BTF data set. The images are arranged so that each pixel corresponds to a single sample point on the surface sample. Each filter in the filter bank is applied at each pixel of each image. A filter applied to an entire image is just another image called a "filter image." Figure 9.6 illustrates this schematically. There is one filter image for each filter in the bank, and one set of filter images for each image in the BTF data set. In Figure 9.6, the filter-response vectors for a single image can be viewed as 1D vertical sections of the filter image stacks at the right.

The next step is to cluster the filter-response vectors into 3D textons. This is illustrated schematically in Figure 9.7. For each pixel, the filter-response vectors of all the images are concatenated into a single vector: if there are 48 filters and n images, then the filter-response vectors have $48n$ elements. The response vector for sample point therefore contains the responses to all the filters in all the lighting/viewing combinations available in the BTF data set. Clustering is done using the k-means algorithm, which produces a set of clusters corresponding to the 3D textons. Again, the idea of clustering is that all the response vectors in each cluster are essentially equivalent, and the center response vector serves as the representative.

Each vector is assigned to the cluster such that the distance from the center of the cluster (the norm of the difference of vectors) is minimized. For sample points assigned to the same cluster, their appearances in the small local neighborhood have similar characteristics under the different viewing and lighting directions. Therefore, every vector assigned to the same cluster is approximated by the rep-

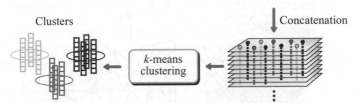

Figure 9.7   Clustering via the *k*-means algorithm. (After [Leung and Malik 01].)

resentative vector of the cluster (the mean of all the vectors in the cluster). The
3D textons are these individual clusters, or the centers thereof; they correspond
to common surface features in the image, such as ridges and groves, as well as
simple markings.

Leung and Malik's work had the goal of using 3D textons to represent and
analyze the appearance of 3D mesostructures. Much of the paper is devoted to
the idea of constructing a basic "vocabulary" of textons that could be used to
describe the appearance of *any* material. The relevance to computer graphics is
that the texton representation may provide a way of rendering a surface using BTF
data from novel lighting and viewing directions; i.e., textons can be used for BTF
synthesis.

9.2.3   BTF Synthesis Using 3D Textons

The paper entitled "Synthesis of Bidirectional Texture Functions on Arbitrary
Surfaces" by Xin Tong, Jingdan Zhang, Ligang Liu, Xi Wang, Baining Guo, and
Heung-Yeung Shum presents a BTF rendering method for arbitrary surface geometry [Tong et al. 02]. The method employs the 3D texton approach: 3D textons
are constructed to represent the entire BTF data set.

The details of the texton-based BTF synthesis are rather involved, but the
basic idea is conceptually simple. Three-dimensional textons are constructed for
the entire BTF data set (although in practice, not all the images are used for all
the textons). This produces a texton "vocabulary," which is a kind of basis for
the texton representation of the surface points under arbitrary lighting/viewing
arrangements. Each pixel in the stack of images, i.e., each surface point in the
captured BTF data, is assigned a single texton "label" from the texton vocabulary.
This label is a single texton, and is chosen by the closest match to the response
vector for the point. The correspondence between surface points and texton labels
is described as a 2D "texton surface map." An analogous map is constructed for
the neighborhood of each point to be rendered. Then, for the distance measure,
the distance between 3D textons that does not depend on BTF geometry is used,
which enables BTF synthesis to handle the arbitrary mesostructure geometry.

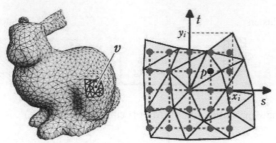

Figure 9.8   Flattening a surface mesh for matching 3D textons (From [Tong et al. 02] © 2002 ACM, Inc. Included here by permission.)

The paper considers the more general problem of mapping a synthesized BTF image onto a geometric model. The process begins by creating an analogous 2D texton surface map on the model as was done on the sample surface. The model surface is assumed to be a triangulated mesh, so the first step is to assign a texton to each mesh vertex. The BTF synthesis is done in the local frame of each triangle vertex, which enables BTF synthesis to handle arbitrary surface geometry. BTF synthesis results in assigning an appropriate pixel coordinate in the appropriate reference image to the vertex. In the rendering process, the appropriate pixel in the original BTF data is copied to the vertex. The synthesis process works by locally flattening the mesh surface onto the tangent plane at a vertex, as illustrated in Figure 9.8. Next, 3D textons are assigned to this rectangular grid by interpolating the textons at the triangular vertices. Finally, the neighborhood of each point p in the mesh is matched with a neighborhood of pixels in the BTF image data set, and the pixel corresponding to p is copied to the output image. This matching computation is efficiently done using 3D textons.

Three-dimensional textons also play an important role in reducing the amount of data and computation cost of the distance computation. As response vectors are often high-dimensional vectors, the computation cost of operations on them is high. However with 3D textons, if the dot product of every possible pair of representative vectors of 3D textons is precomputed (if there are n textons, the number of dot products is of the order n^2), the distance between any two 3D textons can be calculated from the dot products. Therefore, the representative vectors of 3D textons need not be stored explicitly. This reduces the data storage and computation requirements substantially. Moreover, the precomputed dot products of 3D textons are also used for interpolating 3D textons.

Because the response vector contains all the filter responses, as do the textons, the matching of a texton label includes the appearance in a neighborhood around the point in the spatial and lighting/viewing directions. In contrast, the

BTF synthesis method described above, the color of a pixel from BTF data is copied directly to a point to be rendered. The 2D texture synthesis works by searching the image for pixels based on the best match of the neighborhood of the pixel to that of the rendered image. In general, the neighborhood similarity is determined by summing the corresponding pixel differences in the neighborhood. In contrast, 3D textons fit the local neighborhood over images from a collection of viewpoints and lighting directions by their very construction.

In terms of BTF synthesis, the importance of the texton method is that it enables BTF synthesis to handle arbitrary mesostructure BTF geometry as well as arbitrary surface geometry onto which the BTF is mapped. It can be said that this progress pushed BTF synthesis into the practical stage. As will be described in Chapter 10), this method influenced the development of "bi-scale" (mesoscale and macroscale) precomputed radiance transfer [Sloan et al. 02].

9.3   BTF Models

The BTF synthesis methods introduced in the previous section involve copying an appropriate pixel value from the BTF sample data set directly to every location on the surface of the object to be rendered. This approach is intuitive and easily understandable, but it cannot avoid tiling or general synthesis, simply because the surface to be rendered is normally much larger than the original BTF sample surface. Moreover, the methods assume that the BTF data is sampled densely enough for interpolation to be applicable. It is not impossible to prepare such BTF data, but it may be infeasible in practice. Therefore, specific mathematical models that capture how the appearance of the textures change with the lighting/viewing directions have been studied. Such methods are based on advances in image-based rendering, from which several mathematical models have arisen that make BTF image synthesis more efficient.

9.3.1   Algebraic Analysis for Image-Based Representation

BTF synthesis is a kind of interpolation problem: it involves synthesizing a new image from the existing images captured from nearby lighting/viewing directions. For example, suppose images A and B were captured from the same viewpoint, but with slightly different lighting directions. Synthesizing a new image for the same viewpoint with a lighting direction somewhere between the lighting directions of A and B is a straightforward interpolation problem. Simple linear interpolation between the pixels of A and B can be applied to synthesize the new image (although the visual plausibility would depend on the particular surface and lighting directions). If the new lighting direction does not lie strictly between that of A and B, then the synthesized image could be interpolated from A and B and a third image C, and possibly even more images. In general, deciding which images to interpolate is a nontrivial problem in itself. The interpolation problem becomes more complicated still when a different viewing direction is considered along with a different lighting direction.

The BTF synthesis methods described above do not directly interpolate pixels; rather, they perform a kind of extrapolation from a reference object. In the basic synthesis method of Liu et al., this reference object is a reference image taken from the BTF image data set. The template image is synthesized from recovered geometry, which is obtained from a kind of interpolation. In the texton method, the reference object is the set of textons, which were likewise formed by a kind of interpolation (filtering by all the filters in the filter bank can be viewed as a kind of interpolation.)

The key to image-based representations is how the acquired image data is interpolated. Recent research has looked to algebraic methods to improve inter-polation. The basic idea of algebraic analysis is to look for a kind of basis set for the image data. Armed with such a basis, an image from an arbitrary viewing (and lighting) direction can be synthesized from a combination of the basis elements. The texton method of Section 9.2.3 employs one kind of basis: the basis elements are the textons, or more properly, the appearance vectors.

Matrix analysis is a more algebraic way of looking at the basis for a set of images. Consider a basic set of BTF images, i.e., a set of images of an object or surface sample captured from various lighting/viewing directions. Each captured image can be represented by a single vector by "flattening" the image pixels from a 2D array to a 1D array (a vector). There is one such vector for each image in the data set, and the collection of all these vectors can be placed into the columns of a matrix. This matrix is large: the matrix for a typical BTF data set has several hundred columns, and as many as several million rows. Each row represents the variation in the appearance of a point as the lighting/viewing directions change; each column represents the appearance of points over the surface of the object for a fixed lighting/viewing direction. This matrix is known as the *response matrix* R; the vector columns are *response vectors*. Suppose there are n captured images, each of which contains measurements for m points. The response matrix R is an $m \times n$ matrix in this case.

The appearance of the object for an arbitrary lighting/viewing direction can be represented as an m-dimensional column vector just like the other columns of the response matrix. Such a vector is a *synthesized* response vector. For definite-ness, let V denote the set of response vectors for all lighting/viewing directions.

The basic assumption is that V is a subset of the column space (the linear space spanned by the columns) of the response matrix R; i.e., each vector in V is a linear combination of the columns of R. But at the same time, the column space of R greatly exceeds V—many linear combinations of the columns of R do not represent the appearance of the object from a real lighting/viewing direction. After all, the set of lighting/viewing directions comprise four parameters, so V is in some sense a four-parameter space. The column space of R is a subset of that space, as each column is the response vector of a particular lighting/viewing direction. Consequently, it is likely that the column space of R itself has a basis of fewer than n elements. A similar line of reasoning was applied in the "data-driven" approach to BRDF representation of Matusik et al. described in Chapter 8, although that work looks to nonlinear basis elements [Matusik et al. 03].

The basic idea of algebraic analysis is to find a small set of basis vectors that approximates V, the space of all valid object appearance images. From a carefully chosen set of basis vectors, response vectors can be approximated as a linear combination of these basis vectors, which reduces the representation of an image under a new lighting/viewing direction to a set of linear coefficients. That is, each synthesized lighting/viewing direction is a weighted sum of the representative basis vectors. Linear approximation is especially useful for real-time rendering. For example, large matrix multiplications are not performed efficiently on GPUs (4×4 matrix multiplications are normally *very* fast), but linear combinations of large vectors is a natural GPU operation if each vector is stored as a texture map.

9.3.2   SVD and PCA

The notion of an *approximate basis* of a set is a collection of vectors or functions that can be combined to approximate any element of the set. One way of constructing such a basis is to use *principal component analysis* (PCA), which provides, in some sense, the most significant directions in a data set. PCA was originally conceived as a method of data analysis used to reveal the covariance structure of a set of data points. However, the technique has many other applications.

Originally, PCA was done using eigenvector analysis. Basic theory of eigenvalues and eigenvectors are a standard part of an elementary linear algebra course. An *eigenvector* $\vec{x}$ of a square matrix A is a kind of fixed point of the matrix A:

$$A\vec{x} = \lambda\vec{x}. \tag{9.4}$$

That is, transforming an eigenvector $\vec{x}$ by A is equivalent to a scalar multiple of $\vec{x}$. The scalar λ is an *eigenvalue* of the matrix A. The span of all eigenvectors is the *eigenspace* of the matrix. A nonsingular $n \times n$ matrix A has at most n real eigenvalues; if none of the eigenvalues are complex, then the matrix A can be decomposed in the form

$$A = U \Lambda U^T \qquad (9.5)$$

where U is a matrix of orthogonal eigenvectors, and Λ is a diagonal matrix of the eigenvalues. The eigenvectors corresponding to the smallest eigenvalues are regarded as the least important in PCA. Setting small eigenvalues to zero in Equation (9.5) results in an approximation to A.

Eigenvalue analysis has some limitations: it only works on a square matrix, only certain square matrices have only real eigenvalues. Furthermore the eigenvalue decomposition is numerically difficult unless the matrix is symmetric. Originally, principal component analysis was applied to a specially constructed matrix that had properties amenable to eigenvalue analysis. PCA is generally applied to a matrix AA^T, which is necessarily symmetric. A more general matrix decomposition is the *singular value decomposition* (SVD), which is a factorization of an arbitrary matrix M into a product of the form

$$M = \begin{bmatrix} u_1 & u_2 & \cdots & u_m \end{bmatrix} \begin{bmatrix} \sigma_1 & & & \\ & \sigma_2 & & \\ & & \ddots & \\ & & & \sigma_n \end{bmatrix} \begin{bmatrix} v_1^T \\ v_2^T \\ \vdots \\ v_n^T \end{bmatrix} = U \Sigma V^T. \qquad (9.6)$$

(The process of computing the SVD is an important problem in numerical linear algebra.) The diagonal elements of Σ are the *singular values*; normally the singular values are arranged in decreasing order of absolute value. The matrices U and V are orthonormal square matrices consisting of the *left-singular* and *right-singular* vectors, which are the eigenvectors of MM^T and $M^T M$, respectively. Figure 9.9 illustrates the concept graphically. The singular value decomposition can be regarded as an eigenvalue decomposition for a nonsquare matrix M. In fact, there is a direct connection to the eigenvalues of MM^T and $M^T M$:

$$M^T M = V \left(\Sigma^T \Sigma \right) V^T, \qquad (9.7)$$

$$MM^T = U \left(\Sigma \Sigma^T \right) U^T. \qquad (9.8)$$

In other words, the singular values of M are the square roots of the eigenvalues of $M^T M$ and MM^T; V consists of the eigenvectors of $M^T M$, and U consists of the eigenvectors of MM^T.

The application of the SVD to principal component analysis comes from the interpretation of the singular values. Each singular value σ_k corresponds to a left-singular vector and a right-singular vector, and in a manner of speaking, provides the "weight" of those vectors. Setting σ_k to zero "turns off" the corresponding

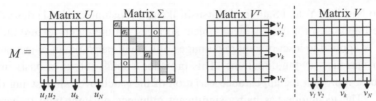

$$M =$$

Matrix U Matrix Σ Matrix V^T Matrix V

Figure 9.9   A graphical representation of the singular value decomposition. A matrix M is decomposed into the product of three matrices: $M = U\Sigma V^T$; U has left-singular vectors in its columns, V^T has right-singular vectors in its rows, and Σ has the singular values on its diagonal. The matrix V^T is so written because the rows of this matrix are the relevant singular vectors, while usually a matrix is regarded as collection of column vectors.

singular vector. Consequently, the product $U\Sigma V^T$ with the last few singular values set to zero results in a matrix that is fairly close to M, but has lower rank. That is, the rows and columns have a smaller linear span. Setting the smallest singular values to zero therefore removes the least important basis elements. In effect, this is a kind of lossy data compression algorithm for the span of the matrix. The number of singular values set to zero depends on the particular application. For example, when the matrix M corresponds to pixels in a grayscale image, there is often a particular SVD threshold where the grayscale image of the approximate matrix ceases to be recognizable.

PCA is often used for analyzing physical responses to a discrete input signal, such as the response to sound or the response to an external force acting on an object in the finite-element method. Rendering an object can be regarded as computing its response to light at a specific position on the surface of the object, due to a specific lighting/viewing direction. A PCA approximation isolates the most significant parts of the response.

9.3.3 Eigen-Textures

An early paper that uses PCA to approximate responses that represent the appearance of an object, "Face Recognition Using Eigenfaces" by Matthew Turk, and Alex Pentland was published in the field of image recognition in 1991 [Turk and Pentland 91]. This paper describes the application of PCA to the image data of various human faces with various facial expressions, in order to create faces (called "eigenfaces") that best represent the characteristics of all the faces in the data set. These eigenfaces are then used as a way to identify a person from a new face image. The paper was considered a landmark result in the field of image recognition, and is one of the most cited papers in the field. The paper "Eigen-Texture Method: Appearance Compression and Synthesis Based on a 3D Model" by Ko Nishino, Yoichi Sato, and Katsushi Ikeuchi [Nishino et al. 01] described a related approach for more general object surfaces. In the eigen-texture method, PCA is applied to a set of captured images of a small patch on an object surface under various viewing directions. This provides a small subset of basis images that best represent the appearance variation of the patch over all viewing directions. The technique has had a significant influence on light field research in general.

In light field rendering (Chapter 5), the radiance from an object is captured in a collection of directions to construct the light field, then the appearance of the object from any surface point can be reconstructed by interpolating the light field radiance values. The reconstruction does not consider the specific geometry of the object, which is one of the strengths of the method. However, it does have the drawback of regarding all parts of the object as having equal visual importance. Furthermore, the lack of any specific geometric representation can cause problems with the appearance of interpolated shadows. The goal of the eigen-texture method was to construct a representation similar to the light field that also accounts for changes in the lighting/viewing direction and the geometry of the particular object. The paper considered a restricted version of the problem, where the viewpoint and light direction remain fixed and the object is rotated. Consequently the lighting/viewing directions are functions of only one parameter, the rotation angle.

In the eigen-texture method, the object surface is divided into small triangular patches, and the analysis is done on each patch. Images of the object are captured from the various rotation angles. Then these images are registered so that the parts of the images corresponding to each patch can be extracted. Each triangular patch is warped to a fixed-size right triangle, called a "cell" in the paper, and the appearance of a cell from a particular viewpoint is a "cell image." A sequence of cell images represents the appearance of a patch for all viewing directions (Figure 9.10). Synthesizing a cell image for an arbitrary rotation angle θ could be done by interpolating the appropriate image cells separately in each image cell sequence, but the authors were interested in something better. A model typically consists of thousands of patches, each of which requires a large number of cell images. The storage requirements are therefore quite large, and one goal of the method was to develop a compact representation of the view-dependent texture. The eigen-texture method, as the name suggests, employs eigenvector-based PCA to compress the sequence of cell images. The color channels of the cell image pixels are included in the PCA analysis. Some interpolation methods for color images work on each color component separately. In the eigen-texture method, the color channels are separated and concatenated into cell image column vectors

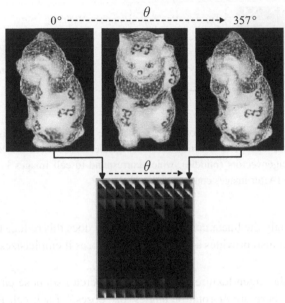

Figure 9.10   Construction of the cell images for a single surface patch. The appearance of the patch is
               extracted from all the images, then warped to a right triangle. The sequence of cell images,
               which are tiled into the lower image, represents the appearance of the cell for each rotation
               angle. The tiled image is purely for illustration and has no relation to the response matrix.
               (After images courtesy of Ko Nishino.)

as described below. The method uses a normalized luminance/chrominance space
instead of RGB colors.

The compression process works as follows. First, the values of each cell image are flattened (aligned vertically) into a column vector, then these vectors are
placed into the columns of a matrix. As in the general response matrix described
above, each row of this matrix therefore contains the variation in a particular pixel
with view direction; each column contains the spatial variation over the patch for
a particular view direction. Next, the average value of the matrix elements is
subtracted from each matrix element. This way, the average value of the matrix
elements is zero, and each matrix element contains what is called the *deviation
from the mean*.   PCA is then applied to the resulting cell matrix. A small number of basis eigenvectors are selected to serve as the approximate basis for the
eigenspace; these are the *eigen-texture* of the cell. The remaining eigenvectors are
projected onto these basis vectors and the resulting linear coefficients (weights)
are recorded in place of the vectors themselves. By virtue of the additivity of light,
the synthesis of an image from an arbitrary rotation angle can be accomplished by

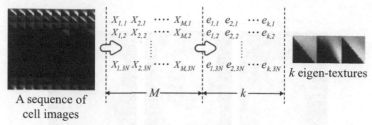

Figure 9.11   Cell images (left) are converted to a matrix M where each column consists of the pixel values in a cell image. The selection of basis eigenvectors reduces the M columns to k representative eigenvectors (middle), which correspond to cell images known as eigen-textures (right). (After images courtesy of Ko Nishino.)

interpolating only the linear coefficients. Not only does this reduce the amount of computation, it also provides a better interpolation, as it emphasizes the strongest details.

To make the eigen-texture process more concrete, suppose each image has N pixels, and there are M rotation angles, or "poses." Each cell image has $3N$ values (three color channels per pixel), which results in a $3N \times 1$ column vector X_m for the image cell corresponding to pose i, and an $M \times 3N$ matrix X for all poses. The PCA is actually applied to the (symmetric) matrix $Q = XX^T$, and a set of representative basis eigenvectors $\vec{e}_1, \vec{e}_2, \ldots, \vec{e}_k$ are selected corresponding to the k largest eigenvalues. The choice of k depends on the particular data set, but as mentioned above, it is much less than $3N$. Because the basis vectors are orthogonal, the projection of each remaining eigenvector $\vec{v}_m$ onto the basis set is just a dot product, $a_{m,i} = \vec{v} \cdot \vec{e}_i$. Each basis vector still has $3M$ entries, but only k such coefficients are needed to represent each eigenvector; this is a significant reduction from the $3N$ elements in the original (unprojected) vectors. In total, the storage requirements are reduced from $3MN$ to $kM + 3kN$. Figure 9.11 illustrates the basic reduction, and a particular set of eigen-textures.

As noted previously, synthesis of an image from a new rotation angle is done directly from the basis eigenvectors and the projection coefficients. For simplicity in the interpolation, the basis eigenvectors can themselves be represented by k trivial projection coefficients. Figure 9.12 illustrates the concept of a linear approximation of a synthesized cell image from eigen-textures.

The eigen-texture method uses PCA effectively; it selects basis vectors from the eigenvectors of the response matrix based on the value of the eigenvalues, starting with the largest. The largest PCA eigenvalue usually corresponds to the phenomenon that is most numerically significant. Unfortunately, it is not always the most visually significant. For example, diffuse reflection usually has more

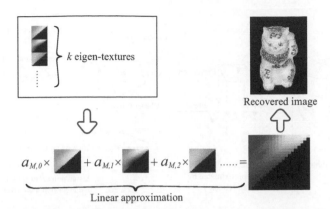

Figure 9.12 Synthesis of an image from a linear combination of basis vectors (eigen-textures). Different image cells have different eigen-textures. (After images courtesy of Ko Nishino.)

numeric statistical strength than specular reflection. Consequently, the selected eigen-textures tend to overemphasize diffuse reflection and can miss specular highlights. This is particularly true if too few basis basis vectors are selected: although this improves the compression ratio, other radiometric phenomena such as specular reflection may not be captured accurately. The authors of the eigen-textures paper got around this by increasing the number of basis vectors for cell image sequences that include specular reflection. However, specular reflection is still problematic for the method, because it is a highly nonlinear process and is therefore difficult to approximate as a linear subspace.

9.3.4 Concept of Local PCA

Natural objects, geometry, functions, responses, etc., are seldom linear; however, linear approximates often work well for local representation. For example, a plane is an absurdly poor approximation to a sphere on the global scale, but at small scale, a tangent plane is a very good approximation (see Figure 9.13(a)). An entire sphere can be covered with a set of local tangent-plane approximations, although it is difficult to get the associated planar coordinates to line up between neighboring tangent planes. This is a very general concept: fundamentally, derivatives and differentials are locally linear approximations. As noted above, a problem with interpolating specular reflection comes from the nonlinearity of specular lobes. In terms of PCA, the problem is that the response matrix is difficult to approximate with a linear subspace. One way around this is to split the response matrix into separate sections and perform PCA separately on each. This approach is called *local PCA*, or *clustered PCA* (CPCA).

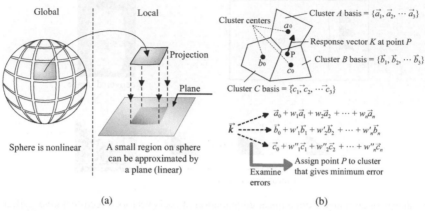

Figure 9.13   Local PCA (Leen's iterative PCA).

Applying local PCA to the response matrix defined above can improve the quality of the compression and therefore the interpolated images. Each column contains the cell image for a particular view direction, and each row contains the change in appearance of each point in the cell with changing view direction. Rows with less variation among the values correspond to points that appear similar from any viewpoint; clustering these rows together leaves rows for points whose appearance differs substantially. These points are those that fall in and out of shadow and exhibit specular reflection, and the corresponding rows can be clustered together. PCA can be applied to the clusters separately, as rows of a separate matrix, which results in a different set of basis eigenvectors for each cluster. Fewer basis vectors are necessary for the cluster having the least variation in pixel appearance.

The key to effective local PCA is the method of clustering. The k-means PCA algorithm (Section 8.1) is one way to perform the clustering. In order to perform clustering that most accurately approximates all the response vectors in the region, the PCA computation is performed simultaneously with the clustering calculation, which is more efficient than performing PCA calculation after the clustering is done. This simultaneous approach is known as *Leen's iterative PCA* algorithm. Its process is as follows (see also Figure 9.13).

1. Cluster centers are initialized, and the entire data set is partitioned into N initial regions.

2. Basic PCA is employed in each cluster to compute basis vectors for the cluster.

3. The clusters are reconstructed according to the approximation error in the sets of basis vectors. That is, each response vector in the entire data set is projected onto the set of basis vectors for each cluster. The response vector is moved, if necessary, to the cluster for which the approximation has the smallest error.

4. The existing basis vectors are discarded, and PCA is applied to construct a new set of basis vectors for each cluster. A representative cluster mean is computed from the mean of the updated PCA basis vectors, and this is subtracted from each cluster response vector before PCA is applied. This way, the vectors contain the "deviation from the mean" values as described earlier.

5. Steps 3 and 4 are repeated until the approximation error for every response vector is sufficiently small.

This iterative PCA algorithm may seem computationally expensive, but the clustering method is highly accurate. As a result, only a few basis vectors are necessary for each cluster, which makes the computation of the approximation error very fast. As a result, memory consumption and computation time in the whole process is significantly reduced. Another advantage of this kind of clustering in general is that once the basis vectors are constructed, the synthesis (rendering) step is very fast, and is also independent of the other clusters.

9.3.5 Local PCA and BTF Rendering

In the image-capture method described in the eigen-textures paper, the object is placed on a turntable and the lighting and viewing direction remain fixed. The captured image set is much smaller than that of a BTF data set, as it does not include relative variations in the lighting/viewing directions. However, the technique itself can be applied to more general sets of captured images. An extension of the eigen-texture approach to full BTF data sets was presented in the paper "Compression and Real-Time Rendering of Measured BTFs using Local PCA" by Gero Muller, Jan Meseth, and Reinhard Klein [Muller et al. 03].

The basic idea is similar to that of the eigen-texture method. In that method, the response vectors come from the captured image "cells." In the technique of Gero Muller et al., all the pixels corresponding to a particular small area on the surface for all the images are collected from BTF data and arranged into a single response vector. Each response vector thus represents the response to the change in lighting and viewing directions at each sample point on the object. In this sense, each response vector represents the total characteristics of reflection at each sample point. In principle, the surface BRDF could be extracted from this data, but doing so requires geometry recovery to remove shadows and issues. Arranging all the response vectors into the columns of a matrix produces the response matrix. Columns of this matrix depict the response of light to the variation in lighting and viewing direction; rows of this matrix depict the variation in the BRDF across the surface of the object. The response vectors that best represent the spatial variation in the BRDF, obtained by PCA, are called *eigen-BRDFs*. A linear combination of eigen-BRDFs becomes a BRDF, of sorts, at the point to be rendered.

As previously mentioned, accurately reproducing nonlinear effects such as specular reflection requires too many basis vectors if PCA is applied to the entire response matrix. So local PCA is applied to the matrix to compute the eigen-BRDFs. As described above, this involves clustering the rows of the response matrix and applying PCA (specifically, Leen's iterative PCA) to each cluster. Proper clustering assures that only a few eigen-BRDFs are needed to accurately represent the reflectance behavior in each cluster, regardless of how it may vary. The paper shows that specular reflection can also be approximated accurately by using only a very few eigen-BRDFs. The paper describes how the final rendering process can be implemented by GPU shaders to perform real-time rendering.

The process of constructing eigen-BRDFs for the BTF data works as follows. First, BTF data is constructed from captured images. The arrangement employs a locally linear approximation to the object surface: the u-axis and v-axis of the BTF data correspond, respectively, to an x-axis and y-axis on the tangent plane at each sample point on the surface. One texture image is created for each pair of lighting and viewing direction (Figure 9.14(a)). From each texture in the BTF data, the pixels corresponding to the same location on the object are collected and arranged into a texture image such that the horizontal direction corresponds to changing viewing directions, and the vertical direction corresponds to changing lighting directions (Figure 9.14(b)). Each such texture is described as a "BTF_{BRDF}" texture. One BTF_{BRDF} texture is created for each location in each pixel of the BTF data. For each BTF_{BRDF} texture, all the pixels in the texture are placed into a column vector, which serves as the response vector, then these column vectors are arranged side by side into the columns of a response matrix. Columns of this matrix thus represent the response variation with changing viewing directions and lighting directions, while the rows represent the response variation with changing location in the small area (Figure 9.15). Finally, local PCA is applied to the response matrix. As a result, each point on the surface is contained in a unique cluster. The appearance variation of the point with changing viewing and lighting directions is represented by a linear combination of the PCA basis vectors (eigen-BRDFs) for that cluster (Figure 9.16).

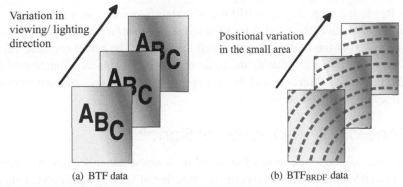

(a) BTF data (b) BTF_{BRDF} data

Figure 9.14   BTF data and BTF$_{BRDF}$ data.

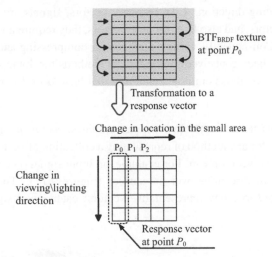

BTF$_{BRDF}$ texture at point P_0

Transformation to a response vector

Change in location in the small area

P_0 P_1 P_2

Change in viewing\lighting direction

Response vector at point P_0

Figure 9.15   Construction of the response matrix.

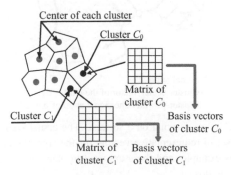

Center of each cluster

Cluster C_0

Matrix of cluster C_0

Basis vectors of cluster C_0

Cluster C_1

Matrix of cluster C_1

Basis vectors of cluster C_1

Figure 9.16   Local PCA is applied while clustering the rows.

Rendering with the eigen-BRDFs is straightforward. For a given point on the object surface, the relative location in the local surface neighborhood is determined, as is the PCA cluster to which it belongs. The actual response vector is constructed by interpolating the basis vector coefficients as a function of the lighting/viewing direction, and the appropriate pixel value is extracted from the interpolated response vector.

9.3.6 General Approximation of Signals

The term *response vector* has been used to describe the collection of radiance values reflected from a surface point as a function of varying lighting/viewing directions. In general, a response vector represents the response of a system due to a stimulus known as a *signal*. In the context of BTFs, a signal is a particular lighting/viewing direction. Like response vectors, signals are usually high-dimensional vectors, and also like response vectors, they require a vast amount of storage space. Consequently, various methods for compressing and approximating signals have been conceived. Some typical methods for doing so are considered next. These methods employ techniques that have been frequently used in this book.

VQ (vector quantization). In computer graphics, *vector quantization* (VQ) is a general term for any method of representing a collection of vectors by a single vector, e.g., by the vector mean. For example, an input signal on a surface might consist of a set of directions over the surface (Figure 9.17). These directions may be *quantized* to a few representative vectors; each actual signal vector is

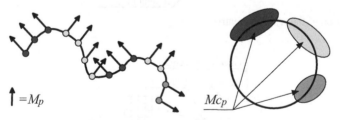

M_p : Signal at point p
M_{cp} : Cluster center vector of the cluster C_p
C_p : Cluster to which the signal at point p is assigned

Figure 9.17   Vector quantization (VQ) of a signal on a surface. The actual signal (not shown) varies over the surface. A set of representative vectors for the signal is chosen by a clustering method (three, in this example) and these are used in place of the actual signal vectors. (Courtesy of Peter-Pike Sloan.)

"snapped" to the closest representative. Vector quantization is frequently used for compression of light field data.

PCA (principal component analysis). In this method, all the signal vectors over the whole region are approximated by a linear combination of a few basis vectors. The signal vectors are replaced by their projection coefficients, which are computed by projecting the vectors onto each basis vector. Calculations involving signals on the region are replaced by calculations with the projection coefficients, which can make computations involving signals more efficient. This technique is used for compression and approximation of data in IBR and BTF rendering in several methods described in this book. Figure 9.18 illustrates the approach on a surface signal.

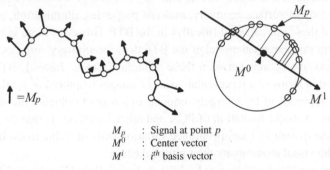

M_p : Signal at point p
M^0 : Center vector
M^i : i^{th} basis vector

Figure 9.18 Principal Component Analysis (PCA). The set of signal vectors are shifted by the mean (M^0) and the best vectors approximating the shifted vectors are selected. In this example, only one such vector is shown. (Courtesy of Peter-Pike Sloan.)

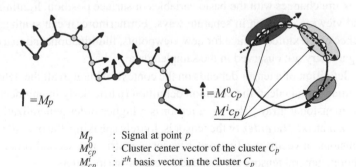

M_p : Signal at point p
M^0_{cp} : Cluster center vector of the cluster C_p
M^i_{cp} : i^{th} basis vector in the cluster C_p

Figure 9.19 Local PCA (clustered PCA) works by grouping similar vectors into clusters, and applying PCA on each. The cluster approximations are generally much better than an approximation to the entire set of vectors. (Courtesy of Peter-Pike Sloan.)

Local PCA (clustered PCA). As described earlier, local PCA selects basis vectors for local clusters rather than for the entire data as is done in normal PCA. As a result, approximation of signals can be performed with a few basis vectors. This method is well suited to a situation where each portion of the signal distribution has some characteristics, e.g., specular reflection. The method of Muller et al. described in Section 9.3.5 for compressing and rendering BTF data is an example of this technique. It is also used for precomputed radiance transfer, as will be described in Chapter 10. Figure 9.19 illustrates local PCA on a surface signal.

9.3.7 TensorTextures

The appearance of a textured surface can vary in a complex manner according to the interaction of surface geometry, material properties, illumination, and imaging. All of these are captured (ideally) in the BTF. However, there is no known closed form mathematical model of the BTF that, for arbitrary surfaces, captures the physical interactions between these different factors. Instead, BTF data is represented in terms of a representative set of images (captured or synthetic); the statistical approach of PCA largely amounts to a way of reducing the storage requirements. A major limitation of PCA and related methods is that they attempt to model the overall surface appearance variation without trying to explicitly distinguish the visual elements by their physical cause.

In the paper "TensorTextures: Multilinear Image-Based Rendering," M. Alex O. Vasilescu and Demetri Terzopoulos introduced an advanced statistical model that accurately approximates arbitrary BTFs in a multifactor manner [Vasilescu and Terzopoulos 04]. The method, which the authors call *TensorTextures*, captures how a texture changes with the basic variables of surface position, lighting direction, and viewing direction in separate ways. Furthermore, it can synthesize the appearance of a textured surface for new viewpoints, illumination, and to a certain extent, geometry not observed in the sampled data.

The definition of a tensor depends on the context. Although all the definitions are essentially equivalent, the common definition (particularly in engineering) is a multidimensional array. That is, a tensor is a higher-order generalization of a vector or a matrix. The *order* of the tensor is, loosely speaking, the overall number of dimensions: a vector is a first-order tensor; a matrix is a second-order tensor. In this book, general tensors are denoted by capital script letters.

As usual, the TensorTextures approach starts by capturing a set of images from different lighting/viewing directions. Each image is "vectorized" by arranging all the pixels into a single vector. Given a collection of sample images of a textured surface captured from I_V different viewpoints, each under I_L different illumination

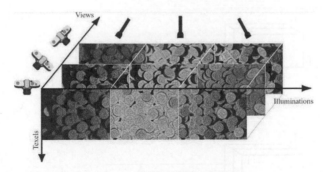

Figure 9.20   TensorTexture image organization. The ensemble of acquired images is organized in a third-order tensor with texels, illumination, and view modes. Although the contents of the texel mode are vectorized images, for clarity they are displayed as 2D images in this and subsequent figures. (From [Vasilescu and Terzopoulos 04] © 2004 ACM, Inc. Included here by permission.)

directions, the TensorTextures approach organizes the vectorized images, each of which have I_x texels (pixels) into a *data tensor* $\mathscr{D}$. This data tensor is a third-order tensor, and has dimensions $I_x I_L I_V$. Figure 9.20 illustrates a data tensor for a set of captured images.

The obvious next step would be to apply principal component analysis to the data tensor. This would be done using the singular value decomposition, but according to the authors there is no true generalization of the SVD to general tensors. There are, however, a number of different tensor decompositions. The authors employ a generalization of the SVD to sections of tensors, known as the *M-mode SVD*. The *M*-mode SVD was first employed by Vasilescu and Terzopoulos in the context of computer vision.[3] The technique, known as *Tensor-Faces* [Vasilescu and Terzopoulos 02] was applied to the problem of face recognition. The authors adapted this work to BTF data in the "TensorTextures" paper. Describing the *M*-mode SVD requires more definitions.

A *mode-m* vector is a subset of a tensor in dimension *m*; column vectors are mode-1 vectors of a matrix (second-order tensor), row vectors are mode-2 vectors. The general *mode-m* product is a generalization of a matrix product to tensors. Although there is a formal definition, it is perhaps easier to understand in terms of *matricized* (flattened) tensors. Matricizing a tensor involves arranging all its mode-*m* vectors into the columns of a matrix. Figure 9.21 illustrates the three ways of matricizing an third-order tensor. In general, the mode-*m* matricized tensor $\mathscr{A}$ is denoted $A_{[m]}$. The *mode-m product*, of a matrix B and a tensor $\mathscr{A}$ is

---

[3]Tensor methods were not new in computer graphics; James Arvo used tensors effectively to simulate non-Lambertian reflectance [Arvo 95].

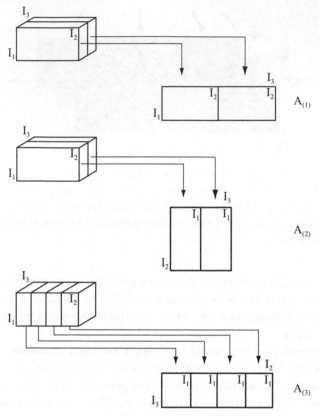

Figure 9.21   Matricizing a third-order tensor. The tensor can be matricized in three ways, to obtain matrices having its mode-1, mode-2, and mode-3 vectors as columns. (From [Vasilescu and Terzopoulos 04] © 2004 ACM, Inc. Included here by permission.)

the ordinary matrix product of B and the mode-m matricized tensor

$$C_{[m]} = BA_{[m]}. \tag{9.9}$$

The mode-m product is denoted by $\times_m$.

To understand the M-mode SVD , it is helpful to see how the SVD works on a matrix regarded as a tensor. As described in Section 9.3.2, the SVD decomposes a matrix D into a product of a diagonal matrix and two orthonormal matrices associated with the column and row spaces of D:

$$D = U_1 \Sigma U_2{}^T \tag{9.10}$$

(here U_1 and U_2 are used in place of U and V). Because a matrix is a second-order tensor, this can be written in tensor form by using the mode-1 and mode-2

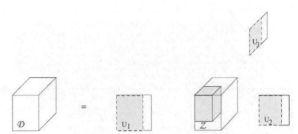

Figure 9.22 The M-mode SVD, illustrated for the case $M = 3$. (From [Vasilescu and Terzopoulos 04] ⓒ 2004 ACM, Inc. Included here by permission.)

products,

$$D = \Sigma \times_1 U_1 \times_2 U_2. \tag{9.11}$$

Equation (9.11) can be readily generalized to express the M-mode SVD of an order-M tensor $\mathcal{D}$ into the product of a tensor $\mathcal{Z}$ and M orthonormal matrices:

$$\mathcal{D} = \mathcal{Z} \times_1 U_1 \times_2 U_2 \cdots \times_m U_m \cdots \times_M U_M. \tag{9.12}$$

The tensor $\mathcal{Z}$ is the *core tensor*, which governs the interaction between the M matrices U_m and is analogous to σ in the ordinary matrix SVD; however, it is no longer diagonal. The orthonormal matrices U_m are called *mode matrices*, and are analogous to the orthonormal row and column matrices in the matrix SVD of Equation (9.10). Figure 9.22 illustrates the M-mode SVD for the case $M = 3$; details of the computation can be found in the paper.

The data tensor created from typical BTF data is of third order, and the dimensions are the number of texels I_x, the number of different illumination conditions I_L, and the number of different viewing directions I_V. The tensor modes correspond to the variation in spatial pixels (texels), the variation in viewing direction, and the variation in lighting direction. It is more convenient to call these modes by name: "pixel mode" (or "texel mode"), "view mode," and "illumination mode," respectively. The respective subscripts x, V, and L are used in place of integer indices.

Because the two primary variables in the BTF are the viewing and illumination directions, the data tensor is decomposed in terms of the illumination and view modes:

$$\mathcal{D} = \mathcal{T} \times_L U_L \times_V U_V. \tag{9.13}$$

The two mode matrices U_L and U_V contain the illumination and viewing variations, respectively. The *basis tensor* $\mathcal{T}$ governs the interaction between the mode matrices, and is defined as

$$\mathcal{T} = \mathcal{Z} \times_x U_x, \tag{9.14}$$

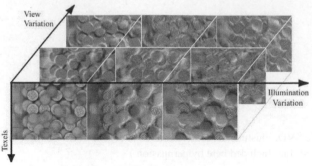

Figure 9.23   A partial visualization of the $\mathcal{T} \in \mathbb{R}^{230400 \times 21 \times 37}$ TensorTextures bases of the coins image ensemble. (From [Vasilescu and Terzopoulos 04] © 2004 ACM, Inc. Included here by permission.)

where $\mathcal{Z}$ is the core tensor in the M-mode SVD above, and U_x is the texel mode matrix. Figure 9.23 illustrates part of $\mathcal{T}$ for the tensor illustrated in Figure 9.20. A more efficient way of computing the TensorTextures basis is

$$\mathcal{T} = \mathcal{D} \times_L U_L^T \times_V U_V^T. \tag{9.15}$$

In order to create a compact multilinear BTF model, U_L, U_V and $\mathcal{T}$ are dimensionally reduced by truncation and optimized using an alternating least squares algorithm.

As is illustrated in Figure 9.24, the TensorTextures basis can be used as a *generative* model to synthesize textures according to the expression

$$\vec{d}_{\text{new}} = \mathcal{T} \times_L \vec{l}_{\text{new}}^T \times_V \vec{v}_{\text{new}}^T, \tag{9.16}$$

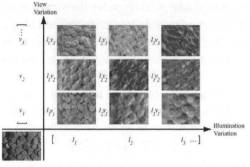

Figure 9.24   TensorTextures texture synthesis. The lower left image is rendered by modulating each of the TensorTextures basis vectors with the coefficients in the view coefficient vector $\vec{v}^T = [v_1\ v_2\ v_3 \dots]$ and illumination coefficient vector $\vec{l}^T = [l_1\ l_2\ l_3 \dots]$. (From [Vasilescu and Terzopoulos 04] © 2004 ACM, Inc. Included here by permission.)

where $\vec{d}_{\text{new}}$ is the synthesized vectorized texture and the vectors $\vec{v}_{\text{new}}$ and $\vec{l}_{\text{new}}$ are the view and illumination representation vectors associated with the new view and illumination directions. These will in general be *novel* directions, in the sense that they will differ from the observed directions in the original captured images. In order to generate a new texture that was not part of the original sampled BTF image data, the view and illumination representations contained in U_V, U_L are blended. More precisely, $\vec{v}_{\text{new}}^T = \vec{w}_V^T U_V$ and $\vec{l}_{\text{new}}^T = \vec{w}_L^T U_L$ where $\vec{w}_V, \vec{w}_L$ are the blending parameters that allow interpolation and extrapolation between the known view and illumination representations. The coins in the image of Figure 9.25 were rendered onto a planar surface by way of Equation (9.16). The method accurately captures the effect of shadows and apparent relief.

If the surface on which the texture is to be rendered is nonplanar, the entire texture cannot normally be synthesized at once. This is because parallax causes the apparent position of the texels to vary with respect to each other. As a result, the texture must be generated by synthesizing values for every texel according to the formula

$$d_t = \mathscr{T}_t \times_L \vec{l}_t^T \times_V \vec{v}_t^T, \tag{9.17}$$

Figure 9.25   The chest contains a TensorTexture mapped onto a planar surface, which appears to have considerable 3D relief when viewed from various directions (top and center) and under various illuminations (center and bottom). (From [Vasilescu and Terzopoulos 04] © 2004 ACM, Inc. Included here by permission.)

where t denotes the texel on the surface. A primary advantage of the TensorTextures model is that it works well even for a sparsely sampled BTF data set.

The TensorTextures paper contains a comparison of the accuracy of BTF approximation using PCA with that using the M-mode SVD, in terms of both numerical accuracy and rendered image quality. For the same number of basis vectors, the TensorTextures method is generally better in both respects. Furthermore, the authors contend that even when the TensorTextures method incurs a larger numerical error, the rendered images tend to have better visual quality.

Two papers were presented at SIGGRAPH 2006 that considered the representation of time-varying reflectance character, i.e., the temporal extension of a BTF [Gu et al. 06, Wang et al. 06]. Matrix-based methods are not well suited to this problem, as they are inherently two-dimensional. In contrast, the Tensor-Textures method can be extended to include time variation by simply adding another dimension (mode) to the data tensor. A drawback of TensorTextures and the matrix-based methods alike is the difficulty in representing "high frequency" reflectance characteristics, such as highly specular reflection. Nonetheless, Tensor-Textures seems a promising approach for use in future computer graphics applications.

10

Radiance Transfer

Much of the history of computer graphics has been devoted to photorealistic rendering, the goal of which is to simulate the real-world interaction and transfer of light. As evidenced by the work described in the earlier chapters, much progress has been made toward the completion of this goal. The rendering equation introduced in Chapter 2 is a fundamental expression governing global illumination, a key component of photorealistic rendering; however, the lack of volumetric effects, including participating media and subsurface scattering, is an intrinsic limitation. Chapters 3 and 4 described methods for rendering these effects. Various optimizations have improved accuracy and efficiency, but accurate interactive GI computation remains difficult.

The emergence of programmable graphics hardware brought the possibility of GI rendering entirely in graphics hardware. The existence of programmable GPUs has been a driving force in research into improvements in image-based approaches. As explained in Part II, image-based lighting (rendering from environment maps) in its basic form reduces rendering to texture lookup and simple linear operations. This is well suited to hardware rendering, as GPUs are optimized for just these operations. However, a drawback to this method is the inability to handle local shadowing and indirect lighting. By computing these effects in a preprocess simulation, then combining the results on the GPU at render time, a final rendering can be generated very quickly. This is the basic idea of the *precomputed radiance transfer* (PRT) method originally introduced in 2002 by Peter-Pike Sloan, Jan Kautz, and John Snyder [Sloan et al. 02]. In the paper entitled "Precomputed Radiance Transfer for Real-Time Rendering in Dynamic, Low-Frequency Lighting Environments," these authors described a technique that can process GI almost entirely on a GPU.

The representation of precomputed radiance transfer simulation is a major issue in PRT because the simulation results must be passed to the GPU in an appropriate format. The original PRT method represents the incident and reflected light in terms of a spherical-harmonics expansion, which is a linear combination of SH basis functions as described in Chapter 7. Even though the SH basis functions themselves are nonlinear, they can be computed on a GPU or precomputed and passed to the GPU at render time. This enables dynamic real-time rendering of objects, including effects such as shadowing and interreflection, that was not possible before the creation of the PRT technique.

PRT has gathered a great deal of attention since it was first introduced in 2002, and has had a substantial impact in the field of real-time rendering. The original PRT method had many limitations: the approximated light could only represent very soft shadows under diffuse lighting, specular reflection was included only to a limited extent, and the shapes of the objects had to be fixed (although they could move with respect to each other). Much of the subsequent work has involved generalizing the basic method and improving its versatility. New approaches have been proposed that replaced the SH basis functions with more general basis sets, such as wavelets. Sloan, Kautz, and Snyder, who originally developed the method, have been actively involved in this subsequent research, and have published several improvements to the original method. This final chapter introduces the basic PRT method, and explores some of the subsequent developments in precomputed transfer for rendering.

10.1   PRT Fundamentals

The work described in the original PRT paper was primarily concerned with a single object illuminated by a distant environment map. The reflected radiance (or the outgoing radiance, in general) at a set of sample points on the object is represented by an expansion in spherical harmonics, which represents the outgoing radiance from any viewpoint. The coefficients of the SH approximation can be calculated quickly from the incident illumination using precomputed *transfer functions*. This allows the object to be rendered at interactive rates as the viewpoint and incident illumination are controlled by a user of the rendering system.

Shadowing and interreflection are included in the precomputation and therefore change according to the lighting. The paper also describes how the method can be applied to more than one object, where there is significant shadowing and interreflection between the objects.

10.1.1   Light Approximations using SH Basis Functions

Spherical harmonics (SH) were introduced in Chapter 7 in the context of approximating and filtering environment maps as functions on a sphere. Specifi-

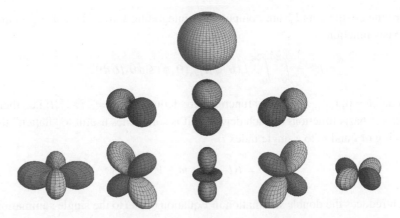

Figure 10.1   Spherical harmonic (SH) basis functions. (Courtesy of Peter-Pike Sloan.)

cally, spherical harmonics are a collection of orthogonal functions defined on the unit sphere. To review, the real SH basis functions are defined as (from Equation (7.2.4))

$$
Y_{l,m} = \begin{cases}
\sqrt{2} K_l^m \cos(m\phi) P_l^m(\cos\theta), & m > 0 \\
\sqrt{2} K_l^m \sin(-m\phi) P_l^{-m}(\cos\theta), & m < 0 \\
K_l^0 P_l^0(\cos\theta), & m = 0
\end{cases}
$$

for each $l = 0, 1, 2, \ldots$ and $m = -l, \ldots, l$; K_k^m is a normalizing factor, and P_l^m are the associated Legendre polynomials described in Chapter 7. The first few real SH basis functions are listed in Table 7.1, and illustrated in Figure 10.1. The SH basis functions $Y_{l,m}$ depend on two variables, θ and ϕ, which are the usual spherical coordinates: θ is the angle of the z-axis (the colatitude) and ϕ is the angle in the xy-plane (the *longitude* or *azimuth*). The index l is the *degree* of the basis function. A particular basis function has at most l oscillations in θ and ϕ, so l also provides the angular frequency of the basis function. When $m = 0$, the SH basis function $Y_{l,0}$ depends only on θ.

The spherical-harmonic expansion of a given spherical function $L(\theta, \phi)$ is a sum of the form

$$
\tilde{L}(\theta, \phi) = \sum_{l=0}^{n-1} \sum_{m=-l}^{l} L_l^m Y_{l,m}(\theta, \phi), \tag{10.1}
$$

where the coefficients L_l^m are computed by integrating L over the corresponding SH basis function:

$$L_l^m = \int_0^\pi \int_0^{2\pi} L(\theta, \phi) Y_{l,m}(\theta, \phi) \sin\theta \, d\phi \, d\theta.$$

For each $l = 0, 1, 2, \ldots$ the basis functions are defined for $m = -l, \ldots, l$; i.e., there are $2l + 1$ basis functions of each degree l. It is sometimes useful to "flatten" the indexing of l and m to a single index i,

$$i = l(l+1) + m + 1,$$

which reduces the double summation in Equation (10.1) to the single summation

$$\sum_{i=1}^{n^2} \ell_i y_i(\theta, \phi). \tag{10.2}$$

To avoid ambiguity, the single-index SH basis functions and corresponding co-efficients are denoted by y_i and ℓ_i, respectively, in Equation (10.2). The upper limit on the summation n^2 comes from the the total number of SH basis functions through degree l which is $1 + 3 + 5 + \cdots + 2n + 1 = (l+1)^2$; $n = l + 1$ is the *order* of the expansion.

Another useful optimization available for real spherical harmonics was employed in Chapter 7. The spherical coordinates θ and ϕ appear only in sine and cosine functions. If a point on the sphere is represented by a unit vector $\vec{s}$, these trigonometric functions can be represented directly in terms of the rectangular coordinates of $\vec{s} = (x, y, z)$, where $x^2 + y^2 + z^2 = 1$. For example, $\cos\theta = z$,

		$Y_{2,-2} = \sqrt{\frac{15}{16\pi}}(x^2 - y^2)$
	$Y_{1,-1} = -\sqrt{\frac{3}{4\pi}}\, x$	$Y_{2,-1} = -\sqrt{\frac{15}{4\pi}}\, xz$
$Y_{0,0} = \sqrt{\frac{1}{4\pi}}$	$Y_{1,0} = \sqrt{\frac{3}{4\pi}}\, z$	$Y_{2,0} = \sqrt{\frac{5}{16\pi}}(3z^2 - 1)$
	$Y_{1,1} = -\sqrt{\frac{3}{4\pi}}\, y$	$Y_{2,1} = -\sqrt{\frac{15}{4\pi}}\, yz$
		$Y_{2,2} = \sqrt{\frac{15}{16\pi}}2xy$

Table 10.1   Real spherical harmonics for $l = 0, 1, 2$ in rectangular coordinates ($x^2 + y^2 + z^2 = 1$).

$\sin\theta\cos\phi = x$, and $\sin\theta\sin\phi = y$. Table 10.1 contains the first few real SH basis functions in rectangular coordinates. The rectangular form is often used in the PRT literature; $y_i(\theta,\phi)$ in Equation (10.2) is often replaced with $y_i(\vec{s})$, where it is assumed that the vector $\vec{s}$ is assumed to be a unit vector.

The value of n in Equation (10.1), the order of the SH approximation, bounds the maximum degree of the terms and thereby limits the angular frequency of detail that can be captured by the approximation. Figure 10.2 illustrates how increasing the order affects the detail in an SH approximation to an environment map. The flattened version of Equation (10.2) reveals an important issue with spherical harmonics: to achieve an order-n approximation, n^2 terms are needed. Consequently, the approximation becomes less efficient for larger n. Unfortunately, a large order is often needed to capture even moderate detail; in Figure 10.2, an order-26 approximation (which has 676 terms) barely separates the basic bright spots in the image. This is one reason the original PRT method was restricted to low-frequency environments.

On the other hand, a high-frequency approximation is not always needed. The frequency of the reflection increases with specularity; diffuse and dull reflective surfaces generally have low-frequency reflection. More precisely, the frequency of the surface reflection refers to the order of the SH approximation needed to accurately represent the slice of the BRDF for any fixed incoming (or outgoing) direction. In this context, the frequency of the reflected light distribution at a point is limited by both the frequency of the reflection, and the frequency of the incident illumination. In other words, low-frequency reflection smooths out high-frequency lighting. Therefore, PRT needs only a low-frequency representation of both the incident and reflected light in an environment exhibiting only low-frequency reflection. However, if surfaces in the environment are sufficiently specular, then higher-frequency approximations are needed to represent radiance distributions throughout the environment. For pure mirror reflection, representing light as a set of values at dense sample points on the sphere is more efficient than

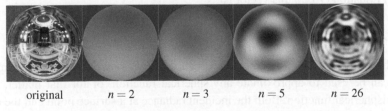

original $n = 2$ $n = 3$ $n = 5$ $n = 26$

Figure 10.2   Approximation of an environment map using SH basis functions of increasing order n. Even at order $n = 26$ much detail is missed, such as the bright spots at the center of the image. (Courtesy of Peter-Pike Sloan.)

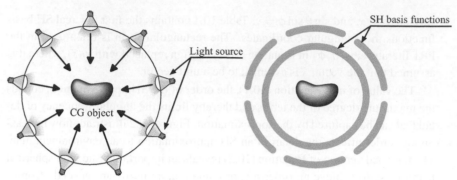

Figure 10.3   Lighting using SH basis functions.

the SH expansion. In short, spherical harmonic representations are not suited for high-frequency (highly specular) environments.

It is worth mentioning that low-frequency SH approximations are useful in themselves. For example, the order-0 approximation is just a constant—the average value of the function over the entire sphere. In Chapter 7 it was explained how the SH approximation is one way of filtering an environment map.

Figure 10.3 illustrates the idea of illuminating an object from a set of light sources. Alternatively, the incident illumination might be from an environment map or some other computed radiance distribution. The figure on the right illustrates schematically how the terms in the corresponding spherical harmonics approximation increase in frequency. The first-order term is constant.

10.1.2   Radiance Transfer and Light Vectors

An advantage of using spherical harmonics, or any other fixed set of basis functions, is that the representation of the incident light (or whatever signal is being approximated) reduces to a set of basis function coefficients. These coefficients can be collected into a single vector. In the case of an order-n SH approximation, as in Equation (10.2), this vector is

$$\vec{\ell} = (\ell_1, \ell_2, \ldots, \ell_{n^2}).$$

In the context of PRT, the vector $\vec{\ell}$ is called a *light vector*. Spherical harmonics can be used to approximate any spherical function, or for that matter, any hemispherical function. Both the incident radiance at a surface point and the outgoing radiance can be approximated with a spherical harmonics expansion, and thus expressed as a light vector. The light vector for the outgoing radiance can be regarded as a function of the incident light vector; this is known as a *trans-*

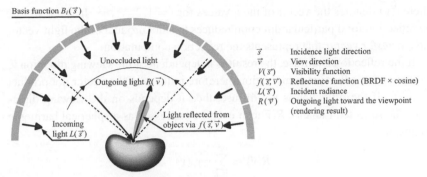

Basis function $B_i(\vec{s})$

Unoccluded light

Outgoing light $R(\vec{v})$

Incoming light $L(\vec{s})$

Light reflected from object via $f(\vec{s}, \vec{v})$

$\vec{s}$	Incidence light direction
$\vec{v}$	View direction
$V(\vec{s})$	Visibility function
$f(\vec{s}, \vec{v})$	Reflectance function (BRDF × cosine)
$L(\vec{s})$	Incident radiance
$R(\vec{v})$	Outgoing light toward the viewpoint (rendering result)

Figure 10.4   Geometry for radiance transfer by reflection.

fer function. The transfer function is necessarily linear, which means that it can be represented by a matrix. In other words, the SH coefficients of the outgoing radiance are a linear function of the SH coefficients of the incident radiance.

To make this more concrete, consider the BRDF model of surface reflection. If $L(\vec{s})$ is the incident radiance function, the reflected (outgoing) radiance R at a point on the surface is given by

$$R(\vec{v}) = \int_{\Omega_{4\pi}} L(\vec{s}) V(\vec{s}) f(\vec{s}, \vec{v}) \, d\vec{s}, \tag{10.3}$$

where $\vec{v}$ is an outgoing direction (i.e., a viewing direction), $V(\vec{s})$ is the visibility function (which is 1 if light coming from direction $\vec{s}$ is visible at the point and 0 otherwise), and $f(\vec{s}, \vec{v})$ is the cosine-weighted BRDF function, i.e., the BRDF function times the cosine of the incidence angle θ. Figure 10.4 illustrates the geometry. The integral is performed over then entire sphere; the visibility function $V\vec{s}$ is zero if the direction $\vec{s}$ lies below the surface.

If the incident radiance $L(\vec{s})$ is represented as a spherical harmonic expansion, Equation (10.3) becomes

$$R(\vec{v}) = \int_{\Omega_{4\pi}} \left(\sum_{i=1}^{n^2} \ell_i y_i(\vec{s}) \right) V(\vec{s}) f(\vec{s}, \vec{v}) \, d\vec{s} = \sum_{i=1}^{n^2} \ell_i \int_{\Omega_{4\pi}} y_i(\vec{s}) V(\vec{s}) f(\vec{s}, \vec{v}) \, d\vec{s}. \tag{10.4}$$

The integral on the right side of Equation (10.4) depends only on the geometry of the object, and can therefore be precomputed. If $t_i(\vec{v})$ denotes the value of the integral for some SH index i and for a specific viewing vector $\vec{v}$, then the reflection can be expressed as

$$R(\vec{v}) = \sum_{i=1}^{n^2} \ell_i t_i(\vec{v}) = \vec{\ell} \cdot \vec{t}(\vec{v}),$$

where $\vec{t}(\vec{v})$ denotes the vector of the t_i values for $i = 1, 2, \ldots, n^2$. In other words, the reflection for a particular direction reduces to a dot product of the light vector and a *transfer vector* that represents the reflection computation.

If the reflection is diffuse, the result is independent of the viewing direction $\vec{v}$, and the entire reflection computation therefore reduces to the vector dot product $R = \vec{l} \cdot \vec{t}$. If the reflection is not diffuse, then it depends on the viewing direction. The reflected radiance $R(\vec{v})$ can itself be expressed as a spherical harmonic expansion

$$R(\vec{v}) \approx \sum_{j=0}^{m^2} r_j y_j(\vec{v})$$

where each coefficient r_j is computed by integrating R against the SH basis function y_j. That is,

$$r_j = \int_{\Omega_{4\pi}} y_j(\vec{v}) \sum_{i=1}^{n^2} \ell_i \int_{\Omega_{4\pi}} y_i(\vec{s}) V(\vec{s}) f(\vec{s}, \vec{v}) \, d\vec{s} \, d\vec{v} \qquad (10.5)$$

$$= \sum_{i=1}^{n^2} \ell_i \int_{\Omega_{4\pi}} \int_{\Omega_{4\pi}} y_j(\vec{v}) y_i(\vec{s}) V(\vec{s}) f(\vec{s}, \vec{v}) \, d\vec{s} \, d\vec{v}, \qquad (10.6)$$

and because the double integral depends only on the geometry, it can be precomputed. If t_{ij} denotes the integral evaluated for a particular i and j, then

$$r_j = \sum_{i=1}^{n^2} t_{ij} \ell_i. \qquad (10.7)$$

Regarding the values of t_{ij} as elements of a matrix T and the SH coefficients r_j as a light vector $\vec{r}$ of the reflected light, the reflection computation amounts to the matrix multiplication

$$\vec{r} = T\vec{l}.$$

This formalizes the notion that the outgoing light vector is a linear function of the incident light vector. The matrix T is the *transfer matrix*, a particular representation of a general *transfer function*.

The derivation of the transfer matrix above assumes a simple BRDF representation of surface reflectance. It also includes shadowing by way of the visibility function V. More effects can be included. For example, the transfer function can account for interreflection between nearby parts of the object, i.e., any light that reflects from the surface at the point hits another nearby point on the object, and bounces back to be reflected in another direction. Multiple bounces can also be included. In general, these effects of occlusion and interreflection are known as *self-transfer*.

Of course, the process of actually computing the elements of the transfer matrix is a major task in itself. Not only does it require evaluation of the double integral of Equation (10.6) for each i and j, it requires simulation of multiple bounces if interreflection is to be considered. This is in fact a scaled down global illumination problem, and it can be simulated, for example, with a form of Monte Carlo path tracing. The simulation has to be done at each point on the surface where an outgoing light vector is to be computed. This involves significant computation, because for most surfaces, a fairly dense set of surface sample points is required. However, the cost of the simulation precomputation is less of a concern than the run-time evaluation. Once the transfer matrices are computed, the radiance transfer computation is just a matrix multiplication, hence the name "precomputed radiance transfer."

10.1.3 Transfer Matrices and Simulation

At a particular sample point on the surface, the transfer matrix can be computed as a sum of the effects of direct lighting and indirect interreflection. A first pass, called a *shadow pass*, is applied to evaluate the integral of Equation (10.6) by sampling over the hemisphere or sphere of directions. The only ray tracing required is the casting of shadow rays, and this is only necessary to determine the value of the visibility function. Figure 10.5 illustrates what is involved in the shadow pass. In practice, the results of the shadow rays are stored and used for other passes. The shadow pass constructs the direct lighting transfer matrix, and can be described as "pass zero." The shadow pass is applied to each sample point.

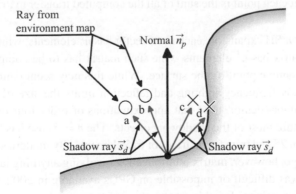

Figure 10.5   The shadow pass in precomputation.

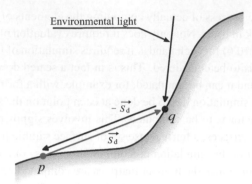

Figure 10.6   The interreflection pass in precomputation.

Because light is additive, the interreflection can be computed separately. At a particular sample point p, the first interreflection pass works as follows. For a set of samples over the hemisphere, rays are cast to test for intersection with the object. Suppose a ray originating at p hits the object at another point q. The directly reflected radiance from q to p is computed from the transfer matrix that was computed in the previous pass: the incident radiance at a sample ray of direction $\vec{s}_d$ is the outgoing radiance at $-\vec{s}_d$ from point q (Figure 10.6). The set of all sample rays over the hemisphere from p are used to construct the indirect transfer matrix at p. The interreflection pass can be repeated using the indirect transfer matrices from the previous interreflection pass to determine the radiance values at the surface intersections. Pass N thus includes light reflected from exactly $N - 1$ bounces, so the outgoing radiance can be expected to drop at each pass. The process is terminated when the values fall below a certain threshold. The final transfer matrix at each point is the sum of all the computed transfer matrices from the N passes.

For an order-n SH expansion, each light vector has n^2 elements, which means each transfer matrix has n^4 elements. One such matrix has to be computed and stored for each sample point on the surface. While this may seem daunting, the assumption of low-frequency lighting and reflection limits the size of the light vectors. The authors demonstrate that approximations of order four or five are sufficient to capture most of the shadowing effects. The $n = 5$ case has light vectors of dimension 25 and transfer matrices of 625 elements. By modern standards, these are not large; however, matrix multiplication involving anything larger than 4×4 matrices was difficult or impossible on GPUs available in 2002 when the original paper was written. For this reason, the surfaces were first assumed to be Lambertian. In this case, the outgoing radiance is constant and the transfer matrix reduces to just a vector ($\vec{t}$, in the notation above), and the transfer computation reduces to just a dot product. For specular reflection the authors used a simple Phong model, which is approximated and evaluated using a technique known as *zonal harmonics* to leverage the symmetry about the direction of reflection.

10.1.4 PRT Rendering

Given the transfer matrices, the rendering process is straightforward. The incident light vector is constructed by projecting the incident light, which can come from an environment map or some other light source, onto the SH basis functions. To render a particular point on the surface, the outgoing radiance light vector is computed by multiplying the incident vector by the transfer matrix, and the value at the particular viewing direction is computed from the SH expansion. In the case of a diffuse surface, this process amounts to a single dot product, as the outgoing radiance is constant. The authors' hardware implementation (in 2002) was able to achieve interactive frame rates for objects having moderately complex geometry. The precomputation, however, required as long as several hours.

10.1.5 PRT Extensions

The method described in the previous subsections for constructing the transfer matrices includes direct reflection, self-shadowing, and interreflection. There is no reason, though, that it has to be limited to these effects. Volumetric effects, such as subsurface scattering, could also be included if the simulation performed in the precomputation accounted for them. The method can be extended to volumetric scattering in a participating medium if the sample points at which an SH representation is constructed is extended from points only on the object surface to points in space. The simulation becomes more complicated in this case, because of the need to compute attenuation and in-scattering and then integrate these effects over each sample ray.

The basic PRT method works on a single object. The volumetric approach can be employed to allow for the interaction of light between two objects, even if they move with respect to each other. Doing this requires a volumetric representation, which is a generalization of an irradiance volume. Each point in the volume contains its own transfer matrix. For definiteness, call the two objects A and B. The process works like the transfer simulation described above for self-transfer, except that the point q is regarded as being in space, and the lighting at each pass is obtained from the transfer matrix at q, even in the shadow pass. This allows object B to be lit depending on the interaction or occlusion of object A, because the effect of A is included at render time. This approach can be applied independent of the shape of object B, and even if object B moves. The ability to move objects around interactively at render time was a remarkable accomplishment.

10.1.6 PRT Limitations

PRT was originally developed to represent low frequency light transfer. The goal was to render a Lambertian object under diffuse lighting conditions, including shadows and interreflection effects, in real time. Spherical harmonics do a good job representing this kind of illumination. An advantage of the SH approach is that relatively few directional samples are needed to get a good approximation with low-degree SH basis functions. This is useful for broad area light sources, which have a large solid angle and therefore would otherwise require a lot of point samples. Furthermore, diffuse lighting generally creates diffuse shadowing, which means the spatial variation in illumination changes slowly. Consequently, the positional dependence can be represented by interpolating relatively sparse samples. Moreover, the computation is well suited to hardware implementation given precomputed transfer functions.

With high-frequency lighting, which arises from small light sources, shadow edges get sharper. As a result, the illumination has to be densely sampled across the surface to properly capture the appearance. This substantially increases the storage requirements as well as the precomputation time. In addition, high-frequency lighting requires a high-order SH approximation to capture the true nature of the light. If there is only one light source, and it is small, the representation is inefficient. A small source requires fewer point samples, so it is more reasonable to just sample the source directly at render time. That is, the benefit of the precomputation drops as the light source decreases in size. However, precomputation of high-frequency lighting can still be effective, especially for indirect lighting. Rendering caustics, which normally requires a very large number of samples, can benefit from precomputation.

High-frequency reflection, i.e., highly specular reflection, causes problems with SH representation as well. Even though reflection does not generally increase the spatial frequency of the incident light, reflections of other scene elements can have high frequency detail (consider a mirror surface reflecting an object having a finely detailed texture). In terms of the transfer matrix, the number of columns corresponds to the dimension of the incident light vector $\vec{\ell}$; the number of rows corresponds to that of the outgoing light vector $\vec{r}$. Increasing the specularity increases the required dimension of the outgoing vector, which in turn increases the number of rows in the matrix. In summary, spherical harmonic approximations work well for low-frequency lighting and reflection, but are poorly suited to medium- and high-frequency effects. A fundamental problem with representing reflected light in general is its inherent quartic complexity: doubling the frequency in all parameters (spatial and angular) causes a sixteen-fold increase in the number of coefficients.

When the original PRT work was developed, it was not practical to represent large matrices on the GPU, so PRT computation of an object with strong specular reflection in real time was considered difficult. The publication of the paper inspired a surge of research into ways of improving PRT and adapting it to more general environments. The application of PRT to general reflection and lighting was considered the primary unsolved problem. The impact of the PRT paper has thus been the subsequent interest in using SH basis functions and other basis functions. PRT has since been developed into versatile real-time methods far beyond the earliest goals of the research.

10.2 Advancing Radiance Transfer

10.2.1 Computation of Reflection Using SH Functions

Adapting PRT for more general surface reflectance requires a method of representing an arbitrary BRDF with spherical harmonics. A BRDF is a function on the Cartesian product of two hemispheres $\Omega \times \Omega$. But because spherical harmonics are defined on the sphere, there is no obvious SH representation for a BRDF. But there are ways of doing it. The method described in this section requires some additional properties of spherical harmonics.

The integral of a product of SH expansions. The integral of the product of two functions $f(\vec{s})$ and $g(\vec{s})$ in terms of their SH expansions

$$\tilde{f}(\vec{s}) = \sum_{i=1}^{n^2} f_i y_i(\vec{s}), \quad \tilde{g}(\vec{s}) = \sum_{i=1}^{n^2} g_i y_i(\vec{s})$$

has a remarkably simple formula:

$$\int_{\Omega_{4\pi}} \tilde{f}(\vec{s})\tilde{g}(\vec{s})\,d\vec{s} = \sum_{i=1}^{n^2} f_i g_i. \tag{10.8}$$

That is, the value of the integral of the product of two SH expansions is the sum of the products of their corresponding coefficients. In terms of light vectors, the right side of Equation (10.8) is the vector dot product $\vec{f} \cdot \vec{g}$. This is a direct result of the orthogonality of SH basis functions: the integral of $y_i(\vec{s})y_j(\vec{s})$ over the sphere is zero if $i \neq j$, and one otherwise. Consequently, all the terms in the product of nonmatching indices vanish in the integration. This property was utilized in the irradiance environment map technique of Ramamoorthi and Hanrahan described in Section 7.2.5.

Rotation of SH expansions. The SH coefficients of a rotated function can be computed from a linear transformation of the SH coefficients of the original function. To make this more precise, suppose R is a general 3D rotation matrix. The function $g(\vec{s}) = f(R\vec{s})$ can be called a *rotation* of the function f by R. Both f and g have SH expansions:

$$\tilde{f}(\vec{s}) = \sum_{l=0}^{n-1} \sum_{m=-l}^{l} f_l^m Y_{l,m}(\vec{s}), \quad \tilde{g}(\vec{s}) = \sum_{l=0}^{n-1} \sum_{m=-l}^{l} g_l^m Y_{l,m}(\vec{s}).$$

For each degree l, the SH coefficient set g_l^m ($m = -l, \dots, l$) of g can be computed from a linear transformation of the SH coefficient set f_l^m of f. (The actual transformation depends on the matrix R, and is rather involved.) The SH expansion of a rotated function can thus be computed by transforming the SH coefficients. This property is very useful in PRT, because it means that rotating an SH expansion in global coordinates to or from a local surface coordinate system can be effected by matrix multiplications.

10.2.2 BRDF representation in spherical harmonics

In terms of the BRDF, the reflection in a particular direction at a surface point is the integral of the product of the cosine-weighted BRDF and the incident radiance function, normally over the hemisphere of directions above the surface point. As was done in the irradiance environment map method of Chapter 7, the integral can be extended to the entire sphere by introducing a clipping term:

$$R(\vec{v}) = \int_{\Omega_{4\pi}} L(\vec{s}) \underbrace{f_r(\vec{s}, \vec{v}) \max(\cos\theta, 0)}_{b(\vec{s}, \vec{v})} d\vec{s},$$

where f_r is the BRDF function, θ is the angle $\vec{s}$ makes with the surface normal, and $\vec{v}$ is a (fixed) viewing direction. The clipping term $\max(\cos\theta, 0)$ zeros all values below the surface and thereby restricts the integral to incident directions above the surface. The function $b(\vec{s}, \vec{v})$ thus represents the BRDF, the cosine, and the surface clipping function.

If both $b(\vec{s}, \vec{v})$ and the incident radiance function $L(\vec{s})$ are expanded in spherical harmonics, then by virtue of the SH product integration formula of Equation (10.8), the computation of reflectance reduces to a multiplication of the SH coefficients. This major simplification results in very efficient rendering; however, there are some complications. One problem involves differing coordinate systems: the incident irradiance is normally expressed in a global coordinate system, while the BRDF and the clipping term are in the local coordinate system at the particular surface point. A rotation must therefore be performed on one set of SH coefficients before the product formula can be applied. A more serious problem arises from the dependence of the BRDF on both the incoming and outgoing angles. The SH expansion has to be separately computed for each outgoing direction $\vec{v}$; fortunately, these expansions are independent of the incident radiance function so they can be precomputed.

BRDF textures. An attempt to solve these problems was described in a paper entitled "Fast, Arbitrary BRDF Shading for Low-Frequency Lighting Using Spherical Harmonics" by Jan Kautz, Peter-Pike Sloan, and John Snyder [Kautz et al. 02]. In this method, the SH expansion for the clipped and weighted BRDF function is in the local coordinates at each sample point on the surface of an object. As usual, the local coordinate system has the z-axis coincident with the surface normal, and the x-axis is chosen either arbitrarily, or to align with the principal direction of anisotropy if the BRDF is not isotropic. The incident radiance function L is rotated at render time to the local coordinate system; the authors employ a fast algorithm to compute the linear coefficients if the lighting or the object changes dynamically at render time.

An SH expansion of the (cosine-weighted and clipped) BRDF function is performed for a fixed set of outgoing vectors $\vec{v}$, each in the local coordinate system. This produces a set of BRDF SH coefficients $b_i(\vec{v})$ for each $\vec{v}$, where i runs from 1 to n^2 (n is the approximation order). The authors use an order-5 approximations, which results in 25 SH coefficients for each approximation. The BRDF coefficients values are stored in texture maps called *BRDF textures*. A separate texture, or subtexture, is used to store all the values of $b_i(\vec{v})$ for a given i; that is, the position in the BRDF texture of index i corresponds to the direction $\vec{v}$.

The process of rendering using BRDF textures is illustrated in Figure 10.7. For the purposes of illustration, it is assumed that the illumination comes from a distant environment map. That way, the incident light function is the same at every point on the object. The first step is to compute the SH expansion of the environment map. The resulting coefficients are stored in a light vector (Step 1 in Figure 10.7). The precomputed BRDF textures, which contain the BRDF SH coefficients, are constructed in the local surface coordinates of the point to be rendered, while the incident light is expanded in global coordinates. Consequently, the SH coefficients contained in the light vector have to be rotated to the local surface coordinate system. As described above, this rotation is effected by a linear transformation, which in the case of the 25-dimensional approximations used by the authors, is a 25×25 matrix (Step 2a in Figure 10.7). Next, the SH coefficients

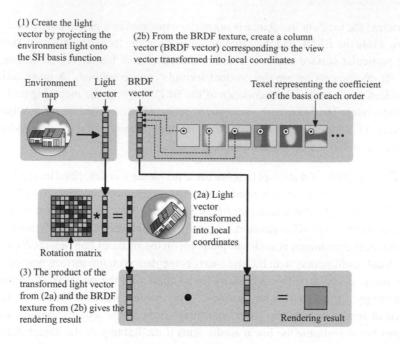

(1) Create the light vector by projecting the environment light onto the SH basis function

(2b) From the BRDF texture, create a column vector (BRDF vector) corresponding to the view vector transformed into local coordinates

Environment map   Light vector   BRDF vector

Texel representing the coefficient of the basis of each order

(2a) Light vector transformed into local coordinates

Rotation matrix

(3) The product of the transformed light vector from (2a) and the BRDF texture from (2b) gives the rendering result

Rendering result

Figure 10.7   The process of constructing and rendering with a BRDF texture. (Courtesy of Jan Kautz.)

for the particular viewing direction $\vec{v}$ are obtained by looking up the values in each of the BRDF textures (Step 2b in Figure 10.7) for the surface point. These are collected into a BRDF vector matching the light vector for the incident illumination, and the dot product of the two vectors computes the reflection integral, via Equation (10.8) (Step 3 in Figure 10.7).

The rendering algorithm illustrated in Figure 10.7 assumes the viewpoint, lighting, and surface BRDF can all be changed interactively at render time. An optimization is possible if the viewing position is fixed and the lighting is the only thing that changes, because the viewing direction at each surface sample point is also fixed. Because of this, the BRDF texture lookup need only be done once for each viewing direction. Furthermore, it is more efficient to rotate these fixed BRDF vectors to the global coordinate system rather than rotate the light vector to each local coordinate system. However, graphics hardware at the time the paper was written (2002) was not capable of performing a 25×25 matrix multiplication; that had to be computed on the CPU and then uploaded to the GPU at render time. Even so, the authors were able to achieve interactive frame rates under the restriction of a fixed viewpoint. In the more general case, the incident light, the viewpoint, and the surface BRDFs can all change dynamically at render time. This requires recomputing the BRDF textures, which slows the process substantially. Nonetheless, the computation is still relatively fast.

BRDF textures and PRT. BRDF textures can be used in precomputed radiance transfer. As described earlier in this chapter, the key element to PRT is the construction of transfer matrices that convert SH coefficients (light vector) of the incident light to SH coefficients of the outgoing light. Transfer matrices can be constructed to account for various effects, including self-shadowing, interreflection, and subsurface scattering. How a BRDF texture is incorporated into a transfer matrix depends on the particular effect the matrix handles.

The simplest case is self-shadowing, which accounts for occlusion of the incident light before it hits the object surface. In this case, the incident radiance $L(\vec{s})$ in the reflection integral (Equation (10.4)) is the occluded incident radiance. Multiplying the environment map light vector by the self-shadowing transfer matrix produces the locally occluded environment map light vector. This is then used in place of the original light vector in the BRDF texture rendering. In other words, accounting for self-shadowing amounts to multiplying the constructed incident light vector by the transfer matrix.

In contrast, BRDF textures are more difficult to incorporate into PRT involving interreflection, because the interreflection depends on the particular BRDF. The surface BRDF therefore has to be included in the simulation step, which means that it cannot be changed dynamically at render time. Multiple sample points on the surface of the object are used to compute the transfer matrix during the simulation, and each point has its own local coordinate system. Therefore it is more efficient to perform the SH expansion in a common global coordinate system.

The composition of the BRDF texture, the rotation matrix, and the transfer matrix can (theoretically) be applied to any surface with any reflection characteristics. However, both the BRDF texture approach and the original PRT approach assumed low-frequency lighting and reflection. For the reasons described above, the practical application of spherical harmonics in representing more general surface reflection is considered rather limited. Recent research, e.g., [Sloan 06,Lehtinen 07], has proposed the use of other bases such as wavelets (described in Section 10.2.4).

BRDF Matrices. As described above, a separate SH expansion of the weighted and clipped BRDF $b(\vec{s},\vec{v})$ is needed to apply the dot product formula (Equation (10.8)) to evaluate the reflection integral of Equation (10.4) for each viewing vector $\vec{v}$. The BRDF texture method uses a set of fixed sample vectors $\vec{v}$, and stores the SH coefficients $b_i(\vec{v})$ for each i in a texture. In general, $b_i(\vec{v})$ for a given

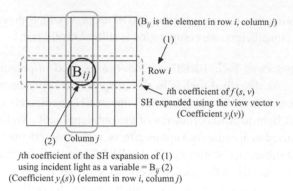

Figure 10.8   BRDF matrix.

i is a function of the viewing direction $\vec{v}$, i.e., is a function on the sphere, and can therefore be approximated by an expansion in spherical harmonics. Coefficient j of the SH expansion of $b_i(\vec{v})$ is denoted by b_{ij}; these coefficients collectively form a *BRDF matrix* (Figure 10.8).

The construction of a BRDF matrix is similar to the construction of a transfer matrix described in Section 10.1.2. The SH coefficient $b_i(\vec{v})$ of the function $b(\vec{s}, \vec{v})$ is computed from projecting $b(\vec{s}, \vec{v})$ onto the SH basis function of index i:

$$b_i(\vec{v}) = \int_{\Omega_{4\pi}} b(\vec{s}, \vec{v}) y_i(\vec{s}) \, d\vec{s}$$

and coefficient j of the SH expansion of $b_i(\vec{v})$ is

$$b_{ij} = \int_{\Omega_{4\pi}} b_i(\vec{v}) y_j(\vec{v}) \, d\vec{v} = \int_{\Omega_{4\pi}} \int_{\Omega_{4\pi}} b(\vec{s}, \vec{v}) y_i(\vec{s}) y_j(\vec{v}) \, d\vec{s} \, d\vec{v} \qquad (10.9)$$

Rows of a BRDF matrix correspond to the variation in the viewing direction; columns of a BRDF matrix correspond to the variation in the light direction.

The BRDF matrix as defined in Equation (10.9) predates PRT by a full decade, having been introduced in 1992 by Stephen H. Westin, James Arvo, and Kenneth E. Torrance in the paper "Predicting Reflectance Functions from Complex Surfaces" [Westin et al. 92]. This work was concerned with photorealistic rendering of surfaces having complex mesostructure, and it succeeded—the paper contains some of the most realistic (synthetically generated) surface renderings ever produced. The application of spherical harmonics by Westin et al. in 1992 had a substantial impact on PRT research in the following decade. Equation (10.9) is very similar to the construction of the transfer matrix given in Equation (10.6). In fact, a transfer matrix is a kind of generalization of a BRDF matrix: both transform an incident light vector (a vector of SH coefficients) to an outgoing light vector. The principal difference is that BRDF matrices include only the surface reflection according to the BRDF, while general transfer matrices can include local geometry effects, including shadowing, interreflection, and even subsurface scattering.

10.2.3 Efficient PRT

Exit transfer matrices. Incorporating a BRDF matrix into the precomputed radiance transfer method is even simpler than it is for BRDF textures, because the BRDF matrix is itself just another transfer matrix. There is, however, the coordinate system compatibility problem: normally the incident light vector is expanded in a global coordinate system, while the BRDF matrix is constructed in local surface coordinates. Whether a transfer matrix applies to a light vector in local or global coordinates depends on the particular assumptions (or the particular implementation). In any case, the transformation from global to local coordinates is a rotation, and as described above, the corresponding transformation of SH coefficients is itself a linear transformation represented by a high-dimensional "rotation" matrix. If the surface is fixed and rigid, this matrix can be precomputed for each surface point. If the surface is allowed to rotate or deform after the precomputation phase, then the rotation matrix must be recomputed. As described earlier, this is not a fast computation, but it is not very complicated either. The cost of this computation depends on the size of the light vectors, i.e., the order of the SH approximations.

Assuming that the transfer matrix accounts for self-shadowing only (i.e., there is no interreflection involved) then the transfer matrix is independent of the BRDF matrix. Assuming also that the transfer matrix is constructed in a global coordinate system, then the outgoing radiance light vector at a surface point p can be computed from the source light vector in three steps. First, the transfer matrix T_p is applied to the source light vector $\vec{\ell}$, which produces an incident light vector accounting for self-shadowing. This light vector is then transformed to the local surface coordinates by a rotation matrix R_p, and finally the BRDF matrix B is applied to produce the outgoing light vector. The composition of all three transformations—the self-shadowing transfer, the rotation, and the reflection— can be combined into a single matrix by the ordinary matrix product

$$\vec{e}_p = BR_pT_p\vec{\ell} = M_p\vec{\ell}. \tag{10.10}$$

The combined matrix M_p is known as the *exit transfer matrix* (see also Figure 10.9).

The precise formulation of an exit transfer matrix depends on the coordinate systems of the light vectors and transfer matrices, which in turn depends on the

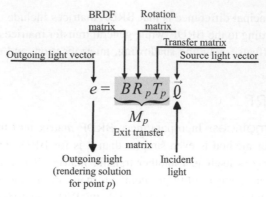

Figure 10.9   Exit transfer matrix.

particular render-time assumptions. For example, it might be more efficient to transform the BRDF matrices to the global coordinate system if the viewpoint remains fixed as described above. The exit transfer matrix also depends on which effects the transfer matrix includes. But the basic idea is always the same: the incident light vector is transformed to an outgoing light vector by a single matrix. As the outgoing light vector contains the SH coefficients of the outgoing radiance function, the actual outgoing radiance is therefore the value of the SH approximation in the viewing direction $\vec{v}$:

$$r_p(\vec{v}) = \sum_{i=1}^{n^2} e_{p,i} y_i(\vec{v}).$$

In Equation (10.10), the SH approximation is in local surface coordinates at p, so the viewing vector $\vec{v}$ also has to be in local surface coordinates at p.

A principal benefit of the exit transfer matrix is that it represents all the rendering steps in a single matrix, including the effects of shadows, and interreflections (if they are included).   At render time, the rendering computation reduces to a matrix-vector product and vector dot products. Although the sizes of the vectors and matrices are much larger than the 3D or 4D vectors and matrices normally used in computer graphics, the computation is still quite fast, and enables real-time computation on contemporary hardware. The exit transfer matrix depends only on the geometry; changing the incident light vector does not affect the matrix. In fact, if the BRDF matrix is independent of the transfer matrix (which is not the case if interreflection is included) then the surface reflectance can be recomputed dynamically at render time as well. Another very useful property of the approach is that the outgoing radiance is represented as a smooth function, approximated by an expansion in spherical harmonics. The outgoing radiance in any viewing direction is therefore computed directly from the SH expansion, which eliminates the need for interpolating the radiance in the viewing direction.

A drawback, however, is that the accuracy and visual quality of the representation depends on the intrinsic properties of spherical harmonics. The fact that more specular reflection and increased detail in the environment map or a small light source all increase the requisite order of the SH expansion is a serious problem. The irradiance environment map technique described in Chapter 7 uses an order-3 approximation, but this is not sufficient for PRT even if the reflection is totally diffuse simply because it does not represent shadowing well enough. The "standard" PRT approach employs an order-5 approximation, which results in 25-dimensional light vectors and 25×25 transfer matrices. Merely doubling the frequency to an order-10 approximation results in a 100×100 transfer matrix at each sample point. The storage cost alone makes this impractical.

Using PCA. The spherical harmonics representation eliminates interpolation in the viewing direction, but not in the sample points on the surface. This means that the surface points may have to be sampled densely enough for the interpolation to be useful. Each sample point p requires (at least) a 25×25 exit transfer matrix, so the storage requirements can be a problem. Much of this storage is likely redundant; on smoother parts of the surface, the exit transfer matrices are not likely to change very fast. A few representative sample points are therefore likely to suffice, from which the values at other sample points can be interpolated. In this case, the exit transfer matrices themselves are what is interpolated. Another benefit of this approach of selecting representative sample points is that when rendering the entire surface, only a few of the full matrix computations are necessary. This makes it much easier to perform real-time rendering.

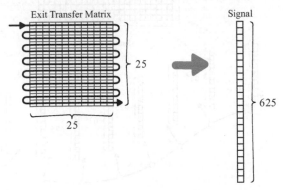

Figure 10.10 Signal construction.

Principal component analysis (PCA) was described in Chapter 9 for the purpose of selecting representative texture samples in bidirectional texture function representations. A similar approach can be used for exit transfer matrices. PCA is applied to a matrix, the columns of which are the "signals" in the language of Section 9.3.6. The matrix for PCA is therefore constructed by flattening the transfer matrix of each sample point into a column vector (Figure 10.10), and the column vectors are then arranged into the columns of the data matrix. If there are N sample points, and each transfer matrix has dimension 25×25, the resulting data matrix has 625 rows and N columns (Figure 10.11).

Basis vectors are extracted by applying PCA to the data matrix. The PCA is actually applied to the covariance matrix of this data matrix: the data matrix has each element replaced by its "deviation from the mean" (i.e., the average value of the matrix is subtracted from each element) and then is multiplied by its transpose. This results in a 625×625 symmetric matrix, which typically has significantly fewer columns than the original $625 \times N$ data matrix. PCA is applied to the symmetric matrix, and M basis vectors are extracted. These correspond to (flattened) exit transfer matrices at surface points that best represent the radiance transfer and reflection. The remaining vectors (matrices) are constructed from a linear combination of these basis vectors; the coefficients (weights) are found

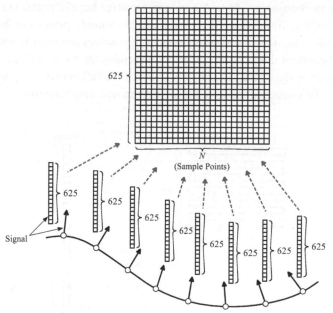

Figure 10.11 Data matrix construction.

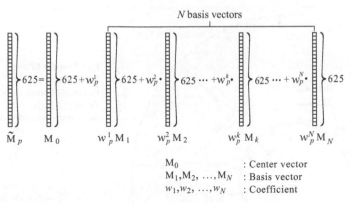

$$\tilde{M}_p \qquad M_0 \qquad w_p^1 M_1 \qquad w_p^2 M_2 \qquad w_p^k M_k \qquad w_p^N M_N$$

M_0 : Center vector
$M_1, M_2, \ldots, M_N$: Basis vector
$w_1, w_2, \ldots, w_N$: Coefficient

Figure 10.12 Approximation using basis vectors.

by projecting the corresponding vectors onto the basis vectors (Figure 10.12). This reduces each transfer matrix, which ordinarily has 625 elements, to just M coefficients.

The data compression using PCA can be significant, especially if the surface is densely sampled. But it actually increases the computational load, because the exit transfer matrix at each sample point has to be reconstructed from the basis elements. Fortunately, there is a better way of doing the interpolation. Because all the operations are linear, the basis function coefficients serve as the coefficients to interpolate the *computed* outgoing radiance values. In other words, the outgoing radiance can be computed at each representative sample point, and the interpolated outgoing radiance at all the other sample points comes from a linear combination of these values.

Data compression with local PCA. The vectors extracted from principal component analysis span a linear subspace; the idea is that this subspace sufficiently approximates the span of the columns (the column space) of the original matrix. As in the other applications of PCA, the column space contains elements that are not physically meaningful. The actual set of valid exit transfer matrices is a nonlinear subspace that may not be well approximated by a linear subspace. The PCA approach is suboptimal in this case, as it creates a single linear approximation to the true nonlinear subspace. The method of local PCA (also called clustered PCA) described in Chapter 9 works by partitioning the data into clusters small enough to be regarded as locally linear subspaces. PCA is then applied to each cluster. If the clusters are properly chosen, a very few basis elements are needed to adequately approximate all the elements in each cluster. In 2003, a year after the original PRT paper was published, Peter-Pike Sloan, Jesse Hall,

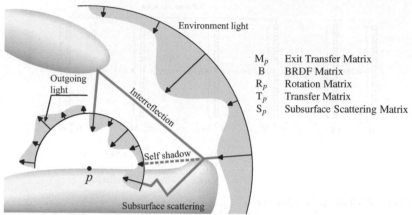

Figure 10.13 Exit radiance transfer conceptual diagram. (After [Sloan et al. 03a].)

John Hart, and John Snyder introduced a local PCA method for PRT in the paper entitled "Clustered Principal Components for Precomputed Radiance Transfer" [Sloan et al. 03a].[1]

Figure 10.13 illustrates the conceptual process of exit radiance transfer simulation described in the 2003 paper. In addition to employing local PCA, transfer matrices are generalized to include both interreflection and subsurface scattering. The layered method described in Chapter 4 is used to compute the subsurface scattering component. It is diffuse, and therefore view-independent, so it only affects the constant term of the outgoing radiance SH expansion. This subsurface scattering component can be expressed as a transfer matrix, but only the top elements (corresponding to the constant SH terms) will be nonzero. The actual exit transfer matrix is therefore

$$BR_pT_p + S_p,$$

although in practice the subsurface scattering is normally handled separately.[2]

Figure 10.14 contains examples of renderings using precomputed transfer matrices with the local PCA compression. From left to right, more basis elements are used to represent each cluster. The rightmost images are the result of rendering using the actual exit transfer matrix on each sample point; i.e., PCA is not ap-

---

[1]This paper introduced Leen's PCA algorithm into computer graphics; the application to BTF data described in Chapter 9 actually came later.

[2]The fact that the reflection integral is actually performed over the hemisphere rather than the sphere is handled by the clipping function $\max(\cos\theta, 0)$ implicit in the SH expansion. This is not so easy to approximate with spherical harmonics. Sloan et al. use a separate matrix A^{-1} to "boost" the BRDF matrix and improve the approximation, especially at silhouette edges. The actual exit transfer matrix is $A^{-1}BA^{-1}R_pT_p$.

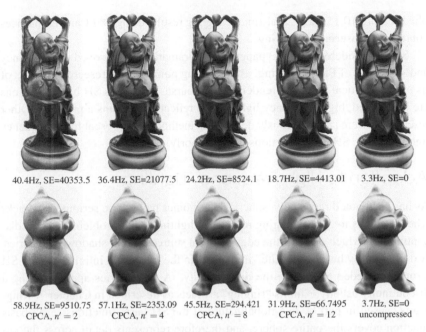

40.4Hz, SE=40353.5 36.4Hz, SE=21077.5 24.2Hz, SE=8524.1 18.7Hz, SE=4413.01 3.3Hz, SE=0

58.9Hz, SE=9510.75 57.1Hz, SE=2353.09 45.5Hz, SE=294.421 31.9Hz, SE=66.7495 3.7Hz, SE=0
CPCA, $n' = 2$ CPCA, $n' = 4$ CPCA, $n' = 8$ CPCA, $n' = 12$ uncompressed

Figure 10.14 Rendering results using exit transfer matrices and local PCA. There are 256 clusters; the number of PCA vectors (left to right) are 2, 4, 8, and 12. The rightmost images use the exit transfer matrices directly without PCA compression. (From [Sloan et al. 03a] © 2003 ACM, Inc. Included here by permission.)

Figure 10.15 Real-time rendering results using exit transfer matrices containing subsurface scattering. (From [Sloan et al. 03a] © 2003 ACM, Inc. Included here by permission.) (See Color Plate XXII.)

plied. Figure 10.15 shows real-time rendering results using exit transfer matrices containing subsurface scattering.

Sloan considered the 2003 paper, which dramatically improved the efficiency and versatility of PRT rendering, as the tipping point of PRT research in terms of its use in practical real-time rendering. Of course, as long as SH basis functions are being used, high-frequency lighting and reflection remains a problem. Other researchers were simultaneously developing methods to represent high-frequency lighting where SH basis functions worked poorly.

10.2.4 Adaption to High-Frequency Lighting

As has been noted repeatedly, spherical harmonics have some serious drawbacks when it comes to approximating real-world lighting. One problem arises at discontinuities, which occur at the edges of light sources and at shadow boundaries. A discontinuity has an "infinite" frequency, in the sense that infinitely many SH terms are needed to capture the discontinuity. A finite series approximating a discontinuity usually exhibits "ringing" artifacts as described in Chapter 7. Ringing is caused in part by the global nature of the SH basis functions: each basis function covers the entire sphere, and therefore represents detail across the entire sphere. In a convergent expansion, the SH coefficients approach zero as the order increases; however, all the terms up to a certain degree are normally required to obtain a particular accuracy. Such problems with spherical harmonics led researchers to investigate other basis functions for representing lighting and reflection, particularly in high-frequency environments. A natural candidate were *wavelets*, which had been used for years in other areas of computer graphics.

Loosely speaking, wavelets are oscillatory functions of arbitrary frequency that are nonzero only on a small part of the domain. The subset of the domain of a function (including the boundary points) on which a function is nonzero is called the *support* of the function. Wavelet functions are said to have *local* or *compact support*—they are only nonzero on a closed bounded subset of the domain.[3] A wavelet basis typically consists of a set of wavelet functions having shrinking support: as the index increases, the region in which the basis function is nonzero decreases. A smaller support means that the oscillation of the function occurs in a smaller region, i.e., has high frequency. In this sense the decreasing support is analogous to increasing frequency.

A wavelet basis is typically constructed from a "mother" wavelet function; the remaining elements come from scaled and translated copies of this function.

---

[3]The compact support property is not strictly necessary; it is just useful. Wavelets derived from Gaussian functions are nonzero across the entire domain, but the values decay so quickly that they are essentially zero far enough away from the peak.

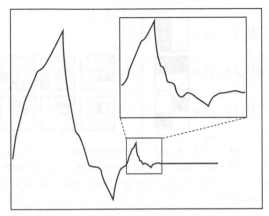

Figure 10.16 Wavelet basis function.

If $\psi(x)$ is the mother wavelet function (in one dimension), then other wavelet functions are created as

$$\psi_{a,b}(x) = \frac{1}{\sqrt{a}}\psi\left(\frac{x-b}{a}\right);$$

these are sometimes known as "child" or "daughter" wavelet functions. In 1D, compact support means that the mother wavelet, and therefore all the child wavelets, are nonzero only in a closed interval. Analogous to a wave, a weighted sum of wavelets having different phase and scale (a and b, respectively) is used to approximate a function. The functions in a wavelet basis are expected to be orthogonal to facilitate projecting a function onto the basis functions. Because of this, not every function works as a wavelet mother function, and the child wavelets cannot be chosen arbitrarily. In fact, constructing mother wavelet functions is a challenging task. The first orthogonal set of continuous wavelets having compact support was constructed by mathematician Ingrid Daubechies in 1988. Figure 10.16 illustrates a *Daubechies wavelet*. The child wavelets are scaled by powers of two; i.e. $a = 2^m$ for integer m (higher-frequency wavelets correspond to negative values of m).

The local nature of the basis functions are a key difference between wavelets and spherical harmonics. In a region of the sphere having little detail, coefficients of the high-frequency wavelets will be very small, or zero, and can therefore be omitted. Conversely, many high-frequency wavelets may be needed to represent high-frequency detail; however, they are only needed at the detailed areas and do not affect the rest of the sphere. The compact support property thus allows detail to be represented only where it is necessary. Detail of much higher frequency can often be represented using the same number of coefficients required for a lower-

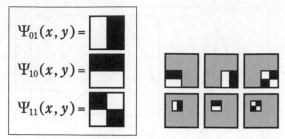

$$\Psi_{01}(x,y) =$$

$$\Psi_{10}(x,y) =$$

$$\Psi_{11}(x,y) =$$

Figure 10.17 The 2D Harr wavelet basis. -1, 0, and 1 are represented by black, gray, and white, respectively. The three "mother" functions are shown at the left; the right image illustrates some daughter wavelets of increasing frequency. (From [Ng et al. 03] © 2003 ACM, Inc. Included here by permission.)

order SH expansion. One advantage of wavelet approximation, and convergent approximations in general, is that the coefficients get smaller as the frequency increases. Consequently, even if the small coefficients cannot be omitted outright, they can sometimes be included at lower precision, which reduces the storage requirements.

A commonly used wavelet basis set is the *Harr basis*, which in some sense is the simplest wavelet basis. Haar wavelets consist of simple step functions having values -1, 0, and 1. In 2D they can visualized as a pattern inside a square. The left side of Figure 10.17 illustrates the three Haar mother functions (in 2D and higher dimensions, several mother wavelets are often employed). The right side of the figure illustrates some child Haar wavelets, which are shifted and scaled versions of the mother functions. To approximate lighting, what is needed is a basis set of wavelets on the sphere. The 2D Haar basis can be mapped onto the sphere as suggested in Figure 10.18: a large cube is centered at the object, and the Haar basis functions on each face of the cube are projected onto the sphere. Alternatively, the spherical environment map or radiance function can be projected onto the faces of the cube and a separate wavelet expansion applied to each face.

In a paper entitled "All-Frequency Shadows Using Non-Linear Wavelet Lighting Approximation," Ren Ng, Ravi Ramamoorthi, and Pat Hanrahan presented a method of using wavelet basis functions in place of SH basis functions to represent high-frequency radiance transfer [Ng et al. 03]. This work was not an extension to the precomputed radiance transfer method of Sloan et al. of the prior year. Rather, it presented an alternative method for a matrix representation of (precomputed) radiance transfer in a problem the authors call *image relighting*. An object is assumed to be viewed from a fixed viewpoint under illumination from

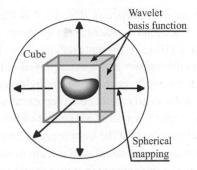

Wavelet
basis function

Cube

Spherical
mapping

Figure 10.18 One approach to wavelet approximation on the sphere is to project a spherical function
onto a concentric cube, then expand the projected function on each face of the cube. Environment maps are often represented as faces on a cube.

an environment map; the object itself is assumed to be stationary and rigid. *Relighting* is the process of recomputing the appearance of the object under a different environment map. This is a more restricted problem than the general PRT
problem, in which the viewpoint can change.

The basic reflectance integral given in Equation (10.3) provides a formula for
the directly reflected radiance in direction $\vec{v}$ from a surface sample point p_i:

$$R(p_i, \vec{v}) = \int_{\Omega_{4\pi}} L(\vec{s}) V(p_i, \vec{s}) f(p_i, \vec{s}, \vec{v}) \, d\vec{s}. \qquad (10.11)$$

The function $f(p_i \vec{s}, \vec{v})$ is the cosine-weighted BRDF, and $L(\vec{s})$ is the incident radiance in direction $\vec{s}$. As usual, the environment map is sufficiently distant that the
incident radiance L does not depend on the surface position. If a set of N directional samples $\vec{s}_j$ are chosen, then the reflectance integral of Equation (10.11) can
be approximated by summing the integrand over the sample points

$$R(p_i, \vec{v}) \approx \frac{4\pi}{N} \sum_j \underbrace{L(\vec{s}_j)}_{l_j} \underbrace{V(p_i, \vec{s}_j) f(p_i, \vec{s}_j, \vec{v})}_{a_{ij}} \qquad (10.12)$$

(the constant factor $4\pi/N$ is hereafter omitted). The $L(\vec{s}_j)$ factor depends on the
lighting; $V(p_i, \vec{s}_j) f(p_i, \vec{s}_j, \vec{v})$ can be precomputed, as the view direction $\vec{v}$ is fixed.
Denoting the former by l_j and a_{ij} for the latter, Equation (10.12) becomes

$$R(p_i, \vec{v}) \approx r_i = \sum_j l_j a_{ij}$$

which can be written as a matrix product

$$\vec{r} = A\vec{l} \qquad (10.13)$$

where $\vec{r}$ is the vectorized set of reflectances $R(p_i, \vec{v})$, $\vec{l}$ is the vectorized set of illumination samples, and A is a matrix consisting of elements a_{ij}.

The matrix A in Equation (10.13) represents radiance transfer, but in a fundamentally different way than the transfer matrices employed in the PRT method as defined in Equation (10.7). One difference is that the light vectors $\vec{\ell}$ contain the SH coefficients, and the transfer matrix elements t_{ij} represent how the coefficients change. The resulting light vector $\vec{r}$ is a set of SH coefficients for the expansion of the outgoing radiance in all directions at the sample point. In contrast, the vector $\vec{l}$ in Equation (10.13) represents point samples in the environment map, and the resulting vector $\vec{r}$ is radiance to the viewpoint at all sample points on the object in the specific view direction. Another difference concerns what the matrices represent: while there is a separate PRT transfer matrix for each sample point on the object, the matrix A represents the transfer over all the sample points on the object.

The matrix product formulation of Equation (10.13) decouples the lighting samples $\vec{l}$ from the visibility and BRDF effects, which are stored in the matrix A. Relighting the scene therefore amounts to simply multiplying A, which is constant for the object and viewpoint, by a different environment map encoded into the elements of $\vec{l}$. However, the computational cost of this operation can be extreme. In the basic case, there is one element l_j for each pixel in the environment map, and one element $R(p_i, \vec{v})$ for each pixel in the image. The matrix A is therefore a *huge* matrix, having something like a *trillion* elements—the storage requirement alone for the matrix A is prohibitive. The PRT transfer matrices are minute by comparison: each has at most 625 elements (although there is one such matrix for each surface sample point).

One way of looking at the matrix A is to consider each directional sample $\vec{s}_j$ as coming from a separate directional light source, as illustrated in Figure 10.19. If the scene is illuminated only by the source corresponding to sample s_j, then only column j of A is relevant in the computation of the outgoing radiance. In other words, the columns of A correspond to the effects of the individual illumination samples. On the other hand, each row of A contributes only to the computation of outgoing sample $r_i = R(p_i)$, which corresponds to a single surface sample point. The summation involved in a row multiplication corresponds to Equation (10.12), which is the reflection integral approximation. The elements in a matrix row therefore correspond to all the samples points over the sphere; each element is the visibility of the associated directional source times the cosine-weighted BRDF. (The matrix A can be extended to include other effects, such as interreflection and subsurface scattering.) The rows of A therefore correspond, loosely, to the transfer vectors in the original PRT paper. The difference is that the PRT vectors assume diffuse reflectance so there is only one radiance value produced, which

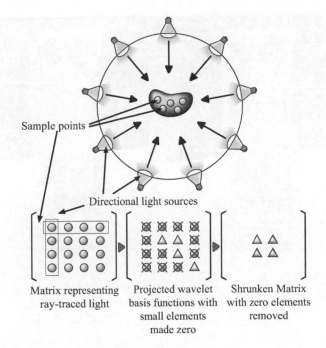

Figure 10.19 Radiance transfer using wavelet basis functions.

corresponds to the radiant exitance (radiosity) or irradiance. The rows of A produce one radiance value at a given surface sample point from a light vector, but that value is in the direction of the viewpoint. (Another difference of course is that the PRT transfer vectors contain SH coefficients rather than sample values.)

Because the directional samples $\vec{s}_j$ correspond to pixels in an environment map (Figure 10.19), each matrix row i corresponds to all the pixels in the environment map at surface sample point p_i. The visibility function $V(p_i, \vec{s}_j)$ can be regarded as the silhouette of the local geometry projected from p_i onto the environment map. The matrix elements a_{ij} in row i can thus be regarded as the silhouette times the cosine-weighted BRDF pixelized in the environment map. The BRDF usually changes slowly and smoothly, except near a specular peak. The visibility function is by nature discontinuous, but the discontinuities are limited to the silhouette edges. The pixelized visibility-BRDF products (which are the rows of A) are therefore well suited to wavelet approximation.

The method described in the 2003 "wavelet lighting" paper actually uses a cube environment map as illustrated in Figure 10.18. A separate matrix A is constructed for each face, with the directional samples corresponding to the pixels in the environment map on the face. A Haar wavelet approximation is then applied

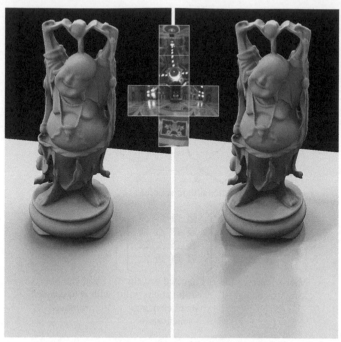

Figure 10.20 Comparison of rendering results using spherical harmonics (left) and wavelet basis functions (right). The faces of the cube environment map are shown in the middle inset. (From [Ng et al. 03] © 2003 ACM, Inc. Included here by permission.)

to each row of each face matrix. As described above, compression works by truncating the small coefficient values to zero (Figure 10.19). An environment map can also be so compressed. The authors show that as few as 1% of the wavelets are needed to accurately represent the light vector representing a complex environment map (as in Figure 10.20), and as few as 0.1% are needed for a simple area light source. However, the compression of the matrix A is not quite as good, and is highly dependent on the sampling frequency. As described above, sometimes a lower precision representation is sufficient for small coefficients. The authors quantize the coefficients to 6 or 7 bits (compared to the usual 32 bits needed for floating-point values). The wavelet approximation combined with this quantization results in compression factors of several thousand.

Figure 10.20 shows the results of rendering a model using SH basis functions (left) and wavelet basis functions (right) under the same environment map illumination. While the left image is visually plausible, it misses the shadow detail caused by the bright windows in the environment map. The order-10 SH basis functions are not able to capture the high-frequency detail necessary to reproduce the shadow boundaries. However, the wavelet approximation assumes a fixed view direction $\vec{v}$, whereas the SH representation handles all viewing directions. Figure 10.20 illustrates an important distinction often made in rendering. The very diffuse shadows in the SH image are *plausible*, in the sense that a casual observer would likely believe that the image is accurate. On the other hand, shadows in the wavelet image on the right are *predictive* in that it is essentially what the shadows would really look like if the original statue were placed on a Lambertian surface inside the actual environment. Interestingly, the "plausible" image might be considered aesthetically superior to the predictive image in this case.

Wavelet approximations do have their own drawbacks compared to other approximation methods. Haar wavelets are the simplest, but they are piecewise constant and therefore can only represent step functions. They converge in the limit, but any finite sum of Haar wavelets has discontinuities. Furthermore, Haar wavelets do not have the smoothing properties of spherical harmonics. Other wavelet bases exist that have better properties, but they are more difficult to compute. Another drawback of wavelet representations on the sphere is the lack of rotational properties exhibited by spherical harmonicss.

For the specific problem of precomputed transfer, the wavelet method described in this section works with only one view direction—the matrix A has to be recomputed in order to render the object from another viewpoint. A year after the publication of their "wavelet lighting" paper, the authors (Ng, Ramamoorthi, and Hanrahan) presented a way of solving this problem in a paper entitled "Triple Product Wavelet Integrals for All-Frequency Relighting" [Ng et al. 04]. The method uses separate wavelet expansions for each of the three different factors in the reflectance integral: the incident light, the reflectance function, and the visibility. These expansions are multiplied together and integrated to compute an outgoing expansion. Shortcuts based on the orthogonality of Haar wavelets are employed to substantially reduce the computational load. The method handles radiance transfer with lighting of arbitrary frequency along with changing view direction. However, the difficulty of rotating the wavelets on the sphere remains, and because of this it is difficult to adapt arbitrary reflection characteristics. Moreover, when compressing a matrix representing radiance transfer, there is still the problem of efficiently uncompressing the wavelet expansion at render time. Even now graphics hardware is not well suited to this.

Progress in the efficiency of PRT, specifically for high-frequency lighting or reflection having strong directionality, drew a great deal of attention from researchers. A variety of new approaches using different basis functions have since been presented (e.g., [Liu et al. 04]). The use of wavelets as presented here focuses on the pioneering use of basis functions other than SH basis functions to efficiently render scenes that would otherwise be unsuitable for PRT.

10.3   PRT and Dynamic Simulation

Soon after the original paper was published in 2002, precomputed transfer found its way into more general applications. Over time, practical experiments to improve the method were attempted, with varying degrees of success. From this work, PRT itself became widely diversified for specific purposes. Animation was one area that immediately benefited from PRT. The paper "Precomputing Interactive Dynamic Deformable Scenes" by Doug L. James and Kayvon Fatahalian presented a pioneering method for applying PRT in dynamic simulation [James and Fatahalian 03]. Doug James had been actively researching real-time dynamic simulation from the late 1990s, and was particularly interested in connecting dynamic simulation with other human senses such as hearing and touch. The 2003 paper introduces a unique way of precomputing physically based deformation that incorporates PRT for rendering.

Deformation is a key aspect of realism in the animation of virtual creatures as well as in general virtual environments, yet physically based animation of deformable models is much more complicated and expensive than it is for rigid models. Physically based deformation requires the simulation of how force propagates through an object. A displacement at a single point on a deformable object can affect the entire object rather than just the neighborhood of the point. In this aspect, deformation is akin to global illumination: the addition of a bright light beam on a small highly reflective object can produce a substantial change of lighting throughout the environment. However, deformation and global illumination have been treated separately in computer graphics despite the conceptual similarity. Precise physically based deformation is apt to be considered of secondary importance in real-time interactive dynamic simulations.

The 2003 paper by James and Fatahalian proposed a new approach for the precomputation of interactive physically based deformable scenes from the perspectives of both deformation dynamics and global illumination. The paper defines a data-driven state space, which combines the dynamic deformation and globally illuminated appearance. It is modeled as a collection of "orbits" that store precomputed values describing the displacement and appearance of each state. The collection of all precomputed orbits comprises a discrete portrait, and it is a subset of the full portrait that describes all possible dynamics required for the scene representation with which a user interacts. The challenge is how to sample and parameterize a representative collection of precomputed orbits so that they can approximate the full dynamics for a particular range of interaction at run-time, as well as supporting the global illumination in the scene for real-time rendering. In both deformable simulation and animation of global illumination effects, data reduction is necessary to limit storage requirements and increase the efficiency of the computation. The key feature of the model reduction described in the "deformable scenes" paper is that the same approach is applied for both deformation and appearance.

10.3.1 Basics of Deformation Simulation

Deformation is normally computed using the finite element method (see Chapter 2). A mesh of points is constructed that represents the shape of the deformable object, along with adjacency information and constraints that represent the interdependence of the points in deformation. There may be other other physical constraints to prevent such things as self intersection. The points along with the interdependencies and the constraints are known as a *deformation model*. If there are several objects, they collectively form a *deformable system*. The *state* of the object or system of objects at time t is represented by the position and velocity of the model points in the object or system. All the positions and velocities (each of which is a 3D vector) are collected into a single large vector $\vec{x}^t$, known as the *system state vector*.

The cloth hanging on the door shown in Figure 10.21 is a representative example of a deformable dynamic system. The cloth is a deformable object, in the sense that outside forces change its shape. The door is rigid, but its movement affects the shape and position of the cloth through direct contact also by imparting other forces, such as air resistance. A regular grid of points on the cloth represents its shape; the state vector of the cloth contains the positions and velocities of all these points combined into a single large vector. Each position and velocity vector has three components, so if there are N points, the state vector has $6N$ elements.

Figure 10.21 Cloth on a moving door. (From [James and Fatahalian 03] © 2003 ACM, Inc. Included here by permission.)

Of course, not all possible state vectors are physically feasible. In the cloth example, self-intersection of the cloth and deformations that imply the cloth is shredded are excluded. Constraints on the deformation dynamics have to be included that limit the set of possible states to those that are reasonable. In fact, the set of state vectors attainable in an particular simulation is much smaller than the set of feasible states simply because the system starts out in a particular initial state and there are limits to the possible deformation forces applied in the simulation. For example, if only the door is allowed to move, the cloth attached to the door can flap around but will not tie itself into knots.

Dynamic simulation is done in a set of discrete time steps. For simplicity, the time between adjacent time steps is constant. A basic deformation describes a discrete change of state from time t to time $t + 1$. The factors that affect the deformation, which includes such things as forces on the object at various points, are collected into a vector of system parameters α^t. The change of state is described abstractly by a function f, as $\vec{x}^{t+1} = f(\vec{x}^t, \alpha^t)$. The system parameters α have to be defined specifically in relation to the deformation model. The function f is an abstract representation of an algorithm used to compute the change in state given a particular set of parameters. But because it is a true function, its values can be precomputed for a collection of representative states, and values at other states can be interpolated from these precomputed values.

For precomputed values, the authors define a *data-driven state space* consisting of a set of state vectors arising from certain specific deformations. The state space is modeled as a set of state vector nodes together with a set of directional connections (arcs or edges, in graph-theory terminology) joining the nodes that represent transitions. A node $\vec{x}_2$ is connected to another node $\vec{x}_1$ if, for some set of parameters (forces) α, $\vec{x}_2 = f(\vec{x}_1, \alpha)$. That is, each node is connected to all other nodes that it can reach in a single time step by a feasible action. The full state space is vastly too large to be precomputed or stored, so the authors consider a subspace of precomputed state vectors that arise from basic deformations. A sequence of connected state vectors is called an *orbit*. An orbit can be regarded as a "motion clip" because it records the shape of the object under a specific deformation sequence across a sequence of time steps. A set of precomputed representative orbits can be reused during the dynamic simulation; "nearby" orbits can be used if the state vectors and forces are sufficiently close.

10.3.2   Impulse Response Function

A set of arbitrary precomputed orbits are not likely to be sufficient in itself to be useful in dynamic simulation. Without a way of handling user control at run time, the simulation would not be truly dynamic—it would reduce to simply replaying the precomputed motion clips. The precomputed orbits therefore have to be carefully chosen and properly indexed for easy lookup in order to give the ability to handle run-time user interactions. The method described in the paper precomputes a number of simple deformation actions expected to be representative of those applied by the user at run time. Such an action is described as an *impulse response*. The idea is that a sudden action is performed at one time step, and this is followed by a persistent forcing action constant in subsequent time steps. The initial action is an *impulse force* (or collection of forces) denoted by α^I; the *persistent forcing state* is denoted by α^F. In the cloth hanging on the door example, the impulse action pushes the door, and the persistent forcing includes the air resistance on the cloth and effect of inertia (angular momentum) as the door swings.

An impulse response on a particular state results in an orbit of sequential states. Starting from the initial state $\vec{x}$, the impulse force α^I is applied first, and then the state is integrated through the remaining $T - 1$ time steps under the persistent forcing α^F. This set of states (the orbit) is denoted by an *impulse response function* (IRF),

$$\xi(\vec{x}, \alpha^I, \alpha^F; T),\tag{10.14}$$

where T is the number of time steps. The IRF orbit is the set of states through which the system passes. Figure 10.22(a) illustrates an impulse response orbit schematically, where the state consists of a reduced displacement vector q and the associated velocity vector $\dot{q}$. The method described in the paper precomputes a collection of IRF orbits to be used at run time. As Equation (10.14) suggests, the IRF orbits are indexed by the initial state $\vec{x}$ and the two system parameters α^I and α^F. An important part of the precomputation is the selection of a set of representative impulse responses. The method uses a set of impulse response pairs (α_i^I, α_i^F), with $i = 1, 2, \ldots, D$ for some fixed D, which the authors call an *impulse palette*. This impulse palette represents a set of deformation actions the user may take. Keeping the number D small bounds the precomputation requirements, although it also limits the range of possible user interactions.

From the standpoint of run-time processing, an IRF is just a time series of precomputed values that describe the displacement of each sequential state. Once an impulse is specified by an index from the impulse palette, the system switches to a nearby IRF of that type and continues to look up the precomputed values until it either reaches the end or is interrupted by another impulse. When a new impulse is applied, the system simply blends the time series of the old and new IRFs. Figure 10.22(b) illustrates a special case where the initial and persistent forces have the same value α, and suggests how the set of orbits can in a sense be parameterized to respond to different user actions.

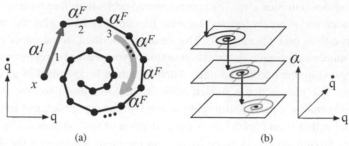

(a)   (b)

Figure 10.22 (a) An impulse response function (IRF) and (b) an impulse response function where the initial and persistent forces are the same. (From [James and Fatahalian 03] © 2003 ACM, Inc. Included here by permission.)

10.3.3 Model Reduction

One problem with general deformable models is the large number of points needed to accurately describe their shape. This is a serious impediment to the precomputation scheme in which the IRF orbits are indexed by state vectors, as state vector can have thousands of components. The authors therefore had to find a way of reducing the complexity of the deformable models without losing too much freedom in deformation.[4]

The deformation model reduction uses information obtained from a collection of simulations. As described above, each time step in a simulation is represented by a state vector $\vec{x}^t$, which consists of the 3D position and velocity vectors of all points in the deformation model:

$$\vec{x}^t = (\vec{v}_1^t, \dot{v}_1^t, \ldots, \vec{v}_M^t, \dot{v}_M^t),$$

where $\dot{v}$ denotes the velocity vector, and there are M points in the model. Each position vector $\vec{v}_i^t$ represents a position on the model in a particular deformation state; subtracting the corresponding position in a representative shape produces a displacement vector $\vec{u}^t$. The collection of M displacement vectors for a set of simulated states can be arranged into a data matrix

$$A_u = [\vec{u}^1 \vec{u}^2 \cdots \vec{u}^N] = \begin{bmatrix} \vec{u}_1^1 & \vec{u}_1^2 & \ldots & \vec{u}_1^N \\ \vdots & \vdots & \ddots & \vdots \\ \vec{u}_M^1 & \vec{u}_M^2 & \ldots & \vec{u}_M^N \end{bmatrix}$$

---

[4]The general problem of deformable model reduction has been well studied, and various reduction methods exist. For example, an interesting general method was recently proposed in the paper "Skipping Steps in Deformable Simulation with Online Model Reduction" by Theodore Kim and Doug L. James [Kim and James 09].

on which principal component analysis can be applied. Here N is the total number of states, and M is the number of points in the deformation model. Each displacement vector $\vec{u}_i^j$ is a 3D column vector, so the matrix A_u is actually a $3M \times N$ matrix.

Row i of the data matrix A_u corresponds to the set of displacements of a particular point i. At nearby points, the corresponding matrix rows are likely to be similar, and therefore redundant. PCA is applied to select a representative basis for the matrix rows. This is done using the singular value decomposition (see Section 9.3): the matrix A_u is decomposed into the product of three matrices

$$A_u = U_u \Sigma_u V_u^T.$$

The sizes of the diagonal elements in the matrix Σ_u represent the importance of the corresponding row in the matrix A_u, and each row of this matrix corresponds to a vertex. Therefore, important vertices in terms of vertices representing the characteristics of deformation can be chosen by setting all components to zero except the largest values of the diagonal elements. Intuitively this SVD reduction amounts to extracting a small number of points that represent the characteristics of the deformation, and this suggests that the dynamic precomputation or the run-time simulation should be performed only on these representative points.

The selection of the reduced coordinates from the SVD thus amounts to selecting the k largest values from the diagonal matrix Σ and setting the remaining diagonal elements to zero (Figure 10.23). Denoting the reduced diagonal matrix

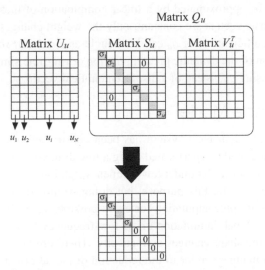

Figure 10.23 Dimensional reduction of state space.

Figure 10.24 Displacement basis vectors (deformation modes). (From [James and Fatahalian 03] © 2003 ACM, Inc. Included here by permission.)

by Σ'_u, the columns of the product

$$Q_u = \Sigma'_u V_u^T = \begin{bmatrix} \vec{q}_u^1 & \vec{q}_u^2 & \cdots & \vec{q}_u^N \end{bmatrix}$$

are thereby truncated to k components. Because $A_u \approx U_u \Sigma'_u V_u^T$, each column of A_u can be approximated by $\vec{u}^j \approx U^u \vec{q}_u^j$. The matrix A_u is thus approximated with the linear combination of N k-dimensional basis vectors $\vec{q}_u^1, \vec{q}_u^2, \dots, \vec{q}_u^N$, which is a reduction from the $3M$-dimensional vectors in the columns of A_u. The vectors $\vec{q}_u$ are the *reduced shape coordinates*, and correspond to representative points in the deformation model.

The basis vectors correspond to the representative deformed shapes. Figure 10.24 illustrates three poses of a dinosaur model corresponding to three basis vectors. In the above approximation, every possible shape generated in the deformation can be approximated by a linear combination of these representative shapes. The basis vectors are constant; only the weight changes along the time. Therefore, a coefficient vector q_u can be thought as a *reduced shape coordinate*, the computation of the dynamic precomputation or run-time simulation can thus be performed using q_u instead of a displacement field vector.

10.3.4 Appearance Model

Once the reduced dynamical system has been constructed, the precomputation of an appearance model is performed using a low-dimensional approximation to the diffuse radiance transfer under low-frequency lighting. Precomputed radiance transfer can be used for this purpose, but doing so directly is too costly, as it requires a separate precomputation for every possible state. In general, the effects of diffuse global illumination under low-frequency lighting do not change notably unless the shape changes dramatically. Therefore the appearance model is reduced in a manner similar to the reduction of the deformation model: a set of representative appearance states is selected, on which the radiance transfer is

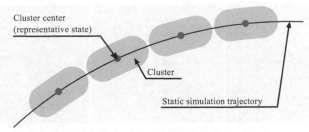

Figure 10.25 Global illumination precomputation state (schematic representation).

precomputed. Ideally, the reduced appearance model would be constructed from a full PRT computation on all the precomputed deformation states. Besides being too costly, in practice it is not necessary because of the redundancy in the appearance of similar shapes. The reduction of the appearance model therefore starts with the simpler problem of computing radiance transfer vectors only at the reduced shape coordinates rather than at every point on the shape model. Also, PRT is applied to a small subset of all the precomputed shapes.

The reflection is assumed to be diffuse, so the PRT transfer matrices reduce to vectors (see Section 10.1.2). The transfer vectors at all the sample points in a particular shape (deformation state) are concatenated into a single vector. The radiance transfer is precomputed for a subset of deformations, which are interpolated across the IRF orbits. The interpolation uses *radial basis functions*, which are suitable for high-dimensional scattered data interpolation. The resulting set of PRT vectors is then clustered using the k-means algorithm (see Section 7.2.2), and the centers of each cluster serve as a collection of N_a representative shapes (Figure 10.25). PRT is then recomputed for these shapes on the original (unreduced) model points, or mesh. This process results in a collection of properly computed PRT vectors for a set of shapes across an IRF orbit.

The N_a PRT vectors are collected into the columns of a matrix A_u:

$$A_a = [X^1 X^2 \cdots X^{N_a}] = \begin{bmatrix} X_{p_1}^1 & X_{p_1}^2 & \cdots & X_{p_1}^{N_a} \\ \vdots & \vdots & \ddots & \vdots \\ X_{p_s}^1 & X_{p_s}^2 & \cdots & X_{p_s}^{N_a} \end{bmatrix}$$

on which principal component analysis is applied. Element $X_{p_i}^j$ of A_u represents the radiance transfer vector at point p_i on shape j (with the mean subtracted); each is actually a vector of dimension $3sn^2$, where s is the number of surface points, and n is the order of the SH approximation. The SVD is used to extract representative basis elements in the same way as in the deformation model reduction. The result is a set of *reduced appearance coordinates* $q_a^1, \ldots, q_a^{N_a}$ which correspond to points on the model surface where the radiance transfer is most significant. The

Figure 10.26 Transfer basis vectors (radiance transfer modes). (From [James and Fatahalian 03] © 2003
ACM, Inc. Included here by permission.)

precomputed transfer is thus limited to these points, and the PRT vectors form the
reduced appearance model. For given state j, the radiance transfer field is computed as the weighted sum of the radiance transfer field precomputed at all the
representative states

$$q_a^j = \sum_{k=1}^{N_a} w_k q_a^k$$

(Figure 10.27). The weight w_k for representative state k is inversely proportional
to the difference of the shapes at state k and state j. The advantage of this method
is that the result of the interpolation reflects the changes of the shape over the
entire deformation.

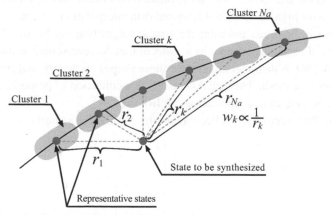

Figure 10.27 Interpolation of radiance transfer fields.

10.3.5 Run-time Synthesis

Through the preprocess described in this section, each IRF orbit stores both the
reduced shape coordinates q_u and the reduces appearance coordinates q_a at each

state node. Also stored are the SVD matrices U_u and U_a, the columns of which are displacement and transfer basis vectors, respectively. It is assumed that an arbitrary deformation can be approximated by the linear combination of IRFs, so at run time there is nothing left to do but synthesize the shape and the appearance for the particular lighting condition and deformation state. This can be done efficiently in graphics hardware.

The method described in the "deformable scenes" paper became a hot topic in both research fields—dynamics and rendering—soon after it was published. It deftly combines the results of the precomputation of dynamic simulation and global illumination. Of course using this kind of union limits the amount of animation that can be performed. Regardless, research to expand radiance transfer to animation increased dramatically as a result of this paper.

10.4   Precomputed Acoustic Transfer

Another area that was influenced, rather unexpectedly, by the PRT work of Sloan et al. was the field of synthetic acoustics, also known as *sound rendering*. The goal of sound rendering is to procedurally synthesize sound in synchronization with computer-generated animation. The paper entitled "Sound Rendering" by Tapio Takala and James Hahn presented at SIGGRAPH is considered to be the genesis of this particular subfield of computer graphics [Takala and Hahn 92]. Mirroring the history of rendering in general, physical accuracy was not initially emphasized; rather, physically based approaches were incrementally added. Sound rendering consists of two processes: sound generation and sound propagation. The research that enabled physically accurate sound generation appeared in the 1990s (e.g., [van den Doel and Pai 96, O'Brien et al. 01, van den Doel et al. 01, Dobashi et al. 03a]). Research related to sound propagation in CG environments had been in progress since the late 1990s, but computing accurate sound radiation from geometrically complex vibrating objects was typically ignored. Diffraction and interreflection effects in an environment are an important part of accurate acoustic modeling, and these were largely ignored until precomputed acoustic transfer (PAT) emerged.

Sound effects caused by global sound radiation are analogous to global illumination effects. Sound and light are both wave phenomena and there are similarities in how their propagation can be simulated; for example, ray tracing in acoustics predates ray tracing for CG rendering by many years. An important difference, though, is that wave effects such as diffraction and interference are typically unimportant in illumination, whereas they can be very important in sound modeling. Doug James, who had connected physically based deformation with

PRT in 2003, presented a paper entitled "Pre-computed Acoustic Transfer (PAT)" coauthored by Jernej Barbič and Dinesh K. Pai describing their investigations into sound preprocessing [James et al. 06]. The authors show that much of the costly transfer phenomena associated with global sound radiation effects can be precomputed to enable real-time sound synthesis.

The preprocess begins by decomposing the sound wave into a weighted summation of basis elements. Each basis element represents a unit sound wave corresponding to a particular frequency band; the weight is the amplitude of the wave. The spatial change of the sound wave as it propagates from a vibrating surface therefore reduces to the change in the weights of the basis waves. This computation is known as *acoustic transfer* and represented sound radiation. Wave motion is governed by the *wave equation*, a well-studied partial differential equation that usually requires a costly numeric solution. James and his coauthors introduced virtual sound sources called *multipoles*, which provide approximate solutions to the wave equation. The sound waves produced by the multipoles can be represented by simple functions. Once appropriate locations and weights are determined for the multipoles in a preprocess, the computation of run-time sound synthesis reduces to a weighted summation of the simple multipole functions, which can be done in real time. Another advantage of the multipole approximation is that it is independent of the geometric complexity of the vibrating objects. This is desirable for CG animation, in which geometrically complex shapes often appear.

One representative application of PAT is the physically based sound rendering of pouring and splashing water, which was described in the paper entitled "Harmonic Fluids" by Changxi Zheng and Doug L. James [Zheng and James 09]. These sounds are caused by the complex vibrations of the rapidly changing water surface. The "harmonics fluids" work models the sound source as a tiny vibrating air particle called an "acoustic bubble" and then computes the sound radiation from a set of appropriate acoustic bubbles. In the preprocess, the sound radiation in the water domain (from the acoustic bubble to the water surface) is computed first. From this, the vibration of the water surface is obtained, which allows for the computation of the sound radiation in the air domain (from the water surface to the observer). The virtual sound sources are used in both domains instead of solving the wave equation directly. The output of preprocess is the locations and weights of multipoles along the time axis associated with the acoustic bubbles.

From the precomputed data, run-time sound synthesis can be done in real time. The behavior of acoustic bubbles is computed using CG fluid simulation methods, and all the precomputation of sound radiation is done in the loop of this fluid simulation (in parallel for all the bubbles), resulting in sound correctly synchronized with the graphics created by the CG fluid simulation. Water animation

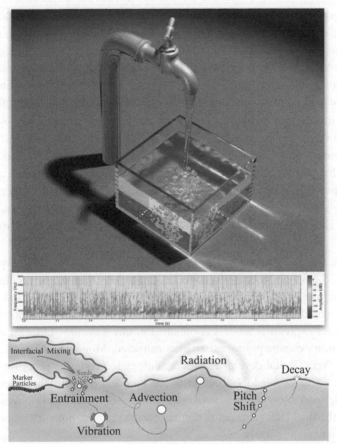

Figure 10.28 Synthesizing the sound of pouring water. (From [Zheng and James 09] © 2009 AMC, Inc. Included here by permission.)

presented at SIGGRAPH using this method demonstrated that such a union of sound and graphics can enhance the realism of computer animation, and largely contributed to an increased popularity of sound rendering [Zheng and James 09].

10.5 Precomputed Radiance Transfer in Movies

The techniques described in this chapter have demonstrated that PRT is sufficiently mature to be ready for practical use. High expectations have been placed on the technology for video game rendering; certainly some games have already utilized PRT to some extent. However, dedicated PRT technology was not used in movie production until James Cameron's stereoscopic film *Avatar* (2009). Weta Digital, the company responsible for the effects in the film, wanted to make the process more interactive as well as producing more realistic rendered results. The goal was to provide the director with the ability to see in real time a visualization of an actor's full performance as it would appear in the final CG character. In this sense, the actors and director could work as if they were filming on a virtual stage.

One of the most notable technologies that reflected this philosophy was the real-time facial capture system. Weta Digital switched from traditional (optical) marker-based facial capture to an image-based facial capture. In this arrangement, a helmet camera is mounted in front of an actor's mouth to capture the displacements of green dots placed on the face. The resulting displacement data is converted to a weighted summation of a facial expressions bases and brought into the system that sculpts a 3D face model with the given facial expression data.[5]

(Note that this "image-based" motion capture is different than those introduced in 5.3.3.) It does not recover a 3D model using stereo reconstruction. MotionBuilder, a commercially available software package, was used to sculpt a 3D face model using the given 2D facial expression data. Once a time series of 3D facial expression models is obtained in this way, the 3D facial animation from arbitrary camera positions can be constructed. Momcilovic Dejan and Mark Sagar at Weta Digital developed the technology to make this processes work in real time. This enabled the director to see the facial performances streamed in live while working with the actors. The same system and pipeline was used for creating the final facial animation that appears in the film, but with more accurate tracking and data analysis.

In *Avatar*, the entire world was represented in CG, and James Cameron wanted the photorealism to exceed that of ordinary live-action films as well as introduce a new level of believability. The ability to view the effects of global illumination with each change of lighting and surface quality evaluation were indispensable to satisfy his demands. However considering the complexity of CG environments in this work, it was very difficult to achieve it using existing approaches. Weta Digital decided that a kind of highly efficient precomputation approach was the best choice. PRT was introduced for this purpose, and a new lighting system was developed by Martin Hill, Nick McKenzie, and Jon Allitt. The PRT in *Avatar*

---

[5]The idea of using facial expression bases, which are commonly called *action units* (AU), came from the *facial action coding system* (FACS) originally invented in the 1970s. Mark Sagar at Weta Digital adapted this idea to establish a new facial animation pipeline in the movie *King Kong* (2005). Each AU corresponds to each part of the face and is combined with a few facial muscles that determine the appearance of that part of the face. Approximating the captured numerical data with the linear combination of AUs produces more natural facial expressions.

inherited the approach of the original PRT paper along with SH representation of BRDFs. Precomputation of radiance transfer was performed, and SH approximations were stored as point clouds for the RenderMan software to read.[6]

Spherical harmonics expansions were applied to both environment lighting and BRDFs. Combining the three components (environment lighting, radiance transfer, and BRDFs) yielded the rendering result. Radiance transfer is a primary realism component yet is costly to compute. Precomputing radiance transfer provides the ability to change both the lighting and surface materials interactively, which greatly contributed to the ease of exploring the lighting and surface expression to get to the desired quality. PRT was also used for the final rendering, and it contributed to the overall quality of all rendered scenes regardless of their type or complexity.

The significant advantage of using PRT in *Avatar* was that there was essentially no difference between final renderings and test iterations—the same PRT was used for both to avoid recomputation. This enabled the artists to work on lighting tests knowing the final renderings would be the same, except at higher pixel resolution. This definitely differs from hardware-accelerated rendering pipelines where the final images are generated by an entirely different software system.

However there was one critical problem in the PRT approach. Spherical harmonics do not work well for high-frequency lighting. In *Avatar*, the scenes include all kinds of lighting and reflection. Instead of SH basis functions, Gaussian functions were employed to represent high-frequency lighting. Lighting was expanded with Gaussian bases and stored, and then convolved with a radiance transfer term derived from the SH and BRDF terms, which were also represented with a Gaussian. This idea proved to be very useful for the representation of high-frequency lighting details, such as sharp specular highlights and reflections. The implementation in the *Avatar* project required lots of ideas different from those presented in the original PRT papers, some of which remain trade secrets. For example, high contrast in the environment lighting could create ringing artifacts in an SH approximation; proprietary methods were developed for suppressing these artifacts at render time.

Until recently, the bottleneck of PRT, in the sense of moving the implementation into movie production, was the costly precomputation process that involves ray tracing. However, ray tracing has come to be more and more prevalent in the motion picture industry since 2008 (as described in Section 2.5.5). The use

---

[6]A "point" in a RenderMan "point cloud" is a kind of little disc having a surface normal, radius, and an area. Point clouds are used to estimate or cache information such as occlusion or one bounce indirect diffuse illumination. The PRT used in *Avatar* mainly computed occlusion in the preprocess and stored the results as a point cloud so that RenderMan can refer to it at render time.

of PRT in movies was likely pushed by this movement, along with increased demands for interactive and real-time technologies. The extensive use of PRT in *Avatar* suggests new potentials that the original researchers could not foresee.

Bibliography

[Adamson and Jenson 01] Andrew Adamson and Vicky Jenson. *Shrek*. VFX: Dream-Works SKG, 2001.

[Adelson and Bergen 91] Edward H. Adelson and J.R. Bergen "The Plenoptic Function and the Elements of Early Vision." In *Computational Models of Visual Processing*, edited by Michael S. Landy and J. Anthony Movshon. Cambridge, MA: MIT Press, 1991.

[Adelson and Wang 92] Edward H. Adelson and John Y. A. Wang. "Single Lens Stereo with a Plenoptic Camera." *IEEE Trans. Pattern Anal. Mach. Intell.* 14:2 (1992), 99–106.

[Agarwal et al. 03] Sameer Agarwal, Ravi Ramamoorthi, Serge Belongie, and Henrik Wann Jensen. "Structured Importance Sampling of Environment Maps." *Proc. SIGGRAPH '03, Transactions on Graphics* 22:3 (2003), 605–612.

[Arvo and Kirk 90] James Arvo and David Kirk. "Particle Transport and Image Synthesis." *Proc. SIGGRAPH '90, Computer Graphics* 24:4 (1990), 63–66.

[Arvo 95] James Arvo. "Applications of Irradiance Tensors to the Simulation of Non-Lambertian Phenomena." In *Proceedings of SIGGRAPH 95, Computer Graphics Proceedings, Annual Conference Series*, edited by Robert Cook, pp. 335–342, Reading, MA: Addison-Wesley, 1995.

[Ashikhmin and Shirley 00] Michael Ashikhmin and Peter Shirley. "An Anisotropic Phong BRDF Model." *J. Graph. Tools* 5:2 (2000), 25–32. Available online (http://portal.acm.org/citation.cfm?id=358644).

[Ashikhmin et al. 00] Michael Ashikhmin, Simon Premože, and Peter Shirley. "A Microfacet-Based BRDF Generator." In *Proceedings of SIGGRAPH 2000, Computer Graphics Proceedings, Annual Conference Series*, edited by Kurt Akely, pp. 65–74, Reading, MA: Addison-Wesley, 2000.

[Bay 01] Michael Bay. *Pearl Harbor*. VFX: Industrial Light & Magic, 2001.

[Beauchemin and Barron 95] S. S. Beauchemin and J. L. Barron. "The Computation of Optical Flow." *ACM Comput. Surv.* 27:3 (1995), 433–466.

[Besson 06] Luc Besson. *Arthur and the Minimoys*. VFX: BUF, 2006.

[Blinn 77] James F. Blinn. "Models of Light Reflection for Computer Synthesized Pictures." *Proc. SIGGRAPH '77, Computer Graphics* 11:2 (1977), 192–198.

[Blinn 82] James F. Blinn. "Light-Reflection Functions for Simulation of Clouds and Dusty Surfaces." *Proc. SIGGRAPH '82, Computer Graphics* 16:3 (1982), pp. 21–29.

[Borshukov and Lewis 03] George Borshukov and J. P. Lewis. "Realistic Human Face Rendering for *The Matrix Reloaded*." *Proc. SIGGRAPH '03, Sketches & Applications* (2003), 1.

[Bradley et al. 08] Derek Bradley, Tiberiu Popa, Alla Sheffer, Wolfgang Heidrich, and Tamy Boubekeur. "Markerless Garment Capture." *Proc. SIGGRAPH '08, Transactions on Graphics* 27:3 (2008), 1–9.

[Brand 03] Matthew Brand. "Charting a Manifold." Technical Report TR-2003-13, Mitsubishi Electric Research Laboratories (MERL), 2003. Available online (http://www.merl.com/publications/TR2003-013/).

[Bridson 08] Robert Bridson. *Fluid Simulation for Computer Graphics*. Wellesley, MA: A K Peters, Ltd., 2008.

[Chadwick et al. 09] Jeffrey N. Chadwick, Steven S. An, and Doug L. James. "Harmonic Shells: A Practical Nonlinear Sound Model for Near-Rigid Thin Shells." *Proc. SIGGRAPH Asia '09, Transactions on Graphics* 28:5 (2009), 1–10.

[Chandrasekhar 50] Subrahmanyan Chandrasekhar. *Radiative Transfer*. Oxford, UK: Oxford University Press, 1950.

[Charette and Sagar 99] Paul Charette and Mark Sagar. *The Jester*. 1999. Available online (http://us.imdb.com/Title?0271019).

[Chen and Williams 93] Shenchang Eric Chen and Lance Williams. "View Interpolation for Image Synthesis." In *Proceedings of SIGGRAPH 93, Computer Graphics Proceedings, Annual Conference Series*, edited by Jmaes T. Kajiya, pp. 279–288, New York: ACM Press, 1993.

[Chen et al. 02] Wei-Chao Chen, Jean-Yves Bouguet, Michael H. Chu, and Radek Grzeszczuk. "Light Field Mapping: Efficient Representation and Hardware Rendering of Surface Light Fields." *Proc. SIGGRAPH '02, Transactions on Graphics* 21:3 (2002), 447–456.

[Chen et al. 04] Yanyun Chen, Xin Tong, Jiaping Wang, Stephen Lin, Baining Guo, and Heung-Yeung Shum. "Shell Texture Functions." *Proc. SIGGRAPH '04, Transactions on Graphics* 23:3 (2004), 343–353.

[Cohen and Wallace 93] M.F. Cohen and J.R. Wallace. *Radiosity and Realistic Image Synthesis*. San Francisco: Morgan Kaufmann, 1993.

[Columbus 02] Chris Columbus. *Harry Potter and the Chamber of Secrets*. VFX: Industrial Light & Magic, and Framestore CFC, 2002.

[Cook and Torrance 82] R. L. Cook and K. E. Torrance. "A Reflectance Model for Computer Graphics." *Proc. SIGGRAPH '82, Computer Graphics* 1:1 (1982), 7–24.

[Cook et al. 84] Robert L. Cook, Thomas Porter, and Loren Carpenter. "Distributed Ray Tracing." *Proc. SIGGRAPH '84, Computer Graphics* 18:3 (1984), 137–145.

[Dana et al. 99] Kristin J. Dana, Bram van Ginneken, Shree K. Nayar, and Jan J. Koenderink. "Reflectance and Texture of Real-World Surfaces." *ACM Trans. Graph.* 18:1 (1999), 1–34.

[de Aguiar et al. 08] Edilson de Aguiar, Carsten Stoll, Christian Theobalt, Naveed Ahmed, Hans-Peter Seidel, and Sebastian Thrun. "Performance Capture from Sparse Multi-view Video." *Proc. SIGGRAPH '08, Transactions on Graphics* 27:3 (2008), 1–10.

[Debevec and Malik 97] Paul E. Debevec and Jitendra Malik. "Recovering High Dynamic Range Radiance Maps from Photographs." In *Proceedings of SIGGRAPH 97, Computer Graphics Proceedings, Annual Conference Series*, edited by Turner Whitted, pp. 369–378. Reading, MA: Addison-Wesley, 1997.

[Debevec et al. 96] Paul E. Debevec, Camillo J. Taylor, and Jitendra Malik. "Modeling and Rendering Architecture from Photographs." Technical Report CSD-96-893, University of California at Berkeley,1996.

[Debevec et al. 99] Paul Debevec, Tim Hawkins, Westley Sarokin, Haarm-Pieter Duiker, Tal Garfinkel, Christine Cheng, and Jenny Huang. "Fiat Lux." In *ACM SIGGRAPH Electronic Art and Animation Catalog*, edited by Alyn Rockwood, p. 133, New York: ACM Press, 1999.

[Debevec et al. 00] Paul Debevec, Tim Hawkins, Chris Tchou, Haarm-Pieter Duiker, Westley Sarokin, and Mark Sagar. "Acquiring the Reflectance Field of a Human Face." In *Proceedings of SIGGRAPH 2000, Computer Graphics Proceedings, Annual Conference Series*, edited by Kurt Akeley, pp. 145–156. Reading, MA: Addison-Wesley, 2000.

[Debevec et al. 04] Paul Debevec, Erik Reinhard, Greg Ward, and Sumanta Pattanaik. "High Dynamic Range Imaging." *Proc. SIGGRAPH '04, ACM SIGGRAPH Course Notes* (2004), 14.

[Debevec 97] Paul Debevec. *The Campanile Movie.* 1997. Available online (http://www.debevec.org/Campanile/).

[Debevec 98] Paul Debevec. "Rendering Synthetic Objects into Real Scenes: Bridging Traditional and Image-Based Graphics with Global Illumination and High Dynamic Range Photography." In *Proceedings of SIGGRAPH 98, Computer Graphics Proceedings, Annual Conference Series*, edited by Michael Cohen, pp. 189–198, Reading, MA: Addison-Wesley, 1998.

[d'Eon et al. 07] Eugene d'Eon, David Luebke, and Eric Enderton. "Efficient Rendering of Human Skin." In *Rendering Techniques 2007: Eurographics Symposium on Rendering, Grenoble, France, June 25–27, 2007*, edited by Jan Kautz and Sumanta Pattanaik, pp. 147–157. Aire-La-Ville, Switzerland: Eurographics Association, 2007.

[Dobashi et al. 03a] Yoshinori Dobashi, Tsuyoshi Yamamoto, and Tomoyuki Nishita. "Real-time Rendering of Aerodynamic Sound Using Sound Textures Based on Computational Fluid Dynamics." *Proc. SIGGRAPH '03, Transactions on Graphics* 22:3 (2003), 732–740.

[Dobashi et al. 03b] Yoshinori Dobashi, Tsuyoshi Yamamoto, and Tomoyuki Nishita. "Real-Time Rendering of Aerodynamic Sound Using Sound Textures Based on Computational Fluid Dynamics." *Proc. SIGGRAPH '03, Transactions on Graphics* 22:3 (2003), 732–740.

[Docter 01] Pete Docter. *Monsters, Inc.* VFX: Pixar Animation Studios. 2001.

[Donner and Jensen 05] Craig Donner and Henrik Wann Jensen. "Light Diffusion in Multi-layered Translucent Materials." *Proc. SIGGRAPH '05, Transactions on Graphics* 24:3 (2005), 1032–1039.

[Donner et al. 08] Craig Donner, Tim Weyrich, Eugene d'Eon, Ravi Ramamoorthi, and Szymon Rusinkiewicz. "A Layered, Heterogeneous Reflectance Model for Acquiring and Rendering Human Skin." *Proc. SIGGRAPH Asia '08, Transactions on Graphics* 27:5 (2008), 1–12.

[Donner et al. 09] Craig Donner, Jason Lawrence, Ravi Ramamoorthi, Toshiya Hachisuka, Henrik Wann Jensen, and Shree Nayar. "An Empirical BSSRDF Model." *Proc. SIGGRAPH '09, Transactions on Graphics* 28:3 (2009), 1–10.

[Drebin et al. 88] Robert A. Drebin, Loren Carpenter, and Pat Hanrahan. "Volume Rendering." *Proc. SIGGRAPH '88, Computer Graphics* 22:4 (1988), 65–74.

[Dür 06] A. Dür. "An Improved Normalization for the Ward Reflectance Model." *J. Graph. Tools* 11:1 (2006), 51–59.

[Eason et al. 78] G. Eason, A. Veitch, R. Nisbet, and F. Turnbull. "The Theory of the Backscattering of Light by Blood." *J. Physics* 11:10 (1978), 1463–1479.

[Edwards et al. 06] Dave Edwards, Solomon Boulos, Jared Johnson, Peter Shirley, Michael Ashikhmin, Michael Stark, and Chris Wyman. "The Halfway Vector Disk for BRDF Modeling." *ACM Trans. Graph.* 25:1 (2006), 1–18.

[Farrell et al. 92] T.J. Farrell, M.S. Patterson, and B. Wilson. "A Diffusion Theory Model of Spatially Resolved, Steady-State Diffuse Reflectance for the Noninvasive Determination of Tissue Optical Properties in Vivo." *Med. Phys* 19:4 (1992), 879–888.

[Fedkiw et al. 01] Ronald Fedkiw, Jos Stam, and Henrik Wann Jensen. "Visual Simulation of Smoke." In *Proceedings of SIGGRAPH 2001, Computer Graphics Proceedings, Annual Confertence Series*, edited by E. Flume, pp. 15–22. Reading, MA: Addison-Wesley, 2001.

[Fincher 99] David Fincher. *Fight Club*. VFX: BUF et al. 1999.

[Fournier 95] Alan Fournier. "Separating Reflectance Functions for Linear Radiosity." In *Rendering Techniques '95: Proceedings of the Eurographics Workshop in Dublin, Ireland, June 12–14, 1995*, edited by P. Hanrahan and W. Purgathofer, pp 296–305. Wien: Springer-Verlag, 1995.

[Fuchs et al. 08] Martin Fuchs, Ramesh Raskar, Hans-Peter Seidel, and Hendrik P. A. Lensch. "Towards Passive 6D Reflectance Field Displays." *Proc. SIGGRAPH '08, Transactions on Graphics* 27:3 (2008), 1–8.

[Georgeiv et al. 06] T. Georgeiv, K.C. Zheng, B. Curless, D. Salesin, S. Nayar, and C. Intwala. "Spatio-angular Resolution Tradeoff in Integral Photography." In *Rendering Techniques 2006: Eurographics Symposium on Rendering, Nicosta, Cyprus, June 26–29, 2006*, edited by Tomas Akenine-Möller and Wolfgang Heidrich, pp. 263–272. Aire-La-Ville, Switzerland: Eurographics Association, 2006

[Gondry 95] Michel Gondry. "Like A Rolling Stone." VFX: BUF. 1995.

[Gortler et al. 96] Steven J. Gortler, Radek Grzeszczuk, Richard Szeliski, and Michael F. Cohen. "The lumigraph." In *Proceedings of SIGGRAPH 96, Computer Graphics*

Proceedings, Annual Conference Series, edited by Holly Rushmeier, pp. 43–54, Reading, MA: Addison-Wesley, 1996.

[Gouraud 71] Henri Gouraud. "Continuous Shading of Curved Surfaces." *IEEE Transactions on Computers* 20:6 (1971), 623–629.

[Gu et al. 06] Jinwei Gu, Chien-I Tu, Ravi Ramamoorthi, Peter Belhumeur, Wojciech Matusik, and Shree Nayar. "Time-Varying Surface Appearance: Acquisition, Modeling and Rendering." *Proc. SIGGRAPH '06, Transactions on Graphics* 25:3 (2006), 762–771.

[Hachisuka and Jensen 09] Toshiya Hachisuka and Henrik Wann Jensen. "Stochastic Progressive Photon Mapping." *Proc. SIGGRAPH Asia '09, Transactions on Graphics* 28:5 (2009), 1–8.

[Hachisuka et al. 08] Toshiya Hachisuka, Shinji Ogaki, and Henrik Wann Jensen. "Progressive Photon Mapping." *Proc. SIGGRAPH Asia '08, Transactions on Graphics* 27:3 (2008), 1–8.

[Hanrahan and Krueger 93] Pat Hanrahan and Wolfgang Krueger. "Reflection from Layered Surfaces Due to Subsurface Scattering." In *Proceedings of SIGGRAPH '93, Computer Graphics Proceedings, Annual Conference Series*, edited by James T. Kajiya, pp. 165–174. New York: ACM Press, 1993.

[Hao et al. 03] Xuejun Hao, Thomas Baby, and Amitabh Varshney. "Interactive Subsurface Scattering for Translucent Meshes." In *Proceedings of the 2003 Symposium on Interactive 3D Graphics, SI3D*, pp. 75–82. New York: ACM Press, 2003.

[Hawkins et al. 04] Tim Hawkins, Andreas Wenger, Chris Tchou, Andrew Gardner, Fredrik Göransson, and Paul Debevec. "Animatable Facial Reflectance Fields." In *Rendering Techniques 2004: Eurographics Symposium on Rendering, Norrk öping, Sweden, June 2123, 2004*, edited by Alexander Keller and Henrik Wann Jensen, pp. 309–319. Aire-La-Ville, Switzerland: Eurographics Association, 2004.

[He et al. 91] Xiao D. He, Kenneth E. Torrance, François X. Sillion, and Donald P. Greenberg. "A Comprehensive Physical Model for Light Reflection." *Proc. SIGGRAPH '91, Computer Graphics* 25:4 (1991), 175–186.

[Hery 05] Christophe Hery. "Implementing a Skin BSSRDF: (Or Several...)." *Proc. SIGGRAPH '05, ACM SIGGRAPH Courses* (2005), 4.

[Hirsch et al. 09] Matthew Hirsch, Douglas Lanman, Henry Holtzman, and Ramesh Raskar. "BiDi Screen: A Thin, Depth-Sensing LCD for 3D Interaction Using Light Fields." *Proc. SIGGRAPH Asia '09, Transactions on Graphics* 28:5 (2009), 1–9.

[Ishimaru 78] Akira Ishimaru. *Wave Propagation and Scattering in Random Media. Vol 1: Single Scattering and Transport Theory*. Academic Press, 1978.

[Jackson 05] Peter Jackson. *King Kong*. VFX: Universal Pictures. 2005.

[Jakob et al. 09] Wenzel Jakob, Jonathan T. Moon, and Steve Marschner. "Capturing Hair Assemblies Fiber by Fiber." *Proc. SIGGRAPH Asia '09, Transactions on Graphics* 28:5 (2009), 1–9.

[James and Fatahalian 03] Doug L. James and Kayvon Fatahalian. "Precomputing Interactive Dynamic Deformable Scenes." *Proc. SIGGRAPH '03, Transactions on Graphics* 22:3 (2003), 879–887.

[James et al. 06] Doug L. James, Jernej Barbič, and Dinesh K. Pai. "Precomputed Acoustic Transfer: Output-Sensitive, Accurate Sound Generation for Geometrically Complex Vibration Sources." *Proc. SIGGRAPH '06, Transactions on Graphics* 25:3 (2006), 987–995.

[Jensen and Buhler 02] Henrik Wann Jensen and Juan Buhler. "A Rapid Hierarchical Rendering Technique for Translucent Materials." *Proc. SIGGRAPH '02, Transactions on Graphics* 21:3 (2002), 576–581.

[Jensen and Christensen 98] Henrik Wann Jensen and Per H. Christensen. "Efficient Simulation of Light Transport in Scences with Participating Media Using Photon Maps." In *Proceedings of SIGGRAPH '98, Computer Graphics Proceedings, Annual Conference Series*, edited by Michael Cohen, pp. 311–320, Reading, MA: Addison-Wesley, 1998.

[Jensen et al. 01a] Henrik Wann Jensen, Frédo Durand, Julie Dorsey, Michael M. Stark, Peter Shirley, and Simon Premože. "A Physically-Based Night Sky Model." In *Proceedings of SIGGRAPH 2001, Computer Graphics Proceedings, Annual Conference Series*, edited by E. Fiume, pp. 399–408. Reading, MA: Addison-Wesley, 2001.

[Jensen et al. 01b] Henrik Wann Jensen, Stephen R. Marschner, Marc Levoy, and Pat Hanrahan. "A Practical Model for Subsurface Light Transport." In *Proceedings of SIGGRAPH 2001, Computer Graphics Proceedings, Annual Conference Series*, edited by E. Fiume, pp. 511–518. Reading, MA: Addison-Wesley, 2001.

[Jensen 96] Henrik Wann Jensen. "Global Illumination Using Photon Maps." In *Rendering Techniques '96: Proceedings of the Eurographics Workshop in Porto, Portugal, June 17 - 19, 1996*, edited by X. Pueyo and P. Schröder, pp. 21–30. Wien: Springer-Verlag, 1996.

[Kajiya and Kay 89] J. T. Kajiya and T. L. Kay. "Rendering Fur with Three Dimensional Textures." *Proc. SIGGRAPH '89, Computer Graphics* 23:3 (1989), 271–280.

[Kajiya and Von Herzen 84] James T. Kajiya and Brian P Von Herzen. "Ray Tracing Volume Densities." *Proc. SIGGRAPH '84, Computer Graphics* 18:3 (1984), 165–174.

[Kajiya 86] James T. Kajiya. "The Rendering Equation." *Proc. SIGGRAPH '86, Computer Graphics* 20:4 (1986), 143–150.

[Kang et al. 03] Sing Bing Kang, Matthew Uyttendaele, Simon Winder, and Richard Szeliski. "High Dynamic Range Video." *Proc. SIGGRAPH '03, Transactions on Graphics* 22:3 (2003), 319–325.

[Kautz and McCool 99] Jan Kautz and Michael D. McCool. "Interactive Rendering with Arbitrary BRDFs Using Separable Approximations." In *Proceedings of SIGGRAPH '99, ACM SIGGRAPH Conference Abstracts and Applications*, p. 253. New York: ACM Press, 1999.

[Kautz et al. 02] Jan Kautz, Peter-Pike Sloan, and John Snyder. "Fast, Arbitrary BRDF Shading for Low-Frequency Lighting Using Spherical Harmonics." In *Rendering Techniques 2002: Proceedings of the Eurographics Workshop in Pisa, Italy, June 26– 28, 2002* , edited by P. Debevec and S. Gibson, pp. 291–296. Aire-La-Ville, Switzerland: Eurographics Association, 2002.

[Kautz et al. 07] Jan Kautz, Solomon Boulos, and Frédo Durand. "Interactive Editing and Modeling of Bidirectional Texture Functions." *Proc. SIGGRAPH '07, Transactions on Graphics* 26:3 (2007), 53.

[Keller 96] Alexander Keller. "Quasi-Monte Carlo Radiosity." In *Rendering Techniques '96: Proceedings of the Eurographics Workshop in Porto, Portugal, June 17 - 19, 1996*, edited by X. Pueyo and P. Schröder, pp. 101–110. Wien: Springer-Verlag, 1996.

[Kim and James 09] Theodore Kim and Doug L. James. "Skipping Steps in Deformable Simulation with Online Model Reduction." *Proc. SIGGRAPH Asia '09, Transactions on Graphics* 28:5 (2009), 1–9.

[Kim et al. 09] Min H. Kim, Tim Weyrich, and Jan Kautz. "Modeling Human Color Perception under Extended Luminance Levels." *Proc. SIGGRAPH '09, Transactions on Graphics* 28:3 (2009), 1–9.

[Kollig and Keller 03] Thomas Kollig and Alexander Keller. "Efficient Illumination by High Dynamic Range Images ." In *Rendering Techniques 2003: Eurographics Symposium on Rendering, Leuven, Belgium, June 25-27, 2003.*, edited by Philip Dutré, Frank Suykens, Per H. Christensen, and Daniel Cohen-Or, pp. 45–51. Aire-La-Ville, Switzerland: Eurographics Association, 2003.

[Lafortune and Willems 93] Eric P. Lafortune and Yves D. Willems. "Bi-directional Path Tracing." In *Proceedings of Third International Conference on Computational Graphics and Visualization Techniques (Compugraphics '93)*, edited by H. P. Santo, pp. 145–153. Alvor, Portugal, 1993. Available online (http://citeseer.ist.psu.edu/lafortune93bidirectional.html).

[Lafortune et al. 97] Eric P. F. Lafortune, Sing-Choong Foo, Kenneth E. Torrance, and Donald P. Greenberg. "Non-linear Approximation of Reflectance Functions." In *Proceedings of SIGGRAPH 97, Computer Graphics Proceedings, Annual Conference Series*, edited by Turner Whitted, pp. 117–126, Reading, MA: Addison-Wesley, 1997.

[Landis 02] H. Landis. "Production-Ready Global Illumination." *ACM SIGGRAPH Course Notes* (2002). New York: ACM Press, 2002.

[Lanman et al. 08] Douglas Lanman, Ramesh Raskar, Amit Agrawal, and Gabriel Taubin. "Shield Fields: Modeling and Capturing 3D Occluders." *Proc. SIGGRAPH Asia '08, Transactions on Graphics* 27:5 (2008), 1–10.

[Lasseter 95] John Lasseter. *Toy Story.* VFX: Pixar Animation Studios. 1995.

[Laveau and Faugeras 94] Stephane Laveau and Olivier Faugeras. "3-D Scene Representation as a Collection of Images and Fundamental Matrices." Technical Report 2205, INRIA, 1994.

[Lawrence et al. 04] Jason Lawrence, Szymon Rusinkiewicz, and Ravi Ramamoorthi. "Efficient BRDF Importance Sampling Using a Factored Representation." *Proc. SIGGRAPH '04, Transactions on Graphics* 23:3 (2004), 496–505.

[Leclerc and Bobick 91] Y.G. Leclerc and A.F. Bobick. "The Direct Computation of Height from Shading." In *Computer Vision and Pattern Recognition 1991: Proc. of IEEE Conf. on Comp. Vision and Patt. Recog.*, pp. 552–558. IEEE Computer Society, 1991.

[Lehtinen and Kautz 03] Jaakko Lehtinen and Jan Kautz. "Matrix Radiance Transfer." In *Proceedings of the 2003 Symposium on Interactive 3D Graphics, SI3D*, pp. 59–64. New York: ACM Press, 2003.

[Lehtinen 07] Jaakko Lehtinen. "A Framework for Precomputed and Captured Light Transport." *ACM Trans. Graph.* 26:4 (2007), 13.

[Leighton 94] T. Leighton. *The Acoustic Bubble.* San Diego, CA: Academic Press, 1994.

[Leung and Malik 01] Thomas Leung and Jitendra Malik. "Representing and Recognizing the Visual Appearance of Materials using Three-dimensional Textons." *Int. J. Comput. Vision* 43:1 (2001), 29–44. Available online (http://dx.doi.org/10.1023/A:1011126920638).

[Levoy and Hanrahan 96] Marc Levoy and Pat Hanrahan. "Light Field Rendering." In *Proceedings of SIGGRAPH '96: Computer Graphics Proceedings, Annual Conference Series*, edited by Holly Rushmeier, pp. 31–42. Reading, MA: Addison-Wesley,1996.

[Levoy 88] Marc Levoy. "Display of Surfaces from Volume Data." *IEEE Comput. Graph. Appl.* 8:3 (1988), 29–37.

[Liang et al. 08] Chia-Kai Liang, Tai-Hsu Lin, Bing-Yi Wong, Chi Liu, and Homer H. Chen. "Programmable Aperture Photography: Multiplexed Light Field Acquisition." *Proc. SIGGRAPH '08, Transactions on Graphics* 27:3 (2008), 1–10.

[Lippmann 08] M. G. Lippmann. "Epreuves reversible donnant la sensation du relief." *Journal de Physique Théorique et Appliquée* 7:1 (1908), 821–825.

[Liu et al. 01] Xinguo Liu, Yizhou Yu, and Heung-Yeung Shum. "Synthesizing Bidirectional Texture Functions for Real-World Surfaces." In *Proceedings of SIGGRAPH 2001, Computer Graphics Proceedings, Annual Conference Series*, edited by E. Fiume, pp. 97–106, Reading, MA: Addison-Wesley, 2001.

[Liu et al. 04] Xinguo Liu, Peter-Pike Sloan, Heung-Yeung Shum, and John Snyder. "All-Frequency Precomputed Radiance Transfer for Glossy Objects." In *Rendering Techniques 2004: Eurographics Symposium on Rendering, Norrköping, Sweden, June 21–23, 2004*, edited by Alexander Keller and Henrik Wann Jensen, pp. 337–344. Aire-La-Ville, Switzerland: Eurographics Association, 2004.

[Lokovic and Veach 00] Tom Lokovic and Eric Veach. "Deep Shadow Maps." In *Proceedings of SIGGRAPH 2000, Computer Graphics Proceedings, Annual Conference Series*, edited by Kurt Akeley, pp. 385–392, Reading, MA: Addison-Wesley, 2000.

[Lorensen and Cline 87] William E. Lorensen and Harvey E. Cline. "Marching Cubes: A High Resolution 3D Surface Construction Algorithm." *Proc. SIGGRAPH '87, Computer Graphics* 21:4 (1987), 163–169.

[Lucas 77] George Lucas. *Star Wars.* VFX: Industrial Light & Magic. 1977.

[Lucas 02] George Lucas. *Star Wars: Episode II: Attack of the Clones.* VFX: Industrial Light & Magic. 2002.

[Lucas 05] George Lucas. *Star Wars: Episode III: Revenge of the Sith.* 2005. VFX: Industrial Light & Magic et al. 2005.

[Mann and Picard 95] Steve Mann and Rosalind W. Picard. "Being 'Undigital' with Digital Cameras: Extending Dynamic Range by Combining Differently Exposed Pictures." In *Proceedings of IS&T 46th Annual Conference*, pp. 422–428, 1995.

[Marschner et al. 00] S. R. Marschner, S. H. Westin, E. P. F. Lafortune, and K. E. Torrance. "Image-Based Bidirectional Reflectance Distribution Function Measurement." *Applied Optics* 39:16 (2000), 2592–2600.

[Marschner et al. 03] Stephen R. Marschner, Henrik Wann Jensen, Mike Cammarano, Steve Worley, and Pat Hanrahan. "Light Scattering from Human Hair Fibers." *Proc. SIGGRAPH '03, Transactions on Graphics* 22:3 (2003), 780–791.

[Matusik et al. 03] Wojciech Matusik, Hanspeter Pfister, Matt Brand, and Leonard McMillan. "A Data-Driven Reflectance Model." *Proc. SIGGRAPH '03, Transactions on Graphics* 22:3 (2003), 759–769.

[Mcallister et al. 02] David K. Mcallister, Anselmo Lastra, and Wolfgang Heidrich. "Efficient Rendering of Spatial Bi-directional Reflectance Distribution Functions." In *Graphics Hardware 2002: Proceedings of the ACM SIGGRAPH / Eurographics Conference on Graphics Hardware*, edited by T. Ertl, W. Heidrich, and M. Doggett, pp. 79–88. Aire-la-Ville, Switzerland: Eurographics Association, 2002. Available online (http://portal.acm.org/citation.cfm?id=569057).

[McMillan and Bishop 95] Leonard McMillan and Gary Bishop. "Plenoptic Modeling: An Image-Based Rendering System." In *Proceedings of SIGGRAPH '95, Computer Graphics Proceedings, Annual Conference Series*, edited by Robert Cook, pp. 39–46, Reading, MA: Addison-Wesley, 1995.

[Mitsunaga and Nayar 99] Tomoo Mitsunaga and Shree K. Nayar. "Radiometric Self Calibration." In *Computer Vision and Pattern Recognition 1999: Proc. of IEEE Conf. on Comp. Vision and Patt. Recog.*, 2, 2. IEEE Computer Society, 1999.

[Moon and Marschner 06] Jonathan T. Moon and Stephen R. Marschner. "Simulating Multiple Scattering in Hair Using a Photon Mapping Approach." *Proc. SIGGRAPH '06, Transactions on Graphics* 25:3 (2006), 1067–1074.

[Moon et al. 08] Jonathan T. Moon, Bruce Walter, and Steve Marschner. "Efficient Multiple Scattering in Hair Using Spherical Harmonics." *Proc. SIGGRAPH '08, Transactions on Graphics* 27:3 (2008), 1–7.

[Muller et al. 03] Gero Muller, Jan Meseth, and Reinhard Klein. "Compression and Real-Time Rendering of Measured BTFs Using Local PCA." In *Proceedings of Vision, Modeling and Visualization* 2003.

[Naemura et al. 01] T. Naemura, T. Yoshida, and H. Harashima. "3-D Computer Graphics Based on Integral Photography." *Optics Express* 8:2 (2001), 255–262.

[Nayar et al. 91] Shree K. Nayar, Katsushi Ikeuchi, and Takeo Kanade. "Shape from Interreflections." *International Journal of Computer Vision* 6:3 (1991), 173–195. Available online (http://dx.doi.org/10.1007/BF00115695).

[Nayar et al. 06] Shree K. Nayar, Gurunandan Krishnan, Michael D. Grossberg, and Ramesh Raskar. "Fast Separation of Direct and Global Components of a Scene Using High Frequency Illumination." *Proc. SIGGRAPH '06, Transactions on Graphics* 25:3 (2006), 935–944.

[Ng et al. 03] Ren Ng, Ravi Ramamoorthi, and Pat Hanrahan. "All-Frequency Shadows Using Non-linear Wavelet Lighting Approximation." *Proc. SIGGRAPH '03, Transactions on Graphics* 22:3 (2003), 376–381.

[Ng et al. 04] Ren Ng, Ravi Ramamoorthi, and Pat Hanrahan. "Triple Product Wavelet Integrals for All-Frequency Relighting." *Proc. SIGGRAPH '04, Transactions on Graphics* 23:3 (2004), 477–487.

[Ng et al. 05] Ren Ng, Marc Levoy, Mathieu Brédif, Gene Duval, Mark Horowitz, and Pat Hanrahan. "Light Field Photography with a Hand-Held Plenoptic Camera." Technical Report CSTR 2005-02, Stanford University, 2005. Available online (http://graphics.stanford.edu/Papers/lfcamera/).

[Ng 05] Ren Ng. "Fourier Slice Photography." *Proc. SIGGRAPH '05, Transactions on Graphics* 24:3 (2005), 735–744.

[Ngan et al. 04] Addy Ngan, Frédo Durand, and Wojciech Matusik. "Experimental Validation of Analytical BRDF Models." *Proc. SIGGRAPH '04, ACM SIGGRAPH Sketches* (2004), 90.

[Nguyen et al. 02] Duc Quang Nguyen, Ronald Fedkiw, and Henrik Wann Jensen. "Physically Based Modeling and Animation of Fire." *Proc. SIGGRAPH '02, Transactions on Graphics* 21:3 (2002), 721–728.

[Nishino et al. 01] Ko Nishino, Yoichi Sato, and Katsushi Ikeuchi. "Eigen-Texture Method: Appearance Compression and Synthesis Based on a 3D Model." *IEEE Transactions on Pattern Analysis and Machine Intelligence* 23:11 (2001), 1257–1265.

[Nishita and Nakamae 94] Tomoyuki Nishita and Eihachiro Nakamae. "Method of Displaying Optical Effects within Water Using Accumulation Buffer." In *Proceedings of SIGGRAPH 94, Computer Graphics Proceedings, Annual Conference Series*, edited by Andrew Glassner, pp. 373–379, New York: ACM Press, 1994.

[Nishita et al. 87] Tomoyuki Nishita, Yasuhiro Miyawaki, and Eihachiro Nakamae. "A Shading Model for Atmospheric Scattering Considering Luminous Intensity Distribution of Light Sources." *Proc. SIGGRAPH '87, Computer Graphics* 21:4 (1987), 303–310.

[Nishita et al. 93] Tomoyuki Nishita, Takao Sirai, Katsumi Tadamura, and Eihachiro Nakamae. "Display of the Earth Taking into Account Atmospheric Scattering." In *Proceedings of SIGGRAPH 93, Computer Graphics Proceedings, Annual Conference Series*, edited by James T. Kajiya, pp. 175–182, New York: ACM Press, 1993.

[O'Brien et al. 01] James F. O'Brien, Perry R. Cook, and Georg Essl. "Synthesizing Sounds from Physically Based Motion." In *Proceedings of SIGGRAPH 2001, Computer Graphics Proceedings, Annual Conference Series*, edited by E. Fiume, pp. 529–536, Reading, MA: Addison-Wesley, 2001.

[Oren and Nayar 94] Michael Oren and Shree K. Nayar. "Generalization of Lambert's Reflectance Model." In *Proceedings of SIGGRAPH 94, Computer Graphics Proceedings, Annual Conference Series*, edited by Andrew Glassner, pp. 239–246, New York: ACM Press, 1994.

[Ostromoukhov et al. 04] Victor Ostromoukhov, Charles Donohue, and Pierre-Marc Jodoin. "Fast Hierarchical Importance Sampling with Blue Noise Properties." *Proc. SIGGRAPH '04, Transactions on Graphics* 23:3 (2004), 488–495.

[Paris et al. 08] Sylvain Paris, Will Chang, Oleg I. Kozhushnyan, Wojciech Jarosz, Wojciech Matusik, Matthias Zwicker, and Frédo Durand. "Hair Photobooth: Geometric and Photometric Acquisition of Real Hairstyles." *Proc. SIGGRAPH '08, Transactions on Graphics* 27:3 (2008), 1–9.

[Peter and Pietrek 98] Ingmar Peter and Georg Pietrek. "Importance Driven Construction of Photon Maps." In *Rendering Techniques '98: Proceedings of the Eurographics Workshop in Vienna, Austria, June 29–July 1, 1998* , edited by G. Drettakis and N. Max, pp. 269–280. Wien: Springer-Verlag, 1998.

[Petersen 06] Wolfgang Petersen. *Poseidon*. VFX: Industrial Light & Magic et al. 2006. Available online (http://imdb.com/title/tt0409182/).

[Petschnigg et al. 04] Georg Petschnigg, Richard Szeliski, Maneesh Agrawala, Michael Cohen, Hugues Hoppe, and Kentaro Toyama. "Digital Photography with Flash and No-Flash Image Pairs." *Proc. SIGGRAPH '04, Transactions on Graphics* 23:3 (2004), 664–672.

[Phong 75] Bui Tuong Phong. "Illumination for Computer Generated Pictures." *Commun. ACM* 18:6 (1975), 311–317.

[Purcell et al. 02] Timothy J. Purcell, Ian Buck, William R. Mark, and Pat Hanrahan. "Ray Tracing on Programmable Graphics Hardware." *Proc. SIGGRAPH '02, Transactions on Graphics* 21:3 (2002), 703–712.

[Purcell et al. 03] Timothy J. Purcell, Craig Donner, Mike Cammarano, Henrik W. Jensen, and Pat Hanrahan. "Photon Mapping on Programmable Graphics Hardware." In *Graphics Hardware 2003: Proceedings of the ACM SIGGRAPH / Eurographics Conference on Graphics Hardware*, edited by W. Mark and A. Schilling, pp. 41–50. Aire-La-Ville, Switzerland: Eurographics Association, 2003. Available online (http://portal.acm.org/citation.cfm?id=844181).

[Ragan-Kelley et al. 07] Jonathan Ragan-Kelley, Charlie Kilpatrick, Brian W. Smith, Doug Epps, Paul Green, Christophe Hery, and Frédo Durand. "The Lightspeed Automatic Interactive Lighting Preview System." *Proc. SIGGRAPH '07, Transactions on Graphics* 26:3 (2007), 25.

[Raimi 04] Sam Raimi. *Spider-Man 2*. VFX: Sony Pictures Imageworks et al. 2004.

[Ramamoorthi and Hanrahan 01a] Ravi Ramamoorthi and Pat Hanrahan. "An Efficient Representation for Irradiance Environment Maps." In *Proceedings of SIGGRAPH 2001, Computer Graphics Proceedings, Annual Conference Series*, edited by E. Fiume, pp. 497–500, Reading, MA: Addison-Wesley, 2001.

[Ramamoorthi and Hanrahan 01b] Ravi Ramamoorthi and Pat Hanrahan. "On the Relationship between Radiance and Irradiance: Determining the Illumination from Images of a Convex Lambertian Object." *Journal of the Optical Society of America A* 18:10 (2001), 2448–2459.

[Raskar and Tumbin 09] Ramesh Raskar and Jack Tumbin. *Computational Photography: Mastering New Techniques for Lenses, Lighting, and Sensors*. Natick, MA: A K Peters Ltd., 2009.

[Raskar et al. 08] Ramesh Raskar, Amit Agrawal, Cyrus A. Wilson, and Ashok Veeraraghavan. "Glare Aware Photography: 4D Ray Sampling for Reducing Glare Effects
of Camera Lenses." *Proc. SIGGRAPH '08, Transactions on Graphics* 27:3 (2008),
1–10.

[Reinhard et al. 02] Erik Reinhard, Michael Stark, Peter Shirley, and James Ferwerda.
"Photographic Tone Reproduction for Digital Images." *Proc. SIGGRAPH '02, Transactions on Graphics* 21:3 (2002), 267–276.

[Ren et al. 06] Zhong Ren, Rui Wang, John Snyder, Kun Zhou, Xinguo Liu, Bo Sun,
Peter-Pike Sloan, Hujun Bao, Qunsheng Peng, and Baining Guo. "Real-Time Soft
Shadows in Dynamic Scenes Using Spherical Harmonic Exponentiation." *Proc. SIG-
GRAPH '06, Transactions on Graphics* 25:3 (2006), 977–986.

[Robinson 01] Ruairi Robinson. *Fifty Percent Grey*. Short film. 2001.

[Rushmeier and Torrance 87] Holly E. Rushmeier and Kenneth E. Torrance. "The Zonal
Method for Calculating Light Intensities in the Presence of a Participating Medium."
Proc. SIGGRAPH '87, Computer Graphics 21:4 (1987), 293–302.

[Rusinkiewicz 98] Szymon M. Rusinkiewicz. "A New Change of Variables for Efficient
BRDF Representation." In *Rendering Techniques '98: Proceedings of the Eurographics Workshop in Vienna, Austria, June 29-July 1, 1998* , edited by G. Drettakis
and N. Max, pp. 11–22. Wien: Springer-Verlag, 1998.

[Sadeghi et al. 10] Iman Sadeghi, Heather Pritchett, Henrik Wann Jensen, and Rasmus
Tamstorf. "An Artist Friendly Hair Shading System." *Proc. SIGGRAPH '10, Transactions on Graphics* 29:4 (2010), 1–10.

[Sagar et al. 94] Mark A. Sagar, David Bullivant, Gordon D. Mallinson, and Peter J.
Hunter. "A Virtual Environment and Model of the Eye for Surgical Simulation."
In *Proceedings of SIGGRAPH 94, Computer Graphics Proceedings, Annual Conference Series*, edited by Andrew Glassner, pp. 205–212, New York: ACM Press,
1994.

[Sagar 00] Mark Sagar. *Young at Heart*. 2000.

[Sand and Teller 04] Peter Sand and Seth Teller. "Video Matching." *Proc. SIGGRAPH
'04, Transactions on Graphics* 23:3 (2004), 592–599.

[Schlick 93] Christophe Schlick. "A Customizable Reflectance Model for Everyday Rendering." In *Proc. of the Fourth Eurographics Workshop on Rendering*, Eurographics
Technical Report Series EG 93 RW, pp. 73–84. Aire-La-Ville, Switzerland: Eurographics Association, 1993.

[Seetzen et al. 03] Helge Seetzen, Lorne A. Whitehead, and Greg Ward. "A High Dynamic Range Display Using Low and High Resolution Modulators." *SID Symposium
Digest of Technical Papers* 34:1 (2003), 1450–1453.

[Seetzen et al. 04] Helge Seetzen, Wolfgang Heidrich, Wolfgang Stuerzlinger, Greg Ward,
Lorne Whitehead, Matthew Trentacoste, Abhijeet Ghosh, and Andrejs Vorozcovs.
"High Dynamic Range Display Systems." *Proc. SIGGRAPH '04, Transactions on
Graphics* 23:3 (2004), 760–768.

[Seitz et al. 05] Steven M. Seitz, Yasuyuki Matsushita, and Kiriakos N. Kutulakos. "A Theory of Inverse Light Transport." In *Proceedings of the Tenth IEEE International Conference on Computer Vision (ICCV '05)*, pp. 1440–1447. Washington, DC: IEEE Computer Society, 2005. Available online (http://dx.doi.org/10.1109/ICCV.2005.25).

[Silberling 04] Brad Silberling. *Lemony Snicket's A Series of Unfortunate Events.* VFX: Industrial Light & Magic. 2004.

[Sloan et al. 02] Peter-Pike Sloan, Jan Kautz, and John Snyder. "Precomputed Radiance Transfer for Real-Time Rendering in Dynamic, Low-Frequency Lighting Environments." *Proc. SIGGRAPH '02, Transactions on Graphics* 21:3 (2002), 527–536.

[Sloan et al. 03a] Peter-Pike Sloan, Jesse Hall, John Hart, and John Snyder. "Clustered Principal Components for Precomputed Radiance Transfer." *Proc. SIGGRAPH '03, Transactions on Graphics* 22:3 (2003), 382–391.

[Sloan et al. 03b] Peter-Pike Sloan, Xinguo Liu, Heung-Yeung Shum, and John Snyder. "Bi-scale radiance transfer." *Proc. SIGGRAPH '03, Transactions on Graphics* 22:3 (2003), 370–375.

[Sloan et al. 07] Peter-Pike Sloan, Naga K. Govindaraju, Derek Nowrouzezahrai, and John Snyder. "Image-Based Proxy Accumulation for Real-Time Soft Global Illumination." Paper presented at the Pacific Conference on Computer Graphics and Applications, Maui, HI, October 29, 2007.

[Sloan 06] Peter-Pike Sloan. "Normal Mapping for Precomputed Radiance Transfer." In *Proceedings of the 2006 Symposium on Interactive 3D Graphics and Games, SI3D '06*, pp. 23–26. New York: ACM Press, 2006.

[Smith 87] Alvy R. Smith. "Volume Graphics and Volume Visualization, A Tutorial." Technical Report 176, Pixar, 1987.

[Song et al. 09] Ying Song, Xin Tong, Fabio Pellacini, and Pieter Peers. "SubEdit: A Representation for Editing Measured Heterogeneous Subsurface Scattering." *Proc. SIGGRAPH '09, Transactions on Graphics* 28:3 (2009), 1–10.

[Stam 95] Jos Stam. "Multiple Scattering as a Diffusion Process." In *Rendering Techniques '95: Proceedings of the Eurographics Workshop in Dublin, Ireland, June 12–14, 1995*, edited by P. Hanrahan and W. Purgathofer, pp. 41–50. Wien: Springer-Verlag, 1995.

[Stam 99] Jos Stam. "Stable fluids." In *Proceedings of SIGGRAPH 99, Computer Graphics Proceedings, Annual Conference Series*, edited by Alyn Rockwood, pp. 121–128, Redaing, MA: Addison-Wesley, 1999.

[Stanton 03] Andrew Stanton. *Finding Nemo.* VFX: Pixar Animation Studios. 2003.

[Stark et al. 05] Michael M. Stark, James Arvo, and Brian Smits. "Barycentric Parameterizations for Isotropic BRDFs." *IEEE Transactions on Visualization and Computer Graphics* 11:2 (2005), 126–138.

[Sun et al. 05] Bo Sun, Ravi Ramamoorthi, Srinivasa G. Narasimhan, and Shree K. Nayar. "A Practical Analytic Single Scattering Model for Real Time Rendering." *Proc. SIGGRAPH '05, Transactions on Graphics* 24:3 (2005), 1040–1049.

[Takala and Hahn 92] "Tapio Takala and James Hahn." *ACM Computer Graphics (Proc. SIGGRAPH '92).* 26:2 (1992), 211–220.

[Takakuwa 93] Masao Takakuwa. "Diffused Ray Tracing." In *The 9th Nicograph*, 1993.

[Tong et al. 02] Xin Tong, Jingdan Zhang, Ligang Liu, Xi Wang, Baining Guo, and Heung-Yeung Shum. "Synthesis of Bidirectional Texture Functions on Arbitrary Surfaces." *Proc. SIGGRAPH '02, Transactions on Graphics* 21:3 (2002), 665–672.

[Tong et al. 05] Xin Tong, Jiaping Wang, Stephen Lin, Baining Guo, and Heung-Yeung Shum. "Modeling and Rendering of Quasi-homogeneous Materials." *Proc. SIG-GRAPH '05, Transactions on Graphics* 24:3 (2005), 1054–1061.

[Torrance and Sparrow 67] K. E. Torrance and E. M. Sparrow. "Theory for Off-Specular Reflection from Roughened Surfaces." *Journal of the Optical Society of America* 57:9 (1967), 1105–1114.

[Tuchin 00] Valery Tuchin, editor. *Tissue Optics: Light Scattering Methods and Instruments for Medical Diagnosis.* Bellingham, WA: SPIE Press, 2000.

[Turk and Pentland 91] Matthew A. Turk and Alex P. Pentland. "Face Recognition Using Eigenfaces." In *Computer Vision and Pattern Recognition 1991: Proc. of IEEE Conf. on Comp. Vision and Patt. Recog.*, pp. 586–591. IEEE Compter Society, 1991.

[van den Doel and Pai 96] K. van den Doel and D.K. Pai. "Synthesis of Shape Dependent Sounds with Physical Modeling." In *Proceedings of the International Conference on Auditory Displays*, International Community for Auditory Display, 1996.

[van den Doel et al. 01] Kees van den Doel, Paul G. Kry, and Dinesh K. Pai. "FoleyAutomatic: Physically-Based Sound Effects for Interactive Simulation and Animation." In *Proceedings of SIGGRAPH 2001, Computer Graphics Proceedings, Annual Conference Series*, edited by E. Fiume, pp. 537–544, Reading, MA: Addison-Wesley, 2001.

[Vasilescu and Terzopoulos 02] M. Alex O. Vasilescu and Demetri Terzopoulos. "Multilinear Analysis of Image Ensembles: TensorFaces." In *ECCV '02: Proceedings of the 7th European Conference on Computer Vision-Part I*, pp. 447–460. London, UK: Springer-Verlag, 2002.

[Vasilescu and Terzopoulos 03] M. Alex O. Vasilescu and Demetri Terzopoulos. "Tensor-Textures." *Proc. SIGGRAPH '03, ACM SIGGRAPH Sketches & Applications* (2003), 1.

[Vasilescu and Terzopoulos 04] M. Alex O. Vasilescu and Demetri Terzopoulos. "Tensor-Textures: Multilinear Image-Based Rendering." *Proc. SIGGRAPH '03, Transactions on Graphics* 23:3 (2004), 336–342.

[Veach and Guibas 97] Eric Veach and Leonidas J. Guibas. "Metropolis Light Transport." In *Proceedings of SIGGRAPH 97, Computer Graphics Proceedings, Annual Conference Series*, edited by Turner Whitted, pp. 65–76, Reading, MA: Addison-Wesley, 1997.

[Veach 97] E. Veach. "Robust Monte Carlo Methods for Light Transport Simulation." Ph.D. diss., Stanford University, 1997.

[Veeraraghavan et al. 07] Ashok Veeraraghavan, Ramesh Raskar, Amit Agrawal, Ankit Mohan, and Jack Tumblin. "Dappled Photography: Mask Enhanced Cameras for Heterodyned Light Fields and Coded Aperture Refocusing." *Proc. SIGGRAPH '07, Transactions on Graphics* 26:3 (2007), 69.

[Verbinski 03] Gore Verbinski. *Pirates of the Caribbean: The Curse of the Black Pearl.* VFX: Industrial Light & Magic et al. 2003.

[Verbinski 06] Gore Verbinski. *Pirates of the Caribbean: Dead Man's Chest.* VFX: Industrial Light & Magic et al. 2006.

[Vlasic et al. 08] Daniel Vlasic, Ilya Baran, Wojciech Matusik, and Jovan Popović. "Articulated Mesh Animation from Multi-view Silhouettes." *Proc. SIGGRAPH '08, Transactions on Graphics* 27:3 (2008), 1–9.

[Wachowski and Wachowski 99] Andy Wachowski and Larry Wachowski. *The Matrix.* VFX: Manex Visual Effects et al. 1999.

[Wachowski and Wachowski 03a] Andy Wachowski and Larry Wachowski. *The Matrix Reloaded.* VFX: ESC Entertainment et al. 2003.

[Wachowski and Wachowski 03b] Andy Wachowski and Larry Wachowski. *The Matrix Revolutions.* VFX: ESC Entertainment et al. 2003.

[Wang et al. 05] Lifeng Wang, Wenle Wang, Julie Dorsey, Xu Yang, Baining Guo, and Heung-Yeung Shum. "Real-Time Rendering of Plant Leaves." *Proc. SIGGRAPH '05, Transactions on Graphics* 24:3 (2005), 712–719.

[Wang et al. 06] Jiaping Wang, Xin Tong, Stephen Lin, Minghao Pan, Chao Wang, Hujun Bao, Baining Guo, and Heung-Yeung Shum. "Appearance Manifolds for Modeling Time-Variant Appearance of Materials." *Proc. SIGGRAPH '06, Transactions on Graphics* 25:3 (2006), 754–761.

[Ward and Heckbert 92] Gregory J. Ward and Paul S. Heckbert. "Irradiance Gradients." In *Proc. of the Third Eurographics Workshop on Rendering.* pp. 85–98. Wien: Springer-Verlag, 1992.

[Ward et al. 88] Gregory J. Ward, Francis M. Rubinstein, and Robert D. Clear. "A Ray Tracing Solution for Diffuse Interreflection." *Proc. SIGGRAPH '88, Computer Graphics* 22:4 (1988), 85–92.

[Ward Larson et al. 97] Gregory Ward Larson, Holly Rushmeier, and Christine Piatko. "A Visibility Matching Tone Reproduction Operator for High Dynamic Range Scenes." *IEEE Transactions on Visualization and Computer Graphics* 3:4 (1997), 291–306.

[Ward 91] Gregory J. Ward. "Adaptive Shadow Testing for Ray Tracing." In *Proc. of the Second Eurographics Workshop on Rendering*, edited by P. Brunet and F. W. Jansen, Wien: Springer-Verlag, 1991.

[Ward 92] Gregory J. Ward. "Measuring and Modeling Anisotropic Reflection." *Proc. SIGGRAPH '92, Computer Graphics* 26:2 (1992), 265–272.

[Westin et al. 92] Stephen H. Westin, James R. Arvo, and Kenneth E. Torrance. "Predicting Reflectance Functions from Complex Surfaces." *Proc. SIGGRAPH '92, Computer Graphics* 26:2 (1992), 255–264.

[Wexler et al. 05] Daniel Wexler, Larry Gritz, Eric Enderton, and Jonathan Rice. "GPU-accelerated High-Quality Hidden Surface Removal." In *Graphics Hardware 2005: ACM SIGGRAPH / Eurographics Symposium Proceedings*, edited by Mark Harris, David Luebke, Mark Segal, and Philipp Slusallek, pp. 7–14. New York: ACM Press, 2005.

[Whitted 79] Turner Whitted. "An Improved Illumination Model for Shaded Display." *Proc. SIGGRAPH '79, Computer Graphics* 13:2 (1979), 14.

[Williams 78] Lance Williams. "Casting Curved Shadows on Curved Surfaces." *Proc. SIGGRAPH '78, Computer Graphics* 12:3 (1978), 270–274.

[Williams 83] Lance Williams. "Pyramidal Parametrics." *Proc. SIGGRAPH '83, Computer Graphics* 17:3 (1983), 1–11.

[Woop et al. 05] Sven Woop, Jörg Schmittler, and Philipp Slusallek. "RPU: A Programmable Ray Processing Unit for Realtime Ray Tracing." *Proc. SIGGRAPH '05, Transactions on Graphics* 24:3 (2005), 434–444.

[Yu et al. 99] Yizhou Yu, Paul Debevec, Jitendra Malik, and Tim Hawkins. "Inverse Global Illumination: Recovering Reflectance Models of Real Scenes from Photographs." In *Proceedings of SIGGRAPH 99, Computer Graphics Proceedings, Annual Conference Series*, edited by Alyn Rockwood, pp. 215–224, Reading, MA: Addison-Wesley, 1999.

[Yuksel and Keyser 08] Cem Yuksel and John Keyser. "Deep Opacity Maps." *Computer Graphics Forum* 27:2 (2008), 675–680.

[Yuksel et al. 09] Cem Yuksel, Scott Schaefer, and John Keyser. "Hair Meshes." *Proc. SIGGRAPH Asia '09, Transactions on Graphics* 28:5 (2009), 1–7.

[Zheng and James 09] Changxi Zheng and Doug L. James. "Harmonic Fluids." *Proc. SIGGRAPH '09, Transactions on Graphics* 28:3 (2009), 1–12.

[Zhou et al. 05] Kun Zhou, Yaohua Hu, Stephen Lin, Baining Guo, and Heung-Yeung Shum. "Precomputed Shadow Fields for Dynamic Scenes." *Proc. SIGGRAPH '05, Transactions on Graphics* 24:3 (2005), 1196–1201.

[Zhou et al. 09] Kun Zhou, Qiming Hou, Zhong Ren, Minmin Gong, Xin Sun, and Baining Guo. "RenderAnts: Interactive Reyes Rendering on GPUs." *Proc. SIGGRAPH Asia '09, Transactions on Graphics* 28:5 (2009), 1–11.

[Zhu and Bridson 05] Yongning Zhu and Robert Bridson. "Animating Sand as a Fluid." *Proc. SIGGRAPH '05, Transactions on Graphics* 24:3 (2005), 965–972.

[Zinke and Weber 07] Arno Zinke and Andreas Weber. "Light Scattering from Filaments." *IEEE Transactions on Visualization and Computer Graphics* 13:2 (2007), 342–356.

[Zinke et al. 08] Arno Zinke, Cem Yuksel, Andreas Weber, and John Keyser. "Dual Scattering Approximation for Fast Multiple Scattering in Hair." *Proc. SIGGRAPH '08, Transactions on Graphics* 27:3 (2008), 1–10.

[Zinke et al. 09] Arno Zinke, Martin Rump, Tomás Lay, Andreas Weber, Anton Andriyenko, and Reinhard Klein. "A Practical Approach for Photometric Acquisition of Hair Color." *Proc. SIGGRAPH Asia '09, Transactions on Graphics* 28:3 (2009), 1–9.

Index